The Thistle Rises

Books By Alan Bold

Poetry

Society Inebrious   The Voyage   To Find The New   A Perpetual Motion Machine   Penguin Modern Poets 15 (with Morgan and Brathwaite)   The State of the Nation   The Auld Symie   He Will be Greatly Missed   A Century of People   A Pint of Bitter   Scotland, Yes   This Fine Day   In This Corner: Selected Poems 1963–83

Stories

Hammer and Thistle (with Morrison)

Criticism

Thom Gunn & Ted Hughes   George Mackay Brown   The Ballad   (ed) Smollett: Author of the First Distinction   (ed) The Sexual Dimension in Literature   The Sensual Scot   Modern Scottish Literature   MacDiarmid: The Terrible Crystal   (ed) Scott: The Long-Forgotten Melody   (ed) Byron: Wrath and Rhyme

Anthologies

The Penguin Book of Socialist Verse   The Martial Muse: Seven Centuries of War Poetry   The Cambridge Book of English Verse 1939–75   Making Love: The Picador Book of Erotic Verse   The Bawdy Beautiful: The Sphere Book of Improper Verse   Mounts of Venus: The Picador Book of Erotic Prose   Drink To Me Only: The Prose (and Cons) of Drinking   A Scottish Poetry Book   The Poetry of Motion

THE THISTLE RISES

An Anthology
of Poetry and Prose
by
Hugh MacDiarmid

edited by
Alan Bold

Hamish Hamilton London

First published in Great Britain 1984
by Hamish Hamilton Ltd
Garden House 57–59 Long Acre London WC2E 9JZ

MacDiarmid Hugh *1892–1978*
  The Thistle Rises
  I. Title
  821'.912   PR6019.053

ISBN 0–241–11171–4

Printed in Great Britain by St Edmundsbury Press
Bury St Edmunds Suffolk

TO NORMAN MacCAIG

My angling friend Norman MacCaig …
And MacCaig has laughed and said
'Let me see you catch anything yet
Big enough not to throw in again'.

Hugh MacDiarmid, *In Memoriam James Joyce*

CONTENTS

PART ONE: POETRY

(*In the list below, the poems marked with an asterisk do not appear in* Complete Poems; *textual sources of these uncollected poems are given where appropriate.*)

INTRODUCTION

It is the intention of this book, which contains previously unpublished and uncollected poetry and prose, to demonstrate the scope and status of Hugh MacDiarmid's genius and bring the whole range of his writing within the reach of the general reader as well as the literary specialist. Although MacDiarmid produced, in *Sangschaw* (1925) and *Penny Wheep* (1926), the most concentrated lyrics – and even asserted 'Wee bit sangs are a' I need' – he was a visionary poet who thought on a grand scale. Built into the thematic repertoire of his masterpiece *A Drunk Man Looks at the Thistle* (1926) is the notion of poetic growth and metaphysical expansion so that the narrator says,

> I doot I'm geylies mixed, like Life itsel',
> But I was never ane that thocht to pit
> An ocean in a mutchkin. As the haill's
> Mair than the pairt sae I than reason yet.

Later in the poem the theme thus introduced is reinforced:

> O ilka man alive is like
> A quart that's squeezed into a pint
> (A maist unScottish-like affair!)

And again,

> But let my soul increase in me,
> God dwarfed to enter my puir thocht
> Expand to his true size again,
> And protoplasm's look befit
> The nature o' its destiny,
> And seed and sequence be nae mair
> Incongruous to ane anither,
> And liquor packed impossibly
> Mak' pint-pot an eternal well.

MacDiarmid's poetic universe, in other words, is an endlessly expanding one.

In packing a MacDiarmidian ocean into a mutchkin (or book-sized half-bottle) I am aware, however, that the poet's concept of size was paradoxical. After all, he considered the subject in his own way by asking and answering the rhetorical question, 'Scotland small? Our multiform, our infinite Scotland *small?*' (see p. 107). For MacDiarmid physical size – in a person or a country – was an earthly limitation that could be transcended by stretching out imaginatively into infinity. This is what he consistently tried to do in his writing so he could transform himself into an example of creative individuality. MacDiarmid has been portrayed in various ways and understandably so, yet the quintessential man contains all the apparent contradictions, even those that have caused most comment. Contemporaries were confused when the Anglophobic advocate of the Scottish literary renaissance contrived his later poems in English; political colleagues were puzzled by the man who was both Scottish Nationalist and Communist, simultaneously materialist and mystic.

Admittedly MacDiarmid can seem an elusive figure anxious to avoid classification: after shaping the lyrics in *Sangschaw* and *Penny Wheep*, he went on to shake the Scots language to its linguistic roots in *A Drunk Man Looks at the Thistle* and then apparently abandoned Scots for an idiosyncratic English. And if poetically he seems to embody an exceptionally restless spirit then his refusal to conform to political conventions likewise caused consternation: in 1928 he helped found the National Party of Scotland which expelled him in 1933 for his Communism while the Communist Party followed suit in 1938 and expelled him for his nationalism. In 1957 when many intellectuals were leaving the Communist Party as a protest against the Russian invasion of Hungary, MacDiarmid rejoined and contributed to the *Daily Worker* of 28 March 1957 an explanation that incidentally pronounced on poetry:

> I am the kind of poet I am because, in living nature, it is the complicated which seems to be nature's climax of rightness. The simple is at a discount. Poetry has nothing to do with religious mysticism, but is entirely an affair of the practical reason.

This from a poet who in 'Lament for the Great Music' proclaimed his 'cosmic consciousness' and in *In Memoriam James Joyce* (1955) discerned 'some loftier perfection/In the universe as a whole'. MacDiarmid was, it must be remembered when considering some of his public statements, a man with a mischievous sense of humour and a literary giant who entirely eschewed Grand Old Mannerisms. He delighted in being provocative and explained, in a letter of 1 July 1964 to George Bruce, 'My job, as I see it, has never been to lay a tit's egg, but to erupt like a volcano, emitting not only flame, but a lot of rubbish.' I hope that this collection is illuminated by the flame that flared, in the first place, in a little Scottish Border town.

Hugh MacDiarmid was born Christopher Murray Grieve in Langholm ('the Muckle Toon') on 11 August 1892, the son of a rural postman. As he explained in his autobiography *Lucky Poet* (1943) he devoured an enormous amount of books at an early age, since the family lived beneath the local library. Both his parents were devout members of Langholm South United Free Church whose minister, from 1901 to 1907, was the Rev. Thomas Scott Cairncross. When Cairncross published, in 1905, a collection of poems *The Return of the Master* Grieve was enormously impressed. Cairncross in turn generally encouraged young Chris Grieve, an accomplished Sunday School teacher at the time, and lent him copies of books he reviewed for the *Irish Times*. Grieve was fortunate in coming into contact with Cairncross in Langholm where he also encountered, at Langholm Academy, the composer Francis George Scott who was later to give the poet moral support when finalising the form of *A Drunk Man Looks at the Thistle*. In Edinburgh, where he arrived in 1908 as a pupil teacher, Grieve found another mentor in George Ogilvie who ran the English department at Broughton Junior Student Centre. Ogilvie introduced his most promising student to A. R. Orage's weekly *The New Age* and the intellectual-cum-evangelical tone of the periodical made an enduring impact on the young man who shared its socialist principles and air of artistic arrogance.

In the First World War, Grieve served with the Royal Army Medical Corps and was invalided home from Salonika suffering from cerebral malaria. During the war he wrote most of the material – including 'A Moment in Eternity' dedicated to Ogilvie – that eventually found its way into his first book *Annals of the Five Senses* (1923). After the war he determined to fight for his own small country and drastically to change the cultural climate of Scotland. Grieve settled in Montrose in 1921 and there embarked on a decade of the most intense artistic and political activity, becoming chief reporter of *The Montrose*

Review, a Labour member of the Town Council, a Justice of the Peace; and also a founder of the Scottish Centre of PEN, the National Party of Scotland and the periodicals *The Scottish Chapbook*, *The Scottish Nation* and *The Northern Review*. It was *The Scottish Chapbook* that provided editor Grieve with a platform for the most successful poetic experiment attempted in modern Scotland.

The first issue of *The Scottish Chapbook* carried, in August 1922, a contribution by one Hugh MacDiarmid: 'Nisbet' (see pp. 318–28), interestingly enough, was a dramatic interlude in English. In the third issue of *The Scottish Chapbook*, October 1922, 'MacDiarmid' was featured on the first page as the author of 'The Watergaw'. This pseudonymous lyric, a memory of the death of the poet's father, was the beginning of the Scottish Literary Renaissance (as MacDiarmid called the movement he generated) and *The Scottish Chapbook* was soon expounding the cause of Synthetic Scots (so called because it drew from all regional dialects) in essays such as 'A Theory of Scots Letters' (see pp. 125–41).

What MacDiarmid had done, in creating his Synthetic Scots, was to combine the strength of the oral tradition with the range of literary words preserved in Jamieson's Etymological Dictionary. Recently Scots had been contaminated, so MacDiarmid felt, by the standards of the kailyard;* by writing with a modernist perspective and an indigenous use of contrast and counterpoint he was bringing the linguistic experimentation of Joyce and Eliot home to Scotland. As I have observed elsewhere, C. M. Grieve created his alter ego Hugh MacDiarmid during the *annus mirabilis* of modernism, for *Ulysses* appeared in February 1922 and *The Waste Land* in October of the same year.

MacDiarmid's early lyrics in *Sangschaw* and *Penny Wheep* spectacularly broke with the post-Burnsian tradition of sentimentality and cosy domesticity. MacDiarmid replaced Burns's Standard Habbie Stanza (which had been *de rigueur* in Scots

---

* The 'Kailyard' (or cabbage-patch) school of writing flourished in Victorian Scotland and was so-called after the epigraph to Ian Maclaren's *Beside the Bonnie Brier Bush* (1894): 'There grows a bonnie brier bush in our kail-yard.' Maclaren, S. R. Crocket and J. M. Barrie were the leading kailyarders, and their sentimentality of style sickened Scottish intellectuals who wanted to present a more realistic picture of Scotland.

poetry since the eighteenth century) with subtly orchestrated stanzas that finished with a witty or philosophical flourish. His characteristic method was to isolate a particular image, then seek out its cosmic implications before bringing it back to earth with a bang (never a whimper). Although he used the slogan 'Dunbar – Not Burns!' in the 1920s, MacDiarmid was as interested in the linguistic innovations of his modernist contemporaries as he was in Scottish precedents. His genius included an ability to achieve unity-in-diversity by making extremes meet in a memorable way. Thus he could be both intimately physical and soaringly metaphyscial, perfectly natural and hauntingly supernatural, audaciously direct and majestically enigmatic.

His technique of revealing unusual aspects by treating a subject as a target to be aimed at from various angles sustained him throughout his masterpiece *A Drunk Man Looks at the Thistle*. In this poem MacDiarmid virtually remade Scotland in his own image. The narrative was suggested by two sources: in 'Tam O'Shanter' Burns's homeward-heading hero encounters a drink-induced vision; in *Ulysses*, Joyce transforms the Homeric odyssey into Everyman's walk through Dublin. MacDiarmid's Drunk Man, during his unsteady odyssey homewards to the bed of his beloved Jean (a figure fusing the nagging wife in Burns's poem with Penelope Bloom), stumbles on a hillside and there – by the light of the full moon – addresses the thistle as a Freudian symbol of Scotland's past and potential. While the alcoholic spirit is strong the metamorphoses are soul-searchingly disturbing but slowly the insobriety is replaced by a spiritual intensity as Scotland rises to rebirth:

> The thistle rises and forever will.
> Getherin' the generations under't.
> This is the monument o' a' they were,
> And a' they hoped and wondered.

The Drunk Man is a Scot who becomes, by his vision of the resurrection that is inside Everyman, an apostle of individuality, a poetic redeemer. MacDiarmid calls him 'A greater Christ, a greater Burns' and is aware of the possibility of martyrdom:

> *A Scottish poet maun assume*
> *The burden o' his people's doom.*
> *And dee to brak' their livin' tomb.*

In the thistle, clearly, MacDiarmid had found the perfect subject but he was certainly not content to rest on his laurels – or accept the crown of thorns without a struggle.

At various stages of his literary career MacDiarmid conceived massive poetic projects so that an expansive theme runs right through his creative lifetime. In his correspondence with George Ogilvie he constantly anticipates extended sequences (of sonnets, for example) and big books. On 6 August 1926 he told Ogilvie of his plans for *A Drunk Man Looks at the Thistle*: 'It's the thing as a whole that I'm mainly concerned with, and if, as such, it does not take its place as a masterpiece – sui generis – one of the biggest things in the range of Scottish Literature, I shall have failed.' Forty years later, in a discussion on the composer Sorabji included in *The Company I've Kept* (1966), he exclaims, 'I'm all for GIANTISM in the arts.' It is generally accepted, of course, that in *A Drunk Man* MacDiarmid not only conceived a work of genius but delivered it to an astonished and admiring world. It is also important to note that some of the poems included in the present book were also conceived as parts of large-scale compositions. In almost every instance the poems have an autonomous power yet it is instructive to recall the original poetic concept.

MacDiarmid followed *A Drunk Man* with *To Circumjack Cencrastus* (1930) which had (as the title implies) the splendid intention of squaring the Celtic circle (Cencrastus being the snake with its tail in its mouth, symbolic of eternity). However the poem turned out to be a hit-and-miss affair alternating between exquisite lyrics such as 'Lourd on my hert' and a parade of personal grudges. Due to distressing personal circumstances culminating in the breakdown of his marriage, MacDiarmid suffered some loss of poetic confidence as is evident in *Cencrastus* with its completely uncharacteristic confessional mood of defeatism. Apparently aware of the flaws in the poem MacDiarmid planned a triumphant poem that would be even more impressive, he hoped, than *A Drunk Man*.

Accordingly MacDiarmid announced a poetic colossus with the collective title *Clann Albann*, a five-volume autobiography in verse. In an article contributed to the *Scots Observer* of 12 August 1933 MacDiarmid glosses the title as meaning 'the children of Scotland – past, present and future' and describes the nature of the first volume. *The Muckle Toon*:

> The first book deals with *The Muckle Toon* [i.e., Langholm, in Dumfriesshire], my birthplace, and my boyhood days; and this involves poems about my parents, about the hills, woods, and streams of that district, about my first contacts with Love and Death, about the Church influence which bulked so largely in my life then, about Border history, and about the actual – and symbolic – significance of the frontier.

In the present book the following poems were originally conceived as parts of *The Muckle Toon*: 'Kinsfolk' (the opening of the volume), 'First Hymn to Lenin', 'At My Father's Grave', 'Prayer for a Second Flood', 'Second Hymn to Lenin', 'Milk-Wort and Bog-Cotton'. 'Water Music', 'Depth and the Chthonian Image', 'Of John Davidson', 'By Wauchopeside', 'Whuchulls', 'Bracken Hills in Autumn'.

When MacDiarmid moved to Shetland in 1933 he virtually abandoned *Clann Albann* and never did assemble the completed parts of the first volume, *The Muckle Toon*, in proper sequence. Instead he redirected his angle of approach in order to cope with a fresh challenge, new conditions and a geologically stimulating environment. The result was a series of Shetland lyrics, like 'With the Herring Fishers', and another ambitious linguistic experiment. Having written his early lyrics and *A Drunk Man* in Synthetic Scots he now evolved what he termed Synthetic English and used this resourceful idiom to fashion dense linguistic structures, the most celebrated of which is 'On a Raised Beach'. He also began to contemplate an epic that would express his Celtic consciousness in the intricately improvisatory manner of the Scottish pibroch. The new sequence was to be called *Mature Art*. It was to be intellectually ostentatious in the manner of Ezra Pound, and as verbally adroit as James Joyce.

MacDiarmid submitted the *Mature Art* sequence, as it then stood, to Faber, and T. S. Eliot replied (on 8 June 1938) saying 'it seems to me an extremely interesting, individual, and indeed very remarkable piece of work. There can be no doubt that it is something that ought to be published, but the question is how, and by whom.' Eliot clearly considered the publication of such an enormous piece of poetry to be commercially unviable, but MacDiarmid placed the work with Jack Kahane's Obelisk

Press in Paris. In a prospectus headed *Mature Art: An Exercise in Schlabone, Bordatini, and Scordattura** MacDiarmid outlined his 20,000-line poem as an epic dealing with

> the interrelated themes of the evolution of world literature and world consciousness, the problems of linguistics, the place and potentialities of the Gaelic genius, from its origin in Georgia to its modern expressions in Scotland, Ireland, Wales, Cornwall, Galicia and the Pays Basque, the synthesis of East and West, and the future of civilisation.
>
> It is a very learned poem involving a stupendous range of reference, especially to Gaelic, Russian, Italian and Indian literatures, German literature and philosophy, and modern physics and the physiology of the brain, and while mainly in English, utilises elements of over a score of languages, Oriental and Occidental.

When Jack Kahane died in 1939 the planned publication of *Mature Art* was delayed and by the time Kahane's son, Maurice Girodias, was in a position to revive the project, the Fall of France prevented it. During the Second World War, MacDiarmid was in Glasgow engaged on war work: first as a fitter on Clydeside, then as a deckhand on a Norwegian ship. Once again circumstances interrupted his poetic plans but he continued to retouch the text of *Mature Art* and bits and pieces of the poem were published in volumes such as *Lucky Poet* (1943), *In Memoriam James Joyce* (1955), *The Kind of Poetry I Want* (1961) and *Dìreadh* (1974). In the present volume the following items are from the *Mature Art* sequence: 'Bagpipe Music', '*from* In Memoriam James Joyce', 'Happy on Heimaey', 'Reflections in a Slum', 'British Leftish Poetry, 1930–40', '*from* 'Dìreadh I', 'Dìreadh III'.

Although I recognise the part that these different projects played in MacDiarmid's poetic outlook I have retained, in the present volume, the order of the poems established in the posthumous *Complete Poems* (1978) – that is, as the poet wished, 'in chronological order according to their year of publication' (which leads to some confusion because of the bibliographical vagaries of MacDiarmid's career). The reason for conforming to that established order is because I believe MacDiarmid's poetry, for all the different linguistic contexts, amounts ultimately to a marvellously unified text. His work has a

---

* In the second impression of *In Memoriam James Joyce* (Glasgow, 1956, p. 35) the spelling was corrected in the line 'In schablone, bordatini, and prolonged scordatura'.

visionary unity which in several poems* he refers to (in a phrase from *Ezekiel* I: xxii) as 'the terrible crystal'. Far from being a muddled mass of contradictions MacDiarmid was quite right to insist, in the 1972 reprint of *Lucky Poet*, that 'under the apparent inconsistencies and contradictions [of my writing] there is a basic unity'. There is indeed. What MacDiarmid always searched for was the source of creative energy which could transform the world, remake it in a glorious image. In his search for 'the terrible crystal' of creativity he delighted in different angles of approach and the display of different facets of his talent. As he says, in 'The Terrible Crystal', this leads him to a stunning creative clarity.

> Clear thought is the quintessence of human life.
> In the end its acid power will disintegrate
> All the force and flummery of current passions and pretences,
> Eat the life out of every false loyalty and craven creed
> And bite its way through to a world of light and truth ...
> This is the hidden and lambent core I seek.
> Like crystal it is hidden deep
> And only to be found by those
> Who will dig deep.
> Like crystal it is formed by cataclysm and central fires;
> Like crystal it gathers into an icy unity
> And a gem-like transparence
> All the colour and fire of life;
> Like crystal it concentrates and irradiates light;
> Like crystal it endures.

While MacDiarmid's literary immortality is assured on the strength of his poetry alone, he was also an astonishingly productive writer (and speaker) of eloquent prose and I wanted to indicate this further facet of his talent. All his life MacDiarmid was a fast and fluent journalist who could turn out copy to order, and in doing so he often illuminated issues crucial to his poetry. He also, however, wrote some impressively imaginative prose and the very best of MacDiarmid's fiction begins to approach the crystalline clarity his poetry proclaims. His first book, *Annals of the Five Senses*, was written predominantly in prose and exhibits some fine Dostoevskean moments of existential anxiety and anguish. A story such as 'The Never-Yet-Explored' alternates between such brittle and frenetic rhythms

---

* See my *MacDiarmid: The Terrible Crystal* (London, 1983) in which I pursue this argument.

and the ebb-and-flow of the stream-of-consciousness narrative style so successfully developed by Virginia Woolf.

During the 1920s MacDiarmid experimented with Scots prose to achieve some dramatic results; he at one time comtemplated writing his own version of *Macbeth*, and although this project came to nothing, he had a dramatist's flair for words that vividly convey physical conditions and mental states. He was well aware that some of the greatest moments in Scottish fiction were associated with the use of a racy Scots to put a narrative under linguistic pressure and bring about a telling sense of urgency. His models were the Scott of 'Wandering Willie's Tale' (from *Redgauntlet*) and the Stevenson of 'Thrawn Janet'. Like Scott and Stevenson, MacDiarmid draws lurid Gothic forms as he touches on the folk imagination and finds it haunted by rumour and speculation, obsessed by the past. Though MacDiarmid's Scots fiction does not have the metaphysical dimension of his Scots poetry it does have a more directly human quality. The poet who habitually poured scorn on 'the feck' (the majority, the rabble) found some fellow-feeling with the folk in his Scots fiction.

Given his prediliction for massive forms it is not surprising that MacDiarmid should have contemplated a novel, a sustained statement that would be the prose equivalent of *A Drunk Man*. However in 1927 he found he was composing Scots stories as fluently as he had written his early Scots lyrics. Thus he wrote to tell Neil Gunn, on 28 February 1927, that Scots prose was now his priority:

> So far as I am concerned I've made a little headway with my own novel (in English) but switched that to one side on a sudden impulse, deciding that my next book would be a collection of short stories in Scots. I've well over half the book written . . . The title of the book will be *The Muckle Toon*.

The title, of course, is one he returned to with the *Clann Albann* project which expresses similar Langholm-induced experience in verse. In the 1930s, when *Clann Albann* was being overtaken by his new plan to write a Celtic epic in Synthetic English, MacDiarmid essayed a more didactic fiction in English though with a thoroughly Scottish subject-matter. An undated letter, obviously written early in 1935, explains to Tom Macdonald (otherwise known as the novelist Fionn Mac Colla) his intention of publishing a book of stories evidently combining the dramatic Scots monologues of the 1920s with the recently written English stories:

> They are of course Scottish short stories – and of a different order to anything of that sort we have yet produced – nothing Kailyairdie about them, very varied, simply and straightforwardly written, anecdotal like Maupassant's in kind and without any involved psychologising.

MacDiarmid offered this book to Routledge and wrote to his friend A. B. Paterson, the firm's sales manager, on 12 April 1935:

> Now I am putting together a book to be called *Thirty Scottish Stories* by Hugh MacDiarmid – all but two entirely new (the two exceptions have already appeared in periodicals) – and I want to find a publisher to bring this out this Autumn. The stories are (if I says it as shouldn't) very varied and represent some of my best work and something new in Scottish fiction but yet not highbrow or limited in appeal. I have twenty of them all ready now – the other ten I am still revising and polishing a little. But I could send the lot in a week or so. Some of them I think will be found very amusing. The total runs to 50,000 to 60,000 words.

Soon after that MacDiarmid parted company with Routledge who refused to accept MacDairmid's political study of *Red Scotland*. At first MacDiarmid agreed to reduce the book to half its length but then despaired when Routledge questioned the quality of the text itself. As a result of this break with Routledge the projected book of stories never materialised in print and *Red Scotland* is now no more than a title since the work itself has long since disappeared.

As the central section of the present book comprises Mac-Diarmid's non-fictional prose, sometimes in abbreviated form, I should explain why I have taken the liberty of occasionally eliminating some illustrative quotations (as I have indicated in headnotes). There are essays by MacDiarmid, in *Scottish Eccentrics* (1936) for example, that consist entirely of long quotations linked by a few phrases by MacDiarmid. While this anthological approach is often fascinating I felt that MacDiarmid's non-fiction prose could not be represented adequately in a single volume if we had to take on board every quotation. Hence the editorial surgery. I believe MacDiarmid would have approved of this, given the design of the book and its omnibus nature. When I was still a student at Edinburgh University he wrote an Introduction for my first book of poems *Society Inebrious* (1965). Not only was he magnanimous enough to do this for me but he followed the manuscript with a letter in which he said I could make cuts in his Introduction if it was too long for the purpose. I did make cuts, then, paring away only quotations, so I approached the present volume with an important editorial precedent. None of MacDiarmid's own prose has been excised and I feel the cutting back of quotations, in certain instances only, reveals the quintessential MacDiarmid. That, and that only, is the purpose of this book.

Alan Bold
May 1983

ACKNOWLEDGEMENTS

I would like to thank Mrs Valda Grieve for making it possible for me to shape this selection of her late husband's writing; and Michael Grieve, the poet's son, for his enthusiasm and co-operation at every stage. I am most grateful for access to the expertise of Duncan Glen, author of *Hugh MacDiarmid and the Scottish Renaissance* (1964); and W. R. Aitken, bibliographer of MacDiarmid and co-editor (with Michael Grieve) of *Complete Poems 1920–1976*. To Linda Christie, Librarian of Broughton High School, I am indebted for providing me with photocopies of Grieve material from the *Broughton Magazine*. The Leverhulme Trust kindly awarded me a Research Grant in connexion with this edition and I am delighted to acknowledge their generosity; to the Phoenix Trust too I am similarly grateful. I also make acknowledgement as follows:

B. T. Batsford Ltd for permission to excerpt 'Islands' (a title adopted for this edition) from *The Islands of Scotland* (1939);

BBC Written Archives Centre for permission to excerpt 'MacDiarmid at Large' (a title adopted for this edition) from D. G. Bridson's interview with MacDiarmid, transmitted on the Third Programme on 4 and 9 March 1960;

BBC Written Archives Centre and George Bruce for permission to edit 'MacDiarmid at Eighty-Five', an interview transmitted on Radio Scotland on 11 August 1977;

BBC Written Archives Centre and Tom Vernon for permission to adapt 'Valedictory' (a title adopted for this edition) from the interview transmitted on Radio 4 on 15 September 1977;

Edinburgh University Library for permission to reprint 'Reflections on the Crux Decussata', 'An Epoch-Making Event' and three poems – 'The Stone of the Dog, in Glen Lyon', 'The Wild Swan', 'The Terns' – from manuscripts in the Library's collection;

Faber and Faber Ltd for permission to reprint '*Satori* in Scotland' from *Memoirs of a Modern Scotland*, edited by Karl Miller;

The Glasgow Herald for permission to reprint the poem 'An October Nightfall' (14 October 1925); and the stories 'The

Common Riding', 'The Waterside', 'The Moon through Glass', 'Maria', 'Andy', 'The Scab' (issues of 12 March 1927, 16 April 1927, 16 July 1927, 27 August 1927, 22 October 1927, 15 August 1932);

Hamish Hamilton Ltd for permission to reprint 'Whisky' (a title adopted for this edition), the foreword to *A Dram Like This* by Alan Reeve-Jones;

Hutchinson Ltd for permission to reprint 'The Dead Harlot', 'A' Body's Lassie', 'Wound-Pie' and 'The Stranger' from *Thirty New Tales of Horror*, edited by John Gawsworth;

Mrs Dora Knight and the National Library of Scotland for permission to print 'The Angus Burghs', an article first commissioned by Mrs Knight's husband Duncan Fraser whose archive is in the National Library of Scotland;

William Maclellan for permission to reprint 'Vouchsafed, A Sign' from *New Short Stories 1945–1946*, edited by John Singer and published by Maclellan in 1946;

Macmillan Publishers Ltd for permission to excerpt 'A Reply to Edwin Muir' (a title adopted for this edition) from *The Golden Treasury of Scottish Poetry*, edited by Hugh MacDiarmid;

Martin Brian and O'Keeffe for permission to reprint poems from the *Complete Poems 1920–1976* of Hugh MacDiarmid, edited (in two volumes) by W. R. Aitken and Michael Grieve;

Walter Perrie for permission to print the full text of 'Metaphysics and Poetry', his interview with MacDiarmid;

Ramsay Head Press for permission to excerpt 'Religion and Art' (a title adopted for this edition) from *John Knox* by Anthony Ross, Campbell MacLean and Hugh MacDiarmid;

Routledge and Kegan Paul Ltd. for permission to excerpt 'This Scottish Strain' (a title adopted for this edition) from *Albyn* by Hugh MacDiarmid; and for permission to excerpt 'An Eccentric Scotswoman' (a title adopted for this edition) from *Scottish Eccentrics* by Hugh MacDiarmid;

Saltire Society for permission to reprint 'Without a Leg to Stand On' from *Saltire Review*, Spring 1960;

The Scots Magazine for permission to reprint 'Murtholm Hill' (issue of April 1927, Vol. 7, No. 1);

R. S. Silver for preserving the text, in galley proof, of 'No Closed Doors, No Religion' and making it available to me;

Gordon Wright for permission to reprint 'Scottish Independence' (a title adopted for this edition), a speech by Hugh MacDiarmid recorded at a 1320 Club Symposium on 6 April 1968 by Gordon Wright and published as *A Political Speech* by Reprographia; and for allowing me to adapt and expand his Chronology from his *MacDiarmid: An Illustrated Biography*.

CHRONOLOGY

(In the Chronology the following abbreviations are used for books by MacDiarmid: LP for Lucky Poet *(1943), SE for* Selected Essays *(1969), Company for* The Company I've Kept *(1966), Annals for* Annals of the Five Senses *(1923), Uncanny for* The Uncanny Scot *(1968).)*

> *My life has been an adventure, or series of adventures, in the exploration of the mystery of Scotland's self-suppression.*
>
> *LP, 381*

1892   *11 August: born at Arkinholm Terrace, Langholm.* I am of the opinion that 'my native place' – the muckle toon of Langholm, in Dumfriesshire – is the bonniest place I know, by virtue, not of the little burgh in itelf ... but of wonderful variety and quality of the scenery in which it is set. (SE, 53)

1894   It was some fourteen months later that I was caught in the act of trying to commit my first murder – attempting, in short, to smash in the head of my newly-born brother [Andrew] with a poker, and, when I was disarmed, continuing to insist that, despite that horrible red-faced object, I 'was still Mummy's boy, too.' (LP, 218–19)

1899   *Enrolled in primary department, Langholm Academy. Moved to house in Library Buildings.* It was that library, however, that was the great determining factor. My father was a rural postman, his beat running up the Ewes Road to Fiddleton Toll, and we lived in the post office buildings. The library, the nucleus of which had been left by Thomas Telford, the famous engineer, was upstairs. I had constant access to it, and used to fill a big washing-basket with books and bring it downstairs as often as I wanted to ... There were upwards of twelve thousand books in the library (though it was strangely deficient in Scottish books), and a fair number of new books, chiefly novels, was constantly bought. Before I left home (when I was fourteen) I could go up into that library in the dark and find any book I wanted ... I certainly read almost every one of them ... (LP, 8–9)

1904 *Transferred to secondary department, Langholm Academy.* But even as a boy ... I drew an assurance that I felt and understood the spirit of Scotland and the Scottish country folk in no common measure, and that that made it at any rate possible that I would in due course become a great national poet of Scotland. (LP, 3)

1905 *Taught in Langholm South United Free Church Sunday School.* My parents were very devout believers and very Churchy people ... (LP, 40) Another poet – Thomas Scott Cairncross, who was, when I was a boy, minister of the church my parents attended, introduced me to the work of many poets ... but ... subsequently ceased to be friendly with me ... (LP, 222) *Taught English by William Burt and Francis George Scott* who were teachers at Langholm Academy when I was a boy ... and, in my opinion, [rank] among the strictly limited number of the best brains in Scotland ... (LP, 228–9)

1908 *Admitted as pupil teacher to Broughton Higher Grade School and Junior Student Centre, Edinburgh.* [George Ogilvie] my English master at the Junior Student Centre in Edinburgh was a man in ten thousand, who meant a very great deal to me ... (LP, 228–9) *Joined the Edinburgh Central Branch of the Independent Labour Party of Great Britain and the Edinburgh University branch of the Fabian Society.*

1909 *Edited* **The Broughton Magazine**.

1911 *Death of father, James Grieve.* A lean, hardy, weather-beaten man, he died at forty-seven after a few days' illness of pneumonia. He had never been ill in his life before. (LP, 18) *Left Scotland to work in South Wales on the* **Monmouthshire Labour News**. My father died suddenly before I was finished at the Junior Student Centre. I took immediate advantage of the fact to abandon my plans for becoming a teacher. That is one thing which I have never, for one moment, regretted ... If I had gone on and qualified and become a teacher, my sojourn in the profession would have been of short duration in any event, and I would have been dismissed as Thomas Davidson and John Maclean and my friend, A. S. Neill, were dismissed. (LP, 228–9)

1912 *Returned to Langholm.* The old Radicalism was still strong all over the Borders, though already a great deal of it had been dissipated away into the channels of religious sectarianism and such moralitarian crusades as the Temperance Movement, the Anti-Gambling agitation, and so forth ... But what I personally owed to the Langholm of that time was an out-and-out Radicalism and Republicanism, combined with an extreme anti-English feeling. (LP, 225) *Moved to Clydebank to work on the* **Clydebank and Renfrew Press**. *Rejoined Independent Labour Party. Moved to Cupar, met Peggy Skinner.*

1913 *Moved to Forfar to work on* **The Forfar Review**.

1915 *Enlisted.* I served in the Royal Army Medical Corps in the First World War, rising to the rank of Quartermaster-Sergeant. From 1916 to 1918 I was in Salonika with the 42nd General Hospital, which, located on the outskirts of the city towards Kalamaria, was established in the marble-floored premises of L'Orphenilat Grec. I was invalided home with malaria in 1918, but, after a period in a malaria concentration centre near Rhyl, was pronounced A1 again and fit for another spell of service overseas. After a brief stay near Dieppe, I was posted to the Section's Lahore Indian General Hospital stationed at the Château Mirabeau at Estaque near Marseilles. This hospital had been established to deal with Indian and other Asiatic soldiers who had been broken down psychologically on the Western Front. We had always several hundred insane there and the death-rate was very high, culminating in the great Influenza Epidemic in 1918 when our patients had little or no power of resistance and died in great numbers. The officers of the hospital were all Indians, mostly Edinburgh-trained, and there were only, in addition to myself, four white NCOs. I returned to Britain and was demobilised in 1920. (Company, 184)

1918 *Married Peggy Skinner.* [1] came back with an *idée fixe* – never again must men be made to suffer as in these years of war. (Annals, 89)

1919 *Found job with* **The Montrose Review** *and moved to Montrose.*

1920 *Moved to Kildermorie, E. Ross and Cromarty. Edited* **Northern Numbers.** Looking back, and recollecting my own conviction even as a mere boy that I was going to be a famous poet, it is surprising that I wrote little or nothing until after I was demobilized in 1919. (LP, 65)

1921 *Returned to Montrose to work for* **The Montrose Review.** *Edited* **Northern Numbers: Second Series.**

1922 *Edited* **Northern Numbers: Third Series.** *Founded and edited* **The Scottish Chapbook.** I became editor-reporter of *The Montrose Review*, and held that position until 1929. I threw myself whole-heartedly into the life of that community and became a Town Councillor, Parish Councillor, member of the School Management Committee and Justice of the Peace for the county. (Company, 184) *Began to use pseudonym Hugh MacDiarmid.* It was an immediate realization of [the] ultimate reach of the implications of my experiment which made me adopt, when I began writing Scots poetry, the Gaelic pseudonym of Hugh MacDiarmid (Hugh has a traditional association and essential rightness in conjunction with MacDiarmid) ... (LP, 6)

1923 *Edited* **The Scottish Chapbook,** *edited* **The Scottish Nation,** *published* **Annals of the Five Senses,** *contributed to* **The New Age.** When Orage gave up *The New Age* [in 1922] and went to America to promulgate the doctrines of

Ouspensky and Gurdjieff I took over the literary editorship of *The New Age* and was a prolific contributor to it over my own name and various pseudonyms for several years – until, in fact, Orage returned to England. (Company, 271)

1924 *Peggy gave birth to Christine. Edited* **The Northern Review**.

1925 **Sangschaw**..

1926 **Penny Wheep**. I was in the thick of the General Strike too. I was the only Socialist Town Councillor in Montrose and a Justice of the Peace for the county, and we had the whole area sewn up. One of my most poignant memories is of how, when the news of the great betrayal came through, I was in the act of addressing a packed meeting mainly of railwaymen. When I told them the terrible news most of them burst into tears – and I am not ashamed to say I did too. (Company, 158) **A Drunk Man Looks at the Thistle. Contemporary Scottish Studies**.

1927 *Founded the Scottish Centre of PEN.* **Albyn. The Lucky Bag. The Present Position of Scottish Music**.

1928 *Founder member of the National Party of Scotland.*

1929 *Peggy gave birth to Walter. Moved to London to edit* **Vox**. In 1929 I left Montrose and went to London to become London editor of *Vox*, a radio critical journal which had been promoted by Compton (afterwards Sir Compton) Mackenzie ... Alas, *Vox* was under-capitalised and premature – radio was not sufficiently far developed to yield an adequate readership concerned with critical assessments of home and foreign programme material of all kinds; and very shortly the venture collapsed. (Company, 186) [In December 1929] I had fallen from the top of a London double-decker motor-bus going at speed, and landed on my head on the pavement, sustaining severe concussion. I did not fracture, but it was a miracle I did not break my neck. (LP, 38)

1930 *Separated from Peggy.* **To Circumjack Cencrastus**. I realized, with terrible distress, that, against my will, the ties between my wife and two children, Christine and Walter, were about to be broken no less completely than I had allowed the ties between myself and my relatives in Langholm and elsewhere to break. (LP, 19) *Moved to Liverpool to work as public relations officer.* After ... one most unfortunate interlude in London, and a subsequent year in Liverpool (equally unfortunate, but for other and far more painful reasons, and owing perhaps to a considerable extent to my own blame), I have been desperately anxious not to leave Scotland again ... (LP, 41)

1931 *Divorced from Peggy. Met Valda Trevlyn in London.* My domestic affairs were in a bad way and I was divorced in 1931. Shortly afterwards I married again. I had, however, no money or income ... (Company, 186) **First Hymn to Lenin and Other Poems**.

1932 *Moved to Thakeham in Surrey. Valda gave birth to Michael.* My friends included, too, such extraordinary characters as Count Geoffrey Potocki de Montalk, editor of the *Right Review* (who went ... about London wearing a long red cloak – as did his brother, Count Cedric – and whose cottage at Thakeham in Sussex I 'took on' while he was in gaol for publishing obscene literature) ... (LP, 48) **Second Hymn to Lenin. Scots Unbound and Other Poems**.

1933 *Moved to the Shetland island of Whalsay.* I came to Whalsay, this little north Isle of the Shetland group, in 1933. I was absolutely down-and-out at the time – with no money behind me at all, broken down in health, unable to secure remunerative employment of any kind, and wholly concentrated on projects in poetry and other literary fields which could bring me no monetary return whatever ... I could not have lived anywhere else ... without recourse to the poorhouse. We were not only penniless when we arrived in Whalsay – I was in exceedingly bad state, psychologically and physically. *Expelled from the National Party of Scotland.* (LP, 41, 45)

1934 *Joined the Communist Party of Great Britain.* My coming to Communist membership was not the resolution of a conflict, but the completion, as it were, of a career ... From the beginning I took as my motto – and I have adhered to it all through my literary work – Thomas Hardy's declaration: 'Literature is the written expression of revolt against accepted things.' (LP, 232) **Stony Limits and Other Poems**. *Death of mother, Elizabeth.* My mother ... and I were always great friends and had a profound understanding of the ultimate worth of each other's beliefs ... (LP, 224)

1935 *Suffered nervous breakdown.* I have been Scotland's Public Enemy No. 1 for over a decade now, and I have certain accounts to settle while (a recent very grave illness prompts the phrase) there is yet time. (LP, 34) **Second Hymn to Lenin and Other Poems**.

1938 *Edited* **The Voice of Scotland**. *Expelled from the Communist Party for Nationalist deviation.*

1941 *Conscripted for National Service.*

1942 *Left Shetland.* In February [1942] I had to abandon my Shetland retreat, and since then I have been doing hard manual labour in big Clydeside engineering shops. Going from one extreme to the other like this is, of course, in keeping with my (and Gurdjieff's) philosophy of life, and, happily, at fifty, my constitution has been able to stand the long hours, foul conditions, and totally unaccustomed, heavy and filthy work perfectly well ... my Leontiev-like detestation of all the bourgeoisie, and, especially, teachers, ministers, lawyers, bankers, and journalists, and my preference for the barbarous and illiterate lower classes of workers, has been completely confirmed by my Clydeside experiences. (LP, xxxiii) *Rejoined the Scottish National Party. Member of SNP National Council.*

1943 *Transferred to the Merchant Service.* I had made a good recovery from a serious general break-down I had had in

1935, but the very rough conditions at Mechans [engineering firm] and the fact that I suffered serious injuries when a stack of copper-cuttings fell on me and cut both my legs very severely led me to seek a transfer to the Merchant Service. This was granted and I became first a deck hand – and then first engineer – on a Norwegian vessel, MFV *Gurli*, chartered by the British Admiralty and engaged in servicing vessels of the British and American Navies in the waters of the Clyde Estuary. (Company, 187) **Lucky Poet**.

1945 *Registered as unemployed in Glasgow. Revived* **The Voice of Scotland**.

1948 *Left the Scottish National Party.*

1950 *Visited Russia with members of the Scottish-USSR Friendship Society. Moved to Dungavel House, Strathaven.* At a meeting of the Saltire Society the Earl of Selkirk praised my work for Scotland and the quality of my lyrics, and a little later at his instance his brother, the Duke of Hamilton, offered me a commodious house adjacent to his Lanarkshire mansion of Dungavel, near Strathaven. Standing in a fine wood, it is an ideal dwelling, but unfortunately we had barely moved in and got ourselves settled when the National Coal Board bought over the whole estate, to establish a School for Miners in the mansion and in the adjoining lodges like ours houses for the school staff. So we had to get out ... *Received a Civil List Pension.* I received a letter from the Prime Minister's office asking if I would accept a Civil List pension. This was a Godsend and put me on my feet at last. (Company, 188, 189)

1951 *Moved into Brownsbank Cottage, near Biggar, Lanarkshire.* It was in a derelict condition, not having been occupied for several years, but it had the supreme advantage of being rent-free, and my wife speedily made it not only habitable but comfortable. We had no 'mod cons', and were getting too old to put up with really primitive conditions. In a year or two, however, some of the Edinburgh University students, members of the Young Communist League, and other friends came to the rescue and did all the necessary digging, draining, etc., and we soon found ourselves equipped with a kitchenette, bathroom, hot and cold water, flush lavatory, and electric light and other gadgets. The long spell of hardship and near destitution was over and after about twenty years' tough struggle we were very comfortably ensconced in a house of our own with every likelihood that it would prove a permanency. (Company, 188–9)

1955 *In Memoriam James Joyce. Again revived* **The Voice of Scotland.**

1956 *Rejoined the Communist Party.* I rejoined at the time of what I would call the suppression of the threatened counter-revolution in Hungary. Those who came out then, I think, did so for reasons I would call purely sentimental. They had probably never been convinced Communists and the party was well shot of most of them. (Uncanny, 170)

1957 *Visited China with the British-Chinese Friendship Society. Awarded Honorary LL.D. by Edinburgh University.*

1959 *Visited Czechoslovakia, Rumania, Bulgaria and Hungary as part of the Burns bi-centenary celebration.*

1961 **The Kind of Poetry I Want.**

1962 **Collected Poems.** It was in 1962, however, that the real break-through came. The occasion of my seventieth birthday was celebrated all over the world. There were scores of articles about my poetry in newspapers and periodicals in every so-called civilised country. I had hundreds of greetings telegrams and letters from many countries – so many that for several days round about 11th August ... Biggar Post Office had to run what was virtually a shuttle-service several times a day to deliver the masses of mail. (Company, 189)

1963 *Presented with the William Foyle Poetry Prize for 1962.*

1964 *Visited Canada. Communist candidate for Kinross and West Perthshire in General Election.* It was essential to oppose the Prime Minister (*Sir Alec Douglas-Home*), as a Communist and as a Scotsman. (Company, 203)

1966 **The Company I've Kept.**

1967 *Visited the USA.*

1971 *Visited Italy.*

1973 *Visited Ireland.*

1976 *Visited Canada.*

1978 *Awarded Honorary Litt. D. by Dublin University. 9 September: died in hospital in Edinburgh. 13 September: buried in Langholm Cemetery.* **Complete Poems.**

PART ONE

Poetry

A Moment in Eternity

The great song ceased
– Aye, like a wind was gone,
And our hearts came to rest,
Singly as leaves do,
And every leaf a flame.

My shining passions stilled
Shone in the sudden peace
Like countless leaves
Tingling with the quick sap
Of Immortality.

I was a multitude of leaves
Receiving and reflecting light,
A burning bush
Blazing for ever unconsumed,
Nay, ceaselessly,
Multiplying in leaves and light
And instantly
Burgeoning in buds of brightness,
– Freeing like golden breaths
Upon the cordial air
A thousand new delights,
– Translucent leaves
Green with the goodness of Eternity,
Golden in the Heavenly light,
– The golden breaths
Of any eternal life,
Like happy memories multiplied,
Shining out instantly from me

And shining back for ever into me,
– Breaths given out

But still unlost,
For ever mine
In the infinite air,
The everlasting foliage of my soul
Visible awhile
Like steady and innumerable flames,
Blending into one blaze
Yet each distinct
With shining shadows of difference.

A sudden thought of God's
Came like a wind
Ever and again
Rippling them as waters over stars,
And swiftlier fanning them
And setting them a-dance,
Upflying, fluttering down,
Moving in orderly intricacies
Of colour and of light,
Delaying, hastening,
Blazing and serene,
Shaken and shining in the turning wind,
Lassoing cataracts of light
With rosy boughs,
Or clamouring in echoing unequalled heights,
Rhythmical sprays of many-coloured fire
And spires chimerical
Gleaming in fabulous airs,
And suddenly
Lapsing again
To incandescence and increase.

And again the wind came
Blowing me afar
In fair fantastic fires,
– Ivies and irises invading
The upland garths of ivory;
Queen daisies growing
In the tall red grass

By pools of perfect peace;
And bluebells tossing
In transparent fields;
And silver airs
Lifting the crystal sources in dim hills
And swinging them far out like bells of glass
Pealing pellucidly
And quivering in faery flights of chimes;
Shivers of wings bewildered
In alleys of virgin dream;
Floral dances and revels of radiance
Whirling in stainless sanctuaries;
And eyes of Seraphim,
Shining like sunbeams on eternal ice,
Lifted toward the unexplored
Summits of Paradise.

And the wind ceased.
Light dwelt in me,
Pavilioned there.
I was a crystal trunk,
Columnar in the glades of Paradise,
Bearing the luminous boughs
And foliaged with the flame
Of infinite and gracious growth,
– Meteors for roots,
And my topmost spires
Notes of enchanted light
Blind in the Godhead!
– White stars at noon!

I shone within my thoughts
As God within us shines.

And the wind came,
Multitudinous and light
I whirled in exultations inexpressible
– An unpicturable, clear,
Soaring and glorying,
Swift consciousness,
A cosmos turning like a song of spheres
On apices of praise,

A separate colour,
An essential element and conscious part
Of successive and stupendous dreams
In God's own heart!

And the wind ceased
And like a light I stood,
A flame of glorious and complex resolve,
Within God's heart.

I knew then that a new tree,
A new tree and a strange,
Stood beautifully in Heaven.
I knew that a new light
Stood in God's heart
And a light unlike
The Twice Ten Thousand lights
That stood there,
Shining equally with me,
And giving and receiving increase of light
Like the flame that I was
Perpetually.
And I knew that when the wind rose
This new tree would stand still
Multiplied in light but motionless,
And I knew that when God dreamt
And His creative impulses
Ran through us like a wind
And we flew like clear and coloured
Flames in His dreams,
(Adorations, Gratitudes, and Joys,
Plenary and boon and pure,
Crystal and burning-gold and scarlet
Competing and co-operating flames
Reflecting His desires,
Flashing like epical imaginings
And burning virgin steeps
With ceaseless swift apotheoses)
One light would stand unmoved.

And when on pinnacles of praise
All others whirled

Like a white light deeper in God's heart
This light would shine,
Pondering the imponderable,
Revealing ever clearlier
Patterns of endless revels,
Each gesture freed,
Each shining shadow of difference,
Each subtle phase evolved
In the magnificent and numberless
Revelations of ecstasy
Succeeding and excelling inexhaustibly,
– A white light like a silence
Accentuating the great songs!
– A shining silence wherein God
Might see as in a mirror
The miracles that He must next achieve!

Ah, Light,
That is God's inmost wish,
His knowledge of Himself,
Flame of creative judgment,
God's interrogation of infinity,
Searching the unsearchable,
– Silent and steadfast tree,
Housing no birds of song,
Void to the wind,
But rooted in God's very self,
Growing ineffably,
Central in Paradise!

When the song ceased
And I stood still,
Breathing new leaves of life
Upon the eternal air,
Each leaf of all my leaves
Shone with a new delight
Murmuring Your name.

O thou,
Who art the wisdom of the God
Whose ecstasies we are!

The Bonnie Broukit Bairn

For Peggy

Mars is braw in crammasy,
Venus in a green silk goun,
The auld mune shak's her gowden feathers,
Their starry talk's a wheen o' blethers,
Nane for thee a thochtie sparin',
Earth, thou bonnie broukit bairn!
– *But greet, an' in your tears ye'll droun*
The haill clanjamfrie!

The Watergaw

Ae weet forenicht i' the yow-trummle
I saw yon antrin thing,
A watergaw wi' its chitterin' licht
Ayont the on-ding;
An' I thocht o' the last wild look ye gied
Afore ye deed!

There was nae reek i' the laverock's hoose
That nicht – an' nane i' mine;
But I hae thocht o' that foolish licht
Ever sin' syne;
An' I think that mebbe at last I ken
What your look meant then.

Reid E'en

Ilka hert an' hind are met
'Neath Arcturus gleamin' bonnie,
Bien the nicht owre a' the warl',
Hey, nonny, nonny!

But my hert sall meet nae maik
This reid-e'en or ony.
Luve an' a' are left behind.
– Hey, nonny, nonny.

Crowdieknowe

Oh to be at Crowdieknowe
When the last trumpet blaws,
An' see the deid come loupin' owre
The auld grey wa's.

Muckle men wi' tousled beards,
I grat at as a bairn
'll scramble frae the croodit clay
Wi' feck o' swearin'.

An' glower at God an' a' his gang
O' angels i' the lift
– Thae trashy bleezin' French-like folk
Wha gar'd them shift!

Fain the weemun-folk'll seek
To mak' them haud their row
– *Fegs, God's no blate gin he stirs up*
The men o' Crowdieknowe!

The Eemis Stane

I' the how-dumb-deid o' the cauld hairst nicht
The warl' like an eemis stane
Wags i' the lift;
An' my eerie memories fa'
Like a yowdendrift.

Like a yowdendrift so's I couldna read
The words cut oot i' the stane
Had the fug o' fame
An' history's hazelraw
No' yirdit thaim.

The Innumerable Christ

*Other stars may have their Bethlehem, and their
Calvary too.*

Professor J. Y. Simpson

Wha kens on whatna Bethlehems
Earth twinkles like a star the nicht,
An' whatna shepherds lift their heids
    In its unearthly licht?

'Yont a' the stars oor een can see
An' farther than their lichts can fly,
I' mony an unco warl' the nicht
    The fatefu' bairnies cry.

I' mony an unco warl' the nicht
The lift gaes black as pitch at noon,
An' sideways on their chests the heids
    O' endless Christs roll doon.

An' when the earth's as cauld's the mune
An' a' its folk are lang syne deid,
On coontless stars the Babe maun cry
    An' the Crucified maun bleed.

Wheesht, Wheesht

Wheesht, wheesht, my foolish hert,
For weel ye ken
I widna ha'e ye stert
Auld ploys again.

It's guid to see her lie
Sae snod an' cool,
A' lust o' lovin' by –
Wheesht, wheesht, ye fule!

'A deid man's never
Feery o' the feet,
Jock, five years buried
Maun be far frae fleet,
Sae, lad ye needna worry,
He'll no' hae's in a hurry.'

Aye, lass! but Resurrection's
The danger that dings a',
We maun up braw an' early
Gin we're to win awa',
Else sune's the trumpet's blared
There'll be twa daiths in oor kirkyaird.

Hungry Waters

FOR A LITTLE BOY AT LINLITHGOW

The auld men o' the sea
Wi' their daberlack hair
Ha'e dackered the coasts
O' the country fell sair.

They gobble owre cas'les,
Chow mountains to san';
Or lang they'll eat up
The haill o' the lan'.

Lickin' their white lips
An' yowlin' for mair,
The auld men o' the sea
Wi' their daberlack hair.

Duncan Gibb o' Focherty's
A giant to the likes o' me.
His face is like a roarin' fire
For love o' the barley-bree.

He gangs through this and the neebrin' shire
Like a muckle rootless tree
– And here's a caber for Daith to toss
That'll gi'e his spauld a swee!

His gain was aye a wee'r man's loss
And he took my lass frae me,
An wi' mony a quean besides
He's ta'en his liberty.

I've had nae chance wi' the likes o' him
And he's tramped me underfit.
– Blaefaced afore the throne o' God
He'll get his fairin' yet.

He'll be like a bull in the sale-ring there.
And I'll lauch lood to see,
Till he looks up and canna mak' oot
Whether it's God – or me!

Scunner

Your body derns
In its graces again
As dreich grun' does
In the gowden grain,
And oot o' the daith
O' pride you rise
Wi' beauty yet
For a hauf-disguise.

The skinklan' stars
Are but distant dirt,
Tho' fer owre near
You are still – whiles – girt
Wi' the bonnie licht
You bood ha'e tint
– And I lo'e Love
Wi' a scunner in't.

Empty Vessel

I met ayont the cairney
A lass wi' tousie hair
Singin' till a bairnie
That was nae langer there.

Wunds wi' warlds to swing
Dinna sing sae sweet,
The licht that bends owre a' thing
Is less ta'en up wi't.

Gairmscoile

Aulder than mammoth or than mastodon
Deep i' the herts o' a' men lurk scaut-heid
Skrymmorie monsters few daur look upon.
Brides sometimes catch their wild een, scansin' reid,
Beekin' abune the herts they thocht to lo'e
And horror-stricken ken that i' themselves
A like beast stan's, and lookin' love thro' and thro'
Meets the reid een wi' een like seevun hells.
... Nearer the twa beasts draw, and, couplin', brak
The bubbles o' twa sauls and the haill warld gangs black.

Yet wha has heard the beasts' wild matin'-call
To ither music syne can gi'e nae ear.
The nameless lo'enotes haud him in a thrall.
Forgot are guid and ill, and joy and fear.
... My bluid sall thraw a dark hood owre my een
And I sall venture deep into the hills
Whaur, scaddows on the skyline, can be seen
– Twinin' the sun's brent broo wi' plaited horns
As gin they crooned it wi' a croon o' thorns –
The beasts in wha's wild cries a' Scotland's destiny thrills.

The lo'es o' single herts are strays; but there
The herds that draw the generations are,
And whasae hears them roarin', evermair
Is yin wi' a' that gangs to mak' or mar
The spirit o' the race, and leads it still
Whither it can be led, 'yont a' desire and will.

I

Wergeland, I mind o' thee – for thy bluid tae
Kent the rouch dirl o' an auld Scots strain,
– A dour dark burn that has its ain wild say
Thro' a' the thrang bricht babble o' Earth's flood.
Behold, thwart my ramballiach life again,
What thrawn and roothewn dreams, royat and rude,
Reek forth — a foray dowless herts condemn –
While chance wi' rungs o' sang or silence renshels them.

(A foray frae the past – and future tae
Sin Time's a blindness we'll thraw aff some day!)
... On the rumgunshoch sides o' hills forgotten
Life hears beasts rowtin' that it deemed extinct,
And, sudden, on the hapless cities linked
In canny civilisation's canty dance
Poor herds o' heich-skeich monsters, misbegotten,
... Streets clear afore the scarmoch advance:
Frae every winnock skimmerin' een keek oot
To see what sic camsteerie cast-offs are aboot.

Cast-offs? – But wha mak's life a means to ony end?
This sterves and that stuff's fu', scraps this and succours that?
The best survive there's nane but fules contend.
Na! Ilka daith is but a santit need.
... Lo! what bricht flames o' beauty are lit at
The unco' een o' lives that Life thocht deid
Till winnock efter winnock kindles wi' a sense
O' gain and glee – as gin a mair intense
Starn nor the sun had risen in wha's licht
Mankind and beasts anew, wi' gusto, see their plicht.

Mony's the auld hauf-human cry I ken
Fa's like a revelation on the herts o' men
As tho' the graves were split and the first man
Grippit the latest wi' a freendly han'.
... And there's forgotten shibboleths o' the Scots
Ha'e keys to senses lockit to us yet
– Coorse words that shamble thro' oor minds like stots,
Syne turn on's muckle een wi' doonsin' emerauds lit.

I hear nae 'hee-haw' but I mind the day
A'e donkey strunted doon a palm-strewn way
As Chesterton has sung; nae wee click-clack
O' hoofs but to my hert at aince comes back
Jammes' Prayer to Gang to Heaven wi' the Asses;
And shambles-ward nae catttle-beast e'er passes
But I mind hoo the saft een o' the kine
Lichted Christ's craidle wi' their canny shine.

Hee-Haw! Click-Clack! And Cock-a-doodle-doo!
– Wull Gabriel in Esperanto cry

Or a' the warld's undeemis jargons try?
It's soon', no' sense, that faddoms the herts o' men.
And by my sangs the rouch auld Scots I ken
E'en herts that ha'e nae Scots 'll dirl richt thro'
As nocht else could – for here's a language rings
Wi' datchie sesames, and names for nameless things.

II

Wergeland, my world as thine 'ca' canny' cries.
And daurna lippen to auld Scotland's virr.
Ah, weel ye kent – as Carlyle quo' likewise –
Maist folk are thowless fules wha downa stir,
Crouse sumphs that hate nane 'bies wha'd wauken them.
To them my Pegasus tae's a crocodile.
Whummelt I tak' a bobquaw for the lift.
Insteed o' sangs my mou' drites eerned phlegm.
... Natheless like thee I stalk on mile by mile,
Howk'n up deid stumps o' thocht, and saw'in my eident gift.

Ablachs, and scrats, and dorbels o' a' kinds
Aye'd drob me wi' their puir eel-droonin' minds,
Wee drochlin' crateurs drutling their bit thochts
The dorty bodies! Feech! Nae Sassunuch drings
'll daunton me. – Tak' ye sic things for poets?
Cock-lairds and drotes depert Parnassus noo.
A'e flash o' wit the lot to drodlich dings.
Rae, Martin, Sutherland – the dowless crew,
I'll twine the dow'd sheaves o' their toom-ear'd corn,
Bind them wi' pity and dally them wi' scorn.

Lang ha'e they posed as men o' letters here,
Dounhaddin' the Doric and keepin't i' the draiks,
Drivellin' and druntin', wi' mony a datchie sneer
... But soon we'll end the haill eggtaggle, fegs!
... The auld volcanoes rummle 'neath their feet,
And a' their shoddy lives 'll soon be drush,
Danders o' Hell! They feel th' unwelcome heat,
The deltit craturs, and their sauls are slush.
For we ha'e faith in Scotland's hidden poo'ers,
The present's theirs, but a' the past and future's oors.

from *A Drunk Man Looks at the Thistle*

I amna fou' sae muckle as tired – deid dune.
It's gey and hard wark coupin' gless for gless
Wi' Cruivie and Gilsanquhar and the like,
And I'm no' juist as bauld as aince I wes.

The elbuck fankles in the coorse o' time,
The sheckle's no' sae souple, and the thrapple
Grows deef and dour: nae langer up and doun
Gleg as a squirrel speils the Adam's apple.

Forbye, the stuffie's no' the real Mackay.
The sun's sel' aince, as sune as ye began it,
Riz in your vera saul: but what keeks in
Noo is in truth the vilest 'saxpenny planet'.

And as the worth's gane doun the cost has risen.
Yin canna throw the cockles o' yin's hert
Wi' oot ha'en' cauld feet noo, jalousin' what
The wife'll say (I dinna blame her fur't).

It's robbin' Peter to pey Paul at least. . . .
And a' that's Scotch aboot it is the name,
Like a' thing else ca'd Scottish nooadays
– A' destitute o' speerit juist the same.

(To prove my saul is Scots I maun begin
Wi' what's still deemed Scots and the folk expect,
And spire up syne by visible degrees
To heichts whereo' the fules ha'e never recked.

But aince I get them there I'll whummle them
And souse the craturs in the nether deeps,
–For it's nae choice, and ony man s'ud wish
To dree the goat's weird tae as weel's the sheep's!)

Heifetz in tartan, and Sir Harry Lauder!
Whaur's Isadora Duncan dancin' noo?
Is Mary Garden in Chicago still
And Duncan Grant in Paris – and me fou'?

Sic transit gloria Scotia – a' the floo'ers
O' the Forest are wede awa'. (A blin' bird's nest
Is aiblins biggin' in the thistle tho'? ...
And better blin' if'ts brood is like the rest!)

You canna gang to a Burns supper even
Wi'oot some wizened scrunt o' a knock-knee
Chinee turns roon to say, 'Him Haggis – velly goot!'
And ten to wan the piper is a Cockney.

No' wan in fifty kens a wurd Burns wrote
But misapplied is a' body's property,
And gin there was his like alive the day
They'd be the last a kennin' haund to gi'e –

Croose London Scotties wi' their braw shirt fronts
And a' their fancy freen's, rejoicin'
That similah gatherings in Timbuctoo,
Bagdad – and Hell, nae doot – are voicin'

Burns' sentiments o' universal love,
In pidgin English or in wild-fowl Scots,
And toastin' ane wha's nocht to them but an
Excuse for faitherin' Genius wi' *their* thochts.

A' *they*'ve to say was aften said afore
A lad was born in Kyle to blaw aboot.
What unco fate mak's *him* the dumpin'-grun'
For a' the sloppy rubbish they jaw oot?

Mair nonsense has been uttered in his name
Than in ony's barrin' liberty and Christ.
If this keeps spreedin' as the drink declines,
Syne turns to tea, wae's me for the *Zeitgeist*!

Rabbie, wad'st thou wert here – the warld hath need,
And Scotland mair sae, o' the likes o' thee!
The whisky that aince moved your lyre's become
A laxative for a' loquacity.

O gin they'd stegh their guts and haud their wheesht
I'd thole it, for 'a man's a man' I ken,
But though the feck ha'e plenty o' the 'a' that',
They're nocht but zoologically men.

I'm haverin', Rabbie, but ye understaun'
It gets my dander up to see your star
A bauble in Babel, banged like a saxpence
'Twixt Burbank's Baedeker and Bleistein's cigar.

There's nane sae ignorant but think they can
Expatiate on *you*, if on nae ither.
The sumphs ha'e ta'en you at your wurd, and, fegs!
The foziest o' them claims to be a – Brither!

Syne 'Here's the cheenge' – the star of Rabbie Burns.
Sma' cheenge, 'Twinkle, Twinkle.' The memory slips
As G. K. Chesterton heaves up to gi'e
'The Immortal Memory' in a huge eclipse,

Or somebody else as famous if less fat.
You left the like in Embro in a scunner
To booze wi' thieveless cronies sic as me.
I'se warrant you'd shy clear o' a' the hunner

Odd Burns Clubs tae, or ninety-nine o' them,
And haud your birthday in a different kip
Whaur your name isna ta'en in vain – as Christ
Gied a' Jerusalem's Pharisees the slip

– Christ wha'd ha'e been Chief Rabbi gin he'd lik't! –
Wi' publicans and sinners to forgether,
But, losh! the publicans noo are Pharisees,
And I'm no' shair o' maist the sinners either.

But that's aside the point! I've got fair waun'ert.
It's no' that I'm sae fou' as juist deid dune,
And dinna ken as muckle's whaur I am
Or hoo I've come to sprawl here 'neth the mune.

That's it! It isna me that's fou' at a',
But the fu' mune, the doited jade, that's led

Me fer agley, or 'mogrified the warld.
– For a' I ken I'm safe in my ain bed.

Jean! Jean! Gin *she's* no' here it's no' *oor* bed,
Or else I'm dreamin' deep and canna wauken,
But it's a fell queer dream if this is no'
A real hillside – and thae things thistles and bracken!

It's hard wark haud'n' by a thocht worth ha'en'
And harder speakin't, and no' for ilka man;
Maist Thocht's like whisky – a thoosan' under proof,
And a sair price is pitten on't even than.

As Kirks wi' Christianity ha'e dune,
Burns Clubs wi' Burns – wi' a'thing it's the same,
The core o' ocht is only for the few,
Scorned by the mony, thrang wi'ts empty name.

And a' the names in History mean nocht
To maist folk but 'ideas o' their ain',
The vera opposite o' onything
The Deid 'ud awn gin they cam' back again.

A greater Christ, a greater Burns, may come.
The maist they'll dae is to gi'e bigger pegs
To folly and conceit to hank their rubbish on.
They'll cheenge folks' talk but no their natures, fegs!

I maun feed frae the common trough ana'
Whaur a' the lees o' hope are jumbled up;
While centuries like pigs are slorpin' owre't
Sall my wee 'oor be cryin': 'Let pass this cup'?

In wi' your gruntle then, puir wheengin' saul,
Lap up the ugsome aidle wi' the lave,
What gin it's your ain vomit that you swill
And frae Life's gantin' and unfaddomed grave?

I doot I'm geylies mixed, like Life itsel',
But I was never ane that thocht to pit
An ocean in a mutchkin. As the haill's
Mair than the pairt sae I than reason yet.

I dinna haud the warld's end in my heid
As maist folk think they dae; nor filter truth
In fishy gills through which its tides may poor
For ony *animalculae* forsooth.

I lauch to see my crazy little brain
– And ither folks' – tak'n' itsel' seriously,
And in a sudden lowe o' fun my saul
Blinks dozent as the owl I ken't to be.

I'll ha'e nae hauf-way hoose, but aye be whaur
Extremes meet – it's the only way I ken
To dodge the curst conceit o' bein' richt
That damns the vast majority o' men.

I'll bury nae heid like an ostrich's,
Nor yet believe my een and naething else.
My senses may advise me, but I'll be
Mysel' nae maitter what they tell's. . . .

I ha'e nae doot some foreign philosopher
Has wrocht a system oot to justify
A' this: but I'm a Scot wha blin'ly follows
Auld Scottish instincts, and I winna try.

For I've nae faith in ocht I can explain,
And stert whaur the philosophers leave aff,
Content to glimpse its loops I dinna ettle
To land the sea serpent's sel' wi' ony gaff.

Like staundin' water in a pocket o'
Impervious clay I pray I'll never be,
Cut aff and self-sufficient, but let reenge
Heichts o' the lift and benmaist deeps o' sea.

Water! Water! There was owre muckle o't
In yonder whisky, sae I'm in deep water
(And gin I could wun hame I'd be in het,
For even Jean maun natter, natter, natter). . . .

And in the toon that I belang tae
– What tho'ts Montrose or Nazareth? –

Helplessly the folk continue
To lead their livin' death! ...

*

Said my body to my mind,
'I've been startled whiles to find,
When Jean has been in bed wi' me,
A kind o' Christianity!'

To my body said my mind,
'But your benmaist thocht you'll find
Was "Bother what I think I feel
– Jean kens the set o' my bluid owre weel,
And lauchs to see me in the creel
O' my courage-bag confined."' ...

I wish I kent the physical basis
O' a' life's seemin' airs and

It's queer the thochts a kittled cull
Can lowse or splairgin' glit annul.

Man's spreit is wi' his ingangs twined
In ways that he can ne'er unwind.

A wumman whiles a bawaw gi'es
That clean abaws him gin he sees.

Or wi' a movement o' a leg
Shows'm his mind is juist a geg.

I'se warrant Jean 'ud no' be lang
In findin' whence this thistle sprang.

Mebbe it's juist because I'm no'
Beddit wi' her that gars it grow! ...

A luvin' wumman is a licht*
That shows a man his waefu' plicht,
Bleezin' steady on ilka bane,
Wrigglin' sinnen an' twinin' vein,

* Suggested by the French of Edmond Rocher.

Or fleerin' quick an' gane again,
And the mair scunnersome the sicht
The mair for love and licht he's fain
Till clear and chitterin' and nesh
Move a' the miseries o' his flesh. . . .

O lass, wha see'est me
As I daur hardly see,
I marvel that your bonny een
Are as they hadna seen.

Through a' my self-respect
They see the truth abject
    – Gin you could pierce their blindin' licht
    You'd see a fouler sicht! . . .

O wha's the bride that cairries the bunch
O' thistles blinterin' white?
Her cuckold bridegroom little dreids
What he sall ken this nicht.

For closer than gudeman can come
And closer to'r than hersel',
Wha didna need her maidenheid
Has wrocht his purpose fell.

O wha's been here afore me, lass,
And hoo did he get in?
    – A man that deed or I was born
    This evil thing has din.

And left, as it were on a corpse,
Your maidenheid to me?
    – Nae lass, gudeman, sin' Time began
    'S hed ony mair to gi'e.

But I can gi'e ye kindness, lad,
And a pair o' willin' hands,
And you sall ha'e my breists like stars,
My limbs like willow wands,

And on my lips ye'll heed nae mair,
And in my hair forget,

The seed o' a' the men that in
My virgin womb ha'e met. . . .

Millions o' wimmen bring forth in pain
Millions o' bairns that are no' worth ha'en'.

Wull ever a wumman be big again
Wi's muckle's a Christ? Yech, there's nae sayin'.

Gin that's the best that you ha'e comin',
Fegs but I'm sorry for you, wumman!

Yet a'e thing's certain – Your faith is great.
Whatever happens, you'll no' be blate! . . .

*

The stars like thistle's roses floo'er
The sterile growth o' Space ootour,
That clad in bitter blasts spreids oot
Frae me, the sustenance o' its root.

O fain I'd keep my hert entire,
Fain hain the licht o' my desire,
But ech! the shinin' streams ascend,
And leave me empty at the end.

For aince it's toomed my hert and brain,
The thistle needs maun fa' again.
– But a' its growth 'll never fill
The hole it's turned my life intill! . . .

Yet ha'e I Silence left, the croon o' a'.

No' her, wha on the hills langsyne I saw
Liftin' a foreheid o' perpetual snaw.

No' her, wha in the how-dumb-deid o' nicht
Kyths, like Eternity in Time's despite.

No' her, withooten shape, wha's name is Daith,
No' Him, unkennable abies to faith

25

–God whom, gin e'er He saw a man, 'ud be
E'en mair dumfooner'd at the sicht than he

–But Him, whom nocht in man or Deity,
Or Daith or Dreid or Laneliness can touch,
Wha's deed owre often and has seen owre much.

O I ha'e Silence left,

               – 'And weel ye micht,'
Sae Jean'll say, 'efter sic a nicht!'

from *To Circumjack Cencrastus*

Lourd on my hert as winter lies
The state that Scotland's in the day.
Spring to the North has aye come slow
But noo dour winter's like to stay
      For guid,
      And no' for guid!

O wae's me on the weary days
When it is scarce grey licht at noon;
It maun be a' the stupid folk
Diffusin' their dullness roon and roon
      Like soot,
That keeps the sunlicht oot.

Nae wonder if I think I see
A lichter shadow than the neist
I'm fain to cry: 'The dawn, the dawn!
I see it brakin' in the East.'
      But ah
      – It's juist mair snaw!

First Hymn to Lenin

To Prince D. S. Mirsky

Few even o' the criminals, cravens, and fools
Wha's voices vilify a man they ken
They've cause to fear and are unfit to judge
As they're to stem his influence again
But in the hollows where their herts should be
     Foresee your victory.

Churchills, Locker-Lampsons, Beaverbrooks'll be
In history's perspective less to you
(And them!) than the Centurions to Christ
Of whom, as you, at least this muckle's true
– 'Tho' pairtly wrang he cam' to richt amang's
     Faur greater wrangs.'

Christ's cited no' by chance or juist because
You mark the greatest turnin'-point since him
But that your main redress has lain where he's
Least use – fulfillin' his sayin' lang kept dim
That whasae followed him things o' like natur'
     'Ud dae – and greater!

Certes nae ither, if no' you's dune this.
It maitters little. What you've dune's the thing,
No' hoo't compares, corrects, or complements
The work of Christ that's ta'en owre lang to bring
Sic a successor to keep the reference back
     Natural to mak'.

Great things ha'e aye ta'en great men in the past
In some proportion to the work they did,
But you alane to what you've dune are nocht
Even as the poo'ers to greater ends are hid
In what's ca'd God, or in the common man,
     Withoot your plan.

Descendant o' the unkent Bards wha made
Sangs peerless through a' post-anonymous days

I glimpse again in you that mightier poo'er
Than fashes wi' the laurels and the bays
But kens that it is shared by ilka man
          Since time began.

Great things, great men – but at faur greater's cost!
If first things first had had their richtfu' sway
Life and Thocht's misused poo'er might ha' been ane
For a' men's benefit – as still they may
Noo that through you this mair than elemental force
          Has f'und a clearer course.

Christ said: 'Save ye become as bairns again.'
Bairnly eneuch the feck o' us ha' been!
Your work needs men; and its worst foes are juist
The traitors wha through a' history ha' gi'en
The dope that's gar'd the mass o' folk pay heed
          And bide bairns indeed.

As necessary, and insignificant, as death
Wi' a' its agonies in the cosmos still
The Cheka's horrors are in their degree;
And'll end suner! What maitters 't wha we kill
To lessen that foulest murder that deprives
          Maist men o' real lives?

For now in the flower and iron of the truth
To you we turn; and turn in vain nae mair,
Ilka fool has folly eneuch for sadness
But at last we are wise and wi' laughter tear
The veil of being, and are face to face
          Wi' the human race.

Here lies your secret, O Lenin, – yours and oors,
No' in the majority will that accepts the result
But in the real will that bides its time and kens
The benmaist resolve is the poo'er in which we exult
Since naebody's willingly deprived o' the good;
          And, least o' a', the crood!

At My Father's Grave

The sunlicht still on me, you row'd in clood,
We look upon each ither noo like hills
Across a valley. I'm nae mair your son.
It is my mind, nae son o' yours, that looks,
And the great darkness o' your death comes up
And equals it across the way.
A livin' man upon a deid man thinks
And ony sma'er thocht's impossible.

Prayer for a Second Flood

There'd ha'e to be nae warnin'. Times ha'e changed
And Noahs are owre numerous nooadays,
(And them the vera folk to benefit maist!)
Knock the feet frae under them, O Lord, wha praise
Your unsearchable ways sae muckle and yet hope
      To keep within knowledgeable scope!

Ding a' their trumpery show to blauds again.
Their measure is the thimblefu' o' Esk in spate.
Like whisky the tittlin' craturs mete oot your poo'ers
Aince a week for bawbees in the kirk-door plate,
– And pit their umbrellas up when they come oot
      If mair than a pulpitfu' o' You's aboot!

O arselins wi' them! Whummle them again!
Coup them heels-owre-gowdy in a storm sae gundy
That mony a lang fog-theekit face I ken
'll be sooked richt doon under through a cundy
In the High Street, afore you get weel-sterted
      And are still hauf-herted!

Then flush the world in earnest. Let yoursel' gang,
Scour't to the bones, and mak' its marrow holes
Toom as a whistle as they used to be
In days I mind o' ere men fidged wi' souls,
But naething had forgotten you as yet,
      Nor you forgotten it.

Up then and at them, ye Gairds o' Heaven.
The Divine Retreat is owre. Like a tidal bore
Boil in among them; let the lang lugs nourished
On the milk o' the word at last hear the roar
O' human shingle; and replenish the salt o' the earth
      In the place o' their birth.

Second Hymn to Lenin

To My Friends Naomi Mitchison and Henry Carr

Ah, Lenin, you were richt. But I'm a poet
(And you c'ud mak allowances for that!)
Aimin' at mair than you aimed at
Tho' yours comes first, I know it.

An unexamined life is no' worth ha'in'.
Yet Burke was richt; owre muckle concern
Wi' Life's foundations is a sure
Sign o' decay; tho' Joyce in turn

Is richt, and the principal question
Aboot a work o' art is frae hoo deep
A life it springs – and syne hoo faur
Up frae't it has the poo'er to leap

And hoo muckle it lifts up wi' it
Into the sunlicht like a saumon there,
Universal Spring! for Morand's richt –
It s'ud be like licht in the air –

> *Are my poems spoken in the factories and fields,*
>   *In the streets o' the toon?*
> *Gin they're no', then I'm failin' to dae*
>   *What I ocht to ha' dune.*
>
> *Gin I canna win through to the man in the street,*
>   *The wife by the hearth,*
> *A' the cleverness on earth 'll no' mak' up*
>   *For the damnable dearth.*
>
> *'Haud on, haud on; what poet's dune that?*
>   *Is Shakespeare read,*
> *Or Dante or Milton or Goethe or Burns?'*
>   *– You heard what I said.*

– A means o' world locomotion,
The maist perfected and aerial o' a'.
Lenin's name's gane owre the haill earth,
But the names o' the ithers? – Ha!

What hidie-hole o' the vineyard d'they scart
Wi' minds like the look on a hen's face,
Morand, Joyce, Burke, and the rest
That e'er wrote; me noo in like case?

Great poets hardly onybody kens o'?
Geniuses like a man talkin' t'm sel'?
Nonsense! They're nocht o' the sort
Their character's easy to tell.

They're nocht but romantic rebels
Strikin' dilettante poses;
Trotsky – Christ, no' wi' a croon o' thorns
But a wreath o' paper roses.

A' that's great is free and expansive.
What ha' they expanded tae?
They've affected nocht but a fringe
O' mankind in ony way.

Barbarian saviour o' civilization
Hoo weel ye kent (we're owre dull witted)
Naething is dune save as we ha'e
Means to en's transparently fitted.

Poetry like politics maun cut
The cackle and pursue real ends,
Unerringly as Lenin, and to that
Its nature better tends.

Wi' Lenin's vision equal poet's gift
And what unparalleled force was there!
Nocht in a' literature wi' that
Begins to compare.

Nae simple rhymes for silly folk
But the haill art, as Lenin gied
Nae Marx-without-tears to workin' men
But the fu' course insteed.

Organic constructional work,
Practicality, and work by degrees;
First things first; and poetry in turn
'll be built by these.

You saw it faur off when you thocht
O' mass-education yet.
Hoo lang till they rise to Pushkin?
And that's but a fit!

> Oh, it's nonsense, nonsense, nonsense,
> Nonsense at this time o' day
> That breid-and-butter problems
> S'ud be in ony man's way.
>
> They s'ud be like the tails we tint
> On leavin' the monkey stage;
> A' maist folk fash aboot's alike
> Primaeval to oor age.
>
> We're grown-up folk that haena yet
> Put bairnly things aside
> – A' that's material and moral –
> And oor new state descried.
>
> Sport, love, and parentage,
> Trade, politics, and law
> S'ud be nae mair to us than braith
> We hardly ken we draw.
>
> Freein' oor poo'ers for greater things,
> And fegs there's plenty o' them,
> Tho' wha's still trammelt in alow
> Canna be tenty o' them –

In the meantime Montéhus' sangs –
But as you were ready to tine
The Russian Revolution to the German
Gin that ser'd better syne,

Or foresaw that Russia maun lead
The workers' cause, and then
Pass the lead elsewhere, and aiblins
Fa' faur backward again,

Sae here, twixt poetry and politics,
There's nae doot in the en'.
Poetry includes that and s'ud be
The greatest poo'er amang men.

– It's the greatest, *in posse* at least,
That men ha'e discovered yet
Tho' nae doot they're unconscious still
O' ithers faur greater than it.

You confined yoursel' to your work
– A step at a time;
But, as the loon is in the man,
That'll be ta'en up i' the rhyme,

Ta'en up like a pool in the sands
Aince the tide rows in,
When life opens its hert and sings
Withoot scruple or sin.

Your knowledge in your ain sphere
Was exact and complete
But your sphere's elementary and sune by
As a poet maun see't.

For a poet maun see in a'thing,
Ev'n what looks trumpery or horrid,
A subject equal to ony
– A star for the forehead!

A poet has nae choice left
Betwixt Beaverbrook, say, and God,
Jimmy Thomas or you,
A cat, carnation, or clod.

He daurna turn awa' frae ocht
For a single act o' neglect
And straucht he may fa' frae grace
And be void o' effect.

> *Disinterestedness,*
> *Oor profoundest word yet,*
> *But hoo faur yont even that*
> *The sense o' onything's set!*

> *The inward necessity yont*
> *Ony laws o' cause*
> *The intellect conceives*
> *That a'thing has!*

Freend, foe; past, present, future;
Success, failure; joy, fear;
Life, Death; and a'thing else,
For us, are equal here.

Male, female; quick or deid,
Let us fike nae mair;
The deep line o' cleavage
Disna lie there.

Black in the pit the miner is,
The shepherd reid on the hill,
And I'm wi' them baith until
The end of mankind, I wis.

Whatever their jobs a' men are ane
In life, and syne in daith
(Tho' it's sma' patience I can ha'e
Wi' life's ideas o' that by the way)
And he's nae poet but kens it, faith,
And ony job but the hardest's ta'en.

The sailor gangs owre the curve o' the sea,
The hoosewife's thrang in the wash-tub,
And whatna rhyme can I find but hub,
And what else can poetry be?

The core o' a' activity,
Changin't in accordance wi'
Its inward necessity
And mede o' integrity.

Unremittin', relentless,
Organized to the last degree,
Ah, Lenin, politics is bairns' play
To what this maun be!

Milk-Wort and Bog-Cotton

To Seumas O'Sullivan

Cwa' een like milk-wort and bog-cotton hair!
I love you, earth, in this mood best o' a'
When the shy spirit like a laich wind moves
And frae the lift nae shadow can fa'
Since there's nocht left to thraw a shadow there
Owre een like milk-wort and milk-white cotton hair.

Wad that nae leaf upon anither wheeled
A shadow either and nae root need dern
In sacrifice to let sic beauty be!
But deep surroondin' darkness I discern
Is aye the price o' licht. Wad licht revealed
Naething but you, and nicht nocht else concealed.

Water Music

TO WILLIAM AND FLORA JOHNSTONE

Wheesht, wheesht, Joyce, and let me hear
  Nae Anna Livvy's lilt,
But Wauchope, Esk, and Ewes again,
  Each wi' its ain rhythms till't.

I

Archin' here and arrachin there,
  Allevolie or allemand,
Whiles appliable, whiles areird,
  The polysemous poem's planned.

Lively, louch, atweesh, atween,
  Auchimuty or aspate,
Threidin' through the averins
  Or bightsom in the aftergait.

Or barmybrained or barritchfu',
  Or rinnin' like an attercap,
Or shinin' like an Atchison,
  Wi' a blare or wi' a blawp.

They ken a' that opens and steeks,
  Frae Fiddleton Bar to Callister Ha',
And roon aboot for twenty miles,
  They bead and bell and swaw.

Brent on or boutgate or beshacht
  Bellwaverin' or borne-heid,
They mimp and primp, or bick and birr,
  Dilly-dally or show speed.

Brade-up or sclafferin', rouchled, sleek,
  Abstraklous or austerne,
In belths below the brae-hags
  And bebbles in the fern.

Bracken, blaeberries, and heather
  Ken their amplefeysts and toves,

Here gangs ane wi' aiglets jinglin',
  Through a gowl anither goves.

Lint in the bell whiles hardly vies
  Wi' ane the wind amows,
While blithely doon abradit linns
  Wi' gowd begane anither jows.

Cougher, blocher, boich and croichle,
  Fraise in ane anither's witters,
Wi' backthraws, births, by-rinnin's,
  Beggar's-broon or blae – the critters!

Or burnet, holine, watchet, chauve,
  Or wi' a' the colours dyed
O' the lift abune and plants and trees
  That grow on either side.

Or coinyelled wi' the midges,
  Or swallows a' aboot,
The shadow o' an eagle,
  The aiker o' a troot.

Toukin' ootrageous face
  The turn-gree o' your mood,
I've climmed until I'm lost
  Like the sun ahint a clood.

But a tow-gun frae the boon-tree,
A whistle frae the elm,
A spout-gun frae the hemlock,
And, back in this auld realm,
Dry leafs o' dishielogie
To smoke in a 'partan's tae'!

And you've me in your creel again,
  Brim or shallow, bauch or bricht,
Singin' in the mornin',
  Corrieneuchin' a' the nicht.

II

Lappin' on the shirrel,
  Or breengin' doon the cleuch,
Slide-thrift for stars and shadows,
  Or sun-'couped owre the heuch'.

Wi' the slughorn o' a folk,
  Sightsmen for a thoosand years,
In fluther or at shire
  O' the Border burns' careers,

Let them popple, let them pirl,
  Plish-plash and plunk and plop and ploot,
In quakin' quaw or fish-currie
  I ken a' they're aboot.

And 'twixt the pavvy o' the Wauchope,
  And the paspey o' the Ewes,
And the pavane o' Esk itsel',
  It's no' for me to choose.

Be they querty, be they quiet,
  Flow like railya or lamoo,
Only turn a rashmill or
  Gar a' the country tew,

As it's froggin' in the hills,
  Or poors pipestapples and auld wives,
Sae Waich Water glents and scrows,
  Reels and ratches and rives.

Some day they say the Bigly Burn
  'll loup oot frae its scrabs and thistles,
And ding the bonnie birken shaw
  A' to pigs and whistles.

And there's yon beck – I winna name't –
  That hauds the fish that aince was hookit
A century syne – the fisher saw't,
  And flew, and a' his graith forsookit.

And as for Unthank Water,
  That seeps through miles o' reeds and seggs,

It's aye at pilliewinkie syne
   Wi' the gowdnie's eggs.

Nae mair than you could stroan yoursel'
   The biggest o' them you may say,
Yet lood and till I see them stoan
   To oceans and the heaven's sway.

Fleetin' owre the meadows,
   Or cleitchin' in the glaur,
The haill world answers to them,
   And they rein the faurest star.

Humboldt, Howard, Maury,
   Hildebrandsson, Hann, and Symons,
A digest o' a' their work's
   In these dour draps or diamonds.

And weel I ken the air's wild rush
   As it comes owre the seas,
Clims up and whistles 'twixt the hills,
   Wi' a' the weather gi'es

O' snaw and rain and thunder,
   Is a single circle spun
By the sun's bricht heat and guided by
   Earth's spin and the shapes o' the grun',

Lappin' on the shirrel,
   Or breengin' doon the cleuch,
I can listen to the waters
   Lang – and no' lang – eneuch.

Wheesht, wheesht, Joyce, and let me hear
   No' Anna Livvy's lilt,
But Wauchope, Esk, and Ewes again,
   Each wi' its ain rhythms till't.

Depth and the Chthonian Image

On looking at a ruined mill and thinking of the greatest

To John Macnair Reid

Absolvitur ab instantia is decreed
In every case against you men array.
Yours is the only nature stiflin' nocht,
Meetin' a' the experiences there are to ha'e
And never meetin' ane o' them raw-edged.
Ripe, reconcilin' mind, sublimely gauged,
Serene receptiveness, nae tongue can speak
Your fair fey form felicitously enow,
Nae subtle mind seek your benmaist howe
And gar your deepest implications beek.
The mills o' God grind sma', but they
In you maun crumble imperceptibly tae.
Nor shadowed nor lit up by ony thocht,
Nae perfect shinin' o' a simmer's day
Vies wi' your ark's assopat speed
In its pure task engaged.
Time and Eternity are no' at odds
In you as in a' that's Man's – and God's,
For nane can look through you as through the sun and see
Some auld adhantare wi' neuked bonnet there,
Urphanömen – o' what? Ah, no, alluterlie
You deal afflufe wi' a' that's fordel and nae gair
In your allryn activity lets kyth
    The faur-side o' your sneith.

As life to death, as man to God, sae stands
This ruined mill to your great aumrie then,
This ruined mill – and every rinnin' mill?
The awte or bait o' everything you ken
And tak' it quicker than a barber's knife
Wi' nocht aclite. There is nae chance o' strife.
Micht a' the canny your abandon see!
Nor ony din they mak' let them forget
Their generations tae and creeds'll yet
Crine to a sic-like laroch while the lets-a-be

41

O' a' your pairts as eidently agree.
Nocht needs your wa's mair audience to gi'e.
Forever ample baith in scouth and skill,
Watchin' your aws by nicht it seems to me
The stars adreigh mimic their drops and 'mang hands
There is nae nearer image gi'en to life
O' that conclusive power by which you rin
Even on, drawin' a' the universe in,
Than this loose simile o' the heavenly hosts
Vainly prefigurin' the unseen jaups
Roond your vast wheel – or mair waesome ghosts
O' that reality man's pairt o' and yet caps
Wi' Gods in his ain likeness drawn
     – Puir travesties o' your plan.

To picture the invisible via the stars
Is the least boutgate that man's speech can gang,
As for your speed the analogy o' sleep,
Your speed and your boon millin' – no' even the lang
Processes o' metamorphosis in rock
Can fetch that ben to him like the shadowy flock
O' atoms in himsel' precariously seen,
Queer dirlin' o' his cells at sic an 'oor,
He whiles can note wha hasna else the poo'er,
Laichest Brownian movements swarmin' to his een
As neath a microscope – a deemless thrang,
To catch their changin' time, and get the hang
O' a' their swift diminishments doon the steep
Chutes o' dissolution, as he lay amang
The mools already, and watched the maggots' wars
Upon his flesh, and sune its finitude mock
Their midgeswarm jaws until their numbers fa'
To a'e toom mou', the fremit last o' a'
The reelin' corruption its vain mudgeons there
Wi' motions that nae measure can seize on
As micht the sun to earth's last look appear
Like yon cart-wheel that raxes to a cone
Afore the spider lets its anchorage slip,
     An insect in its grip.

Nae knowledge its ain offices here
Can seek to magnify and ithers suppress.
An arbiter frae corruption free hauds sway
Unlike man's mind that canna ken unless
It decks its data wi' interpretation
To try to mak' a rational creation.
Hence a' men see contains faur mair than's seen,
Remembrance o' the past, fancy o' the future.
To memory and imagination you stand neuter
As 'twere a scientist confrontin' the gi'en
That nae logical, *a priori*, or ither reasons confess
And yet are carriers o' value that redress
His rational world frae bein' senseless tae,
Tho' here, as in sma'er things, nae inspired guess,
Teleological reasonin' or rapport sheer,
Gi'es minds like his sic valuable dilation.
You're no' its meanin' but the world itsel'.
Yet let nae man think he can see you better
By concentratin' on your aneness either.
He pits his mind into a double fetter
Wha hauds this airt or that, no baith thegither.
You are at aince the road a' croods ha' gane
       And alane wi' the alane.

Alane wi' the alane, yet let us no' forget
Theistic faith's but, extrapolate, plottin' on
The curve o' sae-ca'd knowledge science has made
– Science and theism ha'e their roots in common
(Tho' few can credit sic a teachin' noo!) –
And needs the same redress as sciences do
To say the least. Alane wi' the alane remains
A relative conception as self-betrayed
As heidstrang science dispensin' wi' sic aid
As frae the world's allogic, kept in mind, it gains.
Nae mutual justice, undue claims foregone,
Sympathy wi' divers ootlooks and endeavours shown,
Union o' knowledge's kingdoms piously prayed,
Is less a movement leadin' awa' frae you
Than ony in the opposite airt to it,
Nor can a poet as I am cease to con,
Heedless o' baith, your prime significance

To lead his muse a needle-angel's dance
By hailin' truth a mathematical point
Wi' nae relation to the ooter world,
Whether the times are in or oot o' joint
O' scant concern since a'thing earthly's hurled
– You tae – indifferent, *adiaphora*, faur alow
        Ocht this tak's heed o'.

Aye balk and burral lie the fields o' life.
It fails to acresce a kennin' frae the past,
In a' its fancied contacts wi' what's meant
When it seems shairest in worst backspangs cast;
Its heritage but a bairn's pairt o' gear,
A puir balapat at hairst its fingers speir
And often mairket a toom barley-box;
Aye in bad breid despite their constant toil,
As bairns in their bairnliness, a cursed coil
Hauds men content wi' casual sweetie-pokes
O' a' creation's gear; and little is amassed
Maist folk can life-rent – nocht hain at last.
Yet o' the way-drawn profit wha tak's tent?
The feast is spread yet helplessly they fast,
Aye win an Irishman's rise wi' unco strife,
Cast oot frae a' their dues by the silly fear
That hauds them in habits o' poortith still,
While by them brim the torrents to your mill,
The vast way-drawing that denies mankind
Or pairt or parcel in science or in art
Till bare as worms the feck o' them we find,
Each generation at zero still maun start
And's doomed to end there, wi' a' that they forgaed
        Caught in the suction o' your lade.

Or pairt or parcel in science or in art.
– Or even in life! Hoo few men ever live
And what wee local lives at best they ha'e.
Sirse, science and art might weel rin through the sieve,
Or jow like backfa's when the mill is set.
If maist folk through nae elf-bores dribbled yet
But in some measure lived to a' life is.
Wad that their latent poo'ers 'ud loup alist,

Kyth suddenly a' their wasted past has missed,
And nae mair leave their lives like languages,
– Mere leaks frae streamin' consciousness as if
Thocht roon' itsel' raised wa's prohibitive
O' a' but a fraction o' its possible sway –
But rax in freedom, nocht inhibitive,
In fearless flourishin' amidwart,
Fed by the haill wide world and feedin' it,
Universal life, like an autonomous tongue
In which some vision o' you micht be sung,
Let us remove a' lets and hindrances then
Even as the principle o' limitation, God,
Packed wi' posterity, silent like the deid,
And aye respondin' to a lesser need,
Has vanished like a clood that weighed on men
Owre lang – till your pure radiance glowed.

Ein Mann aus dem Volke – weel I ken
Nae man or movement's worth a damn unless
The movement 'ud gang on withoot him if
He de'ed the morn. Wherefore in you I bless
My sense o' the greatest man can typify
And universalise himsel' maist fully by.
Nocht ta'en at second-hand and nocht let drift,
Nae bull owre big to tackle by the horns,
Nae chance owre sma' for freedom's sake he scorns,
But a' creation through himsel' maun sift
Even as you, nor possible defeat confess,
Forever poised and apt in his address;
Save at this pitch nae man can truly live.
Hence to these ruins I maun needs regress
– As to the facts o' death and a' the past again,
Beast life, plant life, minerals, water, sky,
A' that has been, is, is to be – frae you
Clear seen, still clearer sicht to pursue.
Similia similibus rotantur, a' facts amang
I seek the *Ereigniswerden*'s essence then
That shows a' that seems kent in it wrang
And gars a' else point back to it again,
Their worth to guide wha can use them hence
    To your fulfillin' experience.

Elschaddai. Emelachan.[*] We only want
The world to live and feel its life in us?
But the world lives whether we dae or no',
A's vice that abates life or can blin' us
To your final epopteia – contents us with
The hearin' o' the ear, no' the vision swith,
The life o' shadows, mere tautology,
Ony curious fig-leaf o' the mind whereby
Humanity has socht to hide its sin,
Portentous prison-hooses o' fause thocht we see
'Science' big heicher daily – a' that can pin us
To the spectral frae the live world, come atween us
And the terrible crystal, the ineffable glow.
Diseases o' the will that needs maun fin' us
Less potent to act, and a' the clichés and cant,
Limitations o' personality, pap for pith,
Robotisation, feminism, youth movements,
A' the super-economic programme's intents
Set grey, a hellish parody (oot there
Forenenst your blazin' energy), and its
Perpetual fause alarms, shams o' seemin' fair,
Fixed fallacies auld as man, sheer waste o' wits
– Oh, you are no' the glory mankind desires
      Yet naething else inspires!

The recurrent vividness o' licht and water
Through every earthly change o' mood or scene
Puirly prefigures you – a' Nature's dreamt,
And no' dune, thrang wi' ither plans, has been
A fog twixt you and us. It's nocht to ken
Something has happened – save only when
'Mang mony alternatives sic choice was ta'en.
You aye exclude a' ither possibilities.
A'e voice may cry alood: 'Wha ever sees
You to hairy goon and mossy cell has gane.'
Anither proclaim the vital vision gi'en

[*] *Elschaddai*, the Self-Sufficient One. *Emelachan* means: 'Your spirit is tranquil
and silent, your soul is delicate, your flesh and blood are strong, both easily
roar like the wave of the sea, then gentleness speaks in you: come and be
calm.'

'Ud move to deeds frae care o' consequence clean.
But baith are wrang – the reckless and the fremt.
And in your radiant licht man's first truth's seen
– Tho' still the last and least to matter
In a' their fond affairs to the mass o' men –
The love o' economics is the mainspring
O' a' the virtues. Eternity like a ring,
Virile, masculine, abandoned at nae-turn
To enervatin' luxury
Aboot me here shall ever clearer burn,
And in its licht perchance at last men'll see
Wi' the best works o' art, as wi' you tae,
      Chance can ha'e nocht to dae!

Of John Davidson

I remember one death in my boyhood
That next to my father's, and darker, endures;
Not Queen Victoria's, but Davidson, yours,
And something in me has always stood
Since then looking down the sandslope
On your small black shape by the edge of the sea,
– A bullet-hole through a great scene's beauty,
God through the wrong end of a telescope.

The Skeleton of the Future

At Lenin's Tomb

Red granite and black diorite, with the blue
Of the labradorite crystals gleaming like precious stones
In the light reflected from the snow; and behind them
The eternal lightning of Lenin's bones.

On a Raised Beach

To James H. Whyte

All is lithogenesis – or lochia,
Carpolite fruit of the forbidden tree,
Stones blacker than any in the Caaba,
Cream-coloured caen-stone, chatoyant pieces,
Celadon and corbeau, bistre and beige,
Glaucous, hoar, enfouldered, cyathiform,
Making mere faculae of the sun and moon
I study you glout and gloss, but have
No cadrans to adjust you with, and turn again
From optik to haptik and like a blind man run
My fingers over you, arris by arris, burr by burr,
Slickensides, truité, rugas, foveoles,
Bringing my aesthesis in vain to bear,
An angle-titch to all your corrugations and coigns,
Hatched foraminous cavo-rilievo of the world,
Deictic, fiducial stones. Chiliad by chiliad
What bricole piled you here, stupendous cairn?
What artist poses the Earth échorché thus,
Pillar of creation engouled in me?
What eburnation augments you with men's bones,
Every energumen an Endymion yet?
All the other stones are in this haecceity it seems,
But where is the Christophanic rock that moved?
What Cabirian song from this catasta comes?

Deep conviction or preference can seldom
Find direct terms in which to express itself.
Today on this shingle shelf
I understand this pensive reluctance so well,
This not discommendable obstinacy,
These contrivances of an inexpressive critical feeling,
These stones with their resolve that Creation shall not be
Injured by iconoclasts and quacks. Nothing has stirred
Since I lay down this morning an eternity ago
But one bird. The widest open door is the least liable to
     intrusion,
Ubiquitous as the sunlight, unfrequented as the sun.

The inward gates of a bird are always open.
It does not know how to shut them.
That is the secret of its song,
But whether any man's are ajar is doubtful.
I look at these stones and know little about them.
But I know their gates are open too,
Always open, far longer open, than any bird's can be,
That every one of them has had its gates wide open far longer
Than all birds put together, let alone humanity,
Though through them no man can see,
No man nor anything more recently born than themselves
And that is everything else on the Earth.
I too lying here have dismissed all else.
Bread from stones is my sole and desperate dearth,
From stones, which are to the Earth as to the sunlight
Is the naked sun which is for no man's sight.
I would scorn to cry to any easier audience
Or, having cried, to lack patience to await the response.
I am no more indifferent or ill-disposed to life than death is;
I would fain accept it all completely as the soil does;
Already I feel all that can perish perishing in me
As so much has perished and all will yet perish in these
    stones.
I must begin with these stones as the world began.

Shall I come to a bird quicker than the world's course ran?
        To a bird, and to myself, a man?
        And what if I do, and further?
I shall only have gone a little way to go back again
And be like a fleeting deceit of development,
Iconoclasts, quacks. So these stones have dismissed
All but all of evolution, unmoved by it,
(Is there anything to come they will not likewise dismiss?)
As the essential life of mankind in the mass
Is the same as their earliest ancestors yet.

Actual physical conflict or psychological warfare
        Incidental to love or food
Brings out animal life's bolder and more brilliant patterns
        Concealed as a rule in habitude.
        There is a sudden revelation of colour,

The protrusion of a crest,
The expansion of an ornament,
– But no general principle can be guessed
From these flashing fragments we are seeing,
These foam-bells on the hidden currents of being.
The bodies of animals are visible substances
And must therefore have colour and shape, in the first place
Depending on chemical composition, physical structure,
   mode of growth.
Psychological rhythms and other factors in the case,
But their purposive function is another question.
Brilliant-hued animals hide away in the ocean deeps;
The mole has a rich sexual colouring in due season
Under the ground; nearly every beast keeps
Brighter colours inside it than outside.
What the seen shows is never anything to what it's designed
   to hide,
The red blood which makes the beauty of a maiden's cheek
Is as red under a gorilla's pigmented and hairy face.
Varied forms and functions though life may seem to have
   shown
They all come back to the likeness of stone,
So to the intervening stages we can best find a clue
In what we all came from and return to.
There are no twirly bits in this ground bass.

We must be humble. We are so easily baffled by
   appearances
And do not realise that these stones are one with the stars.
It makes no difference to them whether they are high or low,
Mountain peak or ocean floor, palace, or pigsty.
There are plenty of ruined buildings in the world but no
   ruined stones.
No visitor comes from the stars
But is the same as they are.
– Nay, it is easy to find a spontaneity here,
An adjustment to life, an ability
To ride it easily, akin to 'the buoyant
Prelapsarian naturalness of a country girl
Laughing in the sun, not passion-rent,
But sensing in the bound of her breasts vigours to come

Powered to make her one with the stream of earthlife round
    her,'
But not yet as my Muse is, with this ampler scope,
This more divine rhythm, wholly at one
With the earth, riding the Heavens with it, as the stones do
And all soon must.
But it is wrong to indulge in these illustrations
Instead of just accepting the stones.
It is a paltry business to try to drag down
The arduous furor of the stones to the futile imaginings of
    men,
To all that fears to grow roots into the common earth,
As it soon must, lest it be chilled to the core,
As it will be – and none the worse for that.
Impatience is a poor qualification for immortality.

Hot blood is of no use in dealing with eternity.
It is seldom that promises or even realisations
Can sustain a clear and searching gaze,
But an emotion chilled is an emotion controlled;
This is the road leading to certainty,
Reasoned planning for the time when reason can no longer
    avail.
It is essential to know the chill of all the objections
That come creeping into the mind, the battle between
    opposing ideas
Which gives the victory to the strongest and most universal
Over all others, and to wage it to the end
With increasing freedom, precision, and detachment
A detachment that shocks our instincts and ridicules our
    desires.
All else in the world cancels out, equal, capable
Of being replaced by other things (even as all the ideas
That madden men now must lose their potency in a few
    years
And be replaced by others – even as all the religions,
All the material sacrifices and moral restraints,
That in twenty thousand years have brought us no nearer to
    God
Are irrelevant to the ordered adjustments
Out of reach of perceptive understanding

Forever taking place on the Earth and in the unthinkable
    regions around it;
This cat's cradle of life; this reality volatile yet determined;
This intense vibration in the stones
That makes them seem immobile to us)
But the world cannot dispense with the stones.
They alone are not redundant. Nothing can replace them
Except a new creation of God.

I must get into this stone world now.
Ratchel, striae, relationships of tesserae,
        Innumerable shades of grey.
        Innumerable shapes,
And beneath them all a stupendous unity,
Infinite movement visibly defending itself
Against all the assaults of weather and water,
Simultaneously mobilised at full strength
At every point of the universal front,
        Always at the pitch of its powers,
        The foundation and end of all life.
I try them with the old Norn words – hraun
Duss, rønis, queedaruns, kollyarum;
They hvarf from me in all directions
Over the hurdifell – klett, millya, hellya, hellyina bretta,
Hellyina wheeda, hellyina grø, bakka, ayre, –
        And lay my world in kolgref.

This is no heap of broken images.
Let men find the faith that builds mountains
Before they seek the faith that moves them. Men cannot
    hope
To survive the fall of the mountains
Which they will no more see than they saw their rise
Unless they are more concentrated and determined,
Truer to themselves and with more to be true to,
Than these stones, and as inerrable as they are.
Their sole concern is that what can be shaken
Shall be shaken and disappear
And only the unshakable be left.
What hardihood in any man has part or parcel in the latter?
It is necessary to make a stand and maintain it forever.

These stones go through Man, straight to God, if there is one.
What have they not gone through already?
Empires, civilisations, aeons. Only in them
If in anything, can His creation confront Him.
They came so far out of the water and halted forever.
That larking dallier, the sun, has only been able to play
With superficial by-products since;
The moon moves the waters backwards and forwards,
But the stones cannot be lured an inch farther
Either on this side of eternity or the other.
Who thinks God is easier to know than they are?
Trying to reach men any more, any otherwise, than they are?
These stones will reach us long before we reach them.
Cold, undistracted, eternal and sublime.
They will stem all the torrents of vicissitude forever
With a more than Roman peace.
Death is a physical horror to me no more.
I am prepared with everything else to share
Sunshine and darkness and wind and rain
And life and death bare as these rocks though it be
In whatever order nature may decree,
But, not indifferent to the struggle yet
Nor to the ataraxia I might get
By fatalism, a deeper issue see
Than these, or suicide, here confronting me.
It is reality that is at stake.
Being and non-being with equal weapons here
Confront each other for it, non-being unseen
But always on the point, it seems, of showing clear,
Though its reserved contagion may breed
This fancy too in my still susceptible head
And then by its own hidden movement lead
Me as by aesthetic vision to the supposed
Point where by death's logic everything is recomposed,
Object and image one, from their severance freed,
As I sometimes, still wrongly, feel 'twixt this storm beach and
     me.
What happens to us
Is irrelevant to the world's geology
But what happens to the world's geology
Is not irrelevant to us.

We must reconcile ourselves to the stones,
Not the stones to us.
Here a man must shed the encumbrances that muffle
Contact with elemental things, the subtleties
That seem inseparable from a humane life, and go apart
Into a simple and sterner, more beautiful and more
    oppressive world,
Austerely intoxicating; the first draught is overpowering;
Few survive it. It fills me with a sense of perfect form,
The end seen from the beginning, as in a song.
It is no song that conveys the feeling
That there is no reason why it should ever stop,
But the kindred form I am conscious of here
Is the beginning and end of the world,
The unsearchable masterpiece, the music of the spheres,
Alpha and Omega, the Omnific Word.
These stones have the silence of supreme creative power,
The direct and undisturbed way of working
Which alone leads to greatness.
What experience has any man crystallised,
What weight of conviction accumulated,
What depth of life suddenly seen entire
In some nigh supernatural moment
And made a symbol and lived up to
With such resolution, such Spartan impassivity?
It is a frenzied and chaotic age,
Like a growth of weeds on the site of a demolished building.
How shall we set ourselves against it,
Imperturbable, inscrutable, in the world and yet not in it,
    Silent under the torments it inflicts upon us,
        With a constant centre,
With a single inspiration, foundations firm and invariable;
        By what immense exercise of will,
Inconceivable discipline, courage, and endurance,
        Self-purification and anti-humanity,
            Be ourselves without interruption,
                Adamantine and inexorable?
It will be ever increasingly necessary to find
In the interests of all mankind
Men capable of rejecting all that all other men
        Think, as a stone remains

54

Essential to the world, inseparable from it,
    And rejects all other life yet.
Great work cannot be combined with surrender to the
    crowd.
        – Nay, the truth we seek is as free
From all yet thought as a stone from humanity.
Here where there is neither haze nor hesitation
Something at least of the necessary power has entered into
    me.
I have still to see any manifestation of the human spirit
That is worthy of a moment's longer exemption than it gets
From petrifaction again – to get out if it can.
All is lithogenesis – or lochia;
And I can desire nothing better,
An immense familiarity with other men's imaginings
Convinces me that they cannot either
(If they could, it would instantly be granted
– The present order must continue till then)
Though, of course, I still keep an open mind,
A mind as open as the grave.
You may say that the truth cannot be crushed out,
That the weight of the whole world may be tumbled on it,
And yet, in puny, distorted, phantasmal shapes albeit,
It will braird again; it will force its way up
Through unexpectable fissures? look over this beach.
What ruderal and rupestrine growth is here?
What crop confirming any credulities?
Conjure a fescue to teach me with from this
And I will listen to you, but until then
Listen to me – Truth is not crushed;
It crushes, gorgonises all else into itself.
The trouble is to know it when you see it?
You will have no trouble with it when you do.
Do not argue with me. Argue with these stones.
Truth has no trouble in knowing itself.
This is it. The hard fact. The inoppugnable reality,
Here is something for you to digest.
Eat this and we'll see what appetite you have left
For a world heareafter.
I pledge you in the first and last crusta,
The rocks rattling in the bead-proof seas.

O we of little faith,
As romanticists viewed the philistinism of their days
As final and were prone to set over against it
Infinite longing rather than manly will –
Nay, as all thinkers and writers find
The indifference of the masses of mankind, –
So are most men with any stone yet,
Even those who juggle with lapidary's, mason's, geologist's
    words
        And all their knowledge of stones in vain,
Tho' these stones have far more differences in colour, shape
    and size
        Than most men to my eyes –
Even those who develop precise conceptions to immense
    distances
        Out of these bleak surfaces.
All human culture is a Goliath to fall
To the least of these pebbles withal.
A certain weight will be added yet
To the arguments of even the most foolish
And all who speak glibly may rest assured
That to better their oratory they will have the whole earth
For a Demosthenean pebble to roll in their mouths.

I am enamoured of the desert at last,
The abode of supreme serenity is necessarily a desert.
My disposition is towards spiritual issues
Made inhumanly clear; I will have nothing interposed
Between my sensitiveness and the barren but beautiful
    reality;
The deadly clarity of this 'seeing of a hungry man'
Only traces of a fever passing over my vision
Will vary, troubling it indeed, but troubling it only
In such a way that it becomes for a moment
Superhumanly, menacingly clear – the reflection
Of a brightness through a burning crystal.
A culture demands leisure and leisure presupposes
A self-determined rhythm of life; the capacity for solitude
Is its test; by that the desert knows us.
It is not a question of escaping from life
But the reverse – a question of acquiring the power

To exercise the loneliness, the independence, of stones,
And that only comes from knowing that our function remains
However isolated we seem fundamental to life as theirs.
    We have lost the grounds of our being,
    We have not built on rock.
Thinking of all the higher zones
Confronting the spirit of man I know they are bare
Of all so-called culture as any stone here;
Not so much of all literature survives
As any wisp of scriota that thrives
On a rock – (interesting though it may seem to be
As de Bary's and Schwendener's discovery
Of the dual nature of lichens, the partnership,
Symbiosis, of a particular fungus and particular alga).
These bare stones bring me straight back to reality.
    I grasp one of them and I have in my grip
The beginning and the end of the world,
My own self, and as before I never saw
The empty hand of my brother man,
The humanity no culture has reached, the mob.
Intelligentsia, our impossible and imperative job!

'Ah!' you say, 'if only one of these stones would move
– Were it only an inch – of its own accord.
    This is the resurrection we await,
– The stone rolled away from the tomb of the Lord.
    I know there is no weight in infinite space,
        No impermeability in infinite time,
But it is as difficult to understand and have patience here
        As to know that the sublime
Is theirs no less than ours, no less confined
To men than men's to a few men, the stars of their kind.'
    (The masses too have begged bread from stones,
        From human stones, including themselves,
    And only got it, not from their fellow-men,
    But from stones such as these here – if then.)
Detached intellectuals, not one stone will move,
Not the least of them, not a fraction of an inch. It is not
    The reality of life that is hard to know.
It is nearest of all and easiest to grasp,
But you must participate in it to proclaim it.

– I lift a stone; it is the meaning of life I clasp
Which is death, for that is the meaning of death;
How else does any man yet participate
        In the life of a stone,
How else can any man yet become
Sufficiently at one with creation, sufficiently alone,
Till as the stone that covers him he lies dumb
And the stone at the mouth of his grave is not overthrown?
– Each of these stones on this raised beach,
        Every stone in the world,
Covers infinite death, beyond the reach
Of the dead it hides; and cannot be hurled
Aside yet to let any of them come forth, as love
        Once made a stone move
    (Though I do not depend on that
        My case to prove).
So let us beware of death; the stones will have
Their revenge; we have lost all approach to them,
But soon we shall become as those we have betrayed,
And they will seal us fast in our graves
As our indifference and ignorance seals them;
        But let us not be afraid to die.
No heavier and colder and quieter then,
No more motionless, do stones lie
        In death than in life to all men.
It is not more difficult in death than here
– Though slow as the stones the powers develop
To rise from the grave – to get a life worth having;
And in death – unlike life – we lose nothing that is truly ours.

Diallage of the world's debate, end of the long auxesis,
Although no ébrillade of Pegasus can here avail,
I prefer your enchorial characters – the futhorc of the future –
To the hieroglyphics of all the other forms of Nature.
Song, your apprentice encrinite, seems to sweep
The Heavens with a last entrochal movement;
And, with the same word that began it, closes
Earth's vast epanadiplosis.

With the Herring Fishers

(from *Shetland Lyrics*)

'I see herrin'.' – I hear the glad cry
And 'gainst the moon see ilka blue jowl!
In turn as the fishermen haul on the nets
And sing: 'Come, shove in your heids and growl.'

'Soom on, bonnie herrin', soom on,' they shout,
Or 'Come in, O come in, and see me,'
'Come gie the auld man something to dae.
It'll be a braw change frae the sea.'

O it's ane o' the bonniest sichts in the warld
To watch the herrin' come walkin' on board
In the wee sma' 'oors o' a simmer's mornin'
As if o' their ain accord.

For this is the way that God sees life,
The haill jing-bang o's appearin'
Up owre frae the edge o' naethingness
– It's his happy cries I'm hearin'.

'Left, right – O come in and see me,'
Reid and yellow and black and white
Toddlin' up into Heaven thegither
At peep o' day frae the endless night.

'I see herrin',' I hear his glad cry,
And 'gainst the moon see his muckle blue jowl,
As he handles buoy-tow and bush-raip
Singin': 'Come, shove in your heids and growl!'

The Little White Rose

To John Gawsworth

The rose of all the world is not for me.
I want for my part
Only the little white rose of Scotland
That smells sharp and sweet – and breaks the heart.

Cattle Show

I shall go among red faces and virile voices,
See stylish sheep, with fine heads and well-wooled,
And great bulls mellow to the touch,
Brood mares of marvellous approach, and geldings
With sharp and flinty bones and silken hair.

And through th' enclosure draped in red and gold
I shall pass on to spheres more vivid yet
Where countesses' coque feathers gleam and glow
And, swathed in silks, the painted ladies are
Whose laughter plays like summer lightning there.

Harry Semen

I ken these islands each inhabited
Forever by a single man
Livin' in his separate world as only
In dreams yet maist folk can.

Mine's like the moonwhite belly o' a hoo
Seen in the water as a fisher draws in his line.
I canna land it nor can it ever brak awa'.
It never moves, yet seems a' movement in the brine;
A movin' picture o' the spasm frae which I was born,
It writhes again, and back to it I'm willy-nilly torn.
A' men are similarly fixt; and the difference 'twixt
    The sae-ca'd sane and insane
Is that the latter whiles ha'e glimpses o't
    And the former nane.

Particle frae particle'll brak asunder,
Ilk ane o' them mair livid than the neist.
A separate life? – incredible war o' equal lichts,
Nane o' them wi' ocht in common in the least.
Nae threid o' a' the fabric o' my thocht
Is left alangside anither; a pack
O' leprous scuts o' weasels riddlin' a plaid
    Sic thrums could never mak'.
Hoo mony shades o' white gaed curvin' owre
To yon blae centre o' her belly's flower?
Milk-white, and dove-grey, wi' harebell veins.
Ae scar in fair hair like the sun in sunlicht lay,
And pelvic experience in a thin shadow line;
Thocht canna mairry thocht as sic saft shadows dae.

Grey ghastly commentaries on my puir life,
A' the sperm that's gane for naething rises up to damn
In sick-white onanism the single seed
Frae which in sheer irrelevance I cam.
What were the odds against me? Let me coont.
What worth am I to a' that micht ha'e been?
To a' the wasted slime I'm capable o'
Appeals this lurid emission, whirlin', lint-white and green.

Am I alane richt, solidified to life,
Disjoined frae a' this searin' like a white-het knife,
And vauntin' my alien accretions here,
Boastin' sanctions, purpose, sense the endless tide
I cam frae lacks – the tide I still sae often feed?
O bitter glitter; wet sheet and flowin' sea – and what beside?

Sae the bealin' continents lie upon the seas,
        Sprawlin' in shapeless shapes a' airts,
Like ony splash that ony man can mak'
        Frae his nose or throat or ither pairts,
Fantastic as ink through blottin'-paper rins.
But this is white, white like a flooerin' gean,
Passin' frae white to purer shades o' white,
Ivory, crystal, diamond, till nae difference is seen
Between its fairest blossoms and the stars.
Or the clear sun they melt into,
And the wind mixes them amang each ither
Forever, hue upon still mair dazzlin' hue.

Sae Joseph may ha'e pondered, sae a snawstorm
Comes whirlin' in grey sheets frae the shadowy sky
And only in a sma' circle are the separate flakes seen.
White, whiter, they cross and recross as capricious they fly,
Mak' patterns on the grund and weave into wreaths,
Load the bare boughs, and find lodgements in corners frae
The scourin' wind that sends a snawstorm up frae the earth
To meet that frae the sky, till which is which nae man can say.
They melt in the waters. They fill the valleys. They scale the
    peaks.
There's a tinkle o' icicles. The topmaist summit shines oot.
Sae Joseph may ha'e pondered on the coiled fire in his seed,
The transformation in Mary, and seen Jesus tak' root.

At the Cenotaph

Are the living so much use
That we need to mourn the dead?
Or would it yield better results
To reverse their roles instead?
The millions slain in the War –
Untimely, the best of our seed? –
Would the world be any the better
If they were still living indeed?
The achievements of such as are
To the notion lend no support;
The whole history of life and death
Yields no scrap of evidence for't. –
Keep going to your wars, you fools, as of yore;
I'm the civilisation you're fighting for.

Birth of a Genius Among Men

The night folded itself about me like a woman's hair.
Thousands of dispersed forces drawn as by a magnet
Streamed through the open windows – millions of stars
   poured through;
What destiny were they seeking in us, what outlet?

An immense vigour awoke in my body.
My breast expanded and overflowed into the night.
I was one with Scotland out there and with all the world
And thoughts of your beauty shone in me like starlight.

You were all female, ripe as a rose for the plucking,
I was all male and no longer resisted my need.
The earth obeyed the rhythm of our panting.
The mountains sighed with us. Infinity was emptied.

To both of us it seemed as if we had never loved before.
A miracle was abroad and I knew that not merely I
Had accomplished the act of love but the whole universe
   through me,
A great design was fulfilled, another genius nigh.

Yet I lay awake and as the daylight broke
I heard the faint voices of the Ideas discuss
The way in which they could only express themselves yet
In fragmentary and fallacious forms through us.

Lo! A Child is Born

I thought of a house where the stones seemed suddenly
    changed
And became instinct with hope, hope as solid as themselves,
And the atmosphere warm with that lovely heat,
The warmth of tenderness and longing souls, the smiling
    anxiety
That rules a home where a child is about to be born.
The walls were full of ears. All voices were lowered.
Only the mother had the right to groan or complain.
Then I thought of the whole world. Who cares for its travail
And seeks to encompass it in like lovingkindness and peace?
There is a monstrous din of the sterile who contribute nothing
To the great end in view, and the future fumbles,
A bad birth, not like the child in that gracious home
Heard in the quietness turning in its mother's womb,
A strategic mind already, seeking the best way
To present himself to life, and at last, resolved,
Springing into history quivering like a fish,
Dropping into the world like a ripe fruit in due time. –
But where is the Past to which Time, smiling through her
    tears
At her new-born son, can turn crying: 'I love you'?

The Salmon Leap

I saw one shadow shoot up and over
While ten failed to make it again and again,
But most of the salmon without an effort
In the bottom of the pool all day had lain.

Suddenly, effortlessly, like a flight of birds,
Up and over I saw them all slip.
The secret, I think, was the melted snow
Coming down and flicking them like a whip.

The majority of people make no attempt
In life to explore the infinite,
But who can tell what Death's cold touch
May prompt the lazy louts to yet?

In the Slums of Glasgow

I have caught a glimpse of the seamless garment
And am blind to all else for evermore.
The immaculate vesture, the innermost shift.
 Of high and low, of rich and poor,
The glorious raiment of bridegroom and bride,
  Whoremonger and whore,
I have caught a glimpse of the seamless garment
And have eyes for aught else no more.

Deep under the γνῶθι σεαυτόν of Thales I've seen
The Hindu Atmānam ātmanā pāsya, and far deeper still
In every man, woman, and child in Scotland even
The inseparable inherent cause, the inalienable thrill,
The subtle movement, the gleam, the hidden well-water,
All the lin-gāni of their souls, God's holy will.
As a shining light needs no other light to be seen
The soul is only known by the soul or knows anything still.

It was easier to do this in the slums, as who prefers
A white-faced lass – because the eyes show better, so.
Life is more naked there, more distinct from mind,
Material goods and all the other extraneous things that grow
Hardening over and hiding the sheer life. Behind speech,
 mind and will
Behind sensation, reflection, knowledge, and power – lo!
Life, to which all these are attached as the spokes of a wheel to
 the nave;
The immensity abiding in its own glory of which I have
 caught the glow.

The same earth produces diamonds, rock-crystal, and
 vermilion.
The same sun produces all sorts of plants, the same food
Is converted into hair, nails and many other forms.
These dogmas are not as I once thought true nor as
 afterwards false
But each the empty shadow of an intimate personal mood.
I am indifferent to shadows, possessing the substance now.
I too look on the world and behold it is good.

I am deluded by appearances no more – I have seen
The goodness, passion, and darkness from which all things
    spring,
Identical and abundant in the slums as everywhere else
Taking other forms – to which changing and meaningless
    names cling, –
But cancelling out at last, dissolving, vanishing,
        Like the stars before the rising sun.
Foam, waves, billows and bubbles are not different from the
    sea,
But riding the bright heavens or to the dark roots of earth
    sinking
Water is multiform, indivisible and one,
Not to be confused with any of the shapes it is taking.

I have not gained a single definite belief that can be put
In a scientific formula or hardened into a religious creed.
A conversion is not, as mostly thought, a turning towards a
    belief,
It is rather a turning round, a revolution indeed.
It has no primary reference to any external object.
It took place in me at last with lightning speed.
I suddenly walk in light, my feet are barely touching the
    ground,
I am free of a million words and forms I no longer need.

In becoming one with itself my spirit is one with the world.
The dull, aching tension is gone, all hostility and dread.
All opposing psychic tendencies are resolved in sweet song
My eyes discard all idle shows and dwell instead
In my intercourse with every man and woman I know
On the openings and shuttings of eyes, the motions of mind,
    and, especially, life, and are led
Beyond colour, savour, odour, tangibility, numbers,
    extensions,
Individuality, conjunction, disjunction, priority, posteriority
    – like an arrow sped,
And sheer through intellection, volition, desire, aversion,
Pleasure, pain, merit and demerit – to the fountain-head,
To the unproduced, unproducing, solitary, motionless soul
By which alone they can be known, by which alone we are not
    misled.

I have seen this abhyasa most clearly in the folk of these slums,
Even as I have known the selfless indefatigable love of a
  mother
Concerned only for the highest possible vitality of her children,
Leaving their lives free to them, not seeking to smother
Any jet of their spirits in her own preconceptions or wishes. –
Would such were the love of every one of us for each other!

I have seen this abhyasa most clearly in the folk of these slums
Even as I know how every one of the women there,
Irrespective of all questions of intelligence, good looks,
  fortune's favour,
Can give some buck-navvy or sneak-thief the joy beyond
  compare –
Naked, open as to destitution and death, to the unprudential
Guideless life-in-death of the ecstasy they share –
Eternity, as Boethius defined it, – though few lovers give it his
  terms –
'To hold and possess the whole fulness of life anywhere
In a moment; here and now, past, present and to come.' –
The bliss of God glorifying every squalid lair.

The sin against the Holy Ghost is to fetter or clog
The free impulse of life – to weaken or cloud
The glad wells of being – to apply other tests,
To say that these pure founts must be hampered, controlled,
Denied, adulterated, diluted, cowed,
The wave of omnipotence made recede, and all these lives,
  these lovers,
Lapse into cannon-fodder, sub-humanity, the despised
  slum-crowd.

I am filled forever with a glorious awareness
Of the inner radiance, the mystery of the hidden light in these
  dens,
I see it glimmering like a great white-sailed ship
Bearing into Scotland from Eternity's immense,
Or like a wild swan resting a moment in mid-flood.
It has the air of a winged victory, in suspense
By its own volition in its imperious way.
As if the heavens opened I gather its stupendous sense.

For here too, Philosophy has a royal and ancient seat,
And, holding an eternal citadel of light and immortality,
With Study her only comrade, sets her victorious foot
On the withering flower of the fast-ageing world. – Let all
    men see.
Now the babel of Glasgow dies away in our ears,
The great heart of Glasgow is sinking to rest,
Na nonanunno nunnono nana nananana nanu,
Nunno nunnonanunneno nanena nunnanunnanut.
We lie cheek to cheek in a quiet trance, the moon itself no
    more still.
There is no movement but your eyelashes fluttering against
    me,
And the fading sound of the work-a-day world,
Dadadoduddadaddadi dadadodudadidadoh,
Duddadam dadade dudde dadadadadadodadah.

Bagpipe Music

Let me play to you tunes without measure or end,
Tunes that are born to die without a herald,
As a flight of storks rises from a marsh, circles,
And alights on the spot from which it rose.

Flowers. A flower-bed like hearing the bagpipes.
The fine black earth has clotted into sharp masses
As if the frost and not the sun had come.
It holds many lines of flowers.
First faint rose peonies, then peonies blushing,
Then again red peonies, and behind them,
Massive, apoplectic peonies, some of which are so red
And so violent as to seem almost black; behind these
Stands a low hedge of larkspur, whose tender apologetic
    blossoms
Appear by contrast pale, though some, vivid as the sky above
    them,
Stand out from their fellows, iridescent and slaty as a pigeon's
    breast.
The bagpipes – they are screaming and they are sorrowful.
There is a wail in their merriment, and cruelty in their
    triumph.
They rise and they fall like a weight swung in the air at the
    end of a string.
They are like the red blood of those peonies.
And like the melancholy of those blue flowers.
They are like a human voice – no! for the human voice lies!
They are like human life that flows under the words.
That flower-bed is like the true life that wants to express itself
And does ... while we human beings lie cramped and fearful.

from *In Memoriam James Joyce*

Let the only consistency
In the course of my poetry
Be like that of the hawthorn tree
Which in early Spring breaks
Fresh emerald, then by nature's law
Darkens and deepens and takes
Tints of purple-maroon, rose-madder and straw.

Sometimes these hues are found
Together, in pleasing harmony bound.
Sometimes they succeed each other. But through
All the changes in which the hawthorn is dight,
No matter in what order, one thing is sure
– The haws shine ever the more ruddily bright!

And when the leaves have passed
Or only in a few tatters remain
The tree to the winter condemned
                    Stands forth at last
        Not bare and drab and pitiful,
But a candelabrum of oxidised silver gemmed
By innumerable points of ruby
Which dominate the whole and are visible
Even at considerable distance
As flame-points of living fire.
That so it may be
With my poems too at last glance
Is my only desire.

All else must be sacrificed to this great cause.
I fear no hardships. I have counted the cost.
I with my heart's blood as the hawthorn with its haws
Which are sweetened and polished by the frost!

See how these haws burn, there down the drive,
In this autumn air that feels like cotton wool,
When the earth has the gelatinous limpness of a body dead as
    a whole
While its tissues are still alive!

Poetry is human existence come to life,
The glorious energy that once employed
Turns all else in creation null and void,
The flower and fruit, the meaning and goal,
Which won all else is needs removed by the knife
Even as a man who rises high
Kicks away the ladder he has come up by.

This single-minded zeal, this fanatic devotion to art
Is alien to the English poetic temperament no doubt,
'This narrowing intensity' as the English say,
But I have it even as you had it, Yeats, my friend,
And would have it with me as with you at the end,
I who am infinitely more un-English than you
And turn Scotland to poetry like those women who
In their passion secrete and turn to
Musk through and through!

So I think of you, Joyce, and of Yeats and others who are dead
As I walk this Autumn and observe
The birch tremulously pendulous in jewels of cairngorm,
The sauch, the osier, and the crack-willow
Of the beaten gold of Australia;
The sycamore in rich straw-gold;
The elm bowered in saffron;
The oak in flecks of salmon gold;
The beeches huge torches of living orange.

Billow upon billow of autumnal foliage
From the sheer high bank glass themselves
Upon the ebon and silver current that floods freely
Past the shingle shelves,
I linger where a crack willow slants across the stream,
Its olive leaves slashed with fine gold.
Beyond the willow a young beech
Blazes almost blood-red,
Vying in intensity with the glowing cloud of crimson
That hangs about the purple bole of a gean
Higher up the brae face.

And yonder, the lithe green-grey bole of an ash, with its
   boughs
Draped in the cinnamon-brown lace of samara.
(And I remember how in April upon its bare twigs
The flowers came in ruffs like the unshorn ridges
Upon a French poodle – like a dull mulberry at first,
Before the first feathery fronds
Of the long-stalked, finely-poised, seven-fingered leaves) –
Even the robin hushes his song
In these gold pavilions.

Other masters may conceivably write
Even yet in C major
But we – we take the perhaps 'primrose path'
To the dodecaphonic bonfire.

They are not endless these variations of form
Though it is perhaps impossible to see them all.
It is certainly impossible to conceive one that doesn't exist.
But I keep trying in our forest to do both of these,
And though it is a long time now since I saw a new one
I am by no means weary yet of my concentration
On phyllotaxis here in preference to all else,
All else – but my sense of sny!

The gold edging of a bough at sunset, its pantile way
Forming a double curve, tegula and imbrex in one,
Seems at times a movement on which I might be borne
Happily to infinity; but again I am glad
When it suddenly ceases and I find myself
Pursuing no longer a rhythm of duramen
But bouncing on the diploe in a clearing between earth and
   air
Or headlong in dewy dallops or a moon-spairged fernshaw
Or caught in a dark dumosity, or even
In open country again watching an aching spargosis of stars.

Coronach for the End of the World

Mony a piper has played himsel'
   Through battle and into daith,
And a piper'll rise to the occasion still
   When the warld is brakin' faith!

A trumpet may soond or harps be heard
   Or celestial voices sweet,
But wi' nocht but the cry o' the pipes can Earth
   Or these ... or silence ... meet.

The pipes are the only instrument
   To soond Earth's mortal hour;
But to greet what follows, if onything does,
   Is no' in even *their* power.

Bonnie Birdie, A' Aflocht

Bonnie birdie, a' aflocht!
What's in me to gar ye dreid
Till affward frae the earth it seems
Your wings athwart the sun maun spreid?

Aswaip the lift ye drap again
To tak' anither keek at me.
Or was't the sun I dinna fleg
That smilin'ly encouraged ye?

I wad that like the sun and you
I had a' Space for awmous tae,
And wore it wi' a gallant cant
In sic a bricht astalit way.

Adist, ayont, you come and gang
Inerrand in abandon.
Men say that God's awhaur at aince,
Then you're his imitation!

Ah, no! blithe bird, man's thocht is that,
Invisible as God himsel!
Wad else 'twere mair like you or him
– Or baith, you aefauld miracle!

The Glass of Pure Water

In the de-oxidation and re-oxidation of hydrogen in a single drop of water we have before us, truly, so far as force is concerned, an epitome of the whole life. . . . The burning of coal to move an iron wheel differs only in detail, and not in essence, from the decomposition of a muscle to effect its own concentration.

JAMES HINTON

We must remember that his analysis was done not intellectually, but by an immediate process of intuition; that he was able, as it were, to taste the hydrogen and oxygen in his glass of water.

ALDOUS HUXLEY (of D. H. Lawrence)

Praise of pure water is common in Gaelic poetry.

W. J. WATSON: *Bàrdachd Ghàidhlig*

Hold a glass of pure water to the eye of the sun!
It is difficult to tell the one from the other
Save by the tiny hardly visible trembling of the water.
This is the nearest analogy to the essence of human life
Which is even more difficult to see.
Dismiss anything you can see more easily;
It is not alive – it is not worth seeing.
There is a minute indescribable difference
Between one glass of pure water and another
With slightly different chemical constituents.
The difference betwen one human life and another
Is no greater; colour does not colour the water;
You cannot tell a white man's life from a black man's.
But the lives of these particular slum people
I am chiefly concerned with, like the lives of all
The world's poorest, remind me less
Of a glass of water held between my eyes and the sun
– They remind me of the feeling they had
Who saw Sacco and Vanzetti in the death cell
On the eve of their execution.
– One is talking to God.

I dreamt last night that I saw one of His angels
Making his centennial report to the Recording Angel
On the condition of human life.
Look at the ridge of skin between your thumb and forefinger.
Look at the delicate lines on it and how they change

77

– How many different things they can express –
As you move out or close in your forefinger and thumb.
And look at the changing shapes – the countless
Little gestures, little miracles of line –
Of your forefinger and thumb as you move them.
And remember how much a hand can express,
How a single slight movement of it can say more
Than millions of words – dropped hand, clenched fist,
Snapping fingers, thumb up, thumb down,
Raised in blessing, clutched in passion, begging,
Welcome, dismissal, prayer, applause,
And a million other signs, too slight, too subtle,
Too packed with meaning for words to describe,
A universal language understood by all.
And the angel's report on human life
Was the subtlest movement – just like that – and no more;
A hundred years of life on the Earth
Summed up, not a detail missed or wrongly assessed,
In that little inconceivably intricate movement.
The only communication between man and man
That says anything worth hearing
– The hidden well-water; the finger of destiny –
Moves as that water, that angel, moved.
Truth is the rarest thing and life
The gentlest, most unobtrusive movement in the world.
I cannot speak to you of the poor people of all the world
But among the people in these nearest slums I know
This infinitesimal twinkling, this delicate play
Of tiny signs that not only say more
Than all speech, but all there is to say,
All there is to say and to know and to be.
There alone I seldom find anything else,
Each in himself or herself a dramatic whole,
An 'agon' whose validity is timeless.

Our duty is to free that water, to make these gestures,
To help humanity to shed all else,
All that stands between any life and the sun,
The quintessence of any life and the sun;
To still all sound save that talking to God;
To end all movements save movements like these.

78

India had that great opportunity centuries ago
And India lost it – and became a vast morass,
Where no water wins free; a monstrous jungle
Of useless movement; a babel
Of stupid voices, drowning the still small voice.
It is our turn now; the call is to the Celt.

This little country can overcome the whole world of wrong
As the Lacedaemonians the armies of Persia.
Cornwall – Gaeldom – must stand for the ending
Of the essential immortality of any man controlling
Any other – for the ending of all Government
Since all Government is a monopoly of violence;
For the striking of this water out of the rock of Capitalism;
For the complete emergence from the pollution and fog
With which the hellish interests of private property
In land, machinery, and credit
Have corrupted and concealed from the sun,
From the gestures of truth, from the voice of God,
Hundreds upon hundreds of millions of men,
Denied the life and liberty to which they were born
And fobbed off with a horrible travesty instead
– Self righteous, sunk in the belief that they are human,
When not a tenth of one per cent show a single gleam
Of the life that is in them under their accretions of filth.

And until that day comes every true man's place
Is to reject all else and be with the lowest,
The poorest – in the bottom of that deepest of wells
In which alone is truth; in which
Is truth only – truth that should shine like the sun,
With a monopoly of movement, and a sound like talking to
    God . . .

Happy on Heimaey

Meanwhile, the last of the human faculties
To be touched by the finger of science,
Still unanalysed, still immeasurable,
The sense of smell is the one little refuge
In the human mind still inviolate and unshareable
Because communicable in no known language,
But some day this the most delicate of perceptions
Will be laid bare too – there will be
Chairs of osmology in our universities,
Ardent investigators searching out, recording, measuring,
Preserving in card indexes
The departing smells of the countryside.
Hayfields will be explained in terms of Coumarin,
Beanfields in Ionone, hedge-roses in
Phenyl-Ethyl-Propionate,
Hawthorn as Di-Methyl-Hodroquinone.
(But will they ever capture the scent of violets
Among the smoke of the shoeing-forge, or explain
The clean smell of a road wet with summer rain?)
Until that day, on Heimaey, 400 miles due North-West
Of Rona in the Hebrides, I am content to walk out
Into an unreal country of yellow fields
Lying at the foot of black volcanic cliffs
In the shadow of dead Helgafell,
And watch a few farmers scything
(Careful of the little birds' nests,
Iceland wheatear, snow bunting, white wagtail, meadow
    pipit,
And leaving clumps of grass to protect them)
A sweet but slender hay-crop
And tell its various constituents to myself
– White clover, chickenweed, dandelion,
A very large buttercup, silverweed, horsetail,
Thrift, sorrel, yellow bedstraw,
Poa, carex, and rushes –
Or look out of my bedroom window
In the farmhouse near Kaupstadur
On a garden planted with angelica,
Red currant, rhubarb, and the flower of Venus,

Or at midnight watch the sun
Roll slowly along the northern horizon
To dip behind the great ice-caps
And jokulls of distant Iceland.
'Mellach lem bhith ind ucht ailiuin
    for beind cairrge,
Conacind and ar a mheinci
    feth na fairrci,'*
Ah me! It is a far better thing to be sitting
Alive on Heimaey, bare as an egg though it were,
Than rolled round willy-nilly with yonder sun.

Crystals Like Blood

I remember how, long ago, I found
Crystals like blood in a broken stone.

I picked up a broken chunk of bed-rock
And turned it this way and that,
It was heavier than one would have expected
From its size. One face was caked
With brown limestone. But the rest
Was a hard greenish-grey quartz-like stone
Faintly dappled with darker shadows,
And in this quartz ran veins and beads
Of bright magenta.

And I remember how later on I saw
How mercury is extracted from cinnebar
– The double ring of iron piledrivers
Like the multiple legs of a fantastically symmetrical spider
Rising and falling with monotonous precision,
Marching round in an endless circle
And pounding up and down with a tireless, thunderous force,
While, beyond, another conveyor drew the crumbled ore
From the bottom and raised it to an opening high
In the side of a gigantic grey-white kiln.

* From an ancient poem ascribed to Colum Cille, meaning: 'Pleasant,
  methinks, to be on an isle's breast, on a pinnacle of rock, that I might see
  there in its frequency the ocean's aspect.'

So I remember how mercury is got
When I contrast my living memory of you
And your dear body rotting here in the clay
– And feel once again released in me
The bright torrents of felicity, naturalness, and faith
My treadmill memory draws from you yet.

The North Face of Liathach

The north face of Liathach
Lives in the mind like a vision.
From the deeps of Coire na Caime
Sheer cliffs go up
To spurs and pinnacles and jagged teeth.
Its grandeur draws back the heart.
Scotland is full of such places.
Few (few Scots even) know them.

I think of another
Stupendous wall of rock
On the west coast of Foula
Rising eleven hundred feet from the sea.

Keep all your 'kindly brither Scots,'
Your little happinesses,
Your popular holiday resorts,
Your damned democracy.
This is no place for children
Or for holiday dawdling.
It has no friendly sand or cove.
It is almost frightening
In its lack of anything in common
With Dunoon or Portobello or Aberdeen.
It has no modern conveniences at all
– Only its own stark magnificence
Overwhelming the senses.
Every Scot should make a pilgrimage here
Just once, and alone.

And thereafter pick shells at Montrose,
Or admire our rich Hebridean rock pools,
Or go to 'the island that likes to be visited'
In the Loch of Voshimid in Harris
Or seek like Selma Lagerlöf
For 'the butterfly changed into an island'
And 'pervaded ever since with an intense yearning
To be able to fly again
And go with the birds beyond the horizon.'
And so regain the proper holiday feelings
The proper human feelings,
Surprised at no wildness of belief among
A people who can swallow the Incarnation theory,
The Christian feelings of those of whom Meredith
    said
'If you can believe in a God
You can believe in anything.'

Seen through a murky patch of fog,
Violent, ruthless, incalculable.
I have seen a head blood-drained to this hue.
But this cliff is not dead.
It has an immense life of its own
And will loom, as if it could come rushing
To beat, to maim, to kill
(Damned anti-climax of a notion!)
Just as it looms to-day
After every human being now alive
Has returned, not to rock but to dust.

What does it remind me of?
Why since extremes meet,
Of the life of a great city perhaps,
The compelling sense of the *vécu ensemble*
The *zusammenerlebt*,
Any of man's great *unanimes*
And their place in the history
Of human stupidity.

No flower, no fern,
No wisp of grass or pad of moss
Lightens this tremendous face.

Otherwise it might remind me of my mother.
  The education she gave me was strict enough,
  Teaching me a sense of duty and self-reliance
  And having no time for any softness.
  Her tenderness was always very reserved,
  Very modest in its expression
  And respect was the foremost of my feelings for
    her.
No. Not of my mother.
But of many other women I have known
As I could not know her.
It is with them I have found the soul most exposed,
Something not of this world,
Which makes you tremble with delight and
    repulsion
When you see it so close.

A lot of the old folk here – all that's left
Of them after a lifetime's infernal thrall
Remind me of a Bolshie the 'Whites' buried alive
Up to his nose, just able to breathe, that's all.

Watch them. You'll see what I mean. When found
His eyes had lost their former gay twinkle.
Ants had eaten *that* away; but there was still
Some life in him ... his forehead *would* wrinkle!

And I remember Gide telling
Of Valéry and himself;
'It was a long time ago. We were young.
We had mingled with idlers
Who formed a circle
Round a troupe of wretched mountebanks.
It was on a raised strip of pavement
In the boulevard Saint-Germain,
In front of the statue of Broca.
They were admiring a poor woman.
Thin and gaunt, in pink tights despite the cold.
Her team-mate had tied her, trussed her up,
Skilfully from head to foot,
With a rope that went around her
I don't know how many times,
And from which, by a sort of wriggling,
She was to manage to free herself.

'Sorry image of the fate of the masses!
But no one thought of the symbol.
The audience merely contemplated
In stupid bliss the patient's efforts.
She twisted, writhed, slowly freed one arm,
Then the other, and when at last
The final cord fell from her
Valéry took me by the arm:
"Let's go now! *She has ceased suffering*." '

Oh, if only ceasing to suffer
They were able to become men.

Alas! how many owe their dignity,
Their claim on our sympathy,
Merely to their misfortune.
Likewise, so long as a plant has not blossomed
One can hope that its flowering will be beautiful.
What a mirage surrounds what has not yet blossomed!
What a disappointment when one can no longer
Blame the abjection on the deficiency!
It is good that the voice of the indigent,
Too long stifled, should manage
To make itself heard.
But I cannot consent to listen
To nothing but that voice.
Man does not cease to interest me
When he ceases to be miserable.
Quite the contrary!
That it is important to aid him
In the beginning goes without saying,
Like a plant it is essential
To water at first;
But this is in order to get it to flower,
And I *am concerned with the blossom.*

British Leftish Poetry, 1930–40

Auden, MacNeice, Day Lewis, I have read them all,
Hoping against hope to hear the authentic call.
'A tragical disappointment. There was I
Hoping to hear old Aeschylus, when the Herald
Called out, "Theognis, bring your chorus forward."
Imagine what my feelings must have been!
But then Dexitheus pleased me coming forward
And singing his Bœotian melody:
But next came Chaeris with his music truly
That turned me sick and killed me very nearly.
And never in my lifetime, man nor boy,
Was I so vexed as at the present moment;
To see the Pnyx, at this time of the morning,

Quite empty, when the Assembly should be full'*
And know the explanation I must pass is this
– You cannot light a match on a crumbling wall.

By Wauchopeside

Thrawn water? Aye, owre thrawn to be aye thrawn!
I ha'e my wagtails like the Wauchope tae,
Birds fu' o' fechtin' spirit, and o' fun,
That whiles jig in the air in lichtsome play
Like glass-ba's on a fountain, syne stand still
Save for a quiver, shoot up an inch or twa, fa' back
Like a swarm o' winter-gnats, or are tost aside,
   By their inclination's kittle loup,
   To balance efter hauf a coup.

There's mair in birds than men ha'e faddomed yet.
Tho' maist churn oot the stock sangs o' their kind
There's aiblins genius here and there; and aince
'Mang whitebeams, hollies, siller birks –
     The trees o' licht –
        I mind
I used to hear a blackie mony a nicht
Singin' awa' t'an unconscionable 'oor
Wi' nocht but the water keepin't company
(Or nocht that ony human ear could hear)
– And wondered if the blackie heard it either
Or cared whether it was singin' tae or no'!
O there's nae saying' what my verses awn
To memories like these. Ha'e I come back
To find oot? Or to borrow mair? Or see
Their helpless puirness to what gar'd them be?
   Late sang the blackie but it stopt at last.
   The river still ga'ed singin' past.

O there's nae sayin' what my verses awn
To memories, or my memories to me.

* Aristophanes, *The Acharnians*.

But a'e thing's certain; ev'n as things stand
I could vary them in coontless ways and gi'e
Wauchope a new course in the minds o' men,
The blackie gowden feathers, and the like,
An yet no' cease to be dependent on
The things o' Nature, and create insteed
        Oot o' my ain heid
        Or get ootside the range
                O' trivial change
Into that cataclysmic country which
Natheless a' men inhabit – and enrich.

For civilization in its struggle up
Has mair than seasonal changes o' ideas,
Glidin' through periods o' flooers and fruit,
Winter and Spring again; to cope wi' these
Is difficult eneuch to tax the patience
O' Methuselah himsel' – but transformations,
Yont physical and mental habits, symbols, rites,
That mak' sic changes nane, are aye gaen on,
Revolutions in the dynasty o' live ideals
– The stuff wi' which alane true poetry deals.
Wagtail or water winna help me here,
(That's clearer than Wauchope* at its clearest's clear!)
Where the life o' a million years is seen
Like a louch look in a lass's een.

Diamond Body

In a Cave of the Sea

What after all do we know of this terrible 'matter'
Save as a name for the unknown and hypothetical cause
Of states of our own consciousness? There are not two worlds,
A world of nature, and a world of human consciousness,
Standing over against one another, but one world of nature
Whereof human consciousness is an evolution,

* Wauchope is one of the tributaries of the River Esk, which it joins at the little Dumfriesshire town of Langholm, the author's birthplace.

I reminded myself again as I caught that sudden breathless
   glimpse,
Under my microscope, of unexpected beauty and dynamic
   living
In the world of life on a sliver of kelp
Quite as much as the harpooning of a forty-two foot whale
   shark.

Because, I reminded myself, any assemblage of things
Is for the sake of another, and because of
The existence of active exertion
For the sake of abstraction,
In like manner, as Gaudapada says,
As a bed, which is an assemblage
Of bedding, props, cotton, coverlet, and pillows
Is for another's use, not for its own
And its several component parts
Render no mutual service,
Thence it is concluded that there is a man
Who sleeps upon the bed
And for whose sake it was made
So this world, which is an assemblage
Of the five elements is for another's use,
And there is another for whose enjoyment
This enjoyable body of mine,
Consisting of intellect and all the rest,
Has been produced.

And all I see and delight in now
Has been produced for him –
The sand-burrowing sea urchins with shells
Delicate as those of hen's eggs,
Burrowing by movements of long backwardly-directed spines;
And the burrowing star-fish which settle into the sand
By rows of pointed 'tube feet',
Operated by hydraulic pressure,
On the under-side of each of the five arms;
And the smooth-bodied sand eels and the shrimps
And sea-weeds attached by broad hold-fasts
– Not roots! – to the rocks or boulders,
Brown masses a host of small animals

Grow on or shelter amongst, protected here
From the buffeting of the sea when the tide is in
Or kept moist under the damp weight of weed
When the tide is out. And high up the shore
The limpets wandering about
Grazing on fine encrusting weeds,
And the acorn barnacles, the dog-whelks
Grey-shelled unless they have mussels to feed on
When the change of diet puts brown bands on the shells;
And, in a rock pool, 'crumb of bread' sponge,
Hydroids red, green, purple, or richly patterned
Like the dahlia anemone, yellow sea-lemon, and now and
     again
A rapidly moving snail shell which shows me
It is inhabited by a hermit crab
Much more active than its original occupant.
Countless millions of creatures each essential
To that other, and precisely fashioned
In every detail to meet his requirements.
Millions upon millions of them
Hardly discernible here
In the brilliant light in which sea and sky
Can hardly be distinguished from each other
– And I know there are billions more
Too small for a man to see
Even though human life were long enough
To see them all, a process that can hardly
Be even begun.
Our minds already sense that the fabric of nature's laws
Conceals something that lies behind it,
A greater-unity. – We are beginning more and more
To see behind them something they conceal
For the most part cunningly
With their outward appearances,
By hoodwinking man with a façade
Quite different from what it actually covers.
I am convinced that behind this too
There is another and many more.

Today we are breaking up the chaste
Ever-deceptive phenomena of Nature

And reassembling them according to our will.
We look through matter, and the day is not far distant
When we shall be able to cleave
Through her oscillating mass as if it were air.*
Matter is something which man still
At most tolerates, but does not recognise.
Here in the brilliant light, where the mandala† is almost
  complete,
The circumference of a blinding diamond broken
Only by a few points and dashes of darkness yet,
The shapes and figures created by the fire of the spirit
Are only empty forms and colours. It is not necessary to
  confuse
The dull glow of such figures with the pure white light
Of the divine body of truth, nor to project
The light of the highest consciousness into concretized figures,
But to have the consciousness withdrawn, as if
To some sphere beyond the world where it is
At once empty and not empty,
The centre of gravity of the whole personality
Transferred from the conscious centre of the ego
To a sort of hypothetical point
Between the conscious and the unconscious,
The complete abolition of the original
Undifferentiated state of subject and object;
Thus through the certainty that *something lives through me*
Rather than I myself live‡

* *Vide* the Aphorisms of Franz Marc.
† In 'The Secret of the Golden Flower', symbols having the form of mandalas
  are reproduced. Mandala means circle, specifically 'magic circle': (Jung has
  published the mandalas of a somnambulist in his *Collected Papers on Analytical
  Psychology*). Magic, because the protecting figure of the enclosing circle is
  supposed to prevent any 'out-pouring', that is, to prevent consciousness
  being burst asunder by the unconscious, or by partial psychical systems –
  complexes split off from the whole. At the same time, the mandala gives
  form to the transformation of inward feeling, such as Paul, for instance, has
  in mind when he recognizes that 'it is not I who live, but Christ who lives in
  me' – Christ being here the symbol of the mystical fact of transformation.
  The inner conversion, the assumption of a unique individuality, is described
  by the Chinese as the production of the 'diamond body' or the 'sacred fruit'.
‡ See 'The Secret of the Golden Flower', a Chinese *Book of Life*, translated into
  German and annotated by Richard Wilhelm, with a European commentary
  by C. G. Jung.

A man bridges the gap between instinct and spirit,
And takes hold upon life, attacks life,
In a more profound sense than before.
In the reconciliation of the differentiated
And the inferior function, the 'great Tao
– The meaning of the world' is discovered.

Crossing the island I see the tail of my coat
Wave back and forth and know
It is the waves of the sea on my beach.
And now I am in the cave. A moment ago
I saw the broad leather-brown belts of the tangleweed,
And the minute forms that fix themselves
In soft carmine lace-stencils upon the shingle,
The notched wrack gemmed with lime-white bead-shells
Showing like pearls on a dark braid,
And minute life in a million forms.
And I saw the tide come crawling
Through the rocky labyrinths of approach
With flux and reflux – making inch upon inch
In an almost imperceptible progress.
But now I know it is the earth
And not the water that is unstable,
For at every rise and fall of the pellucid tide
It seems as though it were the shingle
And the waving forest of sea-growth
That moves – and not the water!
And, after all, there is no illusion,
But seeming deception prefigures truth,
For it is a matter of physiographical knowledge
That in the long passages of time
The water remains – and the land ebbs and flows,

I have achieved the diamond body.

Whuchulls*

Gie owre your coontin', for nae man can tell
The population o' a wud like this
In plants and beasts, and needna pride himsel'
On ocht he marks by a' he's boond to miss.
What is oor life that we should prize't abune
Lichen's or slug's o' which we ken scarce mair
Than they o' oors when a' thing's said and dune,
Or fancy it ser's 'heicher purposes'?
The wice man kens that a fool's brain and his
Differ at maist as little 'gainst a' that is
As different continents and centuries,
Time, station, caste, culture, or character –
Triflin' distinctions that dinna cairry faur –
And if at ony point he stops and says:
'My lot has fa'n in mair enlightened days,
I'm glad to be a European, no' a black
– Human, no' hotchin' glaur' ahint his back'
Let him forehear as foolish a future set
Him in a class as seemin' laicher yet,
Or ten pasts damn him for a graceless get.
Original forest, Whuchulls, public park,
Mysel', or ony man, beast, mineral,weed,
I clearly see are a' aside the mark,
The poet hauds nae brief for ony kind,
Age, place, or range o' sense, and no' confined
To ony nature can share Creation's insteed.
First speir this bowzie bourach if't prefers
The simmer or the winter, day or night,
New or forhooied nests, rain's pelts or smirrs,
Bare sticks or gorded fullyery; and syne invite
My choice twixt good and evil, life and death.
What hoar trunk girds at ivy or at fug
Or what sleek bole complains it lacks them baith?
Nae foliage hustle-farrant in windy light

* Local pronunciation of Whitshiels, a wood near Langholm.

Is to the Muse a mair inspirin' sight
Than fungus poxy as the mune; nae blight
A meaner state than flourish at its height.
Leafs' music weel accords wi' gloghole's glug.
Then cite nae mair this, that, or onything.
To nae belief or preference I cling,
Earth – let alane the mucklest mountain in't –
Is faur owre kittle a thing to scho ahint.
I'll no' toy wi' the fragments o't I ken
– Nor seek to beshield *it*, least o' a' men! ...
Yet here's a poem takin' shape again,
Inevitable shape, faur mair inevitable
Than birks and no' bamboos or banyans here,
Impredictable, relentless, thriddin' the rabble
O' themes and aspects in this thrawart scene.
O freedom constrainin' me as nae man's been
Mair constrained wha wasna, as I'll yet be, freer! ...

'Clearlier it comes. I winna ha'e it. Quick
And gi'e me tutors in arboriculture then.
Let me plunge where the undergrowth's mair thick.
Experts in forestry, botany – a' that ken
Mair than I dae o' onything that's here.
I ken sae little it easily works its will.
Fence me frae its design wi' endless lear.
Pile up the facts and let me faurer ben.
Multiply my vocabulary ten times ten.
Let me range owre a' prosody again.
Mak' yon a lammergeir, no' juist a wren.
Is that owre muckle for a Scotsman yet,
Needin' a soupler leid, great skills, he lacks?
Is he in silence safer frae attacks?
Yet wha can thole to see it cavalierly choose
In God's green wud – tak' this and that refuse?
Yon knoul-taed trees, this knurl, at least 't'll use!
Gar memory gie the place fower seasons at aince.'
The world's no' mine. I'll tak' nae hen's care o't.
'Is that Creation's nature you evince,
Sma-bookin' Whuchulls to a rice or twa
Sae arbirtrarily picked, and voidin' a'
The lave as gin it wasna worth a jot?'

There is nae reason but on unreason's based
And needs to mind that often to hain its sense,
Dodo and Mammoth had the same misplaced
Trust in their *données* – and ha'e lang gane hence.
Why fash sae muckle owre Nature's present stock
In view o' a' past changes and to come?
Its wipin' oot 'ud be nae greater shock
Than mony afore; and Poetry isna some
Society for Preservin' Threatened Types,
But strokes a cat or fiddles on its tripes,
And for inclusions or exclusions, fegs,
Needna apologize while a'e bird's eggs
Are plain, anither's speckled, beasts ha'e legs,
Birds wings, Earth here brairds trees, here nocht but seggs.
'Troth it's an insult for a man to seek
A'e woman owre anither. A' woman hae
Their differences and resemblances, but whatna freak
Thinks, frae the latter, ony ane'll dae
Or, frae the former, fain 'ud sair them a'?

The world o' a' the senses is the same.
Creation disna live frae hand to mooth
Juist improvisin' as it gangs, forsooth,
And there's nae meanin' in life that bode to da'
Until we came – or bides a wicer day –
'Yont brute creation, fools, bairns, unborn, deid.
I'd sing bird-mooth'd wi' ony ither creed,
No' wi' Creation's nature and its aim;
Or sing like Miffy – wheesht, world, while he speaks.
In English – hence, the Universal Speech.
He has nae wings; let birds pit on the breeks.
Nae fins. Fish, copy him! And sae let each
O' Nature's sorts be modelled upon him
Frae animalculae to Seraphim.
He is nae poet, but likes the Laureate best.
What, write like that? – Ah! here's the crucial test!
I ha'e the courage to be a Scotsman then
(Nae Scot'll e'er be Laureate we ken!)*
Divided frae ither folk to Eternity's en',
And, if I hadna, ken it wadna maitter.

* 'There are poets little enough to envy even a poet-laureate.' – *Gray*.

I'd be it still. Exclusive forms are nature.
It means to be and comes in Nature's way.
– In its ain nature's, as a' in Nature does.
Supersessions, innovations, variations, display
Nature, no' hide; and Scotland, Whuchulls, us
Interest me less for what they are than as
Facts o' the creative poo'er that, tho' they pass,
'll aye be qualified by their ha'en been.'
It is nae treason then to stell my een
No' on their fleetin' shapes but on their deep
Constituent principles destined to keep
A mystery greater than the sight o' eels
Kelterin' through a' the seven seas reveals.
These to a'e spot converge, but we gang oot
Aye faurer frae oor source – ne'er back, I doot.

'I like to see the ramel gowd-bestreik,
And sclaffer cuit-deep through the birsled leafs.
Here I dung doon the squirrels wi' my sling
And made the lassies brooches o' their paws,
Set girns for rabbits and for arnuts socht,
Herried my nests and blew the eggs, and lit
Fires o' fir-burrs and hag in tinker style.
Hoo faur the interests o' progress warrant
Meddlin' wi' Whuchulls' auld amenities,
And their dependent livelihoods and ploys,
I'm no' to say; I'm glad to see it still
Temporarily triumphant against control.
It's pleasant nae doot for a woman to dream
O' yieldin' hersel' to some buirdly man
Wha kens what he wants and willy-nilly ha'e't
But when the time comes she'll aye find, I think,
Guid reasons for no' yieldin' – bless her hert!
Sae wi' the Whuchulls. May the Lord be praised.'
Nae doot primeval beasts felt juist the same
Aboot the place – tho' different frae this
As only change that's still in store for it.
Hauf saurian-emeritus, hauf prentice spook,
You'll never see the plantin' for the trees,
This Eden where Adam comes fu' circle yet.

There is nae ither way. For weel or woe
It is attained. Tho' idle side-winds blow
In on me still and inferior questions thraw
Their crockets up, a' doots and torments cease.
The road is clear. I gang in perfect peace,
And my idea spreids and shines and lures me on,
O lyric licht auld chaos canna dam!
Celestial, soothin', sanctifyin' course, wi' a'
The high sane forces o' the sacred time
Fechtin' on my side through it till I con
This blainy blanderin' and ken that I'm
Delivered frae the need o' trauchlin' wi't,
Accommodated to't, but in my benmaist hert
Acknowledgmentless, free, condition or reform,
Or sunny lown or devastatin' storm,
Indifferent to me; where the Arts stert
Wi' a' else *corpore vili* – *'God's mercy-seat!'*

The Terrible Crystal

To Sadie McLellan (Mrs. Walter Pritchard)

Clear thought is the quintessence of human life.
In the end its acid power will disintegrate
All the force and flummery of current passions and pretences,
Eat the life out of every false loyalty and craven creed
And bite its way through to a world of light and truth.

Give me the open and unbiased mind
Valuing truth above all prepossessions to such an extent
As to be ready to discard them all
τό κατ' α'υθϱωπόν, and, furthermore,
Is content to approach Metaphysics through Physics,
In the Aristotlean sense in so far
As it recognises that empirical factuality
Can best be attested in that domain,
And is therefore impelled to recognise in the cosmos
A dynamic and teleological character

And by virtue of that recognition
Stands not far from religion
– A teleology essentially immanent,
God's relation to the world being in some general way
Like the relation of our minds to our bodies.

This is the hidden and lambent core I seek.
Like crystal it is hidden deep
And only to be found by those
Who will dig deep.
Like crystal it is formed by cataclysm and central fires;
Like crystal it gathers into an icy unity
And a gem-like transparence
All the colour and fire of life;
Like crystal it concentrates and irradiates light;
Like crystal it endures.

Since only those who have looked upon tragedy
Can dare to behold it.
It is terrible to uninitiated eyes.
Yet in this white stone

Those upon whom tragedy and catastrophe are come
May find their cure and their redemption,
For it has been formed in tragedy
And calcined in catastrophe
I have seen refractions of its purity
In the facets of seers past and present –
Virgil's day-star dawning over ruined Ilium;
Kierkegaard's 'arousal broad awake'
Out of his 'dread and trembling';
Barth's 'horizon light' breaking through the dark obscure;
Brunner's lightning flashes in the midnight of 'eclipse';
Heim's 'two infinitudes' beyond the boundary of dimension,
– Visions of a transcendental country
Stretching out athwart the temporal frontiers;
The sacrificial 'salutation of the cleanness of death'
On the part of Joan the Maid
– All, indeed, but broken lights,
Partial gleams reflecting each in their degree
Some aspect of the white intensity
Of that single central radiance,
But all carrying the same gospel:
'When consciousness is crucified upon circumstance
Give praise!'

The poetry I seek must therefore have the power
Of fusing the discordant qualities of experience,
Of mixing moods, and holding together opposites,
And well I know that the various facets
Of sensibility, sensuous, mental, and emotional,
And its alternating moods
Cannot be fully reconciled
Save in an imaginative integrity
That includes, but transcends, sensibility as such.
Our time opposes such integrity
As much as it demands it
And to struggle through complexity to simplicity
Is therefore as necessary as it is difficult.

A Vision of Scotland

I see my Scotland now, a puzzle
Passing the normal of her sex, going erect
Unscathed through fire, keeping her virtue
Where temptation works with violence, walking bravely,
Offering loyalty and demanding respect.

Every now and again in a girl like you,
Even in the streets of Glasgow or Dundee,
She throws her headsquare off and a mass
Of authentic flaxen hair is revealed,
Fine spun as newly-retted fibres
On a sunlit Irish bleaching field.

Kinsfolk

From 'Work in Progress'
(The Modern Scot, July 1931)

Gin scenic beauty had been a' I sook
I never need ha' left the Muckle Toon.
I saw it there as weel as ony man
(As I'll sune prove); and sin syne I've gane roon'
Hauf o' the warld wi' faculties undulled
      And no' seen't equalled.

But scenic beauty's never maittered much
To me afore, sin poetry isna made
O' onything that's seen, toucht, smelt, or heard,
And no' till lately ha'e the hame scenes played
A pairt in my creative thocht I've yet
      To faddom, and permit.

Gin there's an efter life hoo can I guess
What kind o' man I'll be wha canna tell
What's pairted me here frae my kith and kin
In a' airts mair than Heaven is frae Hell
(To bate the question which is which a wee)
      As't seems to them and me,

Nor tell what brings me unexpectedly back
Whaur't seems nae common thocht or interest's left.
Guid kens it wasna snobbery or hate,
Selfishness, ingratitude, or chance that reft
Sae early, sae completely, ties that last
      Maist folk for life – or was't.

I bein' a man made ither human ties
But they – my choice – are broken (in this case
No' a' my choice) as utterly as those
That bound me to my kin and native place.
My wife and bairns, is't tinin' them that thraws
      Me back on my first cause?

Foreseein' in Christine's or in Walter's mind
A picture o' mysel' as in my ain

My mither rises or I rise in hers
Incredible as to a Martian brain
A cratur' o' this star o' oors micht be
        It had nae point o' contact wi'.

Daith in my faither's case. I ha'e his build,
His energy, but no' his raven hair,
Rude cheeks, clear een. I am whey-faced. My een
Ha'e dark rings roon' them and my pow is fair.
A laddie when he dee'd, I kent little o'm and he
        Kent less o' me.

Gin he had lived my life and wark micht weel
Ha' been entirely different, better or waur,
Or neither, comparison impossible.
It wadna ha' been the same. That's hoo things are.
He had his differences frae some folks aroon'
        But never left the Muckle Toon.

He had his differences but a host o' freen's
At ane wi' him on maist things and at serious odds
In nane, a kindly, gin conscientious, man,
Fearless but peacefu', and to man's and God's
Service gi'en owre accordin' to his lichts
        But fondest o' his ain fireside o' nichts.

Afore he dee'd he turned and gied a lang
Last look at pictures o' my brither and me
Hung on the wa' aside the bed, I've heard
My mither say. I wonder then what he
Foresaw or hoped and hoo – or gin – it squares
        Wi' subsequent affairs.

I've led a vera different life frae ocht
He could conceive or share I ken fu' weel
Yet gin he understood – or understands
(His faith, no' mine) – I like to feel, and feel,
He wadna wish his faitherhood undone
        O' sic an unforeseen unlikely son.

I like to feel, and yet I ken that a'
I mind or think aboot him is nae mair

To what he was, or aiblins is, than yon
Picture o' me at fourteen can compare
Wi' what I look the day (or looked even then).
      He looked in vain, and I again.

Gin he had lived at warst we'd ha' been freen's
Juist as my mither (puir auld soul) and I
– As maist folk are, no' ga'en vera deep,
A maitter o' easy-ozie habit maistly, shy
O' fundamentals, as it seems to me,
      – A minority o' ane, may be!

Maist bonds 'twixt man and man are weel ca'd bonds.
But I'll come back to this, since come I maun,
Fellow-feelin', common humanity, claptrap (or has
In anither sense my comin'-back begun)
I've had as little use for to be terse
      As maist folk ha'e for verse.

My wife and weans in London never saw
The Muckle Toon that I'm concerned wi' noo
(Sittin' in Liverpool), and never may.
What maitters't then, gin a' life's gantin' through,
Biggit on sicna kittle sands as these,
      Wi' like haphazardries?

My clan is darkness 'yont a wee ring
O' memory showin' catsiller here or there
But nocht complete or lookin' twice the same.
Graham, Murray, Carruthers, Frater, and faur mair
Auld Border breeds than I can tell ha' been
      Woven in its skein.

Great hooses keep their centuried lines complete.
Better than I can mind my faither they
Preserve their forbears painted on their wa's
And can trace ilka tendency and trait
O' bluid and spirit in their divers stages
      Doon the ages.

To mind and body I ha' nae sic clue,
A water flowin' frae an unkent source

Wellin' up in me to catch the licht at last
At this late break in its hidden course,
Yet my blin' instincts nurtured in the dark
        Sing sunwards like the lark.

I canna signal to a single soul
In a' the centuries that led up to me
In happy correspondence, yet to a'
These nameless thanks for strength and cleanness gi'e,
And mair, auld Border breeds, ken I inherit,
        And croun, your frontier spirit.

Reivers to weavers and to me. Weird way!
Yet in the last analysis I've sprung
Frae battles, mair than ballads, and it seems
The thrawn auld water has at last upswung
Through me, and's mountin' like the vera devil
        To its richt level!

Bracken Hills in Autumn

These beds of bracken, climax of the summer's growth,
Are elemental as the sky or sea.
In still and sunny weather they give back
The sun's glare with a fixed intensity
      As of steel or glass
      No other foliage has.

There is a menace in their indifference to man
As in tropical abundance. On gloomy days
They redouble the sombre heaviness of the sky
 And nurse the thunder. Their dense growth shuts the narrow
   ways
      Between the hills and draws
      Closer the wide valleys' jaws.

This flinty verdure's vast effusion is the more
Remarkable for the shortness of its stay.
From November to May a brown stain on the slopes
Downbeaten by frost and rain, then in quick array
      The silvery crooks appear
      And the whole host is here.

Useless they may seem to men and go unused, but cast
Cartloads of them into a pool where the trout are few
And soon the swarming animalculae upon them
Will proportionately increase the fishes too.
      Miracles are never far away
      Save bringing new thought to play.

In summer islanded in these grey-green seas where the wind
   plucks
The pale underside of the fronds on gusty days
As a land breeze stirs the white caps in a roadstead
Glimpses of shy bog gardens surprise the gaze
      Or rough stuff keeping a ring
      Round a struggling water-spring.

Look closely. Even now bog asphodel spikes, still alight at the
   tips,
Sundew lifting white buds like those of the whitlow grass

On walls in spring over its little round leaves
Sparkling with gummy red hairs, and many a soft mass
      Of the curious moss that can clean
      A wound or poison a river, are seen.

Ah! well I know my tumultuous days now at their prime
Will be brief as the bracken too in their stay
Yet in them as the flowers of the hills 'mid the bracken
All that I treasure is needs hidden away
      And will also be dead
      When its rude cover is shed.

Facing the Chair

Here under the radiant rays of the sun
Where everything grows so vividly
In the human mind and in the heart,
Love, life, and all else so beautifully,
I think again of men as innocent as I am
Pent in a cold unjust walk between steel bars,
Their trousers slit for the electrodes
And their hair cut for the cap

Because of the unconcern of men and women,
Respectable and respected and professedly Christian,
Idle-busy among the flowers of their gardens here
Under the gay-tipped rays of the sun,
And I am suddenly completely bereft
Of *la grande amitié des choses créées*,
The unity of life which can only be forged by love.

from *Dìreadh I*

Scotland small? Our multiform, our infinite Scotland *small*?
Only as a patch of hillside may be a cliché corner
To a fool who cries 'Nothing but heather!' where in
    September another
Sitting there and resting and gazing round
Sees not only the heather but blaeberries
With bright green leaves and leaves already turned scarlet
Hiding ripe blue berries; and amongst the sage-green leaves
Of the bog-myrtle the golden flowers of the tormentil shining;
And on the small bare places, where the little Blackface sheep
Found grazing, milkworts blue as summer skies;
And down in neglected peat-hags, not worked
Within living memory, sphagnum moss in pastel shades
Of yellow, green, and pink; sundew and butterwort
Waiting with wide-open sticky leaves for their tiny winged
    prey;
And nodding harebells vying in their colour
With the blue butterflies that poise themselves delicately
    upon them;
And stunted rowans with harsh dry leaves of glorious colour.
'Nothing but heather!' – How marvellously descriptive! And
    incomplete!

Dìreadh III

'So, in the sudden sight of the sun, has man stopped, blinded, paralysed and afraid?'

I am reft to the innermost heart
Of my country now,
History's final verdict upon it,
The changeless element in all its change,
Reified like the woman I love.

Here in this simple place of clean rock and crystal water,
With something of the cold purity of ice in its appearance,
Inhuman and yet friendly,
Undecorated by nature or by man
And yet with a subtle and unchanging beauty
Which seems the antithesis of every form of art.

Here near the summit of Sgurr Alasdair
The air is very still and warm,
The Outer Isles look as though
They were cut out of black paper
And stuck on a brilliant silver background,
(Even as I have seen the snow-capped ridges of Hayes
    Peninsula
Stand out stark and clear in the pellucid Arctic atmosphere
Or, after a wild and foggy night, in the dawn
Seen the jagged line of the Tierra del Fuego cliffs
Looking for all the world as if they were cut out of tin,
Extending gaunt and desolate),
The western sea and sky undivided by horizon,
So dazzling is the sun
And its glass image in the sea.
The Cuillin peaks seem miniature
And nearer than is natural
And they move like liquid ripples
In the molten breath
Of the corries which divide them.
I light my pipe and the match burns steadily
Without the shielding of my hands,
The flame hardly visible in the intensity of light
Which drenches the mountain top.

I lie here like the cool and gracious greenery
Of the water-crowfoot leafage, streaming
In the roping crystalline currents,
And set all about on its upper surface
With flecks of snow blossom that, on closer looking,
Show a dust of gold.
The blossoms are fragile to the touch
And yet possess such strength and elasticity
That they issue from the submergence of a long spate
Without appreciable hurt – indeed, the whole plant
Displays marvellous endurance in maintaining
A rooting during the raging winter torrents.
Our rivers would lose much if the snowy blossom
And green waving leafage of the water-crowfoot
Were absent – aye, and be barer of trout too!
And so it is with the treasures of the Gaelic genius
So little regarded in Scotland today.
Yet emerging unscathed from their long submergence,
Impregnably rooted in the most monstrous torrents*
– The cataracting centuries cannot rive them away –
And productive of endless practical good,
Even to people unaware of their existence,
In the most seemingly unlikely connections.

I am possessed by this purity here
As in a welling of stainless water
Trembling and pure like a body of light
Are the webs of feathery weeds all waving,
Which it traverses with its deep threads of clearness
Like the chalcedony in moss agate
Starred here and there with grenouillette.
It is easy here to accept the fact
That that which the 'wisdom' of the past
And the standards of the complacent elderly rulers
Of most of the world today regard
As the most fixed and eternal verities –
The class state, the church,
The old-fashioned family and home,
Private property, rich and poor,
'Human nature' (to-day meaning mainly

* See John Ruskin's description of the spring at Carshalton.

The private-profit motive), their own race,
Their Heaven and their 'immortal soul' –
Is all patently evanescent,
Even as we know our fossil chemical accumulations
Of energy in coal, peat, oil, lignite and the rest
Are but ephemeral, a transitory blaze
Even on the small time-scale of civilized man,
And that running water, though eminently convenient and
    practicable
For the present, will give us a mere trickle
Of the energy we shall demand in the future.

And suddenly the flight of a bird reminds me
Of how I once went out towards sunset in a boat
Off the rocky coast of Wigtownshire
And of my glimpse of the first rock-pigeon I saw.
It darted across one of the steep gullies
At the bottom of which our boat lay rocking
On the dark green water – and vanished into safety
In a coign of the opposite wall
Before a shot could be fired.
It swerved in the air,
As though doubtful of its way,
Then with a glad swoop of certainty
It sped forward, turned upward,
And disappeared into some invisible cranny
Below the overhanging brow of the cliff.

There was such speed, such grace, such happy confidence of
    refuge in that swoop
That it struck me with the vividness of a personal
    experience.
For an instant I seemed to see into the bird's mind
And to thrill with its own exhilaration of assured safety.
Why should this be? It was as though
I had seen the same occurrence,
Or some part of it, before.

Then I knew. Into the back of my mind had come
The first line of the loveliest chorus in *Hippolytus*,
That in which the Troezenian women,
Sympathizing with the unhappy Phaedra,

Who is soon to die by her own hand,
Sing of their yearning to fly away from the palace
Whose sunny terraces are haunted by misery and impending
   doom.
They long to escape with the flight of the sea-birds
To the distant Adriatic and the cypress-fringed waters of
   Eridanus
Or to the fabulous Hesperides,
Where beside the dark-blue ocean
Grow the celestial apple-trees.
It is the same emotion as filled the Hebrew poet
Who cried: 'O for the wings of a dove,
That I might flee away and be at rest.'
'ἠ λιβάτοις ὑ‘πὸ κευθμῶσι γενοίμαν'
The untranslatable word in that line
Is the ὑ‘πὸ. It includes more
Than a single word of English can contain.
Up-in-under: so had the pigeon
Flown to its refuge in 'the steep hiding-places',
So must Euripides have seen a sea-bird
Dart to its nest in the cliffs of Attica.
For an instant, sitting in that swaying boat
Under the red rocks, while the sunset ebbed down the sky
And the water lapped quietly at my side,
I again felt the mind of the poet reaching out
Across the centuries to touch mine.
Scotland and China and Greece!
Here where the colours –
Red standing for heat,
Solar, sensual, spiritual;
Blue for cold – polar, bodily, intellectual;
Yellow luminous and embodied
In the most enduring and the brightest form in gold –
Remind me how about this
Pindar and Confucius agreed.
Confucius who was Pindar's contemporary
For nearly half a century!
And it was Pindar's 'golden snow'
My love and I climbed in that day.
I in Scotland as Pindar in Greece
Have stood and marvelled at the trees

And been seized with honey-sweet yearning for them;
And seen too mist condensing on an eagle,
His wings 'streamlined' for a swoop on a leveret,
As he ruffled up the brown feathers on his neck
In a quiver of excitement;
Pindar, greatest master of metaphor the world has seen,
His spirit so deeply in tune
With the many-sidedness of both Man and Nature
That he could see automatically all the basal resemblances
His metaphors imply and suggest.
Scotland and China and Greece!

So every loveliness Scotland has ever known,
Or will know, flies into me now,
Out of the perilous night of English stupidity,
As I lie brooding on the fact
That 'perchance the best chance
Of reproducing the ancient Greek temperament
Would be to "cross" the Scots with the Chinese.'*
The glory of Greece is imminent again to me here
With the complete justification his sense of it
In Germany – his participation in that great awakening
Taking the form of an imaginative reliving,
On behalf of his people, of the glory of Athens –
Lacked in Hölderlin. I see all things
In a cosmic or historical perspective too.
Love of country, in me, is love of a new order.
In Greece I also find the clue
To the mission of the poet
Who reveals to the people
The nature of their gods,
The instrument whereby his countrymen
Become conscious of the powers on whom they depend
And of whom they are the children,
Knowing, in himself, the urgency of the divine creativeness
    of Nature
And most responsive to its workings in the general world.
'Wer das Tiefste gedacht, liebt das Lebendigste.'

* Sir Richard Livingstone.

And remembering my earlier poems in Scots
Full of my awareness 'that language is one
Of the most cohesive or insulating of world forces
And that dialect is always a bond of union',*
I covet the mystery of our Gaelic speech
In which *rughadh* was at once a blush,
A promontory, a headland, a cape,
Leadan, musical notes, litany, hair of the head,
And *fonn*, land, earth, delight, and a tune in music,†
And think of the Oriental provenance of the Scottish Gael,
The Eastern affiliations of his poetry and his music,
' ... the subtler music, the clear light
Where time burns back about th' eternal embers.'
And the fact that he initiated the idea of civilization
That to-day needs renewal at its native source
Where, indeed, it is finding it, since Georgia,
Stalin's native country, was also the first home of the Scots.

The Gaelic genius that is in this modern world
As sprays of quake grass are in a meadow,
Or light in the world, which notwithstanding
The *Fiat Lux* scores of thousands of years ago,
Is always scanty and dubious enough
And at best never shares the empery of the skies
On more than equal terms with the dark,
Or like sensitive spirits among the hordes of men,
Or seldom and shining as poetry itself.
Quake grass, the 'silver shakers,' with their glumes shaped
    and corded
Like miniature cowrie shells, and wrapped
In bands of soft green and purple, and strung
(Now glittering like diamonds,
Now chocolate brown like partridge plumage)
On slender stems and branchlets, quick
To the slightest touch of air!

So Scotland darts into the towering wall of my heart
And finds refuge now. I give
My beloved peace, and her swoop has recalled

* Sir James Crichton-Browne.
† Macfarlane's *English and Gaelic Vocabularly* (Edinburgh, 1815).

That first day when my human love and I,
Warmed and exhilarated by the sunny air,
Put on our skis and began
A zigzag track up the steep ascent.
There was no sound but the faint hiss and crush
Of the close-packed snow, shifting under our weight.
The cloudless bowl of the sky
Burned a deep gentian. In the hushed, empty world,
Where nothing moved but ourselves,
Our bodies grew more consciously alive.
I felt each steady beat of my heart.
The drawing and holding of my breath
Took on a strange significance.
Nor was I merely conscious of myself,
I began to be equally aware of my love;
Her little physical habits
Sinking into my mind
Held the same importance as my own.

How fragrant, how infinitely refreshing and recreating
Is the mere thought of Deirdre!
How much more exhilarating to see her, as now!

'She said that she at eve for me would wait;
Yet here I see bright sunrise in the sky.'*
Farewell all else! I may not look upon the dead,
Nor with the breath of dying be defiled,
And thou, I see, art close upon that end.

I am with Alba – with Deirdre – now
As a lover is with his sweetheart when they know
That personal love has never been a willing and efficient
    slave
To the needs of reproduction, that to make
Considerations of reproduction dictate the expression of
    personal love
Not infrequently destroys the individual at his spiritual core,
Thus 'eugenic marriages' cannot as a whole
Be succesful so far as the parents are concerned,
While to make personal love master over reproduction

* From a Chinese eight-line lyric, twenty-seven centuries old.

Under conditions of civilization is to degrade
The germ plasm of the future generations,
And to compromise between these two policies
Is to cripple both spirit and germ,
And accept the only solution – unyoke the two,
Sunder the fetters that from time immemorial
Have made them so nearly inseparable,
And let each go its own best way,
Fulfilling its already distinct function,
An emancipation the physical means for which
Are now known for the first time in history!

Let what can be shaken, be shaken,
And the unshakeable remain.
The Inaccessible Pinnacle* is not inaccessible.
So does Alba surpass the warriors
As a graceful ash surpasses a thorn,
Or the deer who moves sprinkled with the dewfall
Is far above all other beasts
– Its horns glittering to Heaven itself.†

An October Nightfall

[Published in *The Glasgow Herald*, 14 October 1925.]

Leafs that ha'e scrauched in the wund a' day
Hing forspent on shaddaws o' trees.
Birds ha'e gane as gin they'd been nocht
But fleetin' ferlies a dream can gie's.

Deasie sheep in the haar are fankled,
Horses dow wi' their heids thegither,
And I'm fell feared that it's Life itsel'
And no' juist Licht that's aboot to wither ...

O whatna cry can I reeze that'll gar
The warld haud hard by its colours and shapes

---

* Of Sgurr Dearg, in Skye.
† See *Volsungakvida en forma*, 41 (*Saemundar Edda* Jónsson).

Or a' thing's tint in the gantin' dark
Like my bonny hen that gaed wi' the gapes?

It'll heist its feathers in whustlin' licht
Nor jouk wi' its eident neb again.
There's nocht but nocht whaur its gleg een glinted
– Maun I tine the warld as I tint my hen.

*On the Island of Little Linga

[Published in *The Broughton Magazine*, issue of Summer 1933.]

> *"That which appears most real to common*
> *consciousness has the least existence"*
>   – PLOTINUS.

It's a' vera weel
   On an island like this,
To lack for a while
   Sae muckle, and no' miss.

But what 'ud I dae
   If I lived here lang,
And never mair mixed
   Other people amang!

Hoo lang could I live
   On the store I had yet,
Frae my previous life,
   At a new store get?

If I'd naething to dae,
   No even work to eat
– The Past gane frae memory,
   And the Future wi't.

That's what'll happen,
   That's why I cam' here
– I'll sune no be able
   Even to think, that's clear.

What'll happen then
   Is juist what I seek
– The communion it's impossible
   To think o', or speak.

*The Stone of the Dog, in Glen Lyon

[Printed from the undated manuscript in Edinburgh University Library.]

This is the Stone of the Dog,
With a neck that comes up to my knee
And a clumsy spatulate head
Going out horizontally,

The stone by which the women believe
They can tell, from the ease with which they can go
Stooping under the head when they're heavy with child,
If their time is to be easy or no'.

*The Wild Swan

[Printed from the undated manuscript in Edinburgh University Library.]

See, Scotland, see how in these desolate days
When all your other birds to kinder countries fare
One wild swan in your freezing waters stays
And strives to keep an open channel there!

But now the encroaching ice is clutching at its feet
And soon in vain its whirling wings may beat!

*The Terns

[Printed from the undated manuscript in Edinburgh University Library.]

Now all about us the terns
Make gestures of incredible grace
– But in human intercourse surely
Only lovelier shapes should ever have place.

Stupid slack girl with a silly sense
Of your human superiority to these,
The lifted wings of any of these little birds
Should suddenly bring you to your knees.

Man with the fat dull eyes just taking for granted
Or indifferent to all this lovely display,
If the sky were like your look it might do for you,
But these snowy wings would go a dirty grey!

*The Unholy Loch

[Published in *Peace Campaign*, issue of January/February 1961.]

'Can you account for it? The Scottish people
Are all opposed to the Polaris base, it's said'.
– It must be some sort of half-forgotten
Self-respect at last raising its ugly head!

The term 'military intelligence', of course,
Is an outsize oxymoron
But for the criminals running Polaris
The first two syllables of the word must be shorn.

The Swedish poet, Harry Martinson,
Has asked in one of his inspired flashes:
'Will Man banish himself from the Paradise of Earth
And crown himself "The King of Ashes"?'

Or will he be able to control his urges
And see the Earth as the only orb where life can find
A land of milk and honey? None will be left
If these maniacs poison Mankind.

Earth is the only ground of human hope, showing now
Unprecedented perspectives for happy fulfilment
Against which only purblind prejudice launches
Its tentiginous genocidal intent.

Some half-forgotten self-respect? By God,
It's high time *that* surged up and prevailed
Before morons, with none, make the whole world
Enurn a humanity that has failed.

Nowhere in Scotland, Europe, American even
Is there a fit place for such a base.
If it must be located anywhere at all
Then Hell itself is the only place.

It's nothing, fools think, to destroy
The population of Glasgow in a second.

That's it – it's *nothing they think* – that's the fact
With which it's high time we reckoned.
Nay, Hell itself it would disgrace.
For a Polaris base there is NO PLACE!

*On the Fishing Grounds

[Printed from the undated manuscript reproduced in *Hugh MacDiarmid: A Festschrift* (1962), edited by K. D. Duval and Sydney Goodsir Smith.]

I am a poet
And beliefs are to me
No more than the sunlight
Is on the deep sea.

Fishers know it's at night
Their harvest is got.
Daylight's only of use
For disposing of the 'shot'.

PART TWO

Matters of Fact and Philosophy

A Theory of Scots Letters

MacDiarmid's linguistic theory was published in three successive issues of The Scottish Chapbook *(Volume 1, nos 7, 8, 9: February, March, April 1923) as part of the regular Causerie by editor C. M. Grieve. At the time MacDiarmid was brooding on ideas that would subsequently find expression in* A Drunk Man Looks at the Thistle. *He is, for example, anxious to associate his theory of Scots with Joycean modernism. Moreover, the Spengler quotation on Dostoevsky – 'The next thousand years belong to the Christianity of Dostoevsky' – is worked into* A Drunk Man *in which the poet describes the Russian novelist as* 'Closer than my ain braith to me,/As close as to the Diety/Approachable in whom appears/This Christ o' the neist thoosand years.'

I

We are in a less happy position than was Thomas Boston, the author of the once-ubiquitous 'Fourfold State' who put on record that 'on Wednesday, 4th August, about eleven o'clock in the forenoon was born to me a son whom . . . I did, after no small struggle with myself, adventure to call Ebenezer.' We have been quite unable to find a more suitable title under which to gather the various lines of argument we propose to simultaneously develop in this paper. Noting our purpose to undertake 'a definite and systematic formulation of our Theory of Scots Letters,' 'Man o' Moray' (who conducts what passes for a literary feature in the *Edinburgh Evening Dispatch* once a week) observes, 'It would be much better not to do so. We have had quite enough of this high-sounding nonsense.' – If we had in view Scottish readers and writers of no higher calibre than 'Man o' Moray' we would be dissuaded by the obvious futility of our task. Doubtless a certain proportion of the readers of our

Chapbook are still of that type. The majority, however, discovered early that 'it was not what they expected it to be' – which, of course, was precisely what we intended. But frankly, the circulation of the *Chapbook* is still too high to be above suspicion. 'If there must be theories of Scots Letters let them be temperately thought out and simply expressed,' continues 'Man o' Moray'. – 'He fails to remember that what is true of a man is true of a book, that the more apparent, obvious, and demonstrated the feelings, the more superficial, unreal and transient they probably are.' And in the sentences which follow that which we have just quoted A. R. Orage in his profound little essay on 'The Criteria of Culture' gives a clue to the spirit in which we are trying to conduct this *Chapbook* – and names the attitude of mind lacking which no reader will find this Theory intelligible, let alone illuminating. 'Culture I define as being, amongst other things, a capacity for subtle discrimination of words and ideas. Epictetus made the discrimination of words the foundation of moral training, and it is true enough that every stage of moral progress is indicated by the degree of our perception of the meaning of words. ... One of the most subtle words, and one of the key-words of culture, is simplicity. Can you discriminate between natural simplicity and studied simplicity, between Nature and Art? In appearance they are indistinguishable, but in reality they are aeons apart: and whoever has learned to distinguish between them is entitled to regard himself as on the way to culture. Originality is another key-word, and its subtlety may be suggested by a paradox which was a commonplace among the Greeks; namely, that the most original minds strive to conceal their originality and that the master minds succeed. Contrast this counsel of perfect originality with the counsels given in our own day, in which the aim of originality is directed to appearing original – you will be brought, thereby, face to face with still another key-idea of Culture, the relation of Appearance to Reality. All these exercises in culture are elementary, however, in comparison with the master-problem of "disinterestedness." No word in the English language is more difficult to define or better worth attempting to define. Somewhere or other in its capacious folds it contains all the ideas of ethics, and even, I should say, of religion. The *Bhagavad Gita* (to name only one classic) can be summed up in the word. Duty is only a pale equivalent to it. I

126

venture to say that whoever has understood the meaning of "disinterestedness" is not far-off understanding the goal of human culture.' Nationalism in literature is the reaction of a distinctive essential of the spirit to the various time-influences to which it is subjected. And that which gives a recognisable if hardly definable unity to the work of all true Scottish writers, whether in English or the Vernacular, is a quality of 'disinterestedness' in the sense in which Orage uses it. This secret of the Scottish soul is laid bare (albeit in a false light of romanticism) by W. H. Hamilton when he sings:

> The lost cause calls me sooner than the true,
> Far sooner than the safe. Perchance I obey
> Some old religious rapture my forbears knew
> The problem unresolved save by this test –
> 'Whoever saves his life hath missed life's best.'

> To die for error ... rather than, being right,
> To rot or slumber or grow wise in my ease,
> – False doctrine, doubtless: be it so! ...

Consider in this connection what Professor Gregory Smith says in this passage from his most searching and stimulating book on *Scottish Literature*: 'There is more in the Scottish antithesis of the real and fantastic than is to be explained by the familiar rules of rhetoric. ... The one invades the other without warning. They are the "polar twins" of the Scottish Muse. ... The douce travesty which stands for the Scot with the general (the methodical, level-headed, self-conscious creature of popular tradition) never says as much as he thinks; he is as calm as a country Sabbath morn on the cantrips of his mind. But he is not the Scot who steps forth self-expressed in the Makars old and new despite the accidents or thwarts of history which stayed or appeared to stay the freer play of his fancy. ... This mingling, even of the most eccentric kind, is an indication to us that the Scot, in that fashion which takes all things as granted, is at his ease in both "rooms of life", and turns to fun and even profanity, with no misgivings. ... [We owe part of our strength] to this freedom in passing from one mood to another. It takes some people more time than they can spare to see the absolute propriety of a gargoyle's grinning at the elbow of a kneeling saint!'

Is not that precisely why the most advanced literature to-day is unintelligible to many highly-educated people even? Professor Gregory Smith has in these words described the great vital characteristic of Scottish literature – a distinguishing faculty, which it can only shape forth poorly in English, but which is potentially expressible in the Vernacular to which it belongs. It is the predominant feature of Scots Literature old and new, and yet, do not the same phrases ('taking all things as granted,' 'freedom in passing from one mood to another') sum up the essential tendencies of the most advanced schools of thought in every country in Europe to-day? We base our belief in the possibility of a great Scottish Literary Renaissance, deriving its strength from the resources that lie latent and almost unsuspected in the Vernacular, upon the fact that the genius of our Vernacular enables us to secure with comparative ease the very effects and swift transitions which other literatures are for the most part unsuccessfully endeavouring to cultivate in languages that have a very different and inferior bias. Whatever the potentialities of the Doric may be, however, there cannot be a revival in the real sense of the word – a revival of the spirit as distinct from a mere renewed vogue of the letter – unless these potentialities are in accord with the newest and truest tendencies of human thought. We confess to having been discouraged when thinking of the Vernacular Movement by the fact that the seal of its approval is so largely set upon the traditional and the conventional. The real enemy is he who cries: 'Hands off our fine old Scottish tongue.' If all that the Movement is to achieve is to preserve specimens of Braid Scots, archaic, imitative, belonging to a type of life that has passed and cannot return, in a sort of museum department of our consciousness – set apart from our vital preoccupations – it is a movement which not only cannot claim our support but compels our opposition. The rooms of thought are choc-a-bloc with far too much dingy old rubbish as it is. There are too many vital problems clamouring for attention. ...

It is a different matter, however, if an effort is to be made to really revive the Vernacular – to encourage the experimental exploitation of the unexplored possibilities of Vernacular expression. 'The letter killeth but the spirit giveth life.' Only in so far as the Vernacular has unused resources corresponding better than English does to the progressive expression of the distinctive characteristics of Scottish life – however much these may have been submerged, subverted, or camouflaged, by present conditions (we shall deal later with the question of the relationship between literature and politics) – has it possibilities of literary value. If the cultural level of work in the Doric is not capable of being raised to equal that in any other living language – if the Doric has not certain qualities which no other language possesses and qualities at that of consequence to modern consciousness as a whole – then all that can be hoped for is a multiplication of equivalents in the Vernacular to work that has already been better achieved in other languages without any special contribution at all from Scotland to the expressive resource of modern life. The Doric unquestionably has a past and, to a very much more limited extent, a present. The question is whether it has a future which will enable it successfully to compete, at any rate along specialised lines, with other languages. Our interest, therefore, should centre not so much in what has been done in the Doric as in what has not but may be done in it. No literature can rest on its laurels.

> We lack the courage to be where we are.
> We love too much to travel on old roads,
> To triumph on old fields; we love too much
> To consecrate the magic of dead things.

For our part we frankly confess that a living dog is worth any number of dead lions, and we unreservedly accept Thomas Hardy's definition that 'literature is the written expression of revolt against accepted things'.

We have been enormously struck by the resemblance – the moral resemblance – between Jamieson's Etymological Dictionary of the Scottish language and James Joyce's *Ulysses*. A *vis comica* that has not yet been liberated lies bound by desuetude and misappreciation in the recesses of the Doric: and its potential uprising would be no less prodigious, uncontrollable, and utterly at variance with conventional morality than was Joyce's tremendous outpouring. The Scottish instinct is irrevocably, continuously, opposed to all who 'are at ease in Zion'. It lacks entirely the English sense of 'the majesty of true corpulence'. Sandy is our national figure – a shy, subtle, disgruntled, idiosyncratic individual – very different from John Bull. And while the Irish may envisage their national destiny as 'the dark Rosaleen' and the thought of England may conjure up pictures of roast beef and stately homes, Scotland is always 'puir auld Scotland'. Dr Walter Walsh recently referred to the affinity between the Scots and the Spartans and voiced a deep national feeling when he deprecated material well-being and comfort of mind or body. It is of first-rate significance, revealing that what really does most profoundly appeal to us is not pleasure but pain, to remember what happened at the concert given by Serge Koussevitzki in Edinburgh recently. (It has a bearing on what we are subsequently to say of the mystical relation of Scotland and Russia.) A newspaper critic described it thus: 'He (Koussevitzki) rose to his greatest heights when he came to the modern Russians. There were the introduction to Moussorgski's opera "Khovanschchina", Rimsky Korsakov's "The Flight of the Bumble Bee", Rachmaninoff's "Vocalise" and Tchaikovski's "Fifth Symphony" ... Two of them had to be repeated, but the symphony marked the climax of the concert. Koussevitzki extracted from it *the last ounce of agony and gloom* with which it is charged. It was all very exciting, and at the close there were scenes unparalleled at these concerts. An Edinburgh audience, reputed to be reserved, rose to its feet, cheered and shouted bravos.' – That's us all over! Joy and gladness are all very well in their way – but gloom is what really gets us and we do enjoy agony! ...

Burns himself had no wish for the increase of mere human self-satisfaction. It is deeply significant that he wrote

> O wad some power the giftie gie's
> To see oorsels as ithers see's

– not, 'Oh gie the gift to ither folk to see us as we see oorsels.'

And one of the most distinctive characteristics of the Vernacular, part of its very essence, is its insistent recognition of the body, the senses. The Vernacular is almost startlingly at one with Rabbi Ben Ezra,

> Let us not always say
> *Spite of this flesh to-day*
> I strove, made head ...

In other words, in Meredith's phrase, the Vernacular can never consent to 'forfeit the beast wherewith we are cross'. This explains the unique blend of the lyrical and the ludicrous in primitive Scots sentiment. It enables us to realise very clearly just what Matthew Arnold meant when he called Burns 'a beast with splendid gleams' – and the essence of the genius of our race, is, in our opinion, the reconciliation it effects between the base and the beautiful, recognising that they are complementary and indispensable to each other.

II

The Scottish Vernacular is the only language in Western Europe instinct with those uncanny spiritual and pathological perceptions alike which constitute the uniqueness of Dostoevski's work, and word after word of Doric establishes a blood-bond in a fashion at once infinitely more thrilling and vital and less explicable than those deliberately sought after by writers such as D. H. Lawrence in the medium of English which is inferior for such purposes because it has entirely different natural bias which has been so confirmed down the centuries as to be insusceptible of correction. The Scots Vernacular is a vast storehouse of just the very peculiar and subtle effects which modern European literature in general is assiduously seeking and, if the next century is to see an advance in mental science equal to that which the last century has marked in material science, then the resumption of the Scots Vernacular into the mainstream of European letters, in a fashion which the most enthusiastic Vernacularist may well hesitate to hope for, is inevitable. The Vernacular is a vast unutilised mass of lapsed observation made by minds whose attitudes to experience and whose speculative and imaginative tendencies were quite different from any possible to Englishmen and Anglicised Scots to-day. It is an inchoate Marcel Proust – a Dostoevskian debris of ideas – an inexhaustible quarry of subtle and significant sound.

As a recent writer on the revival on Irish Gaelic (in which novels as well as poems and plays are now being written) remarks 'the best work done in Gaelic reveals a part of Irish life that has been long silent, with a freshness due to sources that have remained comparatively uninfluenced by alien imagination. ... Most of the writers of the so-called Irish Literary Revival of a decade or so back were ignorant of Gaelic. Even Synge had probably only a patois knowledge. ... A school is now arising among young men having the advantage of an educated knowledge of the tongue, and even the distinctiveness of their work in English is more marked. The new generation will doubtless be increasingly bi-lingual and in possession of the literary traditions of Gaelic life.' The revival of Scots Vernacular is being retarded simply because of the fact that the majority of writers in the Vernacular have only a patois knowledge of it – not an educated knowledge – and are not to any useful extent in possesion of its literary traditions apart from Burns: while they confine their efforts to a little range of conventional forms.

A writer in *The Glasgow Herald* recently pointed out that reflexly the distinctive humour of our Vernacular fulfilled at least three invaluable functions. 'It stimulates the wits and the descriptive and reflective powers. It keeps alive a spirit of brave and virile gaiety. By pricking the bladders of pride and pretension, and nourishing the independence and self-respect of the step-children of Fortune, it brings all sorts and conditions of men to a greatest common measure of sheer humanity, and is thus a powerful preservative of the true spirit of democracy.... The democratic spirit of the Scottish Vernacular speech and literature is strongly allied with an ethical bent which is all the stronger for its fearless realism and its freedom from didacticism or sentiment, and also, with an element of pathos that has suffered somewhat from its dilution and exploitation by certain writers of the Kailyard School.'

The writer goes on to say 'jalouse, dwam, dowie, gurlie, mavis, carline, crouse, gawkie, blate, gaucie, and thrawn are chance selections from a long list of fine old words that usefully express shades of meaning which English either ignores or renders very imperfectly'. To that may be added the fact that the Vernacular abounds in terms which short-circuit conceptions that take sentences to express in English. Take only one – Guyfaul. It takes nine English words to convey its meaning. It means 'Hungry for his meat but not very hungry for his work.'

Just as physiologically we have lost certain powers possessed by our forefathers – the art of wiggling our ears, for example, or of moving our scalps this way and that – so we have lost (but may perhaps reacquire) word-forming faculties peculiar to the Doric for the purposes of both psychological and nature description. There are words and phrases in the Vernacular which thrill me with a sense of having been produced as a result of

132

mental processes entirely different from my own and much more powerful. They embody observations of a kind which the modern mind makes with increasing difficulty and weakened effect. Take the word 'birth,' for instance, meaning a current in the sea caused by a furious tide but taking a different course from it – a contrary motion. It exemplifies a fascinating, exceedingly adroit and purely Scottish application of metaphor. Then there are natural occurrences and phenomena of all kinds which have apparently never been noted by the English mind. No words exist for them in English. For instance – watergaw – for an indistinct rainbow; yow-trummle – meaning the cold weather in July after the sheepshearing; cavaburd – meaning a thick fall of snow; and blue bore – meaning a patch of blue in a cloudy sky. Another feature of the Doric which I will not illustrate here is the fashion in which diverse attitudes of mind or shades of temper are telescoped into single words or phrases, investing the whole speech with subtle flavours of irony, commiseration, realism and humour which cannot be reproduced in English. In onomatopoetic effect, too, the Doric has a wider range and infinitely richer resources than English while the diversity of inherent bias is revealed in unmistakeable fashion.

Whatever the potentialities of the Doric may be, however, there cannot be a revival in the real sense of the word – a revival of the spirit as distinct from a mere renewed vogue of the letter – unless these potentialities are in accord with the newest tendencies of human thought.

Without in any way committing ourselves to agreement with the writers from whom we quote, let us endeavour to show that just as Burns in 'A Man's a Man for a' that' brilliantly forecasted the spirit of the French revolution, so the whole unrealised genius of the Scots Vernacular has brilliantly forecasted – potentially if not actually – tendencies which are only now emerging in European life and literature, and which must unquestionably have a very important bearing upon the future of human culture and civilisation.

Despite the chaos of conflicting opinion on every subject in the world to-day, there seems to be remarkable unanimity among intellectuals of the type who endeavour to form world-opinions in the view that Western civilisation is doomed. Mr H. G. Wells recently wrote: 'I now realise the stupendous instability of the Western world. The system is breaking up. It has neither recuperative nor reconstructive power.' The late Mr Frederic Harrison, in a letter written just before his death, said, 'Every board in civilisation is cracking. The British Empire is melting away, just like the Roman in the year 300, and from the same causes.' Following this same line of thought, Professor Graham Wallas, addressing University Women teachers at Bedford College, said: 'The material world – the world that slowly and painfully created itself upon the fragments of Roman civilisation – is falling in ruins. Right across from the Pacific to the Atlantic, right across the great Eurasian Continent, the old system has fallen in ruins, and the danger we have to face is greater and more intense than the danger with which the world was confronted at the fall of the ancient civilisation. Where there were a few cultivators in the clearings of the woods fifteen hundred years ago, or a few hundred shepherds out in the plains, now there are millions upon millions of industrialised and concentrated factory workers. The very existence of the present population depends upon organisation and to substitute accident and drift and confusion for organisation means to reduce the population to something like what it was at the fall of the Ancient World.' Similar views have been expressed in the books of Samuel Dill and Dr Warde Fowler on the parallels to our own time in the later periods of the Roman Empire and – with immensely greater consequence – by Herr Spengler, the German philosopher, who, in *The Downfall of the Western World* traced the causes of the decline of ancient civilisations and drew an analogy with the present. Spengler's central thesis has already – however ill understood – influenced the literature of every country in Europe: and has given rise to a literature already immense. Spengler is no pessimist: to translate the title of his book, *The Downfall of the Western World*, is to suggest a false idea of it. The idea he seeks to convey is rather 'fulfilment' – the end of one civilsation and the beginning of another – the emergence of a new order. Spengler considers the creative element in his writing to lie in the fact that he has proved by the test of concrete experience that universal history is not a universal succession of occurrences, but a group, so far numbering eight, of high civilisations whose life-histories, completely independent of one another, yet present themselves to us with a perfectly analogous development. It follows that he holds each of these civilisations to have an absolute standard, applicable to itself alone. Every vital idea – including Spengler's own, as he admits – belongs to its own age, its own civilisation, and in the course of history as a whole there are no false or true doctrines any more than there are false or true stages in the growth of a plant. For the man or nation with a true 'historic view' there are no past models to be imitated; there are only examples of the way in which this or that civilisation advanced to its appointed fulfilment. Everything depends upon the way in which men are fulfilling their destiny. He confesses that he discovered his philosophy under the influence of Agadir in 1911, at a time when Darwinian optimism lay like a blight over the European and American world, and ability to face the great tasks implicit in his own civilisation was paralysed in the average West European type of man. Is the position any better to-day? ... He sees tremendous tasks awaiting Western culture before its time of fulfilment arrives – in the realm of jurisprudence, for example, of industry, of the practical tasks of government and administration. Only in art and letters can it be said that there are few or no possibilities of achievement. Our literature is bankrupt. All forms of literary and artistic expression, equally with other phenomena of intellectual and spiritual activity, have reached in our Western civilisation the point beyond which they can go no further. Western Europe, with America, has exhausted her creative energies as Greece, Rome, Assyria, Babylon, exhausted their energies before her. She can add nothing more to the sum of vitally new human knowledge, of fresh and adequate channels of self-expression. We must wait for the inevitable end or rather the new beginning which will come from a civilisation other than ours. .... And he asserted that already is Dostoevsky to be found the first delineation of that new world.

Of the many antitheses out of which Herr Spengler builds up his thesis – which is destined to have an incalculable influence upon the future of human literature – that which predominates in every chapter is the distinction he draws between the 'Apollonian' or classical, and the 'Faustian' or modern type. The Apollonian type is dogmatic, unquestioning, instinctive, having no conception of infinity – in short, your average Englishman or German – and the Faustian mind, on the contrary, is dominated by the conception of infinity, of the

135

unattainable, and hence is ever questioning, never satisfied, rationalistic in religion and politics, romantic in art and literature – a perfect expression of the Scottish race.

It was anticipated that Spengler, in his second book – which has just been published – would reveal the East as the source of the civilisation destined to replace our own, that of the declining West, and in this connection it is well to remember in passing that we Scots are Oriental, the descendants of the lost tribes of Israel (sic) . . . and so he does but only very briefly. Comparing Tolstoy and Dostoevsky he says 'beginning and end meet here. Dostoevsky is a saint, Tolstoy is merely a revolutionary. . . . The Christianity of Tolstoy was a misunderstanding. He spoke of Christ and he meant Marx. The next thousand years belong to the Christianity of Dostoevsky'. And, immediately, Spengler proceeds to align himself with the very conclusions G. K. Chesterton so very differently arrived at in dealing with the difference of Scottish and English literature. Far from being a fatalist, he is an idealist, in the philosophical sense; far from being a cosmopolitan he is a self-assertive nationalist, and he gives the key to his whole political position when he declares in words that are almost a paraphrase of what G. K. Chesterton said of Scottish literature at the London Burns Club dinner: 'A nation is humanity in living form. The practical result of theories of world-betterment is, without exception, a formless and therefore unhistorical mass. All cosmopolitans and enthusiasts for world betterment represent fellaheen-ideals, whether they know it or not. Their success means the abdication of the nation within the historical sphere to the advantage, not of world-progress, but of other nations.' What is the cause of Doric desuetude – of the absence of Doric drama and prose – but lack of fulfilment in the Spenglerian sense? What is this distinction between Appollonian and Faustian types, but just another way of phrasing the contrast between the false Scot – the douce travesty, the methodical level headed self-conscious creature of popular tradition – and the true Scot, rapid in his transitions of thought, taking all things as granted, turning to fun and even to profanity with no misgivings, at his ease in both rooms of life.

The canny Scot tradition has been 'fulfilled' in the Spenglerian sense; and the future depends upon the freeing and development of that opposite tendency in our consciousness which runs counter to the conventional conceptions of what is Scottish. In other words, the slogan of a Scottish literary revival must be the Nietzschean 'Become what you are'.

III

Poet, on people's love set not too high a value,
The momentary noise of frenzied praise will pass
The verdict of a fool, and then the cold crowd's laughter
Thoul't hear: remain unmoved, unruffled and austere,
Thou art a king; live thou alone, the path of freedom
Tread thou; wherever thee thine own free spirit lead,
Perfecting aye the fruits of thy beloved fancy,
Not asking a reward for thine achievement high,
Reward is in thyself – thyself the last tribunal;
More strictly than all else canst thou gauge thine own
    work.
Art thou then satisfied with it, exacting artist?
Art thou then satisfied? then let the crowd find fault,
And on the altar spit whereon thy fire is burning
And in its childish play thy tripod shake.

                              Pushkin.

To explore the Russo-Scottish parallelism a little further leads to some interesting points. The condition of British literary journalism to-day is remarkably similar to that which obtained in Russia after 1855, where a crop of new periodicals appeared, full of vitality and colour. 'This colour,' we read, 'was given them less by their *belles lettres* than by their critical portion, which, indeed, was the outcome of the former but aimed at objects which had nothing to do with it – this is the strength and weakness of Russian criticism – its strength in that the ostensibly "literary" or even "aesthetic" criticism became a moral and socio-political power; it delighted in making use of these literary productions which were suited to the spreading of its ideas and deliberately neglected others often far more important in a literary sense; it relegated aesthetics to ladies' society, and turned its critical report into a sort of pulpit for moral and social preaching. This most 'war-like' criticism, one-sided and purposeful, achieved a colossal effect among the young men, to whom the essays of a Chernychévsky, Dobrolúbov, and a Písarev became revelations, the language of eloquent and fiery agitators, not critics. Therein also lay its weakness, prejudice, and perverseness. One must never let oneself be deceived by its judgments; it extolled or decried the author and his work, as Antonovich did Turgénev in the *Contemporary* because of his Bayárov, not because of the value or no-value of his performance, but for his opinions, his ideas – nay, for the journal in which he published his work. Thus this criticism is often, in spite of all its giftedness, its zeal and fire, only a mockery of all criticism. The work only serves as a peg on which to hang their own views. With a backward society and its mental nonage, its childish dread of dogmas and authorities, this criticism was a means which was sanctified by the end – the spreading of modern and free opinions, the establishment of new ideals. Unhappily, Russian literary criticism has remained till to-day almost solely journalistic, i.e., didactic and partisan. – True, there was also a literary and aesthetic criticism, but against the journalistic, the "real", it could not hold its own.'

In Britain to-day, however, this criticism is not 'soldierly' but 'policeman-like.' It is conservative not revolutionary. In Russia the method was necessary and useful: but in Britain it is not used for the spreading of modern and free opinions, the establishment of new ideals, but in the very opposite direction. Instead of the Russians named we have a 'Claudius Clear', an E. B. Osborn, an Edmund Gosse, and a thousand lesser 'literary' journalists. There are literary and aesthetic critics but against the journalistic and the 'real' they cannot here either hold their own – and, often, indeed the same passage is just as applicable to them, except in so far as the direction of their didacticism and partisanship goes. Scottish literary criticism either of the one kind or the other – as distinct from British (which really means English) – scarcely exists at all.

And – recognising the necessity and usefulness of the method, while quite aware of its weaknesses – what Scotland needs if a Scottish Literary Revival is to be encompassed is criticism like that which Druzhinin, Annenhov, Dobrolúbov, Písarev and Chernychévsky applied in Russia. 'Druzhinin was especially noted as the founder of the society for the support of necessitous literary men and scholars. He took up the cudgels above all against the onesidedness of criticism, against its want of consideration, or total ignorance, e.g. of English literature, against the adherence to pattern of its judgment, its dense repetition instead of a due investigation of current and too hasty judgments, and its love for a moral. He greeted the new men of talent, the new poets, and extolled the energy of literature and the soundness of its trend.' Annenhov dwelt in his criticisms on the necessary and natural connection (apart from any set purpose of the artist's) between works of art, and thought and life. – 'He is the founder of "organic" criticism in contrast to the purely aestheticising and to the "historical" and "realistic". To him a work of art is the organic product of popular life and the historic moment; hence emphasising of the national principle – the co-ordination of art and the national soil. . . . Above all, he demanded from art sincerity, as being its very life.' Chernychévsky 'after the rejection of all metaphysics, decided that the beautiful is life; hence Art has only to subserve the illustrating of life and can never replace or come up to reality . . . Dobrolúbov made the young generation enthusiastic, for it recognised in his "realism", his condemning of all "idealism", the only security for successful development.' Then came Písarev: 'He means his sledge-hammer blows not so much for poetry itself, as for the Conservatives, who made it their pretext, and their reactionary epicureanism.'

Reactionary epicureanism! Scarcely a remark on poetry or *belles lettres* ever appears in any Scottish periodical or book, or anywhere else on the subject of Scottish literature, which does not partake of this nature, allied, also, to Anglicisation, or its more insidious equivalent, 'romantic Nationalism.'

Would that it might be hoped that developing along the lines already indicated by reference to the theories of Spengler and others as inevitable if our latent national potentialities are yet to be realised, Scottish literature might secure a succession of literary critics such as those mentioned, culminating in an equivalent to that moral philosopher and theologian Solovyov (whose religious concepts as the present writer pointed out in a recent article in *The Glasgow Herald* are now being naturalised or re-expressed in Scotland in the writings of Professor J. Y. Simpson of the New College, Edinburgh) 'one of the most interesting phenomena of modern Russia and its mental fermentation – a fearless, fiery proclaimer of the truth, without thought for himself, unselfish, serving only the idea, lastly a contrast to all. His great merit is in times of absolute positivism, nay, indifference to all theory and to metaphysics, to have

139

drawn attention to the "eternal" questions.' Any Scottish Literary Revival worthy of the name must follow in his footsteps:

> In morning mist, with unsure steps, I went
> Towards mysterious and wondrous shores,
> The dawn still battled with the last few stars,
> Dreams still were flying, and, possessed by dreams,
> My soul was praying unto unknown gods.
>
> In the cold light of day my lonely path,
> As erst, I tread toward an unknown land.
> The mist has cleared and plainly sees the eye
> How hard the uphill road and still how far,
> How far away all that was in my dreams,
>
> And until midnight, with no timid steps,
> I shall go on towards the wished-for shores,
> To where upon the hill beneath new stars
> All flaming bright with fires of victory
> There stands awaiting me my promised fame.

The attitude which Scottish poets must adopt towards Scotland if the promises of the present juncture are to be realised to the full must be analogous to that expressed towards Russia by the great Scoto-Russian poet, Lermontov:—

> I love my country, but with a strange love,
> This love my reason cannot overcome:
> 'Tis not the glory bought at price of blood,
> Nor quiet, full of haughty confidence,
> Nor dark antiquity's untouched traditions,
> That move in me a happy reverie,
> But I do love, why I know not myself,
> The cold deep silence of my country's fields,
> Her sleeping forests waving in the wind,
> Her rivers flowing widely like the sea.
> I love to haste through byways on a cart,
> And with slow gaze piercing the shade of night
> And sighing for night's lodging, on each side
> To meet the twinkling light of wretched thorpes.
> I love the smoke above the parching harvest,

The nomad train of waggons on the steppe,
And on the hill amid the yellow crops
A single pair of birches shining white.
I see with joy that many cannot know
A well-filled rickyard with a wooden cabin
Straw-thatched with window shutters neatly carved;
And of a saint's day in the dewy eve
Till midnight I am ready to look on
At dancing, with the stamping and the yells
Accompanied by drunken peasants' talk.

As for the period of stagnation which is now passing in Scotland – this present which is giving place to the future daily – it may be described in another poem of the same great writer's:

To good and bad alike disgracefully indifferent,
We starting our career shall fade without a fight,
In face of perils we are shamefully discouraged
And, despicable slaves, bow to the face of might.

The hate and love we feel are both but accidental.
We sacrifice deny to hate and love in turn;
There reigns within our soul a kind of secret coldness
E'en though within our blood the iron burn.

A gloomy visaged crowd and soon to be forgotten
We shall go through the world without a voice or trace;
No fructifying thought, no work begun with genius
Shall we throw forward for the race.
Posterity, as judge and citizen, with harshness
Our ashes shall insult in some contemptuous verse,
As bitter jibes a son, deceived and disappointed,
Over a spendthrift father's hearse.

This Scottish Strain

MacDiarmid treated G. Gregory Smith's Scottish Literature: Character and Influence *(1919) as a text on which to preach the virtues of his Scottish Literary Renaissance. In this typically trenchant piece of prose, from* Albyn *(1927), he considers some of the implications of the Caledonian Antisyzygy – Smith's term for the Scottish 'zigzag of contradictions'.*

My main purpose here is not to discuss the lets and hindrances which have prevented the development of modern arts in Scotland, nor will my space permit me to analyse the complexities of Scottish character and circumstances responsible for our comparative failure to find expression on the higher levels of culture. But it is curious to find that in relation to the cultures of other countries, or in association with foreign elements in the constitution of the individuals concerned, Scotsmen, or half-Scotsmen have, with a surprising consistency, continued to manifest elements distinctively Scottish which clearly relate them to the Auld Makars, to the ballad makers, to our mediæval Scots musicians, and to that elusive but unmistakable thread of continuity which attaches the work of Norman Douglas, for example, to that of Sir Thomas Urquhart, the translator of Rabelais. Wergeland, the Norwegian poet, was conscious of the idiosyncratic power of the Scottish blood in his veins. So was a greater poet – the Russian Lermontov. So was Hermann Melville; so – to take a living example – is Walter de la Mare, whose *diablerie*, the finest element in his work, is probably attributable to his Scottish blood, as, in his case, were some of Browning's amusing tortuosities and prepossession with dialectical excesses. This Scottish strain is tremendously idiosyncratic, full of a wild humour which blends the actual and the apocalyptic in an incalculable fashion. In his able analysis of the complexities of the Scottish genius Professor Gregory Smith has called it 'the Caledonian antisyzygy' – a baffling zig-zag of contradictions – and he traces it down the centuries in a most interesting fashion, remarking that 'There is more in this Scottish antithesis of the real and fantastic than is to be explained by the familiar rules of rhetoric. .... This mingling, even of the most eccentric kind, is an indication to us that the Scot, in that mediæval fashion which takes all things as granted, is at his ease in both "rooms of life", and turns to fun, and even profanity, with no misgivings. For Scottish literature is more medieval in habit than criticism has suspected, and owes some part of its picturesque strength to this freedom in passing from one mood to another. It takes some people more time than they can spare to see the absolute propriety of a gargoyle's grinning at the elbow of a kneeling saint.' And Professor Gregory Smith goes on to express the opinion that this incalculable Scottish spirit will continue to survive in English arts and letters pretty much as a dancing mouse may manifest itself in a family of orthodox rodents – as something disparate, an ornament, or an excrescence, but irreconcilable to any major tradition and incapable of affording a basis for any higher synthesis of the Scottish genius.

That may be; on the other hand, its expansion may await a conjunction of conditions which have not yet arisen. It has affiliations to the baroque and the rococo, and evidences are not lacking of a widespread renewal of interest in these modes. But a more important fact is that this complicated wildness of imagination is, in Scots literature, associated with a peerless directness of utterance:

> Nae bombast swell,
> Nae snap conceits,

The language of the Greeks is simple and concrete, without *clichés* or rhetoric. English is, by contrast, loose and vague. But what Greek epigram has a more magical simplicity than Burns's

> Ye are na Mary Morison,

or where shall a parallel be found for the terrific concision, the vertiginous speed, of *Tam o' Shanter*? The future of the Scots spirit may depend upon the issue of the great struggle going on in all the arts between the dying spirit of the Renaissance and the rediscovered spirit of nationality. To-day there is a general reaction against the Renaissance. Observe the huge extent to which dialect is entering into the stuff of modern literature in every country. Dialect is the language of the common people; in literature it denotes an almost overweening attempt to express the here-and-now. That, in its principle, is anti-Renaissance. Basil de Selincourt* and many others observe that modern English shows signs of fatigue in comparison with Chaucer's. Chaucer was a poet with this power of plain speech. He never flinched from the life that was being lived at the moment before his eyes. A farmyard, with its straw, its dung, its cocks and hens is not, some people have thought, a poetic subject; Chaucer knew better. Dunbar with the aid of Scots achieved effects beyond Chaucer's compass with an utterance even more simple and straightforward. It has been said that Dunbar had for his highest quality a certain unique intensity of feeling, the power of expressing that passionate and peculiar force which distinguishes and differentiates us people of the North from our Southern neighbours. What is this unique intensity of feeling, this power of direct utterance, but the pre-Renaissance qualities of which I am writing? Braid Scots† is a great untapped repository of the pre-Renaissance or anti-Renaissance potentialities which English has progressively forgone.

> In days when mankind were but callans
> At grammar, logic, and sic talents,
> They took nae pains their speech to balance
>   Or rules to gie,
> But spak' their thoughts in plain braid lallans
>   Like you or me.

But it goes far deeper than language, this 'Caledonian antisyzygy', and music in the long run may utilize it more fully and finely than literature. It is here that I join issue again with my essential theme – to find what I have said concerning the persistence of this queer Scots strain extraordinarily exemplified in modern music in the work of Erik Satie. Satie's middle

* See his *Pomona: or the Future of English*.
† Braid (or broad) Scots, as a term to describe the Scottish dialect, was gradually dropped in favour of Lallans (Lowland Scots).

name was Leslie; his mother was a Scotswoman. Satie was a 'musical joker'. His most distinctive and important work was a species of fantastic experimental clowning, hardening later into satire. His work and his methods should have the special consideration of every Scottish artist – every musician in particular – who is puzzled as to how he may profitably exploit the peculiarities of Scottish psychology of which he is conscious. Paul Landormy calls him 'a freakish musician, more inventor than creator, the composer of "Pieces in the Form of a Pear", of the "Bureaucratic Sonata", and other fantastic products of a whimsical yet quite elegantly witty imagination', but – and this is the vital thing – he admits that 'he furnished certain elements of that new language which the composer of *Pelléas* used for loftier ends'. This is no little understatement of Satie's significance. Dr Eaglefield Hull says: 'This kind of musical irony is the most individual and personal of all types of art. The composer writes for a few detached individual people, who would scoff at the rest of humanity. Only very "superior" people can appreciate such irony, which passes from an elegant wit to a brutal sarcasm.' But he goes on to say: 'Historically Satie was of immense importance. The music on Satie's twelve pages [of his first work, *Sarabandes*, 1887] is even a greater landmark than either Debussy's or Chabrier's work. The "diaphony" of his sevenths and ninths was to become part and parcel of the harmonic decoration of Debussy and the Impressionists. . . . He was the father of atonality in music. Side by side with all his strangeness and boldness are passages of the most amazing commonplaces, which are difficult to explain except as satirical allusions.' Exactly! What is this but the 'Caledonian Antisyzygy' precisely as Professor Gregory Smith describes it, but manifesting itself in modern music to ultimately triumphant effect. There is no need, then, for Dr Hull to say, 'His father was French and his mother Scottish. We wonder to which source his outstanding characteristic of humour is due.' Surely it is along similar lines in Scotland itself that our difficult national characteristics may yet be turned to musical account and make the basis of a new technique, at once completely modern yet intimately related to the whole history of Scots psychology and conjoining in the closest fashion the artists we are about to become, if the Scottish Renaissance realizes its objectives, with the Auld Makars and the ballad-makers whose achievements we have yet to parallel and continue.

As with literature and music so with drama and dancing this tale might be continued. The explanations of Scotland's leeway lie in the Reformation, the Union with England and the Industrial Revolution. If I isolate the second of these as the main cause, it is because it was indispensable to the consummation and continuance of the first and largely determined the effect upon Scotland of the third. There are people who imagine that but for the Union with England Scotland would still be destitute of all the blessings of modern civilization. They find no difficulty in associating this belief with the idea that Scotsmen are thrifty, hardworking, exceptionally well-educated, law-abiding and home-loving. I am not one of them. I believe that the Industrial Revolution would have spread to Scotland much less injuriously if England had suddenly disappeared about 1700. I believe that the concept of the 'canny Scot' is the myth (as M. Delaisi puts it) which has made Scotland governable by England and has prevented the development since the Union of any realistic nationalism worth speaking about. True, it has been so insidiously and incessantly imposed that the great majority of Scots have long been unable for all practical purposes to do other than believe it themselves. Yet there are notable exceptions; the traditions of Highland soldiering, for example – the 'ladies from Hell'. Even the 'canniest' Scot does not repudiate these as un-Scottish. At all events the effect of all these three causes was overwhelmingly repressive and anti-Scottish. The Reformation, which strangled Scottish arts and letters, subverted the whole national psychology and made the dominant characteristics of the nation those which had previously been churl elements. The comparative cultural sterility of the latter is undeniable. A premium was put upon Philistinism. There has been no religious poetry – no expression of 'divine philosophy' – in Scotland since the Reformation. As a consequence Scotland to-day is singularly destitute of aesthetic consciousness. The line of hope lies partially in re-Catholicization, partially in the exhaustion of Protestantism. The Union with England confirmed and secured the effects of the Reformation. It intensified the anglicization that the introduction of an English Bible and the *Shorter Catechism* (with which England itself so promptly dispensed) had initiated. It progressively severed the Scottish people from their past. The extent to which this has gone is almost incredible – especially if taken in conjunction with the general attribution of an uncommon love-of-country to the Scots. English has practically vanquished Scots (which is not a dialect but a sister language to English, with different but not inferior, and, in some ways, complementary, potentialities) and Gaelic. There is very little Scottish Education in Scotland to-day. The type of international Education which is everywhere gaining ground to-day is that which seeks to perfect, and even to intensify, different cultures already existent among different peoples, and sets for its ideal that each people has, first, the right to its own interpretation of life; and, second, the duty of understanding, and sympathizing with, the different interpretations given by its neighbours as fully as possible. Back of this type of international education lies the belief that differentiation in matters of culture is more valuable to life than a stereotyped homogeneity. This, so far as Scotland is concerned, is the aim and object of the Scottish Renaissance movement; and it is high time that the Scottish Educational System was attempting to change-over to this type of education rather than adhering partly to the imperialistic and partly to the eclectic types, both of which, as Professor Zimmern says, 'belong rather to the past than to the present', except, alas, in Scotland, which once prided itself on leading the world in matters of education. A recent Committee of Enquiry, set up by the Glasgow branch of the Educational Institute of Scotland, reports that no schoolbook dealing with Scottish history is of a satisfactory character. This, although a remarkable advance in professional admission, is a sheer understatement. Scottish history is only now in the process of being rediscovered and, once the labours of the new school of Scottish historical researchers come to be synthetized, it will be found that even such comparatively 'Scottish' Scottish Histories as Hume Brown's have to be thrown overboard, as little more than a mass of English propaganda. It is only within recent years that any attempt has been made to teach even such 'Scottish history' in Scottish schools, and then subsidiarily to English, and, as it were, as a make-weight or after-thought – to the older children. Scots literature is in even worse case, although here, too, there has been a slight improvement during the past decade. The increasing – if still insignificant – Scoticization of Scottish Education during recent years is, of course, not a product of the propaganda of the Scottish Renaissance Group. To what is it attributable? How can it be accounted for if the policy of England and, even more determinedly, of Anglo-Scotland, let alone the over-riding tendency of modern industrialism, is towards the complete assimilation of Scotland to England? In my opinion it is a product partly of the latent criticism of the industrial order and partly of a realization of the cultural exhaustion of English (*vide 'Pomona'*) – an instinctive protective re-assembling of the forces suppressed by the existing order of things which has made for the predominancy of English. This explanation accords with the doctrine Spengler expounds in his *Downfall of the Western World*. 'The Caledonian Antisyzygy', instead of being a disparate thing destined to play a baroque, ornamental, or disfiguring rôle – *chacun à son goût* – in English literature may be awaiting the exhaustion of the whole civilization of which the latter is a typical product in order to achieve its effective synthesis in a succeeding and very different civilization. In the history of civilization therefore, the sudden suppression of Scots, with all its unique expressive qualities may prove to have been a providential postponement; it may have been driven underground to emerge more triumphantly later. Its coming musicians and writers must address themselves to it, as Mussorgsky, following Dargomisky's dictum that 'the sound must express the word', addressed himself to Russian – with Mallarmé's 'adoration for the property of words'; just as they must recollect that the 'pure poetry' of some of the contemporary Continental expressionists was anticipated and carried far further long ago in their *Canntaireachd*, or mnemonic notation of the MacCrimmons – a basis upon which they may profitably build.

Growing Up in Langholm

This essay, collected in Karl Miller's symposium Memoirs of a
Modern Scotland *(1970), adapts an article on 'My Native Place' –
contributed to the* Scots Observer *of 2 October 1930 – by adding to it
observations from* Lucky Poet *(1943) and* Francis George Scott
*(1955). The essay was assembled in this form by Duncan Glen as a
broadcast for the poet's seventy-fifth birthday.*

After journeying over most of Scotland, England and central,
southern and eastern Europe, as well as America, Siberia and
China, I am of the opinion that 'my native place' – the
Muckle Toon of Langholm, in Dumfriesshire – is the bonniest
place I know: by virtue not of the little burgh in itself (though
that has its treasurable aspects, and on nights when, as boys,
we used to thread its dim streets playing 'Jock, Shine the
Light', and race over the one bridge, past the factory, and
over the other, with the lamp reflections wriggling like eels at
intervals in the racing water, had an indubitable magic of its
own), but by virtue of the wonderful variety and quality of the
secenery in which it is set. The delights of sledging on the
Lamb Hill or Murtholm Brae; of gathering hines in the
Langfall; of going through the fields of Baggara hedged in
honeysuckle and wild roses, through knee-deep meadow-
sweet to the Scrog Nut Wood and gathering the nuts or
crab-apples there; of blaeberrying on Warblaw or the Castle
Hill; of dookin' and guddlin' or making islands in the Esk or
Ewes or Wauchope and lighting stick fires on them and
cooking potatoes in tin cans – these are only a few of the joys I
knew, in addition to the general ones of hill-climbing and
penetrating the five glens which (each with its distinct
character) converge upon or encircle the town – Eskdale,

149

Wauchopedale, Tarrasdale, Ewesdale and, below the town Carlislewards, the Dean Banks.

As we grew up, too, we learned to savour the particular qualities and rites of Langholm in comparison with other Border burghs: the joys of Langholm Common Riding compared with those at Selkirk or Hawick, for example; the peculiar shibboleths of local pronunciation; the historical associations of our corner of the 'Ballad-land' rife with its tales of raidings and reivings and with the remnants of peels; the wealth of local 'characters' who were still about.

As I grew into my early teens I ranged further afield, and soon all the Borders were within my ken. Many places had their special beauties or points of interest and advantage; but none had the variety of beauty centred round Langholm itself – none seemed so complete a microcosm of the entire Borderland. I knew where to find not only the common delights of hill and forest and waterside (and chiefest of all these to me were the chestnut trees at the sawmill – even now it thrills me to remember the beautiful chestnuts, large and luxurious as horses' eyes, which so surprisingly displayed themselves when we cracked open the prickly green shells, and I remember many huge strops of them I strung and many a fierce competition at Conquerors), but also the various kinds of orchises, and butterwort, sundew, and the like; the various nests – including Terrona crags where ravens nested; how to deal with adders and smoke out wasps' 'bikes', and much other lore of that sort. In short, a boyhood full of country sights and sounds – healthy and happy and able to satisfy its hunger with juicy slices of a big yellow neep stolen from an adjoining field.

I never made any conscious decision that I should be a writer. That was a foregone conclusion from my very early life. I don't know if it originated with myself. When I was nine or ten my teachers seemed to realise that writing was going to be my destiny and I may have absorbed the idea from them. Certainly from a very early age I had begun to try to write for the local paper at Langholm, where my father was the local postman. We lived in the Post Office buildings. The library, the nucleus of which had been left by Thomas Telford, the famous engineer, was upstairs. I had access to it, and used to fill a big washingbasket with books and bring it downstairs as often as I wanted to. There were upwards of 12,000 books in the library, and a fair number of new books, chiefly novels, was constantly bought. Before I left home (when I was 14) I could go up into that library in the dark and find any book I wanted. I read almost every one of them.

My grandfather, John Grieve, was a power-loom tuner in a Langholm tweed mill. I only remember seeing him once – shortly before he died, when I was about four years old. An alert 'jokey' little man, I remember he wore a transparent, butter-coloured waistcoat or linen jacket; and on the occasion I recall I caught him in the act of taking some medicine of a vivid red colour, and somehow or other got it into my childish head that he was drinking blood, and thought of him with horror – not unmixed with envy – for years afterwards. I resemble him physically (in point of leanness and agility, though I am considerably taller) and facially (a big brow and all the features squeezed into the lower half of my face); but when I was a lad the older folk used to tell me I took after him in another respect: 'just like your grandfaither', they used to say, 'aye amang the lassies'. As boys my brother and I wore the Graham tartan. Our mother was Elizabeth Graham. If my father's people were mill-workers in the little Border burghs, my mother's people were agricultural workers. My alignment from as early as I can remember was almost wholly on the side of the industrial workers and not the rural people. I have never had anything but hatred and opposition for deproletarianising and back-to-the-land schemes; my faith has always been in the industrial workers and the growth of the third factor between man and nature – the machine. But even as a boy, from the steadings and cottages of my mother's folk and their neighbours in Wauchope and Eskdalemuir and Middlebie and Dalbeattie and Tundergarth, I drew the assurance that I felt and understood the spirit of Scotland and the Scottish folk in no common measure, and that that made it possible that I would in due course become a great national poet of Scotland. My mother's people lie in the queer old churchyard of Crowdieknowe in the parish of Middlebie.

There was certainly nothing 'lowering', in Lawrence's sense of the word, in Border life when I was a boy. Langholm was full of genial ruffians like the employer to whom, communist though I am, I look back with the utmost relish, who, after carefully instructing a workman whom he was sending up

Westerkirk way as to what he was to do, ended: 'and just call in when you come back and I'll gie you the sack!' Border life was raw, vigorous, rich, bawdy, and the true test of my own work is the measure in which it has recaptured something of that unquenchable humour, biting satire, profound wisdom cloaked in bantering gaiety, and the wealth of mad humour, with not a trace of whimsy, in the general leaping, light-hearted, reckless assault upon the conventions of dull respectability.

My first introduction to my native land was when my mother wrapped me well in a Shetland shawl and took me to the door to see – but, alas, my infant eyesight could not carry so far, nor if it could have seen would my infant brain have understood – the most unusual sight of the Esk frozen over so hard that carts and horses could go upon it for 20 miles as upon a road and the whole adult population were out skating upon it all day, and by the light of great bonfires at night. That, I think, has not happened since – nor anything approaching it.

These were indeed the champagne days – these long enchanted days on the Esk, the Wauchope and the Ewes – and the thought of them today remains as intoxicating as they must have been in actual fact all those years ago. I have been 'mad about Scotland' ever since.

There were scores upon scores of animals and birds I knew far better than I now know the domestic cat, which is the only specimen of the 'lower animals' of which I see much. My eyes may, perhaps, still seek out and recognise and appreciate a dozen or so wild flowers in the course of a year, but my memory recalls – with a freshness and a fullness of detail with which such living specimens cannot vie at all – hundreds I have not seen for over 30 years. My poetry is full of these memories: of a clump of mimulus 'shining like a dog's eyes with all the world a bone'; of the quick changes in the Esk that in a little stretch would far outrun all the divers thoughts of man since time began; of the way in which, as boys, with bits of looking-glass, we used to make the sun jump round about us. Above all, when I think of my boyhood, my chief impression is of the amazing wealth of colour. A love of colour has been one of the most salient characteristics of Scots poetry down to the best work of our contemporary poets, and I have celebrated it again and again in my own work.

Many great baskets of blaeberries I gathered on the hills

round Langholm. Then there were the little hard black cranberries, and – less easy to gather since they grow in swampy places – the speckled craneberries, but above all, in the Langfall and other woods in the extensive policies of the Duke of Buccleuch, there were great stretches of wild raspberry, the fruit of which the public were allowed to pick, and many a splendid 'boiling of jam' I gathered there – gathering more than the raw material of jam, too.

I would come cycling back into Langholm down the Wauchope road with a pillowslipful of crab-apples (as at other times a basket of plovers' egggs) on my carrier; and again there was the Scrog Nut Wood, shaking its bunches of nuts like clenched fists in the windy sunlight. I have nowhere seen loveliness so intense and so diverse crowded into so small a place. Langholm presents the manifold and multiform grandeur and delight of Scotland in miniature – as if quickened and thrown into high relief by the proximity of England.

There is a place at Langholm called the Curly Snake where a winding path coils up through a copse till it reaches the level whence, after passing through a field or two, it runs into the splendid woods of the Langfall. It has always haunted my imagination and has probably constituted itself as the ground-plan of my mind, just as the place called the Nook of the Night Paths in Gribo-Shov, the great forest north of Hillerod, haunted Kierkegaard's.

My boyhood was an incredibly happy one. Langholm was indeed – and presumably still is – a wonderful place to be a boy in. Scotland is not generally regarded as a land flowing with milk and honey. Nevertheless, it can do so more frequently than is commonly understood. It certainly did so in my boyhood – with a bountifulness so inexhaustible that it has supplied all my subsequent poetry with a tremendous wealth of sensuous satisfaction, a teeming gratitude of reminiscence. I still have an immense reservoir to draw upon. My earliest impressions are of an almost tropical luxuriance of nature – of great forests, of honey-scented heather hills, and moorlands infinitely rich in little-appreciated beauties of flowering, of animal and insect life, of subtle relationships of water and light, and of a multitude of rivers, each with its distinct music.

A Plan for the Unemployed

This is the last of eleven essays comprising At the Sign of the Thistle *(1934)*.

The whole problem of unemployement is radically altered by the realization that an ever-increasing proportion of the population will become surplus to industrial and commercial requirements. Science is tending to eliminate all kinds of human drudgery that have hitherto employed masses of workers, and this is a tendency capable of immediate and infinite acceleration as soon as the lets and hindrances to the introduction of new labour-saving and production-increasing devices imposed by the existing economic system (which is based on the necessity of people 'earning their livings') are removed, as they soon must be. The Leisure State is within sight and from this point of view, as Lloyd George says, it is high time to cease thinking of unemployment in the traditional way and begin regarding it as a great opportunity. This is admittedly difficult in a transition period when practically everybody is feeling the economic pinch. It is particularly difficult for the unemployed themselves to realize that they are the vanguard in a great process which will progressively relieve mankind from the necessity of drudgery, as long as they themselves must exist on allowances which debar them from enjoying their leisure. That again, however, is only an unfortunate, and it is to be hoped very temporary, aspect of the transitional period. I am not concerned here with the ways and means whereby the economic system is to be altered, though I have my own very definite views on the matter, and certainly think that these should be the prime concern of all well-disposed persons and particulary of the victims of the present

154

phase themselves. There is, happily, evidence that the latter are concentrating increasingly on the subject. The use they are making of the time on their hands is reflected in the augmented issues of the Free Libraries – and particularly of the issues of books on economic subjects. The main thing perhaps is that they – and other people – should clearly realize that unemployment is a permanent and progressive phenomenon and that there is no possibility, let alone desirability, of the reabsorption of the workless into the productive system. A thorough understanding of this will clear away all manner of absurd arguments and anticipations. That is a necessary preliminary to an adequate view of the phenomenon and the advancement of any useful proposals for dealing with this new state of affairs. Towards public speakers, and others, who are still thinking, talking and writing in terms of a state of affairs which has passed and can never return there ought to be an organized intolerance on the part of all who have a clear view of what is happening, for their obsolescent dogmas only serve to complicate the issue and make comparison worse confounded.

Nor do I intend to deal here with the other type of person who is gravely alarmed at the prospect of people having so much spare time at their disposal and declares that they will not know what to do with it and will inevitably waste it in ways less desirable than the old drudgery and become hopelessly demoralized. I do not believe anything of the sort. The average morale of the lower-paid workers was never very high even when they were fully employed, and I see no signs of any great deterioration due to unemployment. The unemployed, it seems to me, are pretty much the same sort of people as the employed and not a bit worse than the latter in regard to crime or vice of any kind. Any demoralization that is going on is not due so much to the actual fact of unemployment as to its concomitants of insufficient purchasing-power and equivocal social status in the present state of affairs. As soon as they realize that their unemployment is permanent and will in time be shared by the vast majority of the workers, and that they are no longer going to be financially penalized on this account, but on the contrary are to have ample purchasing-power allocated to them, most of the alleged demoralization will disappear. In any case, no one should want to prevent scientific progress or impose needless labour on moral grounds; that is to enforce personal prejudices in an altogether unwarrantable fashion. The proper thing is to trust humanity with all the new opportunities available to it. These may be misused by some people; there may be an interval of chaos and readjustment; but the faculties of humanity will sooner or later achieve an effective equilibrium under the new conditions.

My concern is with the unemployed themselves during the transition phase. I believe that the majority of them are just as diligent and capable and public-spirited as any other section of the population. Footling self-help schemes are a mere evasion of the realities of the situation and not only affect the standards of organized labour on the one hand and enter into competition with established tradesmen on the other, but, taken by and large, represent an effort to re-enter the existing economic system by the back-door and regain and maintain a precarious footing there. Such a manoeuvre is not good for the morale of those concerned either. They are not meeting the implications of their position fairly and squarely and doing man-sized jobs. Expedients such as these will only delay the inevitable reckoning and prolong the agony that comes from a failure to confront the whole situation and deal with it in a rational and adequate manner. What, then, are my proposals?

I think the worst feature of unemployment is the feeling amongst the unemployed that they are regarded by others as failures and a burden on the community. They are nothing of the sort. They are the heralds of a new economic order, and like most pioneers have to suffer for it. But they ought not to conceive their position in terms of a superseded and unreturning condition of affairs. Literally they should realize it as a great opportunity and make the most of it. Freedom from unnecessary toil and ample leisure should be recognized and utilized as great social assets. The unemployed should neither be sensitive about getting – or not getting – 'something for nothing', or about giving it! The idea of others that they ought not to get a decent living unless they work for it, and their own notion that it is unthinkable that they should do anything free, gratis, and for nothing, spring from the same basic misunderstanding, and should cancel each other out. In this transitional phase there are abundant ways and means by which the unemployed can seize their new social opportunity, vindicate themselves against the charges of indolence and demoralization, rehabilitate themselves in the eyes of their fellow-men (and in their own eyes!), and signalize their changed status. The way is not by means of a little amateur tailoring or cobbling on their own behalf, not by petty schemes of mutual assistance, not by a reversion in certain directions to the processes of primitive barter. But the way is by a thorough mobilization of their abilities of all kinds and the application of these in a systematic and disciplined fashion to general public needs. I am referring to purely voluntary work on schemes of real value for the common weal. All manner of important improvements and desirable schemes are at present hung up indefinitely on the plea of economy or because money is not available to carry them out. Resources and amenities of all kinds are going to rack and ruin for the same reason. Let the unemployed, without abating one iota of their claims to proper maintenance, rise above their personal troubles and organize to effect these improvements or discharge these neglected services free, gratis, and for nothing. They have ample ability. It will be a magnificent gesture which cannot fail to impress and win over sections of people who presently regard them with distrust and misunderstanding. It will be the best possible earnest that they themselves, the unemployed, realize their great opportunity and are ready to make the most of it. The schemes they actually carry out in this way will be to their own advantage as well as other people's. The all-impotant thing is to destroy the habit of measuring everything in terms of money value. If they gain nothing financially, at least they will lose nothing – and they will gain a great deal in self-respect and general goodwill. And they will hasten the general process of discerning an immense social asset in the liberation of humanity from all preventible drudgery, and with that hasten the substitution for the present economic system, founded on the gospel of the need to work, of a new and more generous system, based on a realization of the rôle of Science in ushering in the era of leisure and freedom. The speedy, if not the ultimate solution of their present problems of poverty and hardship depends very largely upon the way in which they recognize and use their present chances.

Let them go to those territorial magnates who are bewailing their inability owing to high taxes to look after their lands properly and startle them by offering to do for nothing at all what properly considered is a service to communal property –

the great public asset of our forests and rural areas. Let them embarrass public authorities by offering to do gratuitously all the desirable things these bodies allege they are unable to do owing to the cost. They will speedily reduce to absurdity the upholders of the present financial system. They will exemplify a new spirit in keeping with the coming order, and prove themselves conscious heralds of the greatest advance in the history of humanity.

An Eccentric Scotswoman

In 1936 MacDiarmid published a book of his favourite Scottish Eccentrics *and enthusiastically admitted 'Elspeth Buchan, Friend Mother in the Lord' to the predominantly male company.*

The one Scottish woman with whom I propose to deal in this volume may well be given pride of place, for Scottish women who can be classed as 'eccentrics' are very few and far between, and in most of these the eccentricities displayed are of a very minor and moderate character, scarcely entitling them to more than a little local reputation as 'queer customers'; while their careers as a whole had little or no general interest. Scottish women of any historical importance or interest are curiously rare, and although these may have played dramatic parts in great affairs and manifested no little courage and contriving power, their psychologies present next to nothing that is out of the ordinary. A long list of famous Englishwomen is easy to compile; it is impossible to draw up any corresponding list of Scotswomen. Only half a dozen or so of names come readily to mind, but even these compare poorly with the English 'opposite numbers' whether in beauty, in social sway, or in mental or spiritual interest. For the most part our leading Scotswomen have been shrewd, forceful characters, with keen eyes to the main chance, but almost entirely destitute of exceptional endowments of any sort. Yet the women of Scotland have perhaps played a greater part, influenced the activities of the men to a greater extent, than the women of any other European nation. Can the absence in modern Scotland of all the rarer and higher qualities of the human spirit be attributed to this undue influence of the female sex? It may have something to do with it. It is, at all events, worth recalling that Galton in his study of genius maintains that it seldom comes where the mother's influence is strongest. Scotswomen are overwhelmingly not the sort to be 'fashed with the nonsense' of any attention to the arts, or other precarious and comparatively unremunerative activities on the part of their offspring, as against due concentration on the business of getting on and doing well in a solid material sense.

Especially since the Reformation has this been the case, and the connection between industrial civilisation and Protestantism need not be stressed here. The Church has always been disproportionately – and in recent times to an ever greater extent – dependent upon women, and the subject of this essay deserves pride of place not only because she is the only representative of her sex in my contents-table but because she is a strange exception in the whole history of Scottish religiosity.

It is a curious fact that Scotland, despite the long obsession of its people with religious matters, has produced few religious characters of any great interest to those who are not particularly concerned with the truth (or considered tenability) or otherwise of their tenets, but only with the interest in and for themselves of the personalities in question. The intellectual and psychological processes involved seem incredibly poor and dull in relation to the course of affairs in which these people played such powerful parts. The fact that Scotland has produced practically no religious poetry or other religious literature of quality is probably a consequence of this defect. It is at least noteworthy that Scottish poets who have touched upon religious matters have only done so successfully when they have been in a flippant or sarcastic mood at variance with orthodoxy.

Literary issues apart, the national theological obsession seems to have had a general dehumanising effect, and it is certainly like looking for a needle in a haystack to look for interesting personalities in the interminable host of those bigoted people, any one of whom might well have been interchanged with any other one so far as personal attributes are concerned. Without a special interest in theological – rather than spiritual – matters the life-patterns of the vast majority of Scottish divines are of a singularly commonplace and uninteresting character, and the percentage of these which show significant, let alone sensational, characteristics and complications of temperament and raise curious psychological issues is as small as the occasional divergencies in question are themselves trivial. This great 'cloud of witnessess', characterised by an appalling sameness, has little or no attraction for the connoisseur of human foibles. Whatever light and leading informed them seems to have been contained in the dark lanterns of natures almost as uniformly dingy as the covers of the Book with which they were so abnormally preoccupied. Many Scottish divines played very active and even astonishing parts in affairs, but the interest that attaches is to the affairs themselves – not to the individual personalities of the ministers in question. These historical dramas may be immensely important; the ecclesiastical actors filled their public rôles passionately and portentously enough – but, off the religio-political stage, are seen to have been as a rule very mediocre and insignificant men. To such an extent is this true – so negligible was their contribution to the Spirit of Man – that the hordes of dour and often fanatical Scots take on an extremely depressing aspect as they move through the pages of history, as if engaged in processes to which all that is colourful and vital and valuable in human nature had somehow, inexplicably, become irrelevant. It is with relief that we turn from the spectacle of that devastating steam-roller to the singular problem of Elspeth Buchan.

Elspeth was the daughter of John Simpson, who kept an inn at Fitney-Can, the half-way house between Banff and Portsoy. She was born in 1738 and educated in the Scottish Episcopal Communion. Having been sent when a girl to Glasgow, as a servant-girl, she married Robert Buchan, an employee in her master's pottery, with whom she lived for several years and had several children. 'Having changed her original profession of faith for that of her husband, who was a burgher-seceder, her mind', we are told, 'seems to have become perplexed with religious fancies, as is too often the case with those who alter their creed. She fell into a habit of interpreting the Scriptures literally, and began to promulgate certain strange doctrines, which she derived in this manner from Holy Writ. Having now moved to Irvine, she drew over to her own way of thinking Mr Hugh Whyte, a Relief clergyman, who consequently abdicated his charge and became her chief apostle. The sect was joined by persons of a rank of life in which no such susceptibility was to be expected. Mr Hunter, a lawyer, and several trading people in good circumstances, were among her converts. After having indulged their absurd fancies for several years at Irvine, the mass of the people at length rose in April 1784, and assembled in a threatening and tumultuous manner around Mr Whyte's house, which had become the tabernacle of the new religion, and of which they broke all the windows. The Buchanites felt this insult so keenly that they left the town to the number of forty-six persons, and proceeding through Mauchline, Cumnock, Sanquhar, and Thornhill, did not halt till they arrived at a farmhouse, two miles south of the latter place, and thirteen from Dumfries, where they hired the outhouses for their habitation, in the hope of being permitted, in that lonely scene, to exercise their religion without further molestation. Mrs Buchan continued to be the great mistress of the ceremonies, and Mr Whyte to be the chief officiating priest. They possessed considerable property, which all enjoyed alike, and though several men were accompanied by their wives, all the responsibilities of the married state were given up. Some of them wrought gratuitously at their trades, for the benefit of those who employed them; but they professed only to consent to this in order that they might have opportunities of bringing over others to their own views. They scrupulously abjured all worldly considerations whatsoever, wishing only to lead a quiet and holy life, till the commencement of the Millennium, or the Day of Judgment, which they believed to be at hand.'

The writer of the above account is, however, neither friendly disposed towards his subject nor too scrupulous, or perhaps sufficiently well informed, in matters of detail. What he says of the abandonment of marital relations, for example, carries unwarrantable implications. A fairer account occurs in a letter from the Rev. James Woodrow, minister of Stevenston, to Sir Adam Fergusson of Kilkerran, dated 19th October 1784. Sir Adam had been Member of Parliament for Ayrshire for ten years past; and had just surrendered that seat at the request of his party leaders in order to represent an Edinburgh constituency instead. Apparently he had written to Mr Woodrow asking for some account of the Buchanites, who, although Mrs Buchan had begun her 'ministry' five years previously, had only recently become notorious owing to their flight from Irvine. Mr Woodrow copies out of a Glasgow newspaper a report of their movements, the authorship of which report he ascribes to Mr Millar, the minister of Cumnock. His letter then goes on to give the following picturesque and not unsympathetic account of Mrs Buchan and her followers: 'Mrs Buchan was said to have come originally from Montrose or its neighbourhood, to have lived awhile in Glasgow, her character not good. There, and at Kilmarnock, she made some converts, but very few. She had been at Irvine occasionally for a year or two before, and had resided there constantly during the last winter and spring. She was a pretty old and ill-looking woman (her age at this time was only forty-six), but had something fascinating in her conversation and manners, particularly the appearance of much gentleness and kindness, joined with a cheerful piety and confidence in Heaven. The converts were all made by herself, the influence of her enthusiasm being confined to those who were within the reach of her conversation, and chiefly, though not entirely, to the Relief congregation. It did not spread in the smallest degree in the neighbouring parishes. Mr Whyte (the Relief minister who joined Mrs Buchan's followers) was a cheerful, lively young man of no learning or talents of any kind, except an easy flow of language. He was married and had a young family. Mrs Buchan lived in his house, and after she had in a few weeks infused her own spirit into him and perhaps a fourth part of his congregation, the rest were offended at him, deserted his ministry, and lodged a complaint against him with the Presbytery of Relief. They met at Irvine and without the formality of a trial gave Mr Whyte five or six queries relative to his obnoxious tenets, which he answered in writing immediately and unequivocally, and signed his answer at their desire. They then condemned him on his confession and suspended him from preaching *sine die*. Upon this he gave up the bond he had for his stipend and continued to preach to his little flock in his own house and garden. The people who became Mrs Buchan's disciples had been mostly serious and well-meaning people formerly; some of them of good sense and education. They conceived themselves as quite new creatures, and, indeed, they were strangely changed both in their principles and habits. They rejected and abhorred the doctrines of Election, Reprobation, and other high points for which they had been formerly zealous, and some of them disputed against these things with considerable acuteness, not from the Scriptures, but from other topics. Their turn of mind was cheerful, not gloomy. They entered easily into conversation on their favourite religious points and even attempted to turn every ordinary subject of discourse into that channel as if they had been wholly possessed by their enthusiasm; and in common with all other enthusiasts they had a great difference about the world and neglected business and the care of their families and children. There were more women among them than men, and they parted at last from their relations, their friends, and some of them from their lovers, without the least appearance of reluctance or regret. Besides the kind of inspiration which Mr Millar mentions, some of them, such as Mrs Buchan and Mr Whyte, laid claim to visions and revelations, and lay for many hours in a dark room covered with a sheet in confident expectation of them. One of these visions Mrs Buchan imprudently published, fixing the destruction of the town of Irvine to a particular short day. This exasperated the mob, who considered her a witch, and drove her and Mr Whyte from the town. The rest immediately followed their leaders. Patrick Hunter, a lawyer, was brought back by a warrant on account of some papers belonging to other people in his hands. He continued several days in Irvine, sold his house, a pretty good one, and the rest who had any property in furniture or clothes or shop goods took the opportunity of returning and selling off everything by roup. The money arising from this sale was not put into a common purse and given to Mrs Buchan as was expected, but retained by the individuals. It was still, however, a kind of common stock, for such is their mutual disinterested attachment that everyone was ready to part with whatever he had to any other of the fraternity who needed it. They had in truth a community of goods among them and were suspected by some and accused of having a community of a more criminal kind, yet I never heard anything amounting to a proof or presumption of such licentiousness. They lived together like brothers and sisters. They asked and took provision from other people on the road like those who were entitled to it, telling them that God would repay them, and never offering any payment themselves till it was insisted on.' Mr Woodrow's letter concludes: 'They are, indeed, an object of curiosity to an attentive and inquisitive mind. Several sets of enthusiasts resembling them made their appearance in Holland and Germany about the beginning of the Reformation, and some in America during this century, but the phenomenon is new and singular in Scotland'.

Most of the accounts of the Buchanites were derived from hearsay and without first-hand knowledge, and were mostly prejudiced against them. It is good to find Mr Woodrow discrediting the allegation that they practised 'free love' and insisting that at least there was no evidence to support that charge, which, nevertheless, along with other scandals, was widely retailed against them and all too readily believed in most quarters. Even Burns, in a letter from Mossgiel to his cousin, James Burness, showed a lamentable lack of Mr Woodrow's charitable scepticism in this connection, writing: 'I am personally acquainted with most of them, and I can assure you the above-mentioned are facts.' Burns's short account is, in fact, simply a credulous and unworthy rehash of the malicious countryside gossip. To be seen in its true light it only requires to be set against the account contributed to the *Scots Magazine* in November 1784, by a correspondent who signed himself 'Glasguensis Mercator'. This writer spent two days in their company during the month of August and studied them closely in 'their daily walk and conversation'. He denies all the popular and sensational reports of their conduct and beliefs and ends as follows: 'I found the Buchanites a very temperate, civil, discreet and sensible people, very free in declaring their principles, when they were attended to; but most of their visitants behaved in a rude, wicked, and abandoned way, which improper behaviour they met and bore with surprising patience and propriety.'

Most of the reports do little or nothing to account for Mrs Buchan's strange hold over her followers – followers for the most part of intelligence and substance; and a hold that not only led them cheerfully to abandon all and follow her but did not loosen despite the falsifying of her successive predictions. It was the rowdy and vicious intolerance of the populace that dictated the flight from Irvine and harassed and finally broke up the community in Dumfriesshire – behaviour for which the conduct of the Buchanites, whether in sexual or other matters, seems to have afforded no justification whatever. The absence of the practices popularly imputed to them, however, only makes the problem of their motivation all the stranger and throws the greater stress on the peculiar powers of Mrs Buchan's little-studied personality.

Unfortunately there is altogether insufficient material for an adequate study. It is questionable whether the testimony of a recent writer, Mr A. S. Morton, author of *The Covenanters of Galloway* and other books, is more to be relied on than that of his predecessors when he writes that Elspeth, 'on the death of her mother, was brought up by a distant relative, who taught her to read and write, to sew and cook. This lady married a West India planter, and Elspeth agreed to accompany her to Jamaica, but while waiting for a boat at Greenock she became enamoured of the gay life of the town and deserted her mistress. She entered domestic service, and afterwards married one of her master's workers, a potter named Robert Buchan. He found her wild and wayward, and hoping that she would settle down better in her native district he started a pottery in Banff, but this failed, and he went to Glasgow, leaving his wife and family to shift for themselves. She opened a dame's school, in which she expounded the Scriptures and the Shorter Catechism. Soon she became a religious fanatic, and even fasted for weeks. She neglected her school and her own children, till the neighbours were roused against her, and she found it necessary to return to her husband in Glasgow. Here she continued to neglect her house and family, ran everywhere to religious meetings, and took every opportunity to expound her views, which were far from orthodox.' Mr Morton is wrong, however, when he goes on to say that the Rev. Hugh Whyte, having fallen completely under her sway and adopted her views, failed to appear when he was charged before the Presbytery at Glasgow with heresy, and was ejected from his charge. On the contrary, he appeared and answered the questions put to him in writing, defending the positions he had now taken up, and was temporarily inhibited from his pastoral duties. His final desertion of his ministry was his own action and due to the hostility of the Irvine populace to his continuance in their midst.

Following the heresy trial, as Mr Morton says, 'a Society was formed, and Mrs Buchan received the title, "Friend Mother in the Lord", but to outsiders she was "Luckie Buchan, the witch-wife who had cast her spell over the minister". Violent opposition was raised, and the meeting had to be held after dark. Mrs Buchan proclaimed herself to be the woman described in Revelation xii, 1: "There appeared a wonder in heaven; a woman clothed with the sun, and the moon under her feet, and upon her head a crown of twelve stars". Whyte was the wonder "man-child" of whom she was now spiritually delivered, who was to rule all nations with a rod of iron.'

Mr Morton gives the best account of the subsequent developments. 'The opposition', as he says, 'became more intense, and the Society removed to the house of Patrick Hunter, the Burgh Fiscal, who had been an Elder in the Relief Church, but had joined the new Society. One night the mob smashed the doors and windows of his house, seized Mother Buchan, and started to drive her home to her husband. At Stewarton, eight miles on the way to Glasgow, she managed to escape, and made her way back to Irvine, to the house of James Gibson, one of her supporters. The mob attacked this house, and the magistrates, hastily convened, sent for Hunter and told him that the woman must be removed. She was taken to her husband's house in Glasgow. She and Whyte were invited to Muthill, the birthplace of the most ardent disciple, Andrew Innes. Here Whyte proclaimed his "Friend Mother in the Lord" to be the new Incarnation of the Holy Ghost, and declared that Divine Vengeance would fall on all who did not accept her as such. The Lord, he said, was about to come and translate her and all her followers bodily to Heaven without tasting death, and all unbelievers would perish in the flames. This was too much for the simple folk of Muthill, and they refused to receive him into their houses, so he returned with Mother Buchan and the others to Irvine.

'The opposition was roused again, and the disturbances were renewed. The magistrates decided to banish Mother Buchan, and allowed her two hours to clear out. Burns tells us that her followers "voluntarily quitted the place likewise, and with such precipitation that some of them never shut the door behind them; one left a washing on the green, another a cow bellowing at the crib without food or anyone to mind her". A cart was procured, in which rode Mother Buchan, Whyte, Gibson, and a few others not accustomed to tramping. Other carts were soon added to the procession, and afterwards a white pony, on which rode Mother Buchan, decked in a scarlet robe. The company numbered between forty and fifty, consisting for the most part of "clever chiels and bonnie, spanking, rosy-cheeked lassies, many of them in their teens". They found quarters in the barn at New Cample Farm, tenanted by Thomas Davidson, about a mile south of Thornhill. Here they had all things in common. Marriage was abolished and the children became the property of the Society. They occasionally wrought for neighbouring farmers, but never accepted remuneration. As harvest was approaching, the farmer needed his barn, but offered them ground on which to build a house for themselves. They gladly accepted, and had a place ready before harvest. This the neighbours christened "Buchan Ha'", a name which still survives.

'At first crowds flocked to hear and see them especially Mother Buchan, whom Whyte in his sermons declared to be "the mysterious woman predicted in Revelation, in whom the Light of God was restored to the world, where it had not been since the ascension of Christ, but where it would now continue till the period of translation into the clouds to meet the Lord at his second coming".

'Gradually curiosity gave place to hostility, and, on Christmas Eve 1784, about a hundred men attacked the house, smashed the windows and doors, and searched for Whyte and Mother Buchan, but did not find them. Mr Stewart, factor for Closeburn Estate, had heard of the plot and had persuaded these two to go to Closeburn Hall. Some of the rioters were tried at Dumfries and fined. About this time Whyte published "*The Divine Dictionary*, or a Treatise indicted [*sic*] by Holy Inspiration; containing the Faith and Practice of the people called (by the world) the Buchanites, who are actually waiting for the second coming of our Lord in the air, and so shall they even be with the Lord. *There appeared a great wonder in Heaven – a woman. Rev. chap. xii. v. 1.* Written by that Society." It extended to 124 pages octavo, and is a crude exposition of their beliefs under such heads as – "The propagation of the human race – a demonstration that the soul and person is the same – the person of Christ possessed of a divine nature only – God's method of calling men to true salvation – concerning the end of the world – a divine receipt instructing how all may live for ever – the meeting Christ in the clouds." It is signed "Hugh Whyte – revised and approved by Elspeth Simpson". It showed them to be visionary and rhapsodical, and it is often quite beyond comprehension. Nobody took the slightest notice of it and it fell dead from the press. Mother Buchan was now doing everything to rouse the enthusiasm of her followers. One night when they were all employed as usual, a voice was heard as if from the clouds. The children shouted, clapped their hands, and started singing one of the hymns written by Whyte, beginning

O hasten translation, and come resurrection.
O hasten the coming of Christ in the air.

'Andrew Innes tells us that all the members downstairs instantly started to their feet, shouting and singing, while those in the garret hurried down to the kitchen, "where Friend Mother sat with great composure, while her face shone so white with the glory of God as to dazzle the sight of those who beheld it, and her raiment was as white as snow". The noise attracted the neighbours, and Davidson pressed into the house beseeching Mother Buchan "to save him and the multitude by which the house was surrounded from the pending destruction of the world". She told them, however, to be of good cheer, for no one would suffer that night, for she now saw her people were not sufficiently prepared for the mighty change she intended them to undergo. As the light passed from her countenance she called for a tobacco pipe and took a smoke.'

Another writer says the little republic existed for some time, without anything occurring to mar its happiness, except the occasional rudeness of unbelieving neighbours. But at length, as hope sickened, worldly feelings appear to have returned upon some of the members; and notwithstanding all the efforts which Mrs Buchan could make to keep her flock together a few returned to Irvine. It would seem that as the faith of her followers declined she greatly increased the extravagance of her pretensions and the rigour of her discipline. It was said that 'when any person was suspected of an intention to leave the Society, she ordered him to be locked up and ducked every day in cold water, so that it required some little address in any one to get out of her clutches'. There is no direct or convincing evidence, however, that she was either able or inclined to take any such disciplinary measures or that her adherents were at any time otherwise than perfectly free agents.

Additional particulars, not to be found elsewhere, are set forth in a statement made in 1786 by some of the seceding members on their return to the West, but here again the evidence is to some extent suspect. According to this statement, 'the distribution of provisions she kept in her own hand, and took special care that they should not pamper their bodies with too much food, and everyone behoved to be entirely directed by her. The society being once scarce of money, she told them she had a revelation, informing her they should have a supply of cash from Heaven; accordingly, she took one of the members out with her, and caused him to hold two corners of a sheet, while she held the other two. Having continued for a considerable time, without any shower of money falling upon it, the man at last tired and left Mrs Buchan to hold the sheet herself. Mrs Buchan, in a short time after, came in with £5 sterling, and upbraided the man for his unbelief, which, she said, was the only cause that prevented it coming sooner. Many of the members, however, easily accounted for this pretended miracle, and shrewdly suspected that the money came from her own hoard. That she had a considerable purse was not to be doubted, for she fell on many ways to rob the members of everything they had of value. Among other things, she informed them one evening that they were all to ascend to Heaven next morning; therefore, it was only necessary they should lay aside all their vanities and ornaments, ordering them, at the same time, to throw their rings, watches, etc., into the ash-hole, which many were foolish enough to do, while others more prudently hid every thing of the kind that belonged to them. Next morning she took out all the people to take their flight. After they had waited till they were tired, not one of them found themselves any lighter than they were the day before, but remained with as firm a footing on earth as ever. She again blamed their unbelief – said that want of faith alone prevented their ascension; and complained of the hardship she was under, in being obliged, on account of their unbelief, to continue with them in this world. She at last fell upon an expedient to make them light enough to ascend; nothing less was found requisite than to fast for forty days and forty nights. The experiment was immediately put into practice, and several found themselves at death's door in a very short time. She was then obliged to allow them some spirits and water; but many resolved no longer to submit to such regimen and went off altogether. We know not', thus concludes the statement, 'if the forty days be ended; but a few expedients of this kind will leave her, in the end, sole proprietor of the Society's funds.'

There are , however, no good grounds, so far as research can discover, for attributing any such fraudulent intentions to her, or for alleging that she took advantage of their credulity to enrich herself at their expense. That she did not need to undergo the penances the others had to suffer followed from the assumption of her divine character, and any privileges she had arose equally naturally from her special position amongst them. Nor could her opponents have it both ways; if they believed in the power of faith and in revelation, they were not in a position to deny the revelations she professed to receive nor to disprove that the only thing that prevented the miracles she anticipated taking place was the imperfect faith of her disciples. It is unfortunate that none of them kept a diary. The religious idiom they used, a mixture of Biblical English and Scots vernacular, is little heard to-day and it is therefore difficult to recreate the atmosphere in which they lived, nor are there any materials for a knowledge of the psychologies of even the leading members. Particularly interesting would have been an account book showing the initial capital, the incomings and outgoings, and final financial condition of the Society, but there is, alas, nothing of the sort.

If, however, 'many of the members easily accounted', as we are told, for Mother Buchan's manoeuvres, it is strange that the Society did not fall violently apart; but we hear little or nothing of internal differences and the 'many of the members' in question seem to have been content to continue to be hood-winked. The whole matter of the great fast and of the expected ascension are better described by Mr Morton in an account which significantly differs in many particulars from the fore-going statement:

'She declared that their failure to ascend to Heaven', says Mr Morton, 'was because they had not been sufficently purified from the corruptions of the flesh, and she ordered a forty days' fast – but not for her or Whyte. The authorities were induced to take action, as it was feared that some of the zealots would be starved to death, and there were vague rumours of infanticide. Constables made a thorough search, but discovered nothing incriminating. As the close of the fast drew near the excitement increased, and preparations were made for the triumphant translation to Heaven. Whyte dressed regularly in full clerical costume – gown, bands, and white gloves – and frequently surveyed the heavens for some sign of the coming event. The fateful night at length arrived, and the expectant company assembled on rising ground near the house, where they sang and prayed till midnight. They then proceeded to Templand Hill, the appointed scene of translation, half a mile away. Here they erected a frail wooden staging, which they mounted, with Mother Buchan on a higher platform in the middle. They had all cut their hair short (except Mother Buchan), leaving only a tuft on the top, by which they could be caught up from above, and on their feet they had light bauchels which they could easily kick off when the moment came to ascend. The air was filled with their singing and invocations as they stood stretching their hands towards the rising sun. Suddenly a gust of wind swept along; the flimsy platform collapsed, and instead of ascending to Heaven they crashed down to earth.'

The 'vague rumours of infanticide' were like the charges of 'free love' and other scandals; but it is interesting to point out that, levelled against Roman Catholic convents, they have had a long currency in Scotland, every now and again rising to a fury of denunciation, popular agitation, and demands for thorough inspection of such premises – a vendetta of libel not dissimilar to that connected in other countries with the so-called Ritual Murder alleged to be practised by the Jews. With the general recession of interest in theological matters, scandals of this kind have nowadays found a new and fertile field in politics and the vast majority of intelligent people everywhere are the easy prey of atrocity mongers and find no more difficulty in swallowing the story of the German Corpse Factory or in crediting the Bolshevists with free love and unspeakable sadism than their ancestors had in discovering witches and crediting them with infernal cantrips or in attributing orgies of sexual licence and the practice of infanticide at one time to the Buchanites or at another to the Roman Catholic nuns. The interest attaching to the Buchanites is not that we have here any exceptional manifestation of human credulity and religious fanaticism; these are common enough at all times and the beliefs of the vast majority of people are of substantially the same character as those of the Buchanites. The latter only held opinions which showed a slight deviation from the no less absurd views generally entertained by their contemporaries, but they showed a disposition to insist on these literally and to practise what they preached, an inclination which certainly did not characterise the latter, although the failure of the Buchanites to square their doctrines with the practical requirements of existence was much less serious than it might have been. On the whole, the most that can be said of the attitude of their opponents is that the latter resembled Dr Thomas Somerville, the historian, who, in his *Candid Thoughts on American Independence*, 'maintained those opinions against the claims of the colonists, which were much opposed to the principles on which the Church of Scotland struggled into existence, however much they might accord with those of its pastors after it was firmly established', and displayed 'an affection for the state of things existing at the time of writing, and such a respect for the persons who, by operating great changes, have brought about that existing state, as the writer would have been the last person to feel, when the change was about to be made'. The orthodox mob were far more fanatical – and with no better foundations for their beliefs – than the little flock of the Buchanites, and again to the former may be well applied the phrases used to characterise Somerville's personality: 'an alarmist on principle, he involved in one sweeping condemnation all who entertained views different from his own; and the wild impracticable theorist, and the temperate and philosophical advocate for reform, were with him equally objects of reprobation'.

The fiasco of the Templand Hill ascension reminds me of the Icarian fate of that most interesting personality, James Tytler, a 'poor devil, with a sky-light hat and hardly a shoe to his feet', who nevertheless, in the midst of the most multifarious literary labours, wrote several great songs, including 'I canna come ilka day to woo'. On the commencement of the balloon mania, after the experiments of Montgolfier, Tytler thought he would also try his hand at an aeronautic voyage. Accordingly, having constructed a huge dingy bag, and filled it with the best hydrogen he could procure, he collected the inhabitants of Edinburgh to the spot and prepared to make his ascent. The experiment took place in a garden within the Sanctuary, and the wonder is, we are told, 'that he did not fear being carried beyond it, as in that event he would have been liable to the gripe of his creditors'. There was no real danger, however; the balloon only moved so high and so far as to carry him over the garden wall, and deposit him softly on an adjoining dunghill. The crowd departed, laughing at the disappointed aeronaut, who ever after went by the name, *appropriate on more accounts than one*, of 'Balloon Tytler'.

After the Templand Hill affair there were considerable defections from the Society and, since there had been very few accessions after public hostility first manifested itself, only a remnant of the faithful was left. The Kirk Session of Closeburn summoned Whyte to give security that none of the Society would become a burden on the parish. Whyte could give no such security, and as a consequence the fraternity were all ordered to leave Dumfriesshire on or before 10th March 1787. With the assistance of Davidson, the New Cample farmer, however, they took the farm of Auchengibbert, between Dumfries and Castle-Douglas, and after a temporary residence at Tarbreoch, near Kirkpatrick-Durham, removed there at Whitsunday. They put up fences and erected offices themselves, and all found outlet for their labour, but they no longer worked for nothing. A wheelwright made spinning-wheels, which several of the women used. A tinsmith made articles in his line, and these were bartered for wool to be spun and woven into cloth for both male and female wear. It was dyed light green – the distinctive colour of the dress of the Buchanites, who, in this respect, anticipated the Black Shirts, Brown Shirts, and other similar phenomena of to-day.

It would appear that dissensions were now developing between Mother Buchan and Mr Whyte. 'They no longer attempted to make proselytes,' says Mr Morton, 'but still clung to their own beliefs. Whyte, however, did his utmost to tone down the peculiarities of the Society, and on this he and Mother Buchan disagreed. When she attempted to assert her authority, he threatened to leave and break up the Society.

'Mother Buchan became really ill, but she would not lie down, and no one realised that the end was approaching – it was a cardinal point in their creed that she would never die. When she felt death near, she told them that though she might appear to die, she was only going to Paradise to arrange for their coming and if their faith remained firm she would return at the end of six months and they would all fly to heaven together. If they had not faith she would not return till the end of ten years, and if they were then still unprepared she would not return till the end of fifty years; when her appearance would be the sign of the end of the world and the final judgment of the wicked. Thus she kept up the delusion to the last, for immediately after this extraordinary pronouncement she died on 29th March 1791. Whyte wanted to have her buried, but the others wished to have her secreted about the house. Their dissensions showed that they would require to wait the ten years. The body was accordingly packed in dry feathers and deposited under the kitchen hearth. Sir Alexander Gordon, as Sheriff, had to inquire into the matter, but they hoodwinked him by a temporary burial in Kirkgunzeon Churchyard, and then brought the body back to the house. Ultimately Whyte became so overbearing that Andrew Innes and two others took a neighbouring farm, but informed Whyte they were willing to continue working at Auchengibbert if they got peace to do so, but would keep Larghill too. Whyte would not listen to this, and decided to go to America. The stock at Auchengibbert was accordingly sold and the proceeds divided among the members.

'On 11th June 1792, the seceders started for America. Two carts carried their goods, and thirty people walked beside them to Portpatrick, and eight weeks later they landed at Newcastle on the River Delaware. The remainder removed to Larghill, close to Crocketford, taking the body of Mother Buchan with them. They carried on successfully, and everyone had an allotted task. The women were noted for their spinning, and were the first to introduce into Galloway the two-handed spinning-wheel, in the use of which they were unrivalled. Time passed till the tenth anniversary of Mother Buchan's death arrived, but though they watched and prayed all day their expectations were doomed to disappointment, for nothing happened. As the lease of the farm was not to be renewed, they purchased about five acres of land at Crocketford and built houses, expending about £1,000. For themselves they built Newhouse, which still stands, and the twelve remaining members removed to it, taking with them the body of Mother Buchan. Death gradually reduced their number, and a plot of ground behind the house became their burial ground. One by one they passed away, till only Andrew Innes and his wife remained. As the fiftieth anniversary of Mother Buchan's death approached, Andrew made great preparations for her return;

175

but, alas, the fateful day came and went like any other, and Andrew was never the same again. His wife died in the end of November 1845, and so Andrew was left, the last of the Buchanites. A few weeks afterwards, finding his end drawing near, he sent for his friends and confessed to them for the first time that he had his revered Mother Buchan's body still in his possession, and desired them to bury it in the same grave as himself, but to place his coffin above hers, so that she could not rise without wakening him. Thus they were buried in the little enclosure behind the house.'

I cannot agree that this is in any way an astounding story of religious imposture and childish credulity. The credulity and the element of imposture, or, as I prefer to believe, delusion, seem to me to be essentially the same as are to be found in any and every religion at all times. What I regard as interesting is the fact that the fraternity hung together so long. There was still a compact community of twelve eighteen years after the precipitate flight from Irvine, and Andrew Innes was faithful for an unbroken period of nearly seventy years. I have been unable to find out anything about the career of Whyte and his twenty-nine companions after their emigration to America. It is interesting to remark that after the establishment of the fraternity in Dumfriesshire Mrs Buchan's husband was still living in pursuit of his ordinary trade, and a faithful adherent of the burgher-seceders. One of her children, a boy of twelve or fourteen, lived with the father; two girls of more advanced age were among her own followers. Although the statement must be taken with reserve it is recorded that just before she died Mother Buchan told her disciples that she had one secret to communicate – that she was in reality the Virgin Mary, and mother of our Lord; that she was the same woman mentioned in the Revelations as being clothed with the sun, and who was driven into the wilderness; and that she had been wandering in the world ever since our Saviour's days and only for some time past had sojourned in Scotland. In regard to the Buchanites, however, and particularly their professions and rule of life and the personalities of the leaders, there is, as in so very many other directions in Scottish history, a sorry inadequacy of documentation, and it is impossible at this time of day to effectively check the statements made about them and in any way recapture the precise quality of their communal life. Andrew Innes's final precaution in the matter of the superimposition of his coffin over that of Mother Buchan's is of a type of burial safeguard and anticipation of the contingencies of the Resurrection Morn which informs many Scottish anecdotes from all parts of the country, and the whole conception of the flight to Heaven does not deviate essentially from the ideas of the Last Day, long and perhaps still generally held in our midst.

Certainly in these times of figures like Krishnamurti, and Pastor Russell with his slogan that 'millions now living will never die', and countless freak religionists of greater or less notoriety, the present day is in little condition to point the finger of scorn at Mrs Buchan and her followers. The preservation for over half a century of the unburied body is, of course, an unusual, and gruesome, feature, but the retention of unabated expectation despite disappointment after disappointment is no uncommon thing, and I might cite as a sort of parallel the story told of Sir James Stewart, of Coltness, the father of political economy in Britain – a science that perhaps more than most engenders, or, at least, calls for this quality of undaunted faith!

Among Sir James's intimate friends was Mr Alexander Trotter. Mr Trotter was cut off in early life; and, during his last illness, made a promise to Sir James that, if possible, he would come to him after his death, in an enclosure near the house of Coltness which, in summer, had been frequently their place of study. It was agreed in order to prevent mistake or misapprehension that the hour of meeting should be noon; that Mr Trotter should appear in the dress he usually wore, and that every other circumstance should be exactly conformable to what had commonly happened when they met together. Sir James laid great stress on this engagement. Both before and after his exile (which lasted from 1745 to 1763) he never failed, when it was in his power, to attend at the place of appointment, even when the debility arising from gout rendered him hardly able to walk. Every day at noon, while residing at Coltness, he went to challenge the promise of Mr Trotter, and always returned extremely disappointed that his expectation of his friend's appearance had not been justified. When rallied on the subject, he always observed seriously that we do not know enough of 'the other world' to entitle him to assume that such an event as the reappearance of Mr Trotter was impossible. A very proper conclusion. A similar one may well cover the history of

177

the Buchanites and it is by no means certain that, although their expectations were disappointed in the exact sense in which they were entertained, their faith was not abundantly justified in actual fact.

Islands

From 1933 to 1941 (when he was conscripted for National Service at the age of forty-eight) MacDiarmid lived on the Shetland island of Whalsay. It was a difficult but immensely productive period during which Mac-Diarmid explored, in such poems as 'On a Raised Beach', the expressive resources of the English language. He celebrated his love of islands in The Islands of Scotland *(1939) from which the following observations are excerpted.*

Scotland with her islands (though she is by no means the most be-islanded country in Europe – a distinction which, I think, is Finland's) is like the old woman who lived in a shoe with her children. She doesn't know what to do with them! It would be pleasant to picture her, as some poet of fancy rather than imagination (in the sense Coleridge attached to these two terms) might do, as resembling an eider-duck sailing on the water with her chicks about her. But, alas, the image has only to be conceived to be discarded. The eider-duck marshals her ducklings (or a beautiful sense of discipline in themselves procures the result) with such precision; they are 'dressed' beside her like a file of soldiers on parade. And at any given time they are all about the same age and size. It is not so with Scotland's far more numerous brood. They are of all shapes and sizes. No symmetry of effect is obtainable. She seems to have no control over them. Several groups appear to have escaped from the concerted movement of which she is the centre altogether. And while some remain in groups others are isolated stragglers. It is a chaotic spectacle seen from above. And it is impossible to get them all into focus at once even then.

Scotland has some eight hundred islands. There are over five hundred in the Hebrides. There are nearly sixty in the Orkneys, of which twenty-five, I think, are still inhabited; and over a hundred in the Shetlands. I am not counting the innumerable skerries which are only little snaggles of rock jutting out of the water. Few men can have visited as many of them as I have done – I have landed on most of the skerries even, and, indeed, along with a friend working on H.M. Geological Survey, I landed three or four years ago on several of these in the Shetlands which are not yet marked on the Admiralty Charts. 'Who knows the Scottish islands who only the Scottish islands knows?' But I am intimately acquainted with the Aegean Islands, the Channel Islands, and the little-visited Faroes. And here I must interpolate that not only in their history – at its most interesting stage, and at the stage when it was most autonomous, most independent of, and different from, that of the Scottish mainland – the Hebrides, the Orkneys and Shetlands, and the Faroes formed a sequence linked together by comings-and-goings and mutual interests of so many kinds that even now none of them can be thoroughly understood without adequate knowledge of the other links in that chain of islands, the different main groups of which today seem to have so little in common, to be so discrete; but that, in their pre-history even, there was a similar linkage, known to archaeologists as 'the coast-wise movement from the south-west of the Castle complex' (in the Iron Age), which embraced Cornwall, the Hebrides, and the Orkneys and the Shetlands – in other words, the very line along which my own cultural and other interests have developed. And I believe their future is similarly linked and their problems only susceptible finally of a common solution.

An exact and comprehensive study of the role islands have played in Scottish history would be extremely interesting, for certainly in respect of historical and cultural associations of all kinds and as the scenes of important events the relatively small aggregate area of the Scottish islands – sea-islands and islands of the inland lochs alike – are rich out of all proportion to the rest of the area of Scotland. So much so that whole sections of our history are virtually independent of the history of the Scottish mainland, and often not only almost unrelated to it, but at odds with it to a greater or lesser extent. Scotland in its history and literature resembles very much a many-roomed house, in the different apartments of which, at one and the same time, entirely different activities are going forward, while the people in any one of these rooms have little or nothing in common with those in the other rooms, so that a time at which, on a given summons, all of them would assemble together is unthinkable. Such a general assembly has never, in fact, taken place in the history of Scotland to date, nor does it ever seem likely to do so, for, despite the fact that the difficulty due to the use of different languages has practically ceased to exist, the psychological difficulty, and the difficulties due to difference in tradition, task, and tendency have scarcely lessened and no real coming-together is possible, such apparent comings-together as do take place being for purposes peripheral to the real differences between the various sections, and too often only amounting to the use of a mere Esperanto of mutual intercourse. In other words, Scotland is broken up into islands other than, and to a far greater extent than merely, geographically; and it is perhaps not unreasonable to wish that the process had been physically complete as well, or, at least, to speculate upon the very different course not only Scottish, and English, but world history would have taken if the whole of the mainland of Scotland had been severed from England and broken up into the component islands of a numerous archipelago – as I, for one, heartily wish it had been or still might be – as of course it may! But what I am mainly concerned with just now is that general sense of the nature of Scotland which does not make anything like due allowance for the number, let alone the individual and group differences, of its islands, and fails to realise the high alternative value of a thorough realisation of all of them. 'Though Scotland is a small country', a recent writer says, 'yet there are many Scotlands; South Uist differs more from the Merse, let alone from Motherwell, than Rochdale from Dorset, or even Lille from Béarn.'

It is only now, with the use of the aeroplane, that the Scottish islands (I am thinking particularly of the Hebrides) can be seen effectively, at one and the same time in their individual completeness and in all their connections with each other and with the mainland. Even more important, however, are some of the new aspects in which the earth presents itself to the air-borne.

Mountains lose and gain. They are no longer obstacles demanding a long effort to surmount by transient spectacles. On the other hand, they have ceased to be inert. And to the Highlands and West Coast of Scotland and the Hebrides to a greater degree than almost anywhere else this coming alive of the mountains is a most illuminating novelty. For, as the Rev. Wm. Lewis has said (in an appendix to Mackenzie's *History of the Outer Hebrides*), 'the rock formation of the Outer Hebrides stands out as a solid wall of Archaean age. . . . Standing on these Archaean rocks we really stand on the basement of the geological staircase of the globe.' Or, as Sir Archibald Geikie said, 'The Outer Hebrides, from the Butt of Lewis to Barra Head, no doubt represent a very ancient range of hills which rose along the western border of Europe before the British Isles were separated from the Continent. . . . But the group of islands known as the Inner Hebrides, of which the chief are Skye, Mull, Rum, Eigg, and Canna, belong to a totally different order. They are in large measure composed of terraced, flat-topped, basalt hills, with rich green slopes and long level lines of brown crag. The regularity of their forms stands in strong contrast to the ruggedness of the true Highland mountains.' It is a wonderful experience to fly over this incomparable scenery and witness the vivifying of its geological elements – in particular in those parts of it where, as the Earl of Cottenham has said of a like experience flying in America: 'Looking down, the terrific upthrust of the earth's surface when still malleable, is plainly recognisable although from the ground any idea of it is remote.'

Returning, however, to a less modern or specialised sense in which the nature and inter-relationships of their landscape is unfamiliar to most of the people of Scotland – how many people in Scotland itself, let alone elsewhere, could answer off-hand (to take just one example) how many islands there are in Loch Lomond? There are thirty all told on the Loch. And consider the extent to which these figure in history. To name only a few of them, there are Inchtavannach, or Island of the Monks' House, for there was once a monastery here; Inchconnachan; Inchcruin; Inchfad; Inchailliach, or the Isle of the Old Women, on which there stood a nunnery, founded by Kentigerna, Mother of St. Fillan, one of the most notable of early Scottish missionaries; and Inchmurrin, on the south end of which are the ruins of Lennox Castle. The powerful Earls of Lennox ruled here for centuries, and Earl Malcolm was one of the strongest and ablest supporters of Bruce in the struggle for the independence of Scotland. From the house of Lennox too came Lord Darnley, husband of Mary Queen of Scots, and father of James VI. On this island are also the ruins of the Lady's Bower, to which Isabella, Countess of Albany, retired to end her days after the excecution of her father, her husband, and her two sons by James I on the Heading Hill at Stirling.

But my concern with our islands is nevertheless less with the past than with the future. There is a very generally entertained idea that to live on an island is to be 'out of things' – an assumption that great significance for humanity is more likely to attach itself to big centres of population – to London rather than Eriskay, say. I see no reason for assuming anything of the sort; it is a variant of the assumption that the battle must necessarily be to the strong or the race to the swift. It is a variant, too, of the assumption that brains are brighter in cities and that dwellers in remote country districts are relatively clodhoppers, whereas the fact is that, as Professor Raymond Cattell, in *The Fight for Our National Intelligence*, and other writers have shown, all the available data on the distribution of intellectual ability goes to show that the level of this is highest in out-of-the-way villages untouched by urban influences. 'It is a remarkable fact', writes Th. A. Fischer, author of *The Scots in Germany*, 'that in the history of the development of the human mind the great spiritual movements did not always proceed from the most famous and the most powerful nations or cities, the so-called centres of intelligence, but, similar to the mighty rivers of the world, had their sources in localities small, hidden and unknown. Eisleben (birthplace of Luther) and Haddington were joined to Nazareth, Marbach (birthplace of Schiller) to Stratford, Ecclefechan to Königsberg (birthplace of Kant).' No matter how many millions may be congregated into great cities like London and New York, there is nothing inherently impossible or even improbable in Dr Johnson's remark that 'perhaps, in the revolutions of the world, Iona may be some time again the instructress of the Western regions,' a statement echoing St Columba's own prediction in the verse which, being translated, reads: 'Iona of my heart, Iona of my love! Where now is the chanting of monks, there will be lowing of cattle. But before the world is ended, Iona will be as it was.' The last great revelation came on the island of Patmos; the next – if there is to be one – may just as probably (and indeed, for obvious reasons, far more probably) come on some little island as in London or Leningrad or Berlin or Rome. My general attitude to islands depends upon my realisation that 'the stone the builders rejected' may very well prove the cornerstone, and that it is very dangerous indeed to assume that 'these little ones' (in this case, islands as against mainlands) can be neglected with impunity, or that they are less entitled to a 'life of their own,' or that that life must necessarily be less important than that of bigger land-masses. It is said or felt in many quarters – and perhaps generally – that life on a little island is somehow 'escapist,' a cowardly shirking of the great issues of life, as if somehow these were the peculiar property of the maelstroms of big-city life. This again is the tendency to be on 'the side of the big battalions.' The true view is presented by W. H. Auden in his poem beginning 'Look, stranger, at this island now,' and ending with this magnificent verse:

> Far off like floating seeds the ships
> Diverge on urgent voluntary errands;
> And the full view
> Indeed may enter
> And move in memory as now these clouds do,
> That pass the harbour mirror
> And all the summer through the water saunter.

It is an excellent thing indeed that, thanks to the air services, a man can be in London or Liverpool or Manchester or Glasgow and a few hours later listening to pibroch-playing at a ceilidh in South Uist or landing at Sumburgh in the Shetlands – an excellent thing, and greatly to be encouraged, for the same reason that Mr Aldous Huxley in *Ends and Means* supports the idea (and adduces evidence in regard to its practical business advantages) of changing employees round, often to the most diverse jobs, instead of keeping them always at the same task – the reason, too, that led John Davidson to declare: 'If one has a healthy mind it is wholesome to go from extreme to extreme just as a hardy Russian plunges out of a boiling bath into the snow.' I am concerned mainly with spiritual matters, but they have of course an important practical coefficient, which so shrewd and unmystical an organ as *The Glasgow Herald* recognises well enough when it says, in a leader [of 17 December 1936] on 'Highland and Islands', that the concern over the serious depopulation of these areas, and the decay of their economic life, 'does not spring from sentiment alone – although that is strong – but from the view, based on good economic and social grounds, that the Highlands could contribute materially to Scotland's prosperity, and that the area offers a way of living that is a valuable alternative to, and corrective of, the rush and noise of urban life.' I, too, am concerned enough with, and anxious to facilitate, that alternative way of life, but that is not why the islands appeal most to me – why of all poets I should be the last to cry

> I hate this island steep, this seam of beach,
> This ample desolation of grey rock,

instead of saying with Count Keyserling: 'Once again I probe into the dead stone as a geologist, in order to solve the significance of the living.'

'An island a day ...,' I once began saying to a friend. 'But why?' he protested. 'Apart from details, if you've seen one island you've seen them all. They are essentially as like each other as peas.' On the contrary, I claimed, in order to know any island it is necessary to know many islands, and quoted to my friend these lines of one of my poems in which I say of certain people that

> ... They do not even know why Lothian and Border folk
> Differ as greatly as Volnay and Pommard do,
> And in fact know little of Scotland altogether,
> Oblivious to all those intranational differences which
> Each like a flower's scent by its peculiarity sharpens
> Appreciation of others as well as bringing
> Appreciation of itself, as experiences of gardenia or zinnia
> Refine our experiences of rose or sweet pea.

'Not to know the island', I went on, 'is like having a blunt sensation in the tips of your fingers.' Horrid! But to know a whole lot of islands is like having a portfolio of pictures and an adjustable frame, which enables you to hang up any picture for a day, or a week, or a month. Or in relation to a country they can be used as a man uses and tries to develop his consciousness of some of his rarer faculties. The 'lungs' of a great city is a familiar enough term and idea nowadays; startling speculations aroused by recent experiments in regard to the shape of animals were ventilated at the last meeting of the British Association; what I mean about islands is something analogous and more recondite but no less real. It pleases my patriotism, therefore, and flatters my Scotist love for minute distinctions, that Scotland has so many islands. Above all, they are useful nowadays because an island is an almost startlingly entire thing, in these days of the subdivision, of the atomisation, of life – when, as W. B. Yeats says, we are more and more forced to remark 'how small a fragment of our own nature can be brought to perfect expression, nor that even but with great toil, in a much-divided civilisation'. An island is not an island when it is too big – the United Kingdom, Australia, and the world are islands, but not in the sense in which we use the term; we cannot realise them as such. On an attractive island there must be a happy, hardly definable sense of correspondence in its size to one's sense of the biological limitations of a human individual. So far as I am concerned personally, the fascination islands have for me depends on their size and shape; these appeal in me to something similar to that peculiar liking for geometrical images, images reflecting the mathematical turn of his mind, which leads Zamyatin, the Russian novelist, to symbolise his characters by geometrical figures. Squareness is the principal characteristic of Baryba in *Tales of Country Life*. It is also the main attribute of one of the characters in *Islanders*. In *We*, the two heroines are geometrically contrasted: one is plump and round (and her letter is 'O'); the other is thin and angular (and her letter is 'I').

I have been having a passionate love-affair with Scotland for the past fifteen to twenty years, like Vladimir Soloviev's love-affair with Lake Saima in Finland, and what actuates me in regard to all these islands is sheer love of every inch and particle of the soil which is the natural base of our national life – a regard in which these islands are as the wayward tendrils of a sweet-heart's hair.

A Reply to Edwin Muir

This reply to the central contention of Edwin Muir's Scott and Scotland *(1936) appeared as part of the introduction to MacDiarmid's anthology* The Golden Treasury of Scottish Poetry *(1940); the Colonel Waddell praised by MacDiarmid is L. A. Waddell whose* The British Edda *(1930) demonstrates, according to MacDiarmid, that 'the Edda is not, as has been imagined, a medley of disjointed Scandinavian mythological tales of gods, but one great coherent epic of historical human heroes and their exploits, based upon genuine hoary tradition, and an ancient British (i.e. Celtic), not Scandinavian, epic at that'.*

About a dozen years ago a well-known Scottish (or rather Orcadian) critic wrote: 'No writer can write great English who is not born an English writer and in England: and born moreover in some class in which the tradition of English is pure, and, it seems to me, therefore, in some other age than this.' The facts have not changed; I cannot see that any Scottish writer, writing in English, has managed to write first-class work or to contribute anything essential and indispensable to the central tradition, the main stream, of English literature. But the critic in question has now changed his opinion* and a few years ago wrote a book in which he recommended his countrymen to cast aside Scots altogether as a 'trash of nonsense' and reconcile themselves, with what grace and gratitude they could, to the paradoxical fact that their only chance of writing literature of any worth is to write in English – a strange recommendation, indeed, at a time when we have not only the example of Charles Doughty and the difficulties of vocabulary which have increasingly beset all recent creative writers of any consequence in

* *Scott and Scotland*, by Edwin Muir (1936).

188

English, but when the younger English poets today 'travel back some six centuries to take lessons from Langland, and find in his homely Anglo-Saxon verse a suitable form for their address to the plowman's modern counterpart. Not that the English labourer would understand the idiom of Lewis or Auden, but the vigorous rhythm and marked alliteration of *Piers Plowman* appeals to these poets for its summoning qualities.' With like motives, we Scottish poets must needs travel back in like fashion into Scots and Gaelic. Anglo-Saxon is not for us. (The revival of the literary use of Scots has gone hand in hand with Scottish nationalist political developments, and Mr Muir might well have considered Mr Edgell Rickword's point – that English has developed in keeping with English Imperialism, and may decline with it. Certainly in the Soviet Union minority languages have been encouraged not only alongside but even at the expense of Russian itself. This is a pointer in the right direction.) A recent writer points out that: 'Ninety-two per cent of the Indian people are illiterate. ... For Higher Education there is one college for every 10½ millions of the population. ... Literary education – the *literature of England, of course, not of India!* – predominates over everything else.' In the same way Dr Douglas Hyde in his *Literary History of Ireland*, and many Scottish and Welsh critics, have complained that under the compulsory educational systems imposed on these countries the native literatures have been occluded and English given a virtual monopoly (as William Robertson, the Scottish historian, 1721–1793, foresaw and lamented would be the consequence of Scotland's union with England, instead of a rich synthesis of all the available elements). Professor Joad, for example, recently complained that so much time is devoted at Coleg Harlech to Welsh literature and characterised it as an imbecile waste of time, though he admitted that he knew little or nothing of Welsh literature! This is typical of what has happened all along the line. It is pertinent to wonder to what extent the fame of English literature is due to such methods rather than to its real merits relative to other literatures. Has not American literature in recent years 'found itself' by discarding that over-influence of English literature which was a hang-over from the colonial period before the American War of Independence? There is a great deal more to the problem than even this. Matthew Arnold wrote in the first essay in the first

Essays in Criticism: 'It has long seemed to me that the burst of creative activity in our literature, through the first quarter of this century, had about it in fact something premature; and that from this cause its productions are doomed, most of them, in spite of the sanguine hopes which accompanied and do still accompany them; to prove hardly more lasting than the productions of far less splendid epochs. And this prematureness comes from its having proceeded without having its proper data, without sufficient material to work with. In other words, the English poetry of the first quarter of this century, with plenty of energy, plenty of creative force, did not know enough. This makes Byron so empty of matter, Shelley so incoherent, Wordsworth even, profound as he is, yet so wanting in completeness and variety.' In his *European Balladry* (1940), Professor W. J. Entwistle gives, especially in his chapter entitled 'The Ascent of Ballads', valuable clues to what 'the proper data' of perdurable poetry have proved to be. In the course of a comprehensive survey of those types of poetry from which the generally accepted glories of English literature are a – perhaps very ephemeral – departure, Professor Entwistle writes of the ballads and folk-songs that 'have clung to life, sometimes during four to seven centuries, and that without any aid from courtly society, nor from the schools (who have adored the ancient classics and are now embalming the moderns), nor from official literature, contemptuous of such wild snatches'. Since Scottish poetry has not developed away from these great staples of poetry to anything like the same extent, it is at once a reassurance with regard to it and a warning with regard to English poetry to read the reminder Professor Entwistle gives on the basis of his vast and most thorough survey that the amazing survival and appeal 'in widest commonalty spread' of these kinds of poetry is 'a glory not often achieved by the great artistic poets and, when achieved, it is through some partial endowment of the generous ballad simplicity'. English poetry's development of a greater 'variety of poetic forms' than Scottish poetry certainly wears a very different look in the light of such comprehensive evidence as Professor Entwistle assembles. The rôle English has played in relation to human consciousness throughout the world is well worth thorough reconsideration in view of such a tremendous body of evidence, drawn from neurology, brain physiology, psychiatry and other sciences, as is presented in Count Alfred Korzybski's *Science and Sanity: An Introduction to Non-Aristotelian Systems and General Semantics* (1933). Again, it would be most illuminating and useful to analyse the content of all English poetry accepted as great in some such way as Professor Denis Saurat, in *La Littérature et l'occultisme* (Paris, 1929), tabulates the elements in the work of many of our greatest European poets, including Spenser, Milton, Blake, Shelley and Wordsworth. His table shows the extent to which they have been dependent, without direct recourse to or first-hand knowledge of them, upon certain dubious anti-Christian sources at variance with the ostensible course of that European civilisation of which they are accepted as among the major glories – a fixation largely responsible for the depotentization of human intelligence, and not unlike that early matriarchal control which, as Colonel Waddell shows, delayed the coming of civilisation for thousands of years, just as, in Count Korzybski's words, our 'semantic blockages' perpetuate the state of general unsanity to-day. Mr Muir assumes that Scots may serve our emotions but that we cannot think in it. (Mr Muir seems to give the word 'thought' some peculiar private sense quite different from the sense in which it is commonly used. Scots poetry is far from destitute of 'thought' in the latter sense. Mr Muir's trouble is that he has never realised with Fr Rolfe – and as Scottish poetry incomparably exemplifies – that 'Life is Mind out for a lark', and strives instead to encase it in the strait-waistcoats of dull (platitudes.)) I do not agree with him. He only gives one example, and that a poor one (susceptible of a very different explanation that he supplies) – where, in *Tam o' Shanter*, Burns breaks into pure English for a few lines of reflective poetry. But in contemporary Scots verse I can show Mr Muir scores of instances in which poets, writing in a thin medium of Scots, do not, like Burns, turn to English, but plunge into passages of denser Scots when they seek to express the core of the matter and come to grips with those profounder movements of their spirits for which, naturally, English or near-English Scots affords no possible medium. It is true that Scots is used in print for few purposes save poetry – though there has been a notable increase and great qualitative improvement in the use of Scots alike in novels and in plays in recent years, and I myself have written literary criticism in a full canon of Scots. Yet Scots is used for the full range of discourse by the great majority of Scots still (though, of course, they know English too and can screw themselves up to 'speaking fine' when need be, albeit – in so far as thinking in any language is not a mere metaphor – they think in Scots and have to translate their thought into English utterance). The idea that Scots is an inadequate medium for any expressive purpose has been promulgated by the same agencies and for the same ends as the notion that the Anglo-Saxon age was a crude and uncouth period, a notion concerning which Voċadlo, in his essay on 'Anglo-Saxon Terminology' (vide *Studies in English, by Members of the English Seminar of the Charles University*, Prague, 4th vol,), says, 'in literary culture the Normans were about as far behind the people whom they conquered as the Romans were when they made themselves masters of Greece', and emphasises the significance of Aelfric's Grammar as a test of the fitness of the West-Saxon literary language for the higher functions of science. These are, indeed, welcome reminders when we reflect that not only has English pursued an Ascendancy Policy and refused practically all intercourse with Irish, Welsh, and Scottish Gaelic, the Scots vernacular, and even its own dialects, but that it attempted to disown its own Anglo-Saxon sources in the same fashion, and only the gallant fight put up by the 'Saxon Nymph', Elizabeth Elstob (1683–1756), succeeded against the most obstinate opposition in securing that place for Anglo-Saxon in English Studies without which, today, the latter would hardly be thinkable at all. Besides, Mr Muir gives his own case away – if he may be said to have a case at all – since he contends that the problem of Scots as a literary medium is insoluble,* involving this divorce between a language of the

---

* It is a profound mistake to disparage Scots because it has failed to evolve a prose literature and has remained almost entirely a vehicle for lyrical poetry. May not this be due to the influence of Gaelic just as the comparative lack of prose in old and mediaeval Bengali may be traced to the influence of Sanskrit where also prose works are disproportionately few? As Professor Meiller said in his lecture on the composition of the Gāthās delivered in 1925 at the Upsala University: 'The Buddhist style of composition, prose for explanations, verse for all that is suggestive and all that is to be pronounced with clearness, distinctness, and force, is not an isolated thing in the Indo-European world. It is an antique usage which is found again and again.' Professor Meiller's 'Essai de chronologie des langues indoeuropéennes', in *Bull. de la Soc. de Linguistique*, 1931, xxxii, pp. 1 ff., is one of the documents which, following the discoveries of Winckler and the decipherment of inscriptions by Hrozny, Forrer, and others, have helped to

emotions and a different language to think in, yet he admits that at least one living poet has occasionally solved this difficulty; and if that is so, then others can as well. Plenty are certainly trying to do so. The growing end of Scottish poetry is neither in English nor in Gaelic today but in Scots, and an ever-increasing number of our younger poets are reverting to that medium, and writing in a Scots which is a synthesis of all the dialects into which Scots has degenerated and of elements of Scots vocubulary drawn from all periods of our history. No recent Scottish poet writing in English has written poetry of the slightest consequence; their contemporaries who write in Scots have shown a far higher creative calibre in the opinion of the highest critical authorities of many lands. These new Scots poets (A. D. Mackie, William Soutar, Marion Angus, Helen Cruickshank. and a dozen others) are internationalists in their literary sympathies too, and have translated into Scots a great body of poetry from German, French, Russian, and other European languages. Translations from the Russian of Boris Pasternak by William Soutar, from the Russian of Alexander Blok and the German of Rainer Maria Rilke by myself, from the German of Heine and others by Professor Alexander Gray, from the Dutch of P. C. Boutens and others by Emeritus-Professor Sir H. J. C. Grierson, and from a great array of French poets from Ronsard to Baudelaire by Miss Winefride Margaret Simpson, are included in this tale of recent renderings into Scots, and healthy intromissions with the whole range of European literature, which have been a notable feature of our recent literary history, like a veritable return to the Good Europeanism of our mediaeval ancestors. Scottish Gaelic has shown no similar movement yet, but I have ample evidence that many brilliant young men in our Highlands and Islands are now addressing themselves to that great task. Scotland has

establish that clear conception of the antiquity, the kinship, and even the certain contacts of the Italo-Celtic and Indo-Iranian groups of languages, and their relations with the languages of Asia Minor and Hither Asia, commonly classed together as Hittite, which informs what I say here, apropos Colonel Waddell's and Roger O'Connor's books, of the need to realise that the impetus to civilisation was an Ur-Gaelic initiative and that in the Gaelic genius lies the reconciliation of East and West, in the light of which ineluctable mission of the Gaelic genius the English literary achievement is seen simply as the good which is the deadliest enemy of the best.

idolised Burns but has failed to follow his great example in reverting from English to Scots; this has been long overdue. Mr Muir is only in the unfortunate position of resembling Sir John Squire, who thought it was a pity Burns wrote in Scots, not English. It is an important point that poetry in Scots has still an access, not only to a cultured section but to the working classes, in Scotland, that no English poetry has ever had or, to all appearances, can ever have. 'Hugh Haliburton's' poems were cut out of the newspapers as they appeared and hung up in cottar houses and bothies all over Scotland. My own, in by far the most difficult Scots written in modern times, have won acceptance in every quarter of the world. The use of Scots is no handicap to international recognition.

No Closed Doors, No Religion

Denis Saurat, MacDiarmid's friend, edited (as a contribution to the cultural climate following World War Two) A Symposium On The After War Religion: An Investigation on the Present State and the Future of Religion. *It contained essays by MacDiarmid. Dr R. S. Silver, Jack Lindsay, Seton Pollock, Dr Gerard Adler and Dr L. J. Bendit and reached galley-proof stage when the project was abandoned. MacDiarmid's essay, as printed here, has been abbreviated by omitting lengthy quotations from 'a writer on Maurras', Saurat, Dr Oscar Levy, Dr Rudolf Jordan, Confucius and Dr Lin Yutang.*

Kierkegaard was somewhat prone to premonitions but he never had a truer one, I think, or one the real signifance of which he more completely failed to divine, than he had when on the First Sunday after Easter, April 22nd, 1838, he wrote in his Journal: ,'In case Christ shall come to dwell in me, it must be as in the Gospel of to-day in the almanac: "Christ enters through closed doors."' That is true of all religion – it enters only through closed doors – and the irony is that Kierkegaard penned that fateful and uncomprehending entry *after* he had heard (as he wrongly thought) the authoritative word, 'Awake, thou that sleepest!' For, correctly interpreted and restated in terms of the present day, that Gospel sentence is only another way of saying (and Kierkegaard's, and all, religion only an exemplification of) what Charles S. Peirce says (in his *Chance, Love and Logic*), viz.: 'It is terrible to see how a single unclear idea, a single formula without meaning, lurking in a young man's head, will sometimes act like an obstruction of inert matter in an artery, hindering the nutrition of the brain, and condemning its victim to pine away in the fullness of his intellectual vigour and in the midst of intellectual plenty.' It was for that reason that Christ said: 'Suffer the little children to come unto me', and that all religions have always been so intent on 'catching them young'. It is the sole condition of their continuance, lodgement in the infantile and the perpetuation of infantilisms in those locked rooms which, if Christ penetrated, he was careful to keep to himself and not throw open to the light of day. And, in contradistinction, a true realisation of the significance of that Gospel sentence accounts for the fact that Nietzsche's educational essays though still far too little known and even where known relatively much undervalued, are perhaps his most important productions, though the present writer would be the last to rate too highly the value to European thought of his logical exposure of 'undogmatic Christianity' (for 'the so-called "rationalism" of a David Friedrich Strauss, with its disproof of the supernatural basis of Christianity, did not, for Nietzsche, promise the liberation of the mind which shallow "free-thinkers" welcomed so enthusiastically: rather was it, with its continued loyalty to the moral values inherent in Christian dogma, one more example of a Philistinism which must be destroyed before the Superman could be evolved and the transvaluation of values take effect'), his antithesis of Dionysian and Apollonian, his conception of the Eternal Recurrence, his challenge to objective science divorced from society, his exaltation of the individual, his searching analysis of the values of democracy and nationalism. But some of these great contributions of Nietzschean thought lie outside the scope of this essay, and, though I have listed them in passing. I must make it clear that for my present purpose the invaluable element in Nietzsche's work with which I am concerned is his devastating attack on the social philosophers who thought that you could destroy the whole basis of the Christian religion and yet retain a few of its ethical principles. And I certainly agree with Professor Brinton when he says: 'We are committed by Western tradition to attempt to understand the social process and to guide that process slowly, realistically, with as little violence as possible, by rational means to rational ends ... We understand pathetically little about social change, but we must work with what little we have, or Nietzsche will indeed be enthroned as a prophet.'*

* *Vide* Clare Brinton, *Nietzsche* (Cambridge, Mass., 1942).

It is true of all language usage, as Malinowski said, that 'the fundamental grammatical categories, universal to all human languages, can be understood only with reference to the Weltanschauung of primitive man, and that, through programmatic use of language, the barbarous primitive categories must have deeply influenced the later philosophies of mankind.' And it is equally true and condemnatory of practically all so-called religious thought in particular, that, as Einstein says (*vide The Meaning of Relativity*): 'The only justification for our concepts and system of concepts is that they serve to represent the complex of our experiences; beyond this they have no legitimacy. I am convinced that the philosophers have had a harmful effect upon the progress of scientific thinking in removing certain fundamental concepts from the domain of empiricism, where they are under our control, to the intangible heights of the *a priori*.'

I like to be surrounded with appropriate 'furniture' when I sit down to write. So on the shelf above my writing table I have propped up a number of portraits. The central one is that of Charles Maurras. 'Mr Wallace Fowlie has asserted (*à propos* of Baudelaire),' says a writer on Maurras, 'that "once a Christian, it is impossible to dispossess oneself of the spirit of Christianity. The sacraments leave an indelible mark." Now, Maurras who was at least baptised, confirmed, and made his first communion, is an exception to the rule. For there is nothing in his attitude that recalls that other strange fruit of Catholic education, James Joyce. There is no *odi et amo*. There is only hate. Mr Santayana has recently told us that "Catholicism is the most human of religions, if taken humanly: it is paganism spiritually transformed and made metaphysical". For Mr. Santayana, the Catholicism of a reasonable man is a superior form of paganism; for Maurras it is an inferior form of paganism, tainted with Judaic infection, with the seeds of humanitarianism, with romanticism. It is as hard to imagine Maurras calling, like Mr. Santayana's free-thinking father, for "La Unción y la gallina,' as Mr T. S. Eliot found it to imagine that American semi-Maurrasian, Irving Babbitt, calling like Socrates for that equivalent of the cock of Aesculapius. In each case pride was too strong.'

Next to Maurras's I have set the portrait of David Hume, from an engraving after the painting by Allan Ramsay.' 'I should be most exceedingly surprised,' said Lawrence Herne, 'to hear that David ever had unpleasant contention with any man; and if I should be made to believe that such an event had happened nothing would persuade me that his opponent was not in the wrong, for in my life did I never meet with a being of a more placid and gentle nature.' And a recent writer on Hume has said *à propos* of Mr Ernest Campbell Mossner's book *The Forgotten Hume: Le Bon David* (Columbia University Press, 1943): 'The finished picture is of a thinker whose character is as great as his philosophical explorations into the complexities of human nature in order to explain the world and the laws of life are daring and original. Placidity and gentleness – Sterne's judgment was accurately weighed ... The sub-title of Mr Mossner's book is "Le bon David"; it could have been "A Study in Tolerance." It presents one of the keenest minds in a century of mental keenness in its relations with friends and opponents; and in all circumstances of time and chance – all but one, perhaps it would be safer to say, though that one is an arguable exception – calm, genial, sympathetic, benevolent, courageous, resigned ... Adam Smith, who knew him as intimately as any man, wrote the conclusive tribute: "I have always considered him, both in his lifetime and since his death, as approaching as nearly to the idea of a perfectly wise and virtuous man, as perhaps the nature of human frailty will admit." The value of his History of England can be disputed as history, though not as literature, the importance of his philosophy be variously estimated; but the *goodness* of the Great Infidel is established; it is his very genius and fashion, his thought and his life.'

The remaining portraits I have set up to preside over my work are those of Robert Burns and Paul Valéry. (Not an Englishman amongst them! Four portraits. Two Scots and two French. That is right. 'The strange, shifting, doubling animal Man is generally a negative and often a worthless creature,' wrote Burns, 'of the men called honest and the women called chaste, half of them are not what they pretend to be and many are thought to have even worse faults. But then virtue, everyone knows, is an obsolete business. Some years ago, when I was young, and by no means the saint I am now, I discovered that even a godly woman may be a ... but this is scandal. However respectable *individuals* in all ages may have been, I look on

mankind in the lump as nothing better than a foolish mob.'
Willie Nicol was right when he called him 'Dear Christless
Bobbie!' 'Heresy?' Burns says, in another of his letters, 'I do not
care three farthings for Authorities.'

I prefer Valéry's intellectual integrity to Kierkegaard's
definition – which is also the definition of faith – in *Postscript*:
'Objective uncertainty held fast by the personal appropriation
of the most passionate inwardness is the truth, the highest truth
there is for an existing individual.' And I prefer Valéry to 'the
infinitely interested subjective thinker' Kierkegaard, under his
pseudonym of Climacus, contrasts with the speculative philosopher who, as he is proud to claim, disinterestedly seeks to
ascertain objective truth without any concern about his relation
to it.

My utter repudiation of all religion springs from my agreement with what Dr Oscar Levy in his *Idiocy of Idealism* expresses
when, dealing with the results of the Reformation, he says of the
Puritans: 'Yet if they had been really and truly religious their
own faith might have shown them the way out of the wilderness.
For the religious conscience begot the scientific conscience, and
the scientific conscience ought to produce the intellectual
conscience. Of the latter, Puritanism knew nothing; it has
stopped at the religious and, in few cases, at the scientific
conscience. It fought shy of the last step; it did not allow truth to
enlighten the intellect; it was not honest enough to criticise
moral values, and has thus allowed the world to tumble into
chaos which it tries in vain to organise now by mere reaction, by
still more religion, by still more morality – that is to say, by still
more alcohol for a world of dipsomaniacs.'

The fact is that modern man has come into his estate of
three-dimensional consciousness and one result of this is that
we can nevermore – for good and ill – recover the completely
spontaneous gestures of life; the shameless caress, the swagger
and the prayer. This is a sad thing, no doubt, and in our
petulant adolescence we cry out against those grey-faced tutors
– civilisation, liberalism and protestantism. We see at the
present day a cult of the primitive, the aristocrat, the devotee,
but these are cul-de-sacs which the current of life will pass by,
even if – in the phenomena of communism, fascism, and the
Western neo-catholicism – some of the stagnant water has

mingled with the mainstream. The heirs of the mechanical age will not again accept tribal or village custom, the heirs of the revolutions will not accept class-privilege, the heirs of the 'Enlightenment' will not accept supernatural belief. They would not, even if it should be proved to them that this submission alone could save them from destruction; because, in a Copernican world, their centre is outside them, in irrational impulse, and they can only swing round it blindly.

The ancient Ptolemaic world, which made humanity the centre of the cosmos, symbolised the balanced life of proven commonsense; for man's instinct tells him that the symbol guards reason – which is itself a set of symbols – and that reason pressed to its conclusion leads to the irrational.

But as life advances over our dead bodies, so it advances over shattered symbols, irresistibly, and we can no more bring back the naive, brave, pathetic figures of the past than we can bring back that level immovable stage which supported them all.

Made dizzy by our frantic gyrations through space, by the revolutions of pure abstraction, we search for some hanging-strap to steady ourselves; and find it – perhaps – in the Einsteinian world. There is, then, no great abstract cosmos, no single centre, no far-off divine event to which the whole creation gravitates and in which everything hard and separate will be melted down into one liquid ball of love and equality. The mind is its own centre; and according to its position our universe is rational or irrational. According to our shifting relationship with each other we are each of us in turn savage and the civilised man, the noble and the democrat, the monk and the free-thinker. And this being once recognised we may even accept church and caste, in the knowledge that they can no longer impose on us, because we ourselves are the measure of the world and all things in it. We may once more conform – though with a smile – to cult and custom, seeing in them gracious garments that we can put on and lay aside at our pleasure, and having no fear that we shall again be deceived into thinking, like the child, that it is the habit that makes the monk or the crown that makes the king; nor, like the adolescent, that cowls or crowns could ever come between us and the reality. We shall be able to 'make game' like children, and, unlike children, be perfectly aware that Life is making as much of us. If we shall have lost – and irretrievably – the wonder of the spirit, we shall have gained the freedom of the spirit; and no elders will ever again sadden our days, and no nurse terrify our nights.

What I am pleading for is such a position as that whose obligations Mr Herbert Read in his poem 'A World Within a War' has shouldered bravely – Faith in the self, unbuttressed by faiths, for 'to fight without hope is to fight with grace' (*vide* his 'To a Conscript of 1940'). An austere and no doubt still difficult stand – since space here does not permit me to marshal from the sciences those incontrovertible proofs of the 'semantic block-ages' responsible for the continued sway of religious ideas, of the correspondence of the states of mind so induced with well-known psychopathic conditions, of the evil consequences in every social connection, of the ultimate provenance of these ideas in the basal gangia of the old animal brain and so out of keeping altogether with that development of the cerebral cortex which has been the great feature of the development of man and indicates his proper function and future. I can only name here two books which do assemble all that scientific evidence in the most cogent and unassailable fashion – *The Mind in the Making*, by James Harvey Robinson; and the monumental *Science and Sanity. An Introduction to Non-Aristotelian Systems and General Semantics*, by Count Alfred Karzybski.

But in conclusion I would quote from *The Importance of Living*, by the Chinese writer, Dr Lin Yutang. 'Such religion as there can be in modern life,' says Dr Yutang, 'every individual will have to salvage from the churches for himself. There is always a possibility of surrendering ourselves to the Great Spirit in an atmosphere of ritual and worship as one kneels praying without words and looking at the stained-glass windows, in spite of all that one may think of the theological dogmas. In this sense, worship becomes a true aesthetic experience, an aesthetic experience that is one's own, very similar, in fact, to the experience of viewing a sun setting behind an outline of trees on hills. For that man, religion is a final fact of consciousness, for it will be an aesthetic experience very much akin to poetry.'

Reflections on The Crux Decussata

Printed from the undated manuscript in Edinburgh University Library.

It was interesting to read in the press the other day that, with St Andrew's Day approaching, London's largest chain of teashops began stocking its windows in the Strand, Oxford Street, Piccadilly Circus, and other London thoroughfares with hampers designed to appeal to the Metropolitan Scots population. Each hamper contained Scotch whisky and Scottish raspberries, heather honey, partridge and haggis – canned haggis. Why the latter was included in that unusual – and surely unnecessary – form was not stated, but with the rising fear of Scottish Nationalism in certain quarters in England it may well be there was some apprehension lest the haggis in its natural state might run amok. The Americans are evidently a tougher breed and had no hesitation in allowing 'the largest haggis ever made' to be imported for exhibition in New York, but presumably fire-arms are easier to come by in America than in London and any haggis breaking loose there would get short shrift.

St Andrew's Day has never succeeded in establishing itself as a really national occasion in Scottish observance. We have had, and still have, St Andrew's Societies, of course, and they have done and continue to do excellent work but it is for the most part work concerned with such peripheral issues as the proper display of flags, armorial bearings, and such like technical matters which have little interest for the vast majority of our people and are not really germane to the heart of our national problem.

It may be suggested, however, that precisely because he has no real connection with Scotland and because his cult has never

202

really taken on in our midst St Andrew is a very suitable person to be our patron saint* if, indeed, we need one at all. St Andrew never set foot in Scotland or did anything for it. Only parts of his skeleton were brought here centuries after his martyrdom. So he had no live relationship to use whatever. This lack of any indigenous element and of any relevance to our traditions and needs has militated against his popular acceptance and St Andrew's Day has as a consequence never been effectively observed in our midst. There is nevertheless something very Scottish about all this.

Most of the symbols and institutions in Scotland are similarly devoid of true national significance. Most of them, too, have very questionable foundations. St Andrew became the patron saint of Scotland about the middle of the eighth century. There are various legends which state that the relics of St Andrew were brought under supernatural guidance from Constantinople to the place where the modern St Andrews stands. The oldest stories (preserved in the Colbertine MSS, Paris, and the Harleian MSS in the British Museum) state that the relics were brought by one Regulus to the Pictish King Angus MacFergus, whose dates were about 731 to 761. The only historical Regulus was an Irish monk expelled from Ireland about 573 to 600. There are good reasons for supposing that the relics were originally in the collection of Acca, Bishop of Hexham, who brought them into Pictland when he was driven from Hexham about the year 732 and founded a see on the site of St Andrews, the older names of which were Kilrymont in Gaelic and Muckross in Pictish. As the *Encyclopaedia Britannica* says: 'The connection with Regulus is, therefore, due in all probability to the desire to date the foundation of the church at St Andrews as early as possible.' Our whole accepted history is a tissue of ecclesiastical falsifications, as Major Hay of Seaton demonstrated in his book, *A Chain of Error In Scottish History*, and the very dubious basis on which the acceptance of St Andrew as our patron saint relies is no exception in such connections.

There is more to it than that, however. Scotland's position is full of anomalies of all kinds. We are supposed to have an exceptional love of country, yet that has been paraded and

* Saint George of England is a relative newcomer to the ranks of patron saints. It was only towards the end of the fourteenth century that St George began to gain that position, previously held by St Edward the Confessor.

boasted about alongside an unparallelled ignorance of and indifference to the actual facts of our national position. Unlike any other nation in history we have tamely acquiesced in the relegation of our own history, literature, and languages to a neglible place in our educational system while conceding a virtual monopoly to the history, literature, and languages of an alien people traditionally our greatest (and, indeed, only real) enemy.

The whole state of our arts and affairs is riddled with incredible contradictions of this sort. What more appropriate than that we should be given as our patron saint a man who never had anything to do with Scotland at all? The fact that he was crucified on an unusual shape of cross parallels the extraordinary situation of Scotland itself, since our nation too has been literally crucified on a cross the very shape of which most of our people fail to discern and even mistake for what they call the benefits and blessings that have accrued to us from our Union with England. The cream of the jest, however, lies in the fact that Scotland shares St Andrew as patron saint with Russia, a connection which should give maligners of the Soviet Union 'furiously to think' but which happily underlines the fact that Scotland and Russia have had many important connections in the past and that even today Scotland's economic future is linked to trade with Russia to a far greater degree than applies to England. The *Crux decussata* – as the particular form of the St Andrew's Cross is called – is appropriate enough to our national condition, but if the Saint had been crucified upside down that might have been better still so far as typifying Scotland's position today is concerned.

While St Andrew, and the celebration of 30th November as his day, have never caught on in Scotland, there is no reason why a great deal more should not be done under that name, or, for the matter of that, any other name. The aim should be to powerfully reinforce, with all the strength that can be derived from religious and historical associations coupled with the most realistic recognition of our contemporary problems and potentialities, what has been laid down as the purpose of the Scottish Renaissance Movement, namely, 'to place the soul of the nation in relation to the fundamental facts of life, to express in terms of destiny the *Weltanschauung* of the Scottish people, and plant it deeper in the soil of mystery, myth, history, and

204

prehistory, recognizing clearly that the quiet times in Europe are past and that only a people of united political will, willing never to allow its place in the sun to be challenged, asserting itself in a time of moral and biological decline – only such a people can give proof of its youthfulness and the fulness of its potentialities for the future'.

So far as concerns Canada, America, and other lands overseas where St Andrew's Societies flourish as they have never done in Scotland itself, the pity is that the emotions relied upon are almost wholly sentimental and nostalgic and divorced from reality. Year after year they repeat the old clap-trap about love for Scotland *ad nauseam*; surely it is high time that their speakers turned instead to the actual facts and figures of Scotland's position today, and that the music, songs and poems used in the programmes drew upon our living composers, poets, and vocal and instrumental artistes alive to and in sympathy with the creative developments Scotland has manifested in poetry and music in the past few years. After all, it is forty years ago now since the St Andrew's Society of Glasgow issued a circular drawing attention to the urgent necessity of Scottish schools 'using the classics of Scottish vernacular literature as textbooks' and saying: 'there are at the present hour few young persons in Scotland who know anything of the beauties of Scottish poetry or the vigour of Scottish prose; and within a few years it seems probable that Scotsmen will not be able to read the works of Barbour, Bellenden, and Burns. This is an all-important subject to the Scottish race; but it is more, it is important to the British people generally. Scottish literature is so rich and picturesque, and is so important a branch of British literature generally, that to allow it to die of inanition, as it were, in its native land, would be a national crime.' A good deal has admittedly been done in the interval in Scotland itself, but most of the Scottish Societies abroad remain unaffected by the new creative spirit, and, indeed, even in Scotland itself, most of our young people know no more of the St Andrew's Cross than its use as the multiplication sign, on the one hand, and, on the other, its employment as a symbol for a kiss.

It is forty years ago too, since Judge MacTavish of Canada, replying to Dr W. S. Bruce, the famous Scottish Polar explorer at an Edinburgh St Andrew's Day Dinner, said: 'No matter how low down the thermometer went in Canada, the frost never became so severe as to freeze the warm blood of the Scotsman. In every city and town, and in almost every hamlet in that great country, there was a strong, vigorous and healthy St Andrew's Society. No matter where they were situated, in distant prairies, in cities and towns, not only in the Dominion of Canada, but in the United States, Mexico, and South America, they were with one accord that night thinking of the old country.'

That is still true. Alas, that so much enthusiasm and goodwill should run to waste in mere orations when a very little adaptation could utilise it to real purpose. Scotland's sons and daughters overseas organised with a proper regard for current and prospective realities on the basis of all that is best in our Scottish traditions could, and should, be no mere confederation of sentimentalists but an international factor of great power – the transformation of the *Crux decussata* into a plus sign, a real asset.

The Dour Drinkers of Glasgow—
A Letter from Scotland

From The American Mercury, *March 1952.*

Glasgow! 'This savage, wild, ridiculous city,' as the playwright 'James Bridie' called it, in a speech in which he very properly praised 'the right kind of lunatic, daft, Scottish panache,' an attribute most easily encountered in the pubs, but difficult to find elsewhere except (by accident) in the course of a battle, a political meeting, a love affair, a theological wrangle, or a literary controversy.

I have never been able, despite repeated efforts, to understand the periodicity of those complaints against the Scottish pub which have been made during the past half century. Made, I suspect, when not by women or clergymen, either by English visitors or by Scots who, as Sir Walter Scott said, 'unScotched make damned bad Englishmen'. They are usually accompanied by envious comparisons with the amenities of English inns, which we are told are far more sociable and cater to family parties in a way Scottish pubs do not. For, in the latter, at their most typical, the rule is 'men only' and 'no sitting' – you stand at the counter with your toes in that narrow sawdust-filled trough which serves as a comprehensive combined ash-tray, litter-bin, and cuspidor. So it was when I first began to drink nearly fifty years ago; so it still is for the most part. Certainly nowadays, in addition to the common bars and to the jug (or family) departments to which women, mostly of a shawled, slatternly, and extremely subfusc order, still repair with all the ancient furtiveness, there are bright chromium-fitted saloon bars, cocktail bars, and other modern accessories in the more pretentious places. And even in most of the ordinary bars there is now a fair sprinkling of women not only of the 'lower orders' or elderly at that, but gay young things, merry widows, and courtesans. Men (if you can call them that) even take their wives and daughters along with them to these meretricious, deScotticised resorts.

Now, I am not a misogynist by any means. I simply believe there is a time and a place for everything – yes, literally, *everything*. And like a high proportion of my country's regular and purposive drinkers I greatly prefer a complete absence of women on occasions of libation. I also prefer a complete absence of music and very little illumination. I am therefore a strong supporter of the lower – or lowest – type of 'dive' where drinking is the principal purpose and no one wants to be distracted from that absorbing business by music, women, glaring lights, chromium fittings, too many mirrors unless sufficiently fly-spotted and mildewed, or least of all, any fiddling trivialities of *l'art nouveau*. If there are still plenty of pubs in Glasgow which conform to these requirements and remain frowsy and fusty enough to suit my taste and that of my boon companions, in another respect the old order has changed sadly and I fear irreversibly. Our Scottish climate – not to speak of the soot-laden, catarrh-producing atmosphere of Glasgow in particular – makes us traditionally great spirit-drinkers. That has changed. Most of us cannot afford – or at any rate cannot get – much whisky or, for the matter of that, any other spirit. There are, of course, desperate characters who drink methylated spirits. I have known – and still know – resolute souls partial to a mixture of boot-blacking and 'meth,' and I remember when I was in the Merchant Service during the recent War a few hardy characters who went to the trouble of stealing old compasses off the boats at Greenock (where we had the largest small-boat pool in Europe) in order to extract from them the few drops of spirit (well mixed with crude-oil and verdigris) they contained. But in Glasgow pubs today at least ninety per cent of the drinking is of beer – and mere 'swipes' at that; 'beer' that never saw a hop. I can remember the time when it was the other way about. What beer was consumed was used simply as a 'chaser' to the whisky in precisely the same way as a 'boilermaker' in New York. For of course you get drunk quicker on whisky plus water than on neat whisky, and whisky and soda is an English monstrosity no true Scot can countenance at all.

There are other sorry changes in even the lowest-down pubs which in general hold to the grim old tradition of the true Scottish 'boozer'. The question of hours, for example. In London one can still drink legally twenty-three hours out of twenty-four. That is because London is a congeries of different boroughs which have different 'permitted hours' so that by switching from one borough at closing time it is easy to find another where 'they' will still be open for an hour or two longer. In Glasgow, moreover, unlike London, there are few facilities for drinking outside the permitted hours. For most people, that is. It will hardly be thought that I am pleading for decreased consumption, but I believe that the same amount of strong drink taken in a leisurely way over a fair number of hours is less harmful than the rush to squeeze in the desired number of drinks in the short time the law allows. Our national poet, Robert Burns, was right when he said: 'Freedom and whisky gang thegither.' What he meant is precisely what my own motto means: 'They do not love liberty who fear licence.' I speak for that large body of my compatriots who uphold this great principle and regard respectability and affectations of any kind as our deadliest enemy. There are, of course, clubs and hotels, but *hoi polloi* have nothing to do with either of these.

Only a few years ago there were also Burns Clubs which took advantage of a loophole in the law and did a roaring trade especially on Sundays. You did not require to be introduced. You simply paid half-a-crown at the door and automatically became a member for a day. The difficulty – especially for the thirsty stranger within the gates, and indeed for the bulk of the citizens themselves – was to find these places. One heard about them. One heard, indeed, fantastic tales of the alcoholic excesses which went on there. But they were exceedingly difficult to find. You had to be 'in the know'. Suddenly they disappeared entirely. I have never been able to discover why. There was nothing in the press – and I could learn nothing over my private grapevine either – about police action having been taken. They must have been very profitable to those who ran them, and a substantial source of revenue to the 'liquor trade' generally. They served a very useful purpose since no one not resident in a hotel and not a member of a club could otherwise get a drink in Glasgow on Sundays. (It was – and is still – jolly difficult to get a meal even.)

During these two wars there were all kinds of interferences with the incidence and duration of the 'permitted hours'. Quite a proportion of licence-holders got it into their heads that they could close earlier than the decreed closing-time – and even take a weekly half-holiday and in some cases shut shop and go off for a week's holiday in the summer time. They still do, and act arbitrarily in many other ways. All that is, of course, quite illegal, although the magistracy and police authorities turned a blind eye at these irregularities and even welcomed them. The fact is, of course, as the very term 'public house' shows, that the condition of the licence obliges the licence-holder to have his place at the disposal of citizens at all times – not necessarily for drinking at all; a citizen is entitled to have the use of these places whenever he wants if only to use the lavatory or shelter from the weather, or read his newspaper, or meet a friend. It would, in practice, be virtually impossible to fight this and other corrupt practices the authorites have winked at. Recognising this, some of us tried to organise a 'Consumers' Union', since the consumers are the only unorganised and helpless factor in the liquor situation. It proved impossible; the consumers won't combine. They are far too individualistic. Though such a Consumers' Union might have been very useful in certain connections vis-à-vis the Liquor Trade, the Municipal, State, and Police Authorities and every variety of blue-nosed snooper, I am on many other counts enough of an 'unregenerate sinner' not to regret that the effort failed. Yet at times I like to toy with the idea that if it had been possible to organise even a high proportion of pub-users (leaving out consumers who consume elsewhere) the result would have been one of the strongest organisations in the world. No Trade Union, or combination of Trade Unions, would have been a patch on it.

I trust I have made myself clear. The majority of Glasgow pubs are for connoisseurs of the morose, for those who relish the element of degradation in all boozing and do not wish to have it eliminated by the introduction of music, modernistic fitments, arty effects, or other extraneous devices whatsoever. It is the old story of those who prefer hard-centre chocolates to soft, storm to sunshine, sour to sweet. True Scots always prefer the former of these opposites. That is one of our principal differences from the English. We do not like the confiding, the intimate, the ingratiating, the hail-fellow-well-met, but prefer the unapproachable, the hard-bitten, the recalcitrant, the sinister, the malignant, the sarcastic, the saturnine, the cross-grained and the cankered, and the howling wilderness to the amenities of civilization, the irascible to the affable, the prickly to the smooth. We have no damned fellow-feeling at all, and look at ourselves and others with the eye of a Toulouse Lautrec appraising an obscene old toe-rag doing the double-split. In short, we are all poets (all true Scots – that is, all Scots not encased in a carapace of conventionality a mile thick) of *l'humour noir* and, as William Blake said, 'All poets are of the devil's party.'

There is a well-known story about Carlyle and Emerson spending several hours together without exchanging a word. Carlyle declared it was one of the best nights he ever spent with anybody. A lot of us spend many nights in Scottish pubs in the same way and we agree with Carlyle. Scotland produces a type of man who can dispense more completely than any with what James Joyce called 'the atrocities of human intercourse'.

There is nothing less exportable than a national sense of humour. The Scottish temper I am writing about is little known abroad. Our internationally famous comedians purvey a very different account of us. The sorry joke is that so many Scots believe the latter and model themselves all too successfully on it. Yet what I am trying to express is well-enough known about us in other connections. It is this that for centuries has made the Scottish soldier famous as a bayonet-fighter. A similar preference for naked steel runs through every phase of our life. It is summed up in the old Gaelic proverb: 'Fingal's sword never needs to cut twice.' Burns says in one of his poems that you need not be 'nice' with him. No one need be 'nice' with any true Scotsman – in fact, he will not allow it at all. The only kind of friendships one makes – or wishes to make or could tolerate at all – in such pubs was well described by my Irish friend, the late W. B. Yeats, when he wrote:

> I called him a knave and a fool –
> But friendship never dies!

In other words, the injunction which is as one with the very marrow of our bones is 'woe to him of whom all men speak well'. We have no use for emotions, let alone sentiments, but are solely concerned with passions.

211

One of the best essayists on aspects of Scottish literature, Mr J. D. Scott, has pointed out how deep in Scottish life are the roots of this 'slow and vicious enjoyment', this 'formidable and ferocious scorn'. It is the tremendous animating principle of three of the greatest modern Scottish novels – George Douglas Brown's *House With the Green Shutters*, R. L. Stevenson's unfinished *Weir of Hermiston*, and Sydney Goodsir Smith's super-Rabelaisian story of Edinburgh today (doing for it what Joyce's *Ulysses* did for Dublin), *Carotid Cornucopius*. It is precisely that element, utterly different from English humour, that is the essence of any number of the most typical Scottish anecdotes. Like, for example, the story of the minister who told his congregation that in a dream he had seen them all in Hell suffering the tortures of the damned. 'Ye lifted up your eyes to the Almighty God and ye said to Him, "O Lord, we didna ken it would be like this", and the Lord God Almighty, (*slowly and unctuously*) in His infinite mercy and compassion, looked down upon ye and He said, "Weel, noo ye ken!"'

We (if I may speak for all of us) do not go to pubs for chit-chat, we do not wish them crossed with some sort of café or tea-party or concert or damned *conversazione*; we are fond enough of our women-folk, but there are times when we want away from them as no doubt there are times when they want to be away from us. The keynote of Glasgow life is still expressed in the song sung by Will Fyffe, the great Scottish comedian, which runs:

> I belong to Glasgow,
> Dear old Glasgow toon.
> But what's the matter wi' Glasgow?
> For it's going roon' and roon'.
> I'm only a common old working chap,
> As anyone here can see,
> But when I get a couple o' drinks on a Saturday,
> Glasgow belongs to me.

Our attitude is not inhuman. We are experienced men of the world. We like what we like to be a little grim – in keeping with the facts of life, and loathe facile emotions. We cherish no illusions, and consequently prefer a mutual taciturnity to any sort of social joy, standing shoulder to shoulder with other men we do not know from Adam and do not want to know. We feel no necessity whatever to indulge in any airs and graces, are not fond of promiscuous conversation, at least of any sustained sort, and if our risible faculties are moved at all by the human spectacle, that movement only adorns our faces intermittently with some sort of *risus sardonicus* that in flickering across our features barely interrupts the emission of the dense smoke of the black tobacco going well in our clay pipes. It is, indeed, a sort of fleeting facial comment hardly distinguishable from the effect of that gagging which an unwarily deep swig at what passes for Scotch Whisky is apt to etch on the granitic features of even the most hardened soak.

Elsewhere I have summed up my regard for Glasgow in a brief poem, '*Placenta Previa*', which runs:

> It'll be no easy matter to keep the dirt in its place
> And get the Future out alive in *this* case.

On the last Hogmanay night (New Year's Eve), as on all its predecessors, no matter how dourly and darkly I take my pleasures, the same way some people keep snakes for pets, I once again, with a great upsurge of savage joy, recalled another verse of mine and practised what I preach, namely:

> O this is the time for all mankind
>   To rejoice without a doubt
> – And break the neck of the bottle
>   If the cork will not come out!

And that is precisely how Scots do bring in the New Year. They gather in the public squares of their cities and towns, and as the bells ring out the Old Year and ring in the New, they empty their bottles and smash them on the street. On this most recent Hogmanay I was one of a company of many uproarious hundreds doing this in George Square, Glasgow, undeterred by the fact that a day of gale and sleet was giving way to snow and ice and that hundreds of people in Glasgow alone had been rendered homeless by blown-down houses or injured in the streets by falling chimney-pots and torn-off slates.

A wild night, so our merriment had to be correspondingly wild to lift our hearts above its hazards. A typical incident was the ripping apart of a newly-built school. It was hurled by the gale towards a house occupied by a family of Kellys. One section of the steel-framed school was lifted in the air and wrapped round an electric standard at the Kelly's back fence. That standard saved the Kelly house. If it hadn't been there the school would have gone right through the house.

Hail Caledonia, stern and wild!

Scott Fitzgerald speaks of 'Jay Gatsby breaking up like glass against Tom Buchanan's hard malice'. I sometimes think all the shams and unveracities in the world will break up in the same way against the Scottish spirit of which I am writing. Scots of that particular mettle are the very salt of the earth. I am one of them and so I know. It would not pay anyone to dispute the point in any of the Glasgow pubs I frequent.

Let me finish this Scottish letter on a different note altogether. Otherwise it will not be true to Scotland, which is a country of sharp transitions and extraordinary variety, in its landscape, weather, people and everything else. Glasgow is only a part of it, and utterly unrepresentative of the rest. Well, I was talking to an Edinburgh man yesterday and I said something about the unexpectable character of Scottish scenery, and Scottish life. And he pulled me up at once. 'Nonsense,' he said, 'there is nothing inexplicable – nothing to account for which almost anybody cannot devise at once some reasonable hypothesis.' And he challenged me to give an example. I replied that I was walking across a moor in Ross-shire one summer afternoon. There wasn't a soul in sight, hardly an animal, only a bird or two. It was almost twelve miles to the nearest village. Suddenly among the heather I spied a yellow glove. It was almost brand-new, did not look as if it had been worn at all. I picked it up and as I did so I heard a clicking noise inside it. I took it by the tip of one of the fingers and shook it gently – and out fell four fingernails and a thumbnail, the complete set of nails from one hand. They were perfectly clean, like sea shells. However they had come off it had quite obviously neither been through any disease nor violence. It was impossible to conceive a man drawing off his glove and his nails with it, tossing them into the heather, and walking on unaware, or, if aware, as if nothing has happened. I found it – and find it – impossible to imagine the state of mind of a man who a few miles further on discovered he had done just that. I have been haunted even since by a sense of the horrible blunt feeling of nailless fingertips. I should have thought in such a case a man would have reported the matter to the police or discussed it with friends and that somehow or other news of such an extraordinary occurrence would have got round and out, and even into the papers. I made all sorts of inquiries and found that nothing was known or could be discovered about the matter. I enquired of medical friends and found that no known disease could account for it and that no similar case was cited in any medical or scientific book known to them.

I have never succeeded in solving the mystery or getting any light on it at all. But it can certainly serve as a parable of much that has happened in what has been called 'the self-suppression of the Scot' and the way he has sloughed off his literature, history, native languages, and much else in the past two and a half centuries. Another and equal mystery is the way in which he is today resuming them, just as if the nailless finger-ends were suddenly growing new nails. There is widespread agreement that a great Scottish National Reawakening is in progress. I'd know more about that if I could hit on any explanation of the preceding loss. As matters stand, I take it, in the Scots law phrase, to *avizandum*, i.e. defer for further consideration. And yet I am conscious of my inability to make up my mind to deal with the situation because there are no facts on which one *can* make up one's mind, and a pressing desire to seize on small clues, to build up something in order that one may do something – *anything* – knowing all the time that if one *did* do something it would probably be wrong because the basic facts are missing. Whether I am right or not in fancying that this is something that could only have happened in Scotland, I think it will be agreed that it is exceedingly unlikely ever to have happened anywhere before and highly improbable that it will ever happen again. Above all, I wonder how the hell I invented it at all. Apart from just being Scotch, of course – really Scotch.

The Angus Burghs

In 1953 Duncan Fraser of the Montrose Standard Press planned a monthly pictorial magazine and commissioned an article by MacDiarmid who replied (on 9 January 1954), 'I feel honoured that you should have thought of me nearly quarter of a century since I left Montrose. But I was very fond indeed of Montrose, and of Angus generally, and retain both happy memories of my sojourn there and the liveliest interest in all that goes on there.' Fraser's magazine never materialised but MacDiarmid's manuscript survives in the National Library of Scotland.

There is a limit to everything, and I think that in the world today much of the trouble besetting mankind comes from a loss of proper proportion between the individual human being and his, or her, setting. Few men and women are of world stature, and it might be better if the few who think they are, or are thought to be, were non-existent. We are small creatures with a brief span of life and are not meant to be seen against a world background. There is great virtue in the observation that there is nothing more universal than the local, and, as a professional poet, I have reason to know that the critic was absolutely right who declared that the more local and the more of its own time a poem is the better it is. These are, of course, sentiments that run counter to those most widely held in our modern world. Most poets, for example, think in terms of writing for eternity rather than for their neighbours. The same kind of *folie de grandeur* pervades every branch of human arts and affairs today. The politics of the Parish Pump are in disrepute; there is hardly any Tom, Dick or Harry who lacks ideas for putting the whole world to rights. It is much easier to think globally than to grapple successfully with any little local problem. I think the great majority of women show exemplary commonsense in this way

compared with men. Making a good home is of more consequence than canvassing big ideas on home-making in general.
Given a chance almost any woman can do it, but never as a
result of reading a manual on home-making. What have
observations such as these to do with my subject here, the
Angus Burghs?

Just this. The kind of local chauvinism I am expressing is
largely a product of my life in the Angus burghs, first of all in
Forfar and then, for ten years, in Montrose. In particular my
experience as a member of Montrose Town and Parish Councils reinforced in me what was probably a predisposition (since
I was born and spent my early and most formative years in a
Scottish burgh of less than 4,000 of a population) to think along
these lines. Back in 1935 I was vitally involved in the agitation
against the working of the Local Government (Scotland) Act of
1929. It seemed to me – and seems to me more than ever now –
that the opposition of the Convention of Royal Burghs to the
original bill had been completely justified by the experience
gained after four years' working of the Act. Readers will
remember that, on the administrative side, the Act swept away
Parish Councils and abolished Education Authorities, handing
their functions over to the County Councils, while, in addition,
'small burghs' – that is, burghs with a population of under
20,000 – were deprived of almost all their powers and duties,
with the exception of housing, water, drainage, lighting, and
some minor matters. Many of these burghs were and are
important places. There were 171 of them with a total population of 733,000 and a gross valuation of £6,000,000. They
include the ancient cathedral towns of Elgin and St Andrews,
pleasure resorts like Oban and Rothesay, important fishing
centres like Wick, Peterhead, and Buckie, and industrial towns
like Buckhaven and Methil, Cowdenbeath, Grangemouth, and
many others. Inverness, the Capital of the Highlands, and with
a history going back over 1000 years, only escaped inclusion by
the skin of its teeth. In return for this forfeiture of powers and
privileges the burghs of Scotland have been rewarded with
increased financial burdens, which have steadily mounted year
by year. There is today widespread recognition of the intolerable financial situation that has ensued, of the fact that so little
power has been left to Town Councils that it is hardly worth
while serving on them, and that the indirect effects – in the

217

diminution of local pride, loss of cherished traditions, sapping of initiative, trend to increasing uniformity and so forth – have been disastrous. To counter these evils, since it is useless to talk of repealing the Act of 1929 and scrapping all the elaborate machinery created under it unless there is something better to put in its place, three objects should be aimed at: (1) removal of financial inequalities, (2) revival of interest in local affairs, (3) diminution of bureaucracy and greater decentralisation. I will not expand these points. The problem of Scotland generally is one of the maldistribution of population. Far too big a proportion of it is crammed into the industrial belt. The big cities are faced with the difficulty of acquiring ground for building the thousands of new houses they need; they are proliferating over the surrounding countryside, often at the expense of good farming land we cannot afford to use, and while the creation of new towns at a reasonable remove from the parent megalopolis is the only practicable expedient in the meantime, it is, at best, a poor one, since these new towns are not organic and do not stand – and probably will never come to stand – in proper ecological balance with the locations on which they are dumped. The fourteen new towns now being built in Britain already have a population of more than 200,000. Although it is true that the original concept of the New Towns and the legislation governing them has been admired abroad, there is, nevertheless, a growing disappointment with them. Why? As a recent writer says: 'The main concept is not in question: with proper facilities – churches, halls, playing fields – the social position may yet be retrieved. What has been questioned is the 'wide and open' character of the towns and the 'prairie planning' which leave these towns with so much of the aridity, the 'spottiness' and economically impossible spaces of the old pre-war housing estates, and without either the urbanity or human warmth of the English village or market town. The charge against the New Towns is not that they are wrong in principle, not that individual buildings are bad, but that – in reaction against anarchical nineteenth century overcrowding – they sprawl, undefined, over far more acres than they can ever need, maintain, use or even want.'

Probably a few New Towns to absorb the overspill population of the bigger cities are necessary: but the fewer of these located in Scotland the better, where, so far as the bulk of the country is concerned, a far wiser policy will be to fortify with new pride and a modest degree of expansion through a wise placing of new industries the many small burghs which are the glory of Scotland and in that to be guided by (1) inculcating a thorough appreciation of their close-built urbanity (which in no way runs counter to the provision of modern conveniences of all kinds), (2) conferring on them the benefits of a greatly increased measure of local control of local affairs, and (3) seeing that they get far better social, cultural and recreational facilities than they have had in the past.

That distinguished Montrose author, Tom Douglas Mac-Donald, who writes over the pseudonym of Fionn Mac Colla, and whom I knew when he was a boy in Montrose, in an essay about twenty years ago, made a number of excellent points which require to be hammered home today. He pointed out that in Angus and Mearns are to be found together in one area, and in representative proportion, all the features which are recognized as being most characteristic and typical of Scotland as a whole. There are mountains and glens, fertile straths, a loch or two, the sea; there is the shepherd, the crofter, the large farmer, the fisherman.

It is impossible, I think, to overestimate the value of that variety in the physical setting of the Angus Burghs. But he goes on to make a related but still more important point, I think, when he says: 'It has often been remarked of the towns of Scotland that all, even those that can make the smallest claim to beauty, possess at least character. This is twice true of the burghs of Angus, which are old as well as Scottish. They have character in the sense in which the word connotes a certain quality of strength of boldness and substantiality. And they have also character in the second sense, in which it means a quality of uniqueness or difference by virtue of which each is a town by itself and in no danger of being confused with any other.'

All that would be of little enough consequence were it not for its human bearing, but it is, I hope, still true despite growing standardisation almost everywhere, that each marked difference in the physical aspect of the countryside is reflected as it were among the inhabitants, in a difference of speech, of vocabulary, idiom, intonation, in a variation of habits and customs, even sometimes in a distinctive air and bearing. It will be an infinite pity if the individual characters of the Angus burghs are ever reduced to a common form, and that is, I fear, the greatest danger, arising out of the loss of local autonomy and what I can only call the strangely compelled somnambulistic pace of Westminster Policy in regard to Scottish local issues.

I noticed in *The Scotsman*'s Log the other day a paragraph referring to the extent to which leading Scottish writers, painters, and composers were today living – not in our big cities – but in small towns. George Blake, the novelist, in Dollar; James Veitch in Peebles; Neil Gunn in Dingwall were among the examples. This is a healthy development. It represents, too, a reversal of the romantic escapism which a decade or so ago scattered our writers to the islands of the West and North – Compton Mackenzie in Barra, MacDonald in Benbecula, Macnair Reid in Eigg, Linklater in Orkney, myself in Shetland and so on. A glance at the records of literary history shows – in contradistinction to the old sneer, 'Can any good thing come from Nazareth?' – that few indeed of our writers have been born and written their books in our great cities in comparison to the number belonging to – and preferring to continue working in – our small towns. And in this connection Angus in recent times has certainly more than held its own. (It has always done so. I cannot go here into the statistics of genius in Angus in byegone centuries, though I did so a year or two ago in an essay in the short-lived periodical, *Angus Fireside*, and was able to show that once one went into the matter Angus in this respect could bear comparison well with any other part of the country.) We hear a good deal today about the 'Scottish National Awakening' and the 'new Movement in Scottish Arts and Letters'. It is not so well known perhaps that Scotland owes a very great deal to Angus in regard to this. In a very real sense in the 'Twenties Angus (and particularly Montrose) was the cultural centre of Scotland. There was something in the atmosphere and lay-out of Montrose very conducive to creative work, and most of the discussions on which these new forward-looking movements were based a little over quarter of a century ago took place there, between people like Mr and Mrs Edwin Muir, (then, like myself, living there), Mr A. S. Neill, the educational experimentalist who belongs to Kingsmuir, near Forfar, and such visitors as Mr (now Sir) Compton Mackenzie, Neil Gunn, Dr Pittendreigh Macgillivray, the sculptor and Royal Limner In

Scotland, Sir Herbert Grierson, and many others. These were indeed great times in Montrose and will live in Scottish literary history. Mrs Violet Jacob used to come from House of Dun and discuss the possibilities of Lallans with me; Neil Gunn and I had many an all-night session; the Hon. Ruaraidh Erskine of Marr was another visitor, and Miss Winifred Duke, the novelist, came frequently. One of the outstanding figures in modern Scottish Literature, James Leslie Mitchell ('Lewis Grassic Gibbon'), belonged not to Angus, but near by in the Mearns, and the life of the small towns there, Stonehaven, Bervie and the rest, meant as much to him in his literary development as Kirriemuir meant to that other great Angus writer, the late Sir J. M. Barrie.

All this disproportionate richness in creative productivity on the part of the Angus burghs in comparison with the big centres of population is no accident. It could, I think, be further developed and safeguarded, and ought certainly to engender a sense of local cultural autonomy and result in the strengthening of such things as local amateur dramatic groups, literary and debating societies, and the like. A healthy cultural life has also a direct and most valuable relationship to local well-being in all other respects. It is, in fact, a splendid investment, of consequence to all classes of the community.

I think I have made my point perhaps; certainly I must have made it clear enough why my heart turns so frequently to the Angus burghs. They are one of the great assets of Scotland, bastions of its distinctive culture, and everything possible should be done to preserve them as such and to stimulate them to fresh creativity. The periodical for which I am writing this is, indeed, addressing itself to that task. It deserves the maximum support. Nothing could be more important in the condition of 'civilisation' today. Mr T. S. Eliot, the great poet and dramatist, was right when he said: 'For this immediate future, perhaps for a long way ahead, the continuity of culture may have to be maintained by a very small number of people indeed – and these not necessarily the best equipped with worldy advantages. It will not be the large organs of opinion or the old periodicals; it must be the small and obscure papers and reviews, those which hardly are read by anyone but their own contributors, that will keep critical thought alive and encourage authors of original talent.'

In conclusion, I must remedy an omission. In writing this article I have been so concerned with recalling the very happy and productive years I spent in Angus that I have overlooked the fact that life went on after I left Montrose, but the seed had been sown and in due course came to fruition. In other words, Montrose has continued to produce artistic talents of no mean order. The late William Lamb, for example, the late Edward Baird, and, in literature, a very distinguished writer indeed whom I remember as a mere boy, Stuart Hood, and John Angus, who must have been younger still and whom I cannot recall. There are certainly few towns of like size in Scotland (or anywhere else) who can excel this record. Long may it continue.

MacDiarmid at Large

In October 1959 D. G. Bridson recorded a long conversation with MacDiarmid which was subsequently transmitted, under the title 'Aims and Opinions', on the BBC Third Programme on 4 and 9 March 1960. As broadcast the programmes allowed MacDiarmid to speak for himself as Bridson's contribution was confined to a linking commentary rather than a series of questions. The following remarks were, then, prompted by Bridson but can be read as a series of observations on subjects of special concern to MacDiarmid.

The Scots language had a great body of poetry produced in it by some of our greatest poets. Burns was regarded as Scotland's national poet but he is by no means the greatest poet Scotland had and, in fact, Mr T. S. Eliot was quite right when he said that he thought that Matthew Arnold had been responsible for promulgating the idea that Burns was a sort of forerunner of the English romantic poets, whereas the truth was that he was a degenerate representative of a great alien tradition. And, initially, my object was to try to pick up that tradition at the point where it had lapsed and re-apply it to contemporary needs and carry it forward.

There was still an adequate basis for that because the great majority of Scots people do speak to some measure or other Scots. It is largely a class question. The upper classes have been more Anglicised but the broad mass of the common people still remain Scottish in speech to a degree that the upper classes have lost.

Burns himself reverted from English and wrote his best work in Scots. He was warned by the Edinburgh Literati that in so doing he was likely to confine his reputation to a section of the population of Scotland itself and cut himself off from the great world of the reading public. Whereas if he had written in English he would have had the whole of the reading public of the English-speaking world at his command. Fortunately, Burns disregarded that advice and became probably the most international poet that the world has ever seen through the medium of Scots.

I was demobilised in 1920. When I came back to Scotland I had no knowledge of Scottish literature at all. I had a few poems of Burns – I'm a Scottish Border man – and I knew some of the ballads. And I knew how very different and very much higher in poetical value some of the Scots ballads were to the milk and water ballads produced south of the border. But I had no firm grasp of the distinctive characteristics of Scottish literature, nor any appreciation of the whole sequence of the Scottish literary tradition. So I applied myself as I would apply to learning a foreign language and a foreign literature. The language wasn't foreign to me – it was talked by my father and mother and by the people in the town I belonged to and I had that basis of spoken Scots to work on.

I naturally came to the whole job from a very different angle to that customary amongst Scottish versifiers, because all my interests for years had been not in English literature at all but in Continental literatures, – more particularly French and German literature and I was *au fait* with the latest *avant garde* developments in these literatures. So naturally not having an adequate knowledge of the language and knowing that a great portion of the vocabulary had lapsed out of use I had recourse to the place where the language was kept, that is to say to the dictionary, and I wrote my early Scots lyrics straight out of the dictionary. I think it was a very logical thing to do and they were enormously successful and still are. Naturally, there was a great brouhaha in Scotland. All the old fashioned people who liked the sentimental Kailyard stuff and so on were horrified at my very radical developments and I promulgated a whole programme of working back to a complete canon of Scots.

The idea of a Synthetic Scots was denounced on all hands by people who didn't know that Burns himself didn't write as Scots had ever been spoken or as he spoke it himself. And if we went right further back to the fifteenth century, in Gavin Douglas we had a synthesis of languages that was almost Joycean in its range. He used half the languages of Europe. And assimilated them, quite effectively, to the Scots basis in which he wrote.

Gavin Douglas was a polymath. It sometimes astonishes me when objections are taken to my own multi-linguistic experiments because Gavin Douglas was a multi-linguistic experimenter long before my time but like myself he too was drawn to emphasis the values of Scots itself and of the necessity of maintaining Scots and furthering it. I agree entirely with Ezra Pound when he says that simply because he lived near the sea, because the sound of the sea was in his ears because sea-faring was a thing that he was cognizant of, Gavin Douglas wrote better sea poetry than any English poet has ever written and certainly as a translator he stands virtually in a class by himself.

The further I've studied Scots poetry of the fifteenth and sixteenth centuries the more I have been forced to appreciate the status of Henryson. It is customary of books of literary history and so on to represent him in his great poem about Cresseid inferior to Chaucer. That is nonsense. Henryson's *Cresseid* is one of the great poems of the period and far ahead in my opinion of Chaucer's work and they are very different poets. Chaucer had enormous virtues but in that particular sense it is absurd to talk about Henryson and other Scots poets of that period as Chaucerians. They draw their impetus not from England at that time but as Scots have so often done from Continental sources direct and not via London.

Dunbar attracts me much more than Burns simply because he had a higher intellectuality and because technically he had expertise that Burns could never lay claim to, not even in 'Tam O' Shanter'. Some of the intricate rhyming and so on in Dunbar's poetry has no counterpart in the poetry of any branch of British literature until we come to Swinburne although he had the same technical expertise as Dunbar had but of course with a very different content — if Swinburne had any real content at all.

Burns himself, in so far as he can be said to have had an influence on subsequent verse writing, had a very bad influence. It was the worst elements in Burns that were imitated and it must be remembered that Burns himself was always very shaky on the language question. He was never very certain in most of his work whether he was writing in Scots or in English and as a rule, he was writing in a mixture of the two.

It is generally assumed today that there's very little difference between English people and Scottish people and when any question of Home Rule for Scotland or Scottish separation is raised, we are told it is impossible because England and Scotland are an economic unity. Now, I think there is a very profound difference between the Scots and the English and I don't think it is getting any less. R. L. Stevenson said there are no two adjacent peoples in the world who are so different as the Scots and the English, and in saying that he was only re-echoing what had been said in *The Complaynt of Scotland* in the sixteenth century when the difference between the Scots and the English was equated as between the difference of wolves and sheep! The wolves were the English and have retained that predatory attitude ever since and in fact in my submission to an increasing degree. King James IVth warned his subjects to beware of that quality of their Southern neighbours falsely called 'politeness'. I have another name for it myself – not merely hypocrisy, but a question of 'perfidious Albion' which seems to me to describe what has always been the historical role of the English – but the fact that the English seem to me to be ready to tolerate anything at all provided, by hook or crook, they can persuade themselves that they have a certain cover of legality. After all, Scotland is the oldest independent monarchy in Europe. It is the only white man's country, with the exception of Wales, that hasn't got a measure of Home Rule.

I didn't rejoin the Communist Party until the Hungarian Counter Revolution, when so many members of the Party left it on humanitarian grounds – or other grounds – and I decided the time had come when I must rejoin it. And I rejoined it then, and am now a member of the Communist Party. I regard Communism as the only guarantee of individuality in the modern world. In the Communist countries there is a regard for national minorities and so on that we don't find in the capitalist countries. In China, Soviet Union and the so called satellite countries, Rumania, Bulgaria, Czechoslovakia, the national minorities are recognised, they are not penalised in any way. Their particular languages, their particular cultures and so on, are all encouraged and developed. If the same measure, of recognition and encouragement of our national differences, had obtained under our relationship with England – then I think that would have satisfied most of us, but the contrary is the case.

In the Soviet Union, under the Stalin constitution, provision is made for a very considerable degree of autonomy on the part of the minority peoples of the Soviet Union. The extent to which that is exercised in actual practice is a debatable matter, perhaps: but after all, very little time has elapsed since the October Revolution. In terms of world history, it was an enormous event. A lot of the minority peoples concerned were illiterate – quite unused to democratic procedures – semi-oriental, many of them – and matters of that kind naturally take time. But the fact remains, in the Soviet Union and in Communist China the minority elements are encouraged. The native languages are encouraged in the Soviet Union even at the expense of great Russian itself.

The aim in the Soviet Union and in China is to encourage a diversity in unity rather than a uniformity – and that's precisely what those of us who are concerned with Scottish Nationalism have wanted for our own group of countries in the British Isles. Instead of English Ascendancy we've wanted a real synthesis of the very different contributions that the Scots, the Welsh, the Irish and the Cornish can give, and obviously if that had been obtained we'd have had a great cultural enrichment.

Even as matters stand at the present time – in literature, for example – the role of England in regard to English literature is ceasing to be of first importance; the centre of gravity has shifted. The greatest English poet of recent times was an Irishman, W. B. Yeats. Another poet who established a much greater reputation internationally than any contempory English poet was a Welshman, Dylan Thomas. Two of the most powerful literary influences that have expressed themselves in English in this century are both Americans: Ezra

Pound and T. S. Eliot. But the English in their policy, have hung on to their ascendency even at the expense of losing that possibility of cultural enrichment.

I think Mr T. S. Eliot put his finger on the matter, when he said that there were certain things, certain emotions, certain ideas that could be expressed in Scots that couldn't be expressed in English at all. After all, every language is not only a medium of expression but a determinant of what could be expressed in it. After all, the English language, which isn't a language really at all, but rather a linguistic disease, has drawn its vocabulary from practically all the languages of the world, but it is a very striking fact that it has drawn extremely little from the Scots language. That is because of the radical and unbridgeable difference between the psychology of the Scots people and the English people. The lone words from Scots in the English vocabulary are very few. We have an enormous vocabulary, expressive of psychological moods, feelings, physical sensations, even inflective that have no counterparts at all in the English vocabulary, It's on that basis that we are erecting the new Scots poetry.

I had very little use for English poetry. I agreed, for example, with my friend Ezra Pound that English poetry had been off the rails for centuries, since Chaucer, in fact. Naturally, I couldn't adopt a position like that without taking every precaution to ensure that I could justify it.

But it is a one-way traffic. No English poet has had a corresponding effect on any of the Western European countries. Sir Maurice Bowra, ex-professor of poetry at Oxford, goes even further. He says that post-romantic English poetry depends so largely on a highly specialised use of the English language that it has virtually no counterpart in any other European poetry. Along with that peculiar linguistic development, that sort of cul-de-sac of language into which English poetry has run, has been a progressive denial on the part of English poets that poetry can exercise any real power in the modern world. They say that it must be confined to a margin – it is a marginal activity – and I remember about thirty years ago a very acute critic saying that he had read a volume – an anthology – of modern English poetry without *once* feeling that he was in contact with the intellect of one of the great world powers. I don't think it could be contended by anyone that there has been any improvement in that respect on the part of subsequent English poetry.

If poetry is going to hold itself aloof, deal with what the majority of people feel are trivial themes – artificial themes, themes that don't touch the mainsprings of their lives – then they are not going to be interested. After all, the old ballad poetry was the journalism of its time. It had an enormous vogue, it was largely improvised. I think it is a great pity that we can't have more improvisation today of the poet confronting the audience directly. I think that anything that encourages the poet to meet the audience is a good thing.

In my own case, I have found even with that poetry bourgeois critics might regard as difficult – unlikely to appeal to what they call the 'common people' – that if one read it to them, made certain explanations, told them what one was trying to do, the steps one was taking to achieve certain effects and, in other words, if we took them behind the scenes and showed them how the wheels go round they weren't only capable of following the points we were making perfectly well, but they were keenly interested. And so – it's along these lines, I think, that poetry must proceed.

It won't succeed unless the common people feel a certain sincerity behind it – a real desire to grapple with these issues, to make poetry a matter of consequence again as it was in Classical times for example, as it has been in various stages in world history, and as it has so largely ceased to be for a very long time now. I am quite sure that we must have that reciprocal relation between the readers and the poet himself and without that you tend simply to isolate yourself in an ivory tower – an ivory tower that wouldn't fit in at all with the Scottish landscape although I can imagine ivory towers flourishing in certain English places like Brighton for example where they have already got a facsimile of one.

I outgrew the small lyric. I was no longer able to express my main ideas in small lyrical form. I felt it had become a sort of trick, a sort of thing I could turn out in my off moments, so that forced me back on my whole aesthetic position. And I decided that I must write in bigger forms, that I probably, at any rate for a time, couldn't continue to express myself effectively in Scots because even the revivified Scots that I had developed in my lyrics and in such a long poem as *A Drunk Man Looks at the Thistle* wasn't sufficiently malleable for the expression of the whole range of modern intellectual and artistic interests.

In changing over from the use of Scots to English, I was not abandoning my fight for a continuance of our native Scots literary tradition as opposed to the English tradition. What I was doing was – instead of writing a different kind of poetry from the English in a different language, I was now attacking English from the inside.

The argument against my Scots was that it had been virtually a foreign language. My use of English was even more foreign in many respects to the English reading public. I recognised that a very small portion of the English vocabulary was used or had ever been used by English poets, and it was on these unused elements of the English vocabulary that I proceeded to base a good deal of my work. And I also used a great deal of multi-linguistic diction. But the essence of the matter was that I was dealing with subject matter and expressing ideas that were utterly foreign to the English genius but were demonstrably in keeping with elements in our indigenous Scottish tradition.

I had to take cognizance of the fact that brain physiologists and biologists tell us that out of the infinity, almost, of brain cells that we possess, we are barely using the merest fringe – about 2% of our potentiality. And I want to see not 2% but a very much higher percentage involved. That's to say that the kind of poetry, or kind of statement in any form that I am going to be interested in, isn't one that can come from a single track mind. It must, in some measure or other, involve a knowledge of various disciplines and departments of culture and science and art and so on, and attempt to synthesise these in the interests of a fuller life. And that is precisely what I have been attempting to do in my more recent poetry.

I remember not many years ago a Theatre Workshop conference was called in the North of England of working people from heavy industry and from factories and so on to debate the question as to why more of the working class didn't go to the theatre. It was a delegate conference and speaker after speaker from the floor of the house got up and said, for example, 'I am an engineer, I am accustomed to dealing with extremely powerful machines, and I find the theatre a machine that is completely obsolete, clumsy and slow.' And another delegate would say: 'I am a silk worker from Macclesfield, I run a range of looms and I agree with the previous speaker that the whole business of the theatre as it is available to us now in this country is hopelessly out of date.' I felt precisely the same thing with regard to poetry.

In this country and in other Western European countries, folk poetry occupies a very low level and has done for a century or two. It didn't use to do, and I question, in the long run, if our development of great artistic poetry is going to prove a good thing – is going to prove an adequate *compensation* for the loss of that touch with the common people, which was held all over Europe in the inter-traffic of the ballad traditions and the folk song traditions of the different countries.

We are moving towards a world poetry today, the world is ours and we can open our hearts and minds to take it in, and in attempting to do that I don't think we can ignore the best of Whitman, or belittle in any way what his intentions were – if not his actual achievements. At the time he wrote, he realised and said that poetry of an inclusiveness and range suitable for the masses in the modern world had not yet been attempted anywhere. He himself didn't precisely attempt that. But it remains the task to which I think poets ought to devote themselves, [and they] can learn a great deal from Whitman. The common picture of Whitman that is transmitted in our own British literary criticism and so on, the idea that his work is pretty well confined to a barbaric yawp is completely out of date. Many elements of his work were undoubtedly, from any point of view, amongst the greatest poetry that has been written anywhere in the world.

My reading has kept pace with the general world developments. Science is occupying more and more attention through the world. It is changing the conditions of life to a tremendous extent. There is an unprecedented acceleration of change, and there is every likelihood, I think, that that is going to continue. I remember T. S. Eliot saying that the invention of the internal combustion engine had changed the rhythm of poetry. I agree with him in that respect: I think it has done. I don't think we can go back again to the kind of rhythms and so on that dictated poetry in previous periods.

I have had a very varied life myself. I have been an engineer. I have been a seaman. I was a soldier for years. I have been a journalist, meeting life at all sorts of levels as local journalists do do. And I have had a tremendously wide acquaintance with the Scottish people. I have lived in practically every part of Scotland, and I have been interested in the industries, I have taken the trouble to go to factories and engineering works and talk to the men on the job. And the same thing is true of agriculture. My first book was written for the Fabian Society and dealt with the conditions of agriculture and the need for reform in certain directions.

My reason for writing my later poetry in English now is simply that the revived Scots that I wrote my earlier work in is not sufficiently flexible yet – it will take a generation or two of people writing Scots, following the line that I struck out on, before we can make Scots available again for scientific purposes. After all, Scots ceased to be used before the advent of the scientific age, before the advent of the Industrial Revolution and we have an enormous leeway to make up. I think the resources of Scots are adequate to the purpose: I think we can apply them. But it is not a job that can be done by one man or perhaps even in one lifetime. It may take several generations of intensive work along that line.

Scottish Independence

This speech was deliverd by MacDiarmid at a 1320 Club Symposium at Glasgow University on 6 April 1968.

Mr Chairman, Ladies and Gentlemen,

I think I would have had considerable hesitation in rising to move this motion if the wording hadn't fortunately been altered at the last moment. It read originally, 'A debate on the motion that this house is in favour of devolution which would mean creating some form of parliament in Scotland.' Now, I would have hesitated to move that, and the motion now reads, 'This house is in favour of self-government for Scotland.' I couldn't imagine that it would be easy to find any intelligent Scot, man or woman, who would have moved an amendment to the motion as originally framed, but in the upshot, we didn't find anybody, and after discussing the matter, we agreed to dispense with any mover of the amendment and simply throw the matter open for general debate after I've finished speaking. It would have been a novelty in any case to hear any intelligent person, any presumably intelligent person, putting a case against independence. It's contrary to nature. Most of the world's peoples belong to independent nations, and I know of none of them clamouring to give up that independence. Most of them indeed literally fought to retain it, or, where it has been temporarily lost, recover it. So far as I am concerned the spirit that animates me is that expressed in the passage from the Declaration of Arbroath which reads, 'For so long as one hundred men of us remain alive, we shall never under any conditions submit to the domination of the English. It is not for glory or riches or honours that we fight, but only for liberty, which no good man will consent to lose but with his life.' Earlier on today we had some very subtle arguments as to the lets and hindrances if Scotland recovered a measure of self government, from economists. Last night for about eighty minutes on television another team, including Dr McCrone though, debated the same matter. I don't intend to go into these questions at all. The words in the quotation I have just given you from the Declaration of Arbroath, that we fight not for riches, covers all that. I am not interested in economics. I believe, and my whole nationalist position is grounded in the belief, that where there's a will there's a way, and if we are sufficiently intent on having independence, nothing will stand in our way. We are quite prepared to meet all the sacrifices, if any, that are required. However, it is particularly urgent I think at this juncture – one of the great problems of the modern world is the search for identity – to remember just who we Scots are, and what part we've played in the world. We are too apt to be dismissed by the believers in big units as a small people of no particular consequence in relation to the major problems of modern times; but I think the historian, James Anthony Froude, was right when he said that no small people in the history of the world had so profoundly affected the whole of mankind as the Scots people had done. The debate centres largely in the first instance upon whether there is a real, continuing, irrevocable difference between the Scots and the English. I think the quickest way to arrive at the conclusion of that matter, is perhaps to look through the *Dictionary of National Biography*. We find Scot after Scot holding positions in Civil Service and other government appointments in India and Ceylon, who took an active interest in the culture of the peoples amongst whom he was located, who studied their languages, who wrote books about their arts and so on. If you look at the corresponding number of Englishmen who held similar posts in the same countries, you'll find they contributed nothing, they weren't interested in the cultures of these countries and, in fact, after a very long period of the British Raj in India, what have they to their credit? Two things, two great accomplishments, stand to the immortal glory of the British Empire: pig sticking and cocktails. Now that sums it up pretty well. A recent writer has put the matter in a nut shell when he says, 'A great Scottish idea, the one that Scotland gave to the world out of the agonies of the wars of Independence, is freedom, the 'noble thing' of

Barbour's famous outburst in 'The Bruce'. This is the *sine qua non* of existence, whether of nations or persons, and the tragic irony of Scotland is that she, who gave birth to the idea of national independence and integrity, owing allegiance to no country and no people but itself, should almost alone of European nations, have betrayed and lost this freedom, freedom to create new forms of society and art. Truly such a Scotland is not Scotland, it is only a corpse, breeding and spreading corruption.' He goes on to quote from a poem of mine, a few lines which read as follows:

These denationalised Scots have killed the soul
Which is universally human; they are men without souls;
All the more heavily the judgement falls upon them,
Since it is a universal law of life they have sinned against.

There surely is the answer to the particular kind of treachery found in those Anglo-Scots intellectuals who bleat of a false antithesis, internationalism, not nationalism, as if it were possible to have the one without the other. They sin against the universal law of life which invests life in individuals not conglomerations. Yes, even in the ant hill. In the place of living separate identities, having mostly their differences in common, these ghouls would reduce all to a horrible international, characterless, abstract fog, a devitalised nonentity, but their internationalism in fact equals 'English', and behind the pseudo-internationalism of the Anglo-Scots lurks the face of 'The Auld Enemy', English imperialism. The greatest Scots have always deplored the union with England. The common people had no say in the matter, but they protested violently against it. But the greatest Scots, Burns, for example: 'Alas,' he wrote in one of his letters, 'I have often said to myself, what are all the boasted advantages which my country reaps from the union that can counterbalance the annihilation of her independence and even her very name?' The question is put in a way that implies that the answer must be that there are no such advantages. I have put the same question to myself insistently for nearly half a century, and I have been unable to discover any merit in the connection with England whatsoever. Sir Walter Scott summed up the intolerable character of our relationship with England when he said: 'There has been in England a gradual and progressive system of assuming the management

235

of affairs entirely and exclusively proper to Scotland as if we were totally unworthy of having the management of our own affairs.' I could multiply quotations like these from a host of great Scots, but for my present purpose content myself with observing that there has been lately a remarkable convergence of opinion from the most diverse quarters to the same effect; some of them are quite unexpectable. Lord Reith, for example, in his inaugural address as Lord Rector of this university, stressed the urgent need to preserve and develop Scotland's distinctive traditions and characteristics for the benefit not only of Scotland, but of the world. A few days later, Dr Harry Whitley of St Giles in Edinburgh, spoke to the same effect, and no less a person than the Earl of Dalkeith warned the Government that Scotland was becoming ripe for U.D.I. Is it? It would be astonishing if it were, the denationalising anglicising process of centuries is not so quickly and easily reversed. I am not greatly impressed, though I welcome it as a step in the right direction, by the upsurge of the Scottish National Party and the fact that that party is now the biggest in Scotland with a hundred thousand paid-up members. The best thing about it is that it has now attracted such a huge proportion of our young people; but what do these young people know of Scotland? They have not been put in possession of their natural national heritage. In their schools and colleges, our native Scottish languages, our Scottish literature, even our history, are inadequately taught if at all, and a virtual monopoly is given over instead to the English counterparts of these subjects.

When I was demobbed in 1920, after being abroad for four or five years, in the interests of the rights of small nations, and poor little Belgium and all that, I found I didn't know anything about Scotland. I applied myself to learn. Travelling since in recent years, in most other European countries, talking to university students, I found that most of them didn't realise that Scotland was a separate country, with history, traditions and achievements of its own quite different from those of its southern neighbour. English propaganda had ensured that, by using the adjective English as if it were synonomous with British. The fact that Scotland has a very different and distinctive identity was lost sight of, but that is being overcome at last. Burns and the Edinburgh *literati* were at odds on the subject. The Edinburgh *literati* told Burns that if he persisted wrongheadedly in writing in Scots, he would limit his public to a small fraction of the Scottish reading public, whereas, if he wrote in English, he would have the whole English reading public at his disposal. It didn't turn out that way; there has never been in the history of literature a poet who has achieved such an enormous international reputation as Burns, and even the international song of human amity is couched in the uncouth Scots language. Not in English. The English can't even pronounce 'Syne' properly, they give it a 'Z'. In the last week or two, I have had sent me periodicals in Danish, German, Magyar and Russian, all with articles on contemporary Scottish literature and translations of poems of mine and other contemporary Scottish poets. So that centuries-long position in relation to Scotland is being altered fundamentally. Scotland is emerging again, culturally at any rate, into the modern world as a separate entity with something of its own to say, some contribution to make to the common pool of culture that no other people can make. Certainly not England. If Scotland recovers its own voice fully, that voice will speak in a way that no English voice could ever speak. The sudden upsurge of National Party membership may strike people as wonderful, but far more significant is the fact that after centuries of subordination to England, Scottish literature is at last being taught in an increasing number of Scottish schools, and there are now courses in it in most of our universities. Only a few years ago the Scottish Department of Education ruled that pupils deviating into Scots in the classrooms should not be punished but encouraged. That rule could not be implemented, however, simply because most of the teachers themselves were Anglo-Scots, Scots with no knowledge of the Scots tongue, and none of our independent Scottish literary tradition, which, they said, they could not teach because they had never learned how to evaluate it. That change is more significant than the mere party political quibbling about what seem to be important issues. It is the cultural questions, the language and literary questions, that have been the decisive factor in the national regeneration movements of many European countries, and it will not be otherwise with Scotland. No nation was ever restored to its proper dignity owing to a demand for merely practical measures, better wages, better conditions of employment, better transport, and all the rest of it. These are vitally important, but they are subsidiary and first things must be put first. It is because too many people in the National Party have no concern with the things of fundamental importance, with the great spiritual issues underlying the mere statistics of trade and industry, with the ends to which all other things should merely be means, that I don't feel the destiny of Scotland lies with it. At present they are anxious above all not to go too far, they deprecate anglophobia, many do not envisage armed action. Well, no one in his senses wants warfare, but if we are determined to be absolutely independent, it may be, and almost certainly will be forced upon us. I do not believe the English have learned anything from the Irish affair and I believe that they will be more determined to hang on to Scotland than ever, by fair means or preferably foul, since their world rule has diminished so greatly. In any case, even if it doesn't come to that, we'll have violence anyway in Scotland. Scotland never fought while it was independent any aggressive war but, since the Union, it has been dragged at the heels of England into scores of wars, none of which was of any value to Scotland itself. We have a great deal of violence in Scotland today; I could only wish that it were possible that it could be channelled in better directions.

What is the difference between the Scots and the English, how important is it? Robert Louis Stevenson declared that there were no two adjacent peoples of the world so utterly and irrevocably different as the Scots and the English. In this he was re-echoing what was expressed away back in 1549 in *The Complaynt of Scotland*, which reads: 'In the days of Moses, the Jews dared not have familiarity with the Samaritans, nor with the Philistines, nor the Romans with the Africans, nor the Greeks with the Persians, by reason that each regarded the other as barbarous. For every nation regards another nation as barbarous when their two natures and complexions are contrary to theirs, and there are not two nations under the firmament that are more contrary and different from each other than Englishmen and Scotsmen, howbeit they be within one island, and neighbours, and of one language. For Englishmen are subtle and Scotsmen are facile, Englishmen are ambitious in prosperity and Scotsmen are humane in prosperity, Englishmen are humble when they are subdued by force and violence, and Scotsmen are furious when they are violently subdued.

Englishmen are cruel when they get victory, and Scotsmen are merciful when they get victory. And to conclude, it is impossible that Scotsmen and Englishmen can remain in concord under one government because their natures and conditions are as different as is the nature of sheep and wolves.'

A few words on my own position which puzzles a lot of people in Scotland. This is from an article by Professor David Daiches and he says:

What have the consequences of the union of 1707 proved to be, what has Scotland become, culturally, nationally, psychologically? Is there a viable Scottish identity available to nourish the artist and to provide a vantage point from which to look out on the world? How is Scotland's past related to her present and to her future and what sort of Scottish future do we want anyway? If Scotsmen of imagination and intelligence have been asking these questions and other questions of the same kind more and more fiercely throughout the last forty years, Hugh Mac-Diarmid must take a considerable share of the responsibility. His work for a Scottish renaissance was not simply a literary endeavour, it was bound up with questions of Scottish identity which had for the most part been slumbering for nearly two centuries when he came upon the scene, and not only with questions of Scottish identity but the question of the quality of modern industrial democratic society which prevails over the whole western world is also involved. The anglicisation of Scotland is part of the general *gleichschaltung** of all western culture and an investigation of its nature and causes is therefore bound up with social and political and economic ideas. Arguments about the use of Lallans or the relative merits of Burns and Dunbar or the place of Gaelic in Scottish culture could not therefore, in the context of any adequately conceived Scottish renaissance movement, be merely arguments about a literary trend or skirmishes preliminary to the emergence of something parallel to the pre-Raphaelite movement or the publishing of the Yellow Book. They were in the last resort not only about the meaning of culture, of nationality, or history, they were, to put it quite simply, about the meaning of life. And that is what Hugh MacDiarmid's poems are about. He could have settled for less. He could have stayed at the head of the Scottish literary revival and become a respected Allan Ramsay type of figure writing introductions to Saltire editions of older Scottish writers and blessing the Lallans-writing young. And indeed, he has played some of the parts played by Ramsay but his driving vision of the fulfilled man in the fulfilled society, a vision which is as much responsible for his choice of language, his kind of imagery and the course of his poetic career from lyricist to discursive epic encyclopaedist as it is for his ever shifting synthesis between nationalism and communism, wouldn't leave him alone. It puzzles, distracts and annoys many of his greatest admirers. When he

* Amalgamation (German).

wrote those early Scots lyrics, he was expected to continue in that vein, he didn't, he turned to English, and to make matters worse turned after a while to a special kind of Whitmanesque, up to a point catalogue poetry, whose essential principle of order escaped most critics. There is, it should at once be added, an essential principle of order in these long encyclopaedic poems that is related to MacDiarmid's vision of reality both human and natural rather than to his kind of Scottish nationalism or his role as a Scottish nationalist poet. A major concern of his has long been the search for what Hopkins following Duns Scotus called 'Haeccietas'. This diverseness and individuating reality of things call for a special kind of human response; nationalism for him is only superficially a political programme, at bottom its object is to provide a means of responding properly to experience.

The three great institutions of Scotland safeguarded under the Treaty of Union – although every safeguarding clause in that treaty, of course, has been violated by the English long ago – the three great institutions which were the bulwarks of the independent Scottish tradition were our educational system, our legal system, and our kirk. Lord Snow, C. P. Snow the novelist, summed up the issue so far as education goes when he wrote, 'For over two hundred years, from the end of the sixteenth century to the beginning of the nineteenth, there were four universities in Scotland and two in England. Further, the content and intention of Scottish University education differed deeply from that of the English. Scottish education was much more like European, or the university education of growing up in eighteenth-century New England.' C. P. Snow is referring to a book by Dr George Davie, *The Democratic Intellect*, I think the most important book on any Scottish subject published in my lifetime. And he says, 'This admirable book by Dr Davie is an account of how in the nineteenth century, the Scottish Universities were persuaded, coerced, bullied, and argued into something like English pastiche. Not that this process was straightforward, it is still not quite complete. Scottish education has taken a long time to become undermined and the universities preserved vestiges of an intellectual system and policy radically dissimilar from the English. At its core, the English policy is (*a*) to allow very few students into universities at all; (*b*) to subject those few to courses of intense specialisation. The Scottish policy, in this respect, like the American or Russian policy, or in fact the policy of all advanced countries except England' (note that phrase) 'is (*a*) to regard university education as the normal thing for a high proportion of students, and (*b*) to provide courses of considerable generality. Dr Davie thoroughly believes that (*a*) and (*b*) are linked, that is, if you really believe as a matter of social faith, as Scots, Russians and Americans do, that university education should be a democratic affair, then the education itself will inevitably become wider. If you believe as the English do, alone in the world, that university education ought to be restricted, then inevitably, equally inevitably, the disciplines of study will become narrower and more professionalised.' I stress these two phrases, 'all advanced countries except England' and 'the English alone in the world'. Why then should Scotland ever have been linked with a country so utterly at odds with every other so-called civilised country in the world? No one who has really studied the relationship of England and Scotland can be unaware that hatred and contempt of anything Scottish has been and is still being expressed in England to a far greater extent than hatred of England has ever been expressed in Scotland. One has only to go through the parliamentary speeches recorded in *Hansard* to find that hatred and contempt and ignorance of everything Scottish are expressed time and time again, and there's an unceasing attempt to assimilate everything Scottish to English standards. I point out, in addition to the names I mentioned earlier, Lord Reith, Dr Whitley and others, who have been expressing themselves during this crisis in our affairs, in very similar terms. The two greatest working-class leaders that Scotland has ever thrown up are of the same opinion. Keir Hardie said that if the Scottish Labour MPs in Westminster had only stayed in Scotland, and re-established a parliament in Edinburgh, it would have done more for socialism and more for Scotland, than they could ever achieve at Westminster. The greatest revolutionary working-class leader that Scotland has ever had, John MacLean, went even further. The year before his death in 1923, standing in the Gorbals division of Glasgow, he said, 'I stand as a Scottish Republican.' That's how I stand too, and that's the measure of the devolution that I'm concerned about. I want complete independence, I don't believe in the difficulties that are alleged to exist in the way. I want a Scottish working class republic, based on our ancient traditions, because the difference in democracy in Scotland and England is fundamental and dates back to our Gaelic basis, to the old clan system; we never had the segregations, snobberies, class distinctions that the feudal system gave the English. I'm not an authority on this subject, the subject I'm going to mention (although as you know, I'm an authority on almost everthing else), but I'm not an authority on religion. On the dastardly attempt to undermine the Church of Scotland and assimilate it to Anglicanism I would refer to Professor Ian Henderson's book, *Power and Glory*, in which he sees the attempt to fit the kirk out with Bishops to suit the requirements of Lambeth not as a movement of Holy Spirit, but as a product of historical, geographical, political, sociological and neurotic elements in the relation between England and Scotland. 'Whatever the motives of Anglican imperialism', he says, 'there is no doubt as to its nature. There are two million communicants in the Church of England, in Scotland there are fifty-six thousand and in the United States of America, two million, one hundred and seventy-four thousand, two hundred and two. On the Continent of Europe, the number of Anglicans is as near nil as makes no odds. In all these countries, the Protestant churches are to submit to a complete reconstruction of their power structure, and the extinction of their present ministry, and its replacement by Anglican ordained clergy in order to conform to the preferences of two million Englishmen. This is one of the grossest manifestations of twentieth-century racialism.' But it's in keeping with what we've been accustomed to see England manifesting in all connections during all the time that we've been connected with it. I haven't referred to the great problems of Scotland. The unparalleled drain of emigration from our midst, the dereliction and depopulation of vast areas of our country, our unemployment problem always nearly 50% greater than in the worst hit areas of our southern neighbour. Our tremendous housing problem, the fact that we've got the worst slums in Europe; and alongside these great questions, the questions that do arise from our present parliamentary connections, the way in which the parliamentary time-table is overcrowded, and the ridiculously small amount of time allocated to Scottish issues of all kinds, and even then evoking the impatience of the English members. I haven't referred to legislation by appendix, or to the fact that Scotland under the present system is obliged to suffer squeeze and freeze like England although the balance of payments problem is purely an English one. Scotland doesn't suffer from it at all. No I believe that all these problems and all similar problems can be solved if we get our independence. The Scots people are not inferior in intelligence, in ability, to any people in the world, and if they address themselves to their own affairs, they will speedily find solutions if solutions can be found. The eyes of the fool are on the ends of the earth, and for far too long, the eyes of Scots have been directed away from their own affairs, but they're no use to Scotland, and they certainly can't make any contribution to international culture if they don't first of all put their own house in order, tackle the things that are nearest to the hand, and tackle them with all their might. Those of you who saw the TV programme on Scottish affairs last night will agree that the audience there were emphatically of the opinion that I am about to express. I don't think it is necessary now to argue this question of devolution for Scotland. We are going to have it, and we're going to have it very soon, and we can safely reconcile all our religious and other divergences on the basis of one of the profoundest statements in the Bible, one of the profoundest injunctions in the Bible: 'Be ye not unequally yoked together.' We'll choose our own equals, our own peers. At large, we've been internationalists to a far greater extent than the English ever were, we've never had any imperialist longings, our moral position is infinitely stronger than the position of England in any connection has been for centuries past, and it's on that basis that I suggest to you that we don't allow ourselves to be fobbed off with any talk about the problems and difficulties that varying degrees of devolution would present us with. We don't require to bother about that. We're going for devolution right to the end, that's to say for complete independence and we rest our case on the virtue of our own personality and the strength of our own determination.

Thank you.

Satori in Scotland

An essay contributed to Karl Miller's symposium Memoirs of a Modern Scotland *(1970).*

Most of my early lyrics were published in a little book on the title-page of which I had the foresight to put: *Habent sua fata libelli.* That anticipation has proved more than justified over the 40 years since the lyrics were first published. In a few quarters they were recognised immediately to be of exceptional quality: these included the *Times Literary Supplement*, the *Glasgow Herald* and the *Manchester Guardian*. But they were rare in their appreciation. In Scotland itself I was subjected almost everywhere to ridicule and abuse. Just as the Edinburgh *literati* of the time advised Burns that if he continued to write in Scots, he would confine his readership to a fraction of the Scottish reading public, whereas if he wrote in English he would be available to one that was world-wide, so I was counselled that writing in Scots was foredoomed to failure. Not only that, but I was not even writing in the relatively simple Scots Burns wrote in, but in a far denser linguistic medium. This medium (so it was thought) had been made by taking elements from the different dialects into which Scots had disintegrated, together with obsolete words from the fifteenth- and sixteenth-century Makars, which were no longer understood except by a few scholars. Despite the Edinburgh *literati*, however, Burns achieved a fame unique in literary history. And for my own part, condemned at home and regarded in England as of no account, I was speedily recognised abroad.

Now I may be as over-praised as I was then under-rated. Professor David Daiches, for example, can write: 'Dunbar, Burns and MacDiarmid are the great Scottish trio. Let pedants wrangle over which of these deserves the precedence; there can be little doubt that MacDiarmid is the greatest miracle.' Similar statements have been made in various countries during the last few years, and it was a distinguished Frenchman, Professor Denis Saurat, who early on set the ball rolling: '*Il faut que MacDiarmid prenne la place de Burns. Je ne veux pas dire qu'il est un nouveau Burns. Ce serait une calamité.*' Scottish readers, however, did not want anything new, and above all they did not want Burns supplanted. It had long been generally agreed that the independent Scottish tradition was finished; it had culminated in Burns, who was the be-all and end-all of Scottish poetry. And I was warned of the dire fate in store for me if I tried to oust Burns from that position, or tried to write poems that were not imitative of his. A Moderator of the Church of Scotland denounced my work as not poetry at all, as containing much that could never have emanated from the sane and was reminiscent of nothing so much as Homer without his false teeth. In a recent essay the poet Sydney Goodsir Smith deals with what he calls 'the anti-Scottish lobby in Scottish letters'. He traces the opposition to complete cultural absorption into the British (i.e. English) totality which was shown by Burns and myself and a few others – with, as one commentator put it, 'a mad Japanese courage' – from 1771 to the present day [1970]. One of the defeatists was Edwin Muir in *Scott and Scotland* (1936), though he had spoken previously of my lyrics in terms of the highest praise. Of 'Country Life', he had written: 'It is an almost fantastic economy, a crazy economy, which has the effect of humour and yet conveys a kind of horror, which makes this poem so original and so truly Scottish.'

Habent sua fata libelli. What a complete somersault of opinion these short lyrics of eight or twelve lines have effected. And the revaluation isn't over yet. Sir Compton Mackenzie thought they could bring about the regeneration of Scotland and lead to the regaining of our sovereign independence. Mr Anthony Burgess has said of me: 'Through him that nation becomes articulate again, and great rhetoric serves an end that many Sassenachs hope will be attained. I mean the liberation of Scotland, not necessarily under a Jacobite Royal, but quite possibly under a Jacobin President, who is the greatest poet at present living in these islands.'

What gave this little collection of lyrics this incredible power?

How did I come to write them? I can shed little light on the matter. They just happened. If I am asked when I think I got my first idea about Scotland, I can only reply that I don't think I was ever unaware of it. As Border man, living on the frontier, I was always acutely conscious of the difference between the Scots and the English and I had from the start a certain anti-English feeling. But the first time I applied myself to understand the position and acquire a definite idea of Scotland was after I was demobbed in 1920. That was natural enough. After all, we were fighting a war that was ostensibly for the rights of small nations, poor little Belgium and so on, and when I came back I discovered to my horror that I didn't know anything about Scotland and had never been taught anything about Scots literature. At school we were punished if we lapsed into Scots. 'Standard English' was the rule: a linguistic fiction which doesn't exist in England itself, where there are more dialects than in Scotland – dialects, moreover, which are determined by social status, a state of affairs not found in any other country. Yet most of the people in my home town spoke Scots – my own parents certainly did. So Scots was really my native language. Apart from one or two of the more hackneyed love songs of Burns and the like, however, we got nothing at all at school about Scottish literature and very little about Scottish history.

I am generally credited with having been instrumental in changing all that. A few years ago the Scottish Education Department decreed that dialect (as they called Scots) was to be encouraged in the classrooms. This policy it was found impossible to implement, save in isolated cases, because the majority of the teachers themselves were hopelessly over-Anglicised and didn't know it. Nor could they teach Scottish literature because they themselves had never been taught how to judge it. More recently, however, courses in Scottish literature have been established in most of our universities as part of both the ordinary MA and Honours curricula, and an increasing number of students are now graduating in the subject: my *Drunk Man* has been used as a textbook in these classes. Glasgow Education Authority decreed not long ago that Scottish literature must now be taught in all the city's primary and secondary schools. This is surely a remarkable reversal of policy after two and a half centuries during which English literature and language were given a virtual monopoly. And this reversal can be seen as a sign of the times, now that the remarkable upsurge in membership of the Scottish National Party has made it the largest political party in Scotland and a serious challenge to the three older ones.

I have called this article '*Satori* in Scotland' because *satori* is 'an illumination, a sudden awakening'. Mine was quite unheralded. I had never had any intention of writing poetry in Scots, though I had never had much liking for any English poetry and even in my final years as a schoolboy was quoting Rimbaud, Verlaine, Verhaeren, Richard Dehmel, Else Lasker-Schüler and Renée Vivien in my essays. I have never had much to do with English writers either, but I received great encouragement in the early days, when I needed it most, from Irish writers like Yeats, A. E., Gogarty, Shaw and, above all, Sean O'Casey. Of all the writers I have known personally, O'Casey was in many ways the closest to me.

The Vernacular Circle of the London Burns Club was agitating for the preservation of Scots, but I knew they conceived it only as a medium for the continuance of post-Burnsian doggerel, banality, jocosity and mawkish sentimentality. All of which I hated like hell. I could think of no other literature which had plunged into such an abyss of witless rubbish as had Scots poetry after the great achievements in the fifteenth and sixteenth centuries of poets like Dunbar, Henryson and Gavin Douglas. The Burns cult appeared to be largely to blame, so I opposed the Burns Club's proposals. And then I suddenly wondered if I was being quite fair. It might all depend on the angle from which one approached the question of exploring the expressive potentialities of Scots as a medium for the whole range of modern literary purpose. The language had disintegrated into dialects, but perhaps these could be more or less arbitrarily combined and so provide a basis from which it might be possible to work towards reconstituting a full canon for the language.

So I went to where the words were – to Jamieson's *Dictionary*. My early poems were written straight from that source. They came to me very rapidly, and were generally completed in my head while I was going about my day's work as a journalist, and then written down when I got home at night. As Leon Vivante says, in poetry 'the words find by themselves a thousand

247

avenues, the deepest and truest conceptual affinities; they reconnect forgotten kinships'. This is precisely what happened in my case.

The creation of these lyrics – the whole business of my turning to Scots – was an accident, if you like; it was certainly a phenomenon akin to religious conversion. I just suddenly felt as a Scot what J. S. Machar confesses in his 'Tractate of Patriotism': 'My Czechdom is the portion of my life which I feel, not as delight and bliss, but as a solemn and inborn fealty. My native land is within me alone ... ' And the experience I underwent is exactly described by Ford Madox Hueffer:

> What is the love of one's land? ...
> It is something that sleeps
> For a year – for a day –
> For a month – something that keeps
> Very hidden and quiet and still
> And then takes
> The quiet heart like a wave
> The quiet brain like a spell
> The quiet will
> Like a tornado: and that shakes
> The whole of the soul.

My so-called disciples have seldom got beyond mere dictionary-dredging to achieve the illumination which I have called *satori*. Almost all our contemporary poets in Scotland have developed two rather intractable defects or diseases, and everything as far as the future of Scots poetry is concerned depends on these being cured. The first is a sort of osmotic reluctance, on the part of their mental perceptions, to step through the cilia of what *seems* to be, and reach the vital stream of what actually is. The second is the lack of correspondence, or the essential incongruity, between the words they try to use and the way their minds work, so that their verse is afflicted by a species of *aniseikonia*: a word derived from Greek words meaning 'unequal imagery' and usually applied to the distressing consequences which sometimes result from the fact that images carried to the brain by the two eyes can be quite different both in size and shape. This defect, amongst other things, prevents some people, even of fair intelligence, from comprehending what they read. Even those writers who have a good knowledge of Lallans are divided between it and the English to which they are so hopelessly over-conditioned. As with the difference between the right-eye and the left-eye images, such writers – and readers – in passing from Scots to English, and from English to Scots, have a violent struggle to equate the two things. It must be admitted that all of these readers and writers can only be described as hard-of-thinking – which is the main problem confronting our movement.

Scots – or Lallans, as Burns called it – has a positive advantage simply through being so long disused, or unfamiliar in print: the eye does not run over it so easily but is arrested every now and again and compelled to debate the significance of this or that word. While men like Professor H. J. C. Grierson and John Buchan found it astonishing that 'the speech of simple peasants' could be used successfully as a medium for meta-physical speculation, this was simply because Scots had been so long neglected for the purposes of high poetry, and because they thought of it as just a rustic dialect, instead of a language in the fullest sense of the term (*in posse* if not *in esse*), as I did. The late Sir Alexander Gray was an exemplar of a point of view diametrically opposed to my own in this matter. He was particular about dialect demarcations and believed that if Scots was to be used as a literary medium, this must be done with the authentic usage, limited vocabulary and typical ideas (or lack of ideas) of the sort of people who actually spoke it. Edwin Muir denounced the attempt to write in Scots, declaring that the people who did so thought in English, and that there was thus a fatal division between their mentality and their mode of expression. An even worse disease than *aniseikonia*, no doubt. He instanced the passage of *Tam o' Shanter* which begins, 'But pleasures are like poppies spread . . . ' as representing the case of a Scottish poet, with thoughts that were incapable of expression in Scots, finding it necessary to deviate into English. Muir failed to realise that my own tendency was in precisely the opposite direction – to deepen into quite untranslatable Scots rather than, like Burns, to modulate into English.

Metaphysics and Poetry

*On 29 September 1974 Walter Perrie visited MacDiarmid at Browns-
bank and recorded the following conversation (an abbreviated version of
which was published by Perrie in 1975).*

WP: What would you like to begin with, literature or
      philosophy?

CMG: Whichever you like. I don't draw any line between
      them.

WP: I think of your general philosophical position as
      monist and vitalist. Can you generalise the relation
      between your poetry and your philosophical ideas?

CMG: That's an impossible question because there's no such
      thing as poetry. There are many different kinds of
      poetry. In respect of one kind one might emphasise the
      monism but in others take a different angle of
      approach. I refuse to be screwed down to one par-
      ticular philosophical position.

WP: So the emphasis varies to fit the poem.

CMG: Yes. But the variation of course arises from my own
      personality. I refuse to be labelled as one thing or
      another. As you know, I'm a member of the Commun-
      ist Party and an important thing for me about the
      British Communisty Party was that when the execu-
      tive sent me a congratulatory message on my eightieth
      birthday, it read: 'Mr Grieve has not always agreed
      with us, nor we with him. Nor would we wish it
      otherwise', and that's very important from my point of
      view. It was a very honest declaration.

WP: Do you regard reality as a fundamentally spiritual
      entity, or are you at heart an empiricist?

250

CMG: I see it as a spiritual thing, insofar as reality is conceivable by the human mind. It's possible, of course, to think or to imagine that only a very small portion of reality is accessible to the human mind: which is why I am a materialist and an atheist.

       An interesting point was raised recently about my philosophical position. I find a lot of people who think they are Christians very anxious to call me a Christian poet, perhaps because I use a certain number of references to Christian dogma, because I may show a compassionate spirit in certain connections. Professor MacKinnon who holds the chair of Divinity at Cambridge recently published a little book summarising what he had said in the Gifford Lectures at the University of Edinburgh. He called it *The Problem of Metaphysics*. In it he devotes an entire chapter to one of my poems, and he points out the assurance of atheism which permeates that particular poem, and deprecates the tendency of many Christian apologists to say – 'He really is a Christian poet without knowing it.' He points out that the poem with which he deals confutes that idea entirely. One must remember that both theism and atheism are ontologically based. If you're an assured atheist, there's no reason on earth why you should not create great poetry. As a matter of fact, study of literary history shows that far more of what we call the body of great poetry in Europe has been written by materialists than by believers, and that what is called religious poetry in any of the European literatures is drived largely from non-Christian and, indeed, anti-Christian sources. Not only that, but in British poetry, English poetry if you care to call it, whenever in recent times there's been a recession to Christian belief, the poets who have experienced that recession have lost their creative power: Wordsworth, Auden and so on. Others again, like Yeats, had to flee from it into esoteric religious substitutes – I think that's inevitable.

WP: Do you think then that all good poets are essentially pagans?

CMG: Yes, of course they are.

WP: Difficult to see in a case like Dante's.

CMG: Yes, I agree about that – and there are exceptions in Eastern literature – but then we're talking about Buddhism rather than Christianity.

WP: You perhaps know the essay by John Crowe Ransome on the ontological status of poetry. Is your poetry somehow dependent on the sort of ontology which you specify?

CMG: I should say that it's entirely dependent on the ontology which the poet adopts or expresses. That's one reason why poetry is one of the rarest things in the world. There are all kinds of versifiers but extremely few poets – and it's also one of the reasons why I'm opposed to a great deal of contemporary versifying. Although there is currently an upsurge of popular poetry, it's not poetry. It's not poetry at all. It's anti-poetry, characterised by one or two main qualities or characteristics: emotion without intellect, fancy without imagination, and a tendency to bring the whole thing down to the level of entertainment. I am opposed to all these tendencies.

WP: What role does contradiction play in your thought? It is often said that you present frequent contradictions.

CMG: Like Whitman I would say 'I contradict myself? Very well, I contradict myself.' The variety and the enormity of the world and the infinite possibilities of the human mind are such that contradictions are inevitable for anyone who has a certain depth of intellectual perception. Only shallow minds fancy that they are being consistent. And they can only be consistent within a very narrow ambit. As soon as they endeavour to take in the whole, what Rolfe called the desire and pursuit of the whole, they are lost, completely lost, unless they have learned to juggle with contradications. Lord Raleigh said that the ability to believe two mutually contradictory things at the same time was one of the infallible tests of a good mind in the modern world.

WP: That, of course, is very much a neo-Hegelian view. Have you been influenced directly by the neo-Hegelians? I am thinking of Bradley and Bosanquet.

CMG: Oh, I read them, long ago – before I became a convinced Marxist. They are a very fertile influence, a wonderful breeding ground for poets – unlike those who are opposed to them.

WP: Would you agree that there is a chasm today between sensibility and sensuality so that we no longer have any genuinely sensual poetry – such as the sonnets of Michelangelo, or Yeats's last poems? All that we have is a poetry of the senses.

CMG: Inevitably, the kind of poetry I'm interested in has tended, in the last half-century, to become more and more highly intellectual – more mathematical. I find the same tendency in ultra-modern music and I think the two things are marching together. But it brings me back again to the rarity of poetry. The great majority of people who write verse haven't got to that stage at all. They are full of sensuality – which isn't a bad thing – but it cannot be associated with any sensibility they have without a loss. If they could conjoin the two, or penetrate the one with the other, without losing power, then it would be a very good thing. But they can't do that and there is that lack, as you say, of genuine sensuality in modern poetry. Even those poets to whom I attach most importance in the modern world show that. There's no English poetry of course, we're ruling that out completely – it doesn't exist.

WP: I take it that you regard communism as essentially a spiritual force rather than in materialist terms?

CMG: Yes, I do.

WP: Given the nature and the trends which are evident in the contemporary world, do you see spiritual forces developing coherently in that world? When society is going through a period of great fragmentation, do you see communism as a spiritual force and the practice of poetry developing along fruitful lines?

CMG: It may take time. We are living at a very critical period in world history. But it was, I think, an American who said that the main task confronting the poet today is a great task of assimilation. I agree with that. If poetry is to reassert itself as the Queen of the Arts then what

253

Ezra Pound called 'poppycock', that's to say that store of outworn theories and superstitions, must be swept clean away. Very few poets are attempting to do that. They're still thirled to the 'poetic' which is the worst enemy of poetry. I'm brought back to that by thinking of perhaps the greatest technical change I've seen in poetry. Heine wrote a couple of volumes of song lyrics which were enormously popular – and still are. And then, at a given juncture, he said, 'I'm not going to write any more of that kind of damned thing!' and he spent the remaining years of his life trying to break up the tonality of the lyric and introduce into his work elements up to then considered non-poetical. He succeeded, but his later poetry has, of course, never been popular – and never will be. Pasternak was in the same position. He said, 'The lyric is hopeless in the modern world.' And I've done the same thing, followed the same example. I still adhere to that. One of the reasons is that the lyric, by its very nature, cannot reflect the complexities of modern life. But, apart from that, it necessarily ignores something even more important, and that is the enormous new perspective of the sciences. That can't be encapsulated in a short lyric. It's because of that enormous variety (which ought to be the pre-occupation of poetry and so seldom is) that most modern poetry is trivial and worthless.

WP: You would agree then that an important poem is necessarily a long poem?

CMG: I think so. The epic is the only form which can discharge the duties of the poet in the modern world; not lyric, not any subordinate forms. That's why at the Foyle luncheon which was given when Larkin's *Oxford* anthology came out I made a speech asking why he had left out the greatest poet living in the British Isles – David Jones. He didn't reply. He couldn't reply. It would have confuted the whole basis of his anthology.

WP: What political trends do you see developing in, say, the coming century?

CMG: The greatest force in the modern world is communism. That doesn't necessarily mean that we'll see an extension to other countries of the kind of social system we have today in Russia or in Yugoslavia. But I think they will approximate more and more fully to the idea of a communist state.

WP: And in Britain, will this so-called social democracy ever approximate to communism?

CMG: I think it will, yes. More and more I think the working class are finding out, as the present crisis in this country shows, that right throughout history social democracy has ended up by betraying the workers and the only way to avoid that betrayal is by going further left – to communism.

WP: You regard communism as the philosophy of the future. Does that philosophy leave room for the arts?

CMG: In this country we have a long tradition of popular education and as a result people are less and less well educated. In Russia, despite certain features of the communist regime which I deplore, there has been an enormous advance in educational facilities. They had to face a huge illiteracy problem, and that has been almost entirely eradicated. They are far ahead of us in certain directions, although we must remember the historical background. They were far behind us in certain respects so they had, more or less, to concentrate on scientific development and on large-scale industrialisation; and that has inhibited a corresponding development in aesthetics. But that is temporary. After all, although a great deal of fuss is made in this country about people like Solzhenitsyn, and about Pasternak before that, a tremendous amount of good work had been done in poetry and in other departments of literature of which most people in the West know little or nothing. Solzhenitsyn is a menace. The West has bolstered him up as a great crusader against communist tyranny, for freedom for the artist and all that sort of thing. But he's not an artist at all – he's a reporter – and his reportage is very poor stuff at that. I know half a dozen American writers who for sheer reporting, documentation, are far ahead of him. The *Observer*, for instance, likened him to Tolstoi. He's not fit to brush Tolstoi's shoes.

WP: If we are working towards the emergence of a more egalitarian world, what sort of ideal of man is going to emerge? Will it, for example, be along the lines of *uomo universale* of the renaissance – or might it be some sort of Goethean ideal of the integrated man?

CMG: Most people know nothing, and the educational system equips them only to do a job, not to live, not to become human beings. The fragmentation that is going on whereby specialists in one science are unintelligible to specialists in another has got to end – in the interests of all the sciences. It's that bringing together of these disparate elements again that seems to me to be essential – and it will happen, it's bound to. Not as a result of anyone making a political programme of it but because it's inherent in the nature of things. Otherwise, people are not going to survive.

WP: And you see such a general synthesis coming about in the near future?

CMG: Yes. Yeats, who had a very untrained mind, attempted it in his own way. His ideal was the man who was at home in all the sciences. Wordsworth said it before him, but others have gone a great deal further than that. Somehow or other we've got to get rid of the fact that there's a tremendous amount of indifference on the part of the great majority of people in western, so-called civilised countries: indifference to everything outwith the ambit of their own personal lives. We have to couple that with the fact that it's in the so-called civilised countries that we are seeing this recrudescence of barbarism: torture, massacre and so on. It will happen in this country too. We're going to have an enormous backlash of fascism.

WP: Which literary influences have you consciously rejected?

CMG: I suppose it was inevitable that I should be influenced by most of the English lyric poets, because it was on English lyric poetry that we were fed at school. It wasn't until I turned to the great Scots poets of the fifteenth and sixteenth centuries that I began to see that I had no affiliations whatsoever with English poetry – and rejected it. In my early development I was influenced by the *Arbeiter* poets of Germany, Richard Dehmel and others, but I think that the greatest influence on my ideas about poetry, if not reflected in my actual poetry, was Paul Valéry and the Italians who followed in his wake: Montale and Ungaretti and Quasimodo. I knew both Montale and Quasimodo myself – I've been very lucky that way. It cuts both ways of course. I also knew Yeats and Eliot so there are flaws in my luck. Yeats was very nice to me but I soon got what I regarded as his measure. He was a monologuist and didn't like other people to speak when he was speaking or to introduce new subject matter but on this occasion he wanted to know about Douglas' Social Credit. I hadn't said but a few things to him about it when I discovered that he knew nothing about how the present banking system worked and therefore couldn't possible understand how the other would work. I told him so. We parted amicably.

WP   You have said that there is no English poetry. Why not?

CMG: The whole framework of English society has been against it. Their schooling system kills the imagination – their whole system is opposed to the emergence of aesthetic values. They claim that there is a great tradition of English poetry. Where did it come from? Very little of it was English in an exact sense. In modern times you have two Americans, an Irishman and a Welshman. There are none at the moment. Auden was a complete wash-out. The last thing he said to me was – in a very husky voice – 'Grieve, there's no future in communism.' And I said – 'I don't think there's any future in anything else.'

WP: Do you think there is a connection between the fact that so much fine poetry is now coming out of Central Europe and their, in one sense, more naked experience of the last war?

CMG: I couldn't say about that. I think one of the reasons for it is that they always had to fight for their languages and for the maintenance of their native traditions.

WP: Nationalism in Scotland is currently giving something of a boost to the arts in some respects. Do you think that will last?

CMG: Yes. I think that there is something deeper in the proliferation of nationalisms all over the world. Millions of people have come to feel isolated from their native roots and are trying to reroot themselves in some indigenous tradition, reviving their native languages and so on. That will continue and it is an insistence on maintaining the variety of life. On that level the main objection to capitalism is that it kills. Centralism always comes from the demands of orthodox finance. And if you're standing at an assembly belt doing the same repetitive job day in, day out, six days a week, then of course it will kill everything else stone dead. It dehumanises the workers – which is one of its attractions from the capitalist point of view.

WP Is it not the case that any industrialised society – communist or capitalist – involves this sort of dehumanisation to some extent?

CMG: Oh, so long as you have an industrialised society there will be distasteful jobs which someone has to do, but on the other hand, the perpetuation of that sort of society has been largely due to the fact that capitalism puts into cold storage all sorts of labour-saving, production-increasing devices. There is no reason on earth why at the present time anyone should have to work more than four hours a week. There could be abundant leisure but then all the force of society, the media and so on, prevent people from knowing what in the hell they could do with their spare time. You have to fight all the popular things: the press, radio, television and organised commercial sport.

WP: You have a low opinion of contemporary Scottish literature.

CMG: It's largely a subdivision of English literature. There hasn't been any recurrence to any great extent on the part of Scottish writers to the staples of the independent Scottish tradition. Until that happens I can't see much creative development in Scottish literature. An American professor who runs the *Studies in Scottish Literature* – Professor Roy, he was working in the

258

Mitchell Library in Glasgow – wrote to me and said: we're going to give a double number to contemporary Scottish literature. He wanted a long essay from me. up to about 10,000 words, and was inviting two others to do likewise. Who do you think they were? Eric Linklater and Naomi Mitchison! I wrote back and declined. So far as I was concerned they had nothing to do with contemporary Scottish literature and I wouldn't be associated with them.

WP: In the thirties and later you exercised an obvious influence over a number of writers. Among younger writers that influence is now perhaps less obvious. What effects or influence do you think that you have exercised in this area?

CMG: It's very difficult to tell. I've had this effect, that up until a few years ago there was no systematic teaching of Scottish literature in universities or in senior secondary schools and there's a good deal of it now in all these quarters. Now that's a big change, and it means that those who are students and pupils today will in ten or twenty years time show the benefit of that change. They will know the stuff. Now all these poets who followed my example, who looked up Scots words in dictionaries and so on, they've all faded out. They hadn't got it natively and that's where I had the advantage. I was born into a Scots-speaking community and my own parents and all those round about spoke Scots. But these poets hadn't that advantage and, of course, I have antagonised them – politically and otherwise. I don't think that any of them has really followed my example – certainly not technically. Their poetry has no resemblance to mine except at the mere level of vocabulary and in some uses of the language. But they don't seem to me to be using the language creatively at all. So I don't think I've had a good influence on them. But then, one doesn't expect influences to be good. Basically, I don't think I've been influenced by anybody at all. I'm a great admirer of Valéry and others but I haven't been influenced by them. I'm not writing the kind of stuff they were writing at all. At least, I don't think I am.

259

WP: Do you see any change coming about in the attitudes of educationalists towards the arts, towards poetry in particular?

CMG: No. There's a great deal of activity going on and a lot of facilities being offered – but this business of having poets in residence at universities and so on – it's a bad thing. There's no doubt that there is an enormous frustration of the creative impulses in the modern world. Most people think they could do it with just a little luck but it doesn't work that way at all. You can't multiply the number of poets in a country of five and a half millions overnight. It's a bloody lucky country if it's got one or two. And that's a general thing. I cannot remember offhand who said, but I agree with them, that from the beginnings of recorded human history in all centuries and in all countries, the arts, the sciences, everything that could be regarded as constituent of a civilised order was the work of an infinitesimal proportion of the population, which was a constant. And that if that constant could be eliminated from the mass of humanity, all the rest couldn't do anything to reconstitute the arts and sciences and civilisation in general. I think that's true. Although it may be possible to find techniques for creating a greater proportion of genius to the population than has existed in human history so far.

WP: Genetic engineering and the like?

CMG: Yes, that kind of thing. There's a lot going on in fields such as brain physiology and so on, and that may be one of the hopes for the future. But one thing which we must do if we are to derive the advantage one would wish from that kind of thing is to draw a clear distinction between talent and genius. Talent's the enemy. The good is the enemy of the best. It's too easy. People want it on a plate. They think they have a little talent and can't for the life of them see why they aren't as good as anybody else.

WP: Yes, that's true. Yeats was a case in point. A man who had little or no talent. Who achieved what he did by damn hard work.

CMG: Exactly. It was Kierkegaard who said that if a man's

doing something it's all right so long as he's one of a
number who are doing it. But let him raise his head
above the ruck and he'll be trampled to death under
the feet of geese.

WP: The supernatural, the larger than life, do you agree
that it's essential for poetry?

CMG: I think it's essential for life. Human life itself implies a
belief in, a desire to participate in, the transcendental.
It's inherent in us without reference to any religious
belief. That is the answer to your question.

WP: And how does that square with your materialism?

CMG: The transcendental, if I am right, comes out of the
seeds of things. It's inherent in the original substance
– it's part of the materialism.

Whisky

This glowing tribute to the poet's favourite drink appeared as a foreword to Alan Reeve-Jones's A Dram Like This *(1974).*

Whisky is the safest drink in the world – a fact that is being increasingly appreciated everywhere. The author of this admirable introduction to the historical, literary and social associations of *Usquebaugh* (the water of life) is right when he states: 'Whisky is now a wholly universal drink, selling to more than a hundred and seventy countries of the world.' And he is right, too, when he declares that 'whisky is still a product of Scotland and nowhere else'.

Other countries have tried to distil it – without success. The results – in Spain, in Japan, and elsewhere – have indeed been horrible, and have borne no resemblance whatever to the genuine Scottish article.

In recent years I have travelled in many foreign countries, and one of my difficulties has been to find a short drink I can stay on. There is none at all to equal whisky.

Cognac is no substitute; vodka and aquavita are acquired tastes, which no one used to Scotch is likely to acquire. Other short drinks, like absinthe or mastika or slivovitz, cannot be drunk in more than a sample or two without dire consequences.

That is not the case with whisky, and I have drunk it for nearly seventy years without detriment to my constitution. A couple of years ago, I underwent a major operation, and when the doctor came to change my dressings for the last time he sounded me thoroughly and said all my organs were in a condition that would do credit to a man quarter my age, and there was no reason why I shouldn't live to be a hundred!

I always remember another fact about the health-preserving

virtues of whisky. In the First World War I served in Salonika for a couple of years. The Salonika affair has been called 'a clubbable war'. There was little real fighting; the main enemy was disease, and the consequent casualties were immensely greater than any incurred on the battlefields.

The principal causes were dysentery, blackwater fever, and malaria. It was noted that when there was whisky in the officers' or sergeants' messes there were few recurrences of malaria, but when whisky was not available the recurrence-rate shot up at once.

Alas, many ships were being sunk in the Mediterranean at the time, and suppplies frequently failed to arrive. The Army medical authorities treated malaria with quinine, taken orally or by injection, which caused men's eyesight to be affected and their hair to fall out. Quinine was also expensive.

It would have been cheaper and far more effective to have supplied the sufferers with whisky. But that, of course, was a sensible alternative beyond the Army authorities to contemplate.

'Give a dog a bad name' – and so the widespread prejudice against whisky, inculcated by the Temperance people, prevailed and the death rate steadily increased.

I am not going to take sides in this foreword with one kind of whisky versus another. However, a few years ago malt whisky would not have been available in the majority of pubs – certainly in almost all English pubs. But motoring recently in the Upper Tyne Valley, and coming to lonely little pubs near Falstone or Bewcastle, I found there was no longer this difficulty. All my favourite 'straight malts' were there.

Yet these isolated pubs were only frequented by shepherds, farm-workers and the like. This shows the extent to which the diffusion of the taste for 'pure malt' has increased in recent years to embrace all classes of society.

I have been referring to 'whisky' or 'Scotch', but I am sorry for anyone who asks in a bar for a drink by either of these names instead of nominating the particular brand he wants.

This lack of discrimination entails a great loss of enjoyment. So, too, does the absence of some knowledge of the history and romance of the making and drinking of whisky. A little knowledge of the rich background adds greatly to appreciation of the drink.

That is why I welcome this book. It puts the ordinary drinker in possession of all the main facts, and is, I think, an excellent brief introduction for the general public.

I have said I feel sorry for those who can only ask for 'a whisky' without naming the particular kind they want. But I think this splendid drink deserves to be drunk with due ceremony, whenever possible, and in one of my poems I lament the disappearance of old ritual in this connection:

> Not drinking whisky and soda
> As an Englishman does, which is very dull,
> But with all the splendid old ritual,
> The urn, the rummers, the smaller glasses,
> The silver ladles, and the main essentials.
> The whisky toddy is mixed in a rummer,
> A round-bottomed tumbler on a stem,
> And transferred at intervals with a silver ladle
> Into an accompanying wine-glass
> By way of cooling it
> Sufficiently for consumption.
> Slainte! 'Freedom and whisky gang thegither'. Take aff yer
>   dram!

Religion and Art

In John Knox *(1976) a Roman Catholic (Anthony Ross), a Church of Scotland minister (Campbell Maclean) and a Communist (Mac-Diarmid) contributed to a book on the Scottish Reformer. What follows is the conclusion of MacDiarmid's essay on 'Knox, Calvinism and the Arts'.*

As the late Dr Mary Ramsay showed in her book *Calvinism and Art,* however the particular form it took in Scotland may have been inimical to the Arts, Calvinism in other countries had not had a like disastrous effect. It was a special Scottish misfortune. But the present writer is certain that the effect in question is not only not specially let alone exclusively attributable to Knox, but applies to all religion. It is necessary to remind readers that it is a fact that in actual aesthetic products materialist and sceptical writers have considerably surpassed religious ones. This is hardly true of ancient Greece, of course, where the greatest poets, Homer, Sappho, Aeschylus, Sophocles and Pindar, preceded the age of unbelief. One must remember, however, that it was far easier to be an aesthetic Pagan than it is to be an aesthetic Christian. Apollo, Hermes and Aphrodite were really aesthetic beings, but one must have a marvellous eye for beauty if one can discover it in the Three Persons of the Godhead. Every Latin poet without exception was a materialist or sceptic. Catullus spoke for all when he said:

> *Soles occidere et redire possunt;*
> *nobiscum semel recidit brevis lux*
> *Nox est perpetua una dormienda.**

---

* 'Sins when they sink can rise again, But we, when our brief light has shone,
  Must sleep the long night on and on' (tr. James Michie).

In Italy Dante was religious, but Petrarch, Politian, Ariosto, Machiavelli, Aretino and all the Renaissance poets were sceptical. Tasso lived under the counter-Reformation and was one of the first pupils of the Jesuits, so he may be called religious. Spain must be conceded, I fear. Cervantes, Calderon and Lope de Vega were not merely orthodox, but greatly approved the burning of heretics. In Germany, Schiller may have a touch of religion, but Goethe was on the whole sceptical, and Lessing and Heine were the boldest of mockers. In France nearly all the writers since Voltaire, whether in prose or verse, until after the First World War, have been sceptics. To any doubter of my contention I give Verlaine – unless he objects to take him.

I will not go through the long history of English literature, but in modern times Shelley, Fitzgerald and Swinburne were sceptical enough, and where are there three religious poets to match them in aesthetic power? Tennyson alone can be named. It is a good deal to admit that the author of *In Memoriam* was a believer, but I can afford to be generous. If we had not the recent deplorable cases of T. S. Eliot, Edwin Muir and W. H. Auden, it is interesting to find how devitalising and injurious religion can be for a poet. D. G. James in his *Scepticism and Poetry* says: 'When we consider the tradition of English poetry since the Reformation it is obvious that it is not a Christian poetic tradition. None of the major poets, with the exception of Milton, have written as Christians.'

The fact is that there has been, and remains, an unbroken enmity between religion and art. The Greeks in their best days were an exception, but even in Greece Plato at least appeared with his purer religion and desired to expel poets and musicians from his republic. To this day there are no bells in Mohammedan churches because Mohammed thought music wicked. In Italy beauty was worshipped by the bad Popes, but abhorred by good ones. In the fifteenth century the good Pope Paul II tortured and imprisoned poets, and next century the good Popes of the counter-Reformation waged implacable war against poetry and art. In England the theatres were closed for many years, fiddlers were put in the stocks, and poets had a narrow escape. In France Molière could hardly get buried, and Lully was refused absolution till he burnt an opera he had just composed. Even in the eighteenth century the actress Le Couvreur was refused Christian burial and had to be buried in a field for cattle. There is practically no form of art – neither music nor poetry nor dancing nor the drama nor the novel – which has not been persecuted for ages by every religion.

Writing to John Buchan in 1929, with reference to his (Muir's) book on John Knox, Edwin Muir thanks Buchan 'for your saying that I leave Knox a great figure, for much as we may dislike Knox that seems to be the end of the matter'.

Muir's book, which I thought a thoroughly bad example of debunking, was dedicated to me. And there too I will leave the matter, since that is where the majority of the Scottish people have left it, and I will only add that whatever may be said of Knox's relentless will, we have surely seen enough of athletes of the will in recent years – Hitler, Mussolini, Franco – to have any regard now for that quality.

The most striking example of the gulf between anything that can be called Knoxian and what the Scottish public likes (or has liked, for this is far less the case than it was thirty or forty years ago) is, of course, the position of Robert Burns as Scotland's great national poet. For it is impossible not to think that Knox would have agreed with the English writer who protested that an end should be put to the annual laudation by gatherings in all parts of the world in whose midst appear some of the most eminent in the Church, the Law, Literature and politics of 'one of the lewdest, most drunken, and most dissolute libertines who ever stained human records. ... To drink a toast to a man like Burns ought properly to be considered as an affront to every decent thing in life ... in all the long erratic history of hero-worship there is probably not another such example where a reprobate, a deliberate boasting defaulter from ordinary human decency, has carried his excesses to such repulsive extremes.' The actual facts of Burns's life and character do not, of course, bear this writer out, yet he was sufficiently removed from all the generally accepted moral standards of our people to make it a mystery why he has been so adulated and loved, unless just because he typified what the majority of Scots are, and have always been, under the disguise of respectability under which they have generally concealed their true propensities.

It is a fact, as I have already indicated, that God-fearing, good living, respectable writers in Scotland have been confined to the lower levels of literature while the great names have been more or less flagrantly at odds with the proclaimed standards of our national life.

Whatever influence Calvinism may have had seems to have waned very considerably in recent years. The late J. M. Reid, in his little book *Scotland, Past and Present*, is undoubtedly right when he says: 'The Kirk no longer controls Scottish education. It ceased, more than a century ago, to be the recognised guardian of the poor. The local church is seldom the centre of the life of its parish: indeed, partly as the result of dissensions and reunions, the parochial system itself has broken down, especially in the towns. Congregations are scattered, and intermixed in a way that complicates, though it scarcely cripples, the work of the eldership. It is often said that the Kirk has lost touch with the industrial workers. Perhaps this is rather less true in Scotland than in some other countries. Industrialism has raised barriers against religion in most parts of the world. It is doubtful if there is a Scottish "churchless million". But the days when Scotland lived, intellectually, on the Bible and the Shorter Catechism have certainly gone.'

Whatever doubts there may remain as to the number of our population who have no Church connection of any kind, there is no question, as the General Assembly of the Church of Scotland admitted a few years ago, that Church membership (and the membership of such related bodies as Sunday Schools and Bible Classes) has dropped so greatly that the aggregate belonging to all these represents now only a minority of our people. That minority has undue power, however. Thanks to Lord Reith, for example, the BBC religious broadcasting is out of all proportion to the number of practising believers in the listening public. The means by which this disproportion has been achieved and kept are very questionable and savour of sharp practice out of keeping altogether with the pretensions of the Church. The best equipped recent writers on our Church history have uncovered such a hiatus between professed belief and quotidian practice as to question whether Scotland has ever been a Christian country at all. It would certainly, to put it very mildly, surprise Knox if he could be told that the sort of Scottish ministers who are attracting increasing attention today are such men as Thomas Erskine of Linlathen (who challenged not merely the doctrine of Calvinism but its whole temper), and John McLeod Campbell. Recent publications by men like Andrew L. Drummond and J. Bulloch show (and fully document) the disparity between the claims of the Kirk in relation to the poor, housing and other social problems and the actual facts. It is a horrifying state of affairs that is disclosed and leaves us with no wonder that the minister in our midst is no longer held in reverence, and almost in awe, but retains today little public respect or influence and has hardly any real function except as a 'social worker', or, as was said the other day by a friend of mine, all the pronouncements of the Church and the utterances of individual ministers are simply 'like the telly, all repeats!' The conclusion of A. J. Scott's lectures on Socialism (1860) in criticism of the Owenites and Chartists for their neglect of culture (*op. cit.* pp. 193–5) sums up the whole matter. 'I do not think,' he says, 'we have a great deal of faith. I am not speaking of high mysteries and peculiar doctrines. I do not think that the feeling that there is a God, and that we have to do with God, is practically a very powerful one in this country at all. The feeling that there is a religion, that there is a revelation, that it exercises a strong and beneficial influence in society for smoothness of intercourse, for the maintenance of national organisation, for the preservation of property – all this exists in great force; but a sense of the contact of my own spiritual being with an ever-present and infinite spiritual Being – I cannot but think this has in many ages of the world prevailed far more mightily than now. Now we can only give what we have. We are not to aim, or expect to make others higher and better by anything we have communicated, except that we have the living substance of a higher truth than is practically known to them.'

It is a fact that, with all the advantages of education, the thousands of ministers of the Kirk have contributed little or nothing to literature or the other Arts, and that even the most prominent of them have not even left recognisable names, or any sense of their having done, said, or written anything that outlives them and is of consequence to us now.

What Knox would think if he could view *Christ Superstar* or the American protagonists of the Jesus Cult or the sermonising of the entertainer Billy Connolly and the TV religious programme 'Eighth Day', I can only imagine. What he would think of pop-singing in churches and the other efforts made today to repopularise the Church by giving the people what 'the people want' – by, in other words, descending to the hopelessly anti-intellectual level of the mass of the people – needs no further spelling-out beyond the simple question. My objection to the widely-diffused general derivative of Calvinism – what I have just called a great force – is what I defined forty years ago as one of the planks of the Scottish Renaissance Movement in contemporary Scottish literature, as our determination to 'break out of confinement to a mere earthly endaemonism with Christian nuances; that pseudo-religious mental climate which keeps the harmonies and solutions of our writers on so contemptibly shallower a level than the conflicts and tragedies which encompass our lives'.

The pretence that we are Christians – that the moral standards, the so-called civilised values to which most of us subscribe are other than a myth – is, I think, shown conclusively by the fact that the great ideals of our Labour and Socialist Movement have not led to the production in their name of any literature or other art of any value at all. Knox would be horrified at the increase of Roman Catholicism in Scotland today, but he would have to recognise that our Catholic (convert Catholic) writers have also failed to produce any literature of real value. I am thinking in this connection of such writers as the late Sir Compton Mackenzie, Moray Maclaren, Fionn Mac Colla (T. D. MacDonald) and George Scott-Moncrieff. Our Catholicism has been as null and void as our Protestantism in this connection. Ramsay MacDonald made a few stupid remarks about contemporary Scottish literature and singled out for praise as a novelist, James Welsh, the Ayrshire miner. I wrote protesting that he did not know what he was talking about and that there were other contemporary Scottish writers of much greater significance he had failed to mention. He replied thanking me for my letter and explaining that he did not know much about modern Scottish literature, but he did not explain why then he presumed to pontificate about it. The late Mrs Jean Mann, MP, publicly wished we could have more writers of the calibre of John Buchan. I wrote to her pointing out that Buchan's achievement was hardly on a literary level above contempt. She did not apologise. These two examples are typical of the general attitude of Scottish socialists and literature and the Scots. Matters in this respect have not improved since then.

Dr George Steiner, of the Universities of Cambridge and Geneva, has been rightly described as a man with an exceptionally wide range of knowledge and a familiarity with other literatures, languages and bodies of ideas – whose writings bring out the relative narrowness of most critics' work, and indeed the fragmentariness and lack of exploratory and assimilative vigour in our whole intellectual life. He only quotes one Scottish poet – the present writer – and that in connection with a materialistic poem of mine in which I say:

> The profound kinship of all living substance
> Is made clear by the chemical route.
> Without some chemistry one is bound to remain
> Forever a dumbfounded savage
> In the face of vital reactions.
> The beautiful relations
> Shown only by biochemistry
> Replace a stupefied sense of wonder
> With something more wonderful
> Because natural and understandable.

So far as Poetry is concerned, the majority of so-called educated people in Scotland could not imagine that it was bound to come to pass as I confidently predicted then that 'like far galaxies bending over the horizon of invisibility, the bulk of English poetry is now modulating from active presence into the inertness of scholarly conservation'. Or, as Steiner went on to say, 'Based as it firmly is, on a deep many-branched anatomy of classical and scriptural reference, expressed in a syntax and vocabulary of heightened tenor, the unbroken arc of English poetry, of reciprocal discourse, that relates Chaucer and Spenser to Tennyson and to Eliot, is fading rapidly from the reach of natural reading. A central pulse in awareness, in the language, is becoming archival.'

Yet that 'unbroken arc' (manifestly beyond recovery now) is still the substance of the teaching of literature in our Scottish schools and colleges. The consequence is but for rare exceptions a general minimal literacy in our whole Scottish population. It is not a question of Calvinism or Knox, but simply the refusal of our bourgeoisie to become really civilised at all.

In his book *The Problem of Metaphysics* (Cambridge University Press, 1974) Professor D. M. MacKinnon, the Norris Hulse

Professor of Divinity in the University of Cambridge, in which he summarises his Gifford Lectures, takes to task a familiar type of Scottish religionist today from which I have suffered and regard as a prime example of the unscrupulous use of the myth of our being a Christian people, or, in other words, a 'con trick' of an altogether too common a kind in our midst, when he says: 'MacDiarmid writes as an atheist, and his poem is eloquent testimony that out of an atheist ontology a great poem may spring. To say this is not intended as the insult so often offered by the religious of claiming that no man is a serious atheist. But it is to remember that atheism and theism have this in common: that both alike are ontologies and that in the relatively loose sense of the term on which it may be applied to a conspectus of Aristotle's metaphysics that includes his theology as well as his anatomy of being. If it is insulting to the atheist to speak of him as unknown to himself a religious man, it is permissible to remember that unlike the positivist he allows himself to be concerned with what is, in the very special sense of demanding our unconditional validity for what he says. Hence, indeed, the violence of Lenin's polemics against Bogdanov, for the latter's readiness to substitute Ernst Mach's sensationalism for materialism. No one could call Lenin's *Materialism and Empirio-criticism* philosophy. It is polemic of the kind of which its formidable author is master. Yet it is the sort of work that the philosopher who is concerned with the problem of metaphysics would do well to remember and that not least in the present context as we recall the poetry that MacDiarmid has written in Lenin's honour.'

Without reference to the sources – to Knox's writings or to Calvin's *Institutes* – all manner of people condemn Knox, but he cannot justly be criticised, let alone condemned on such tenth-rate evidence. This anti-Knoxism is something 'that is in the air'. It defies definition. A typical case of this appeared the other day in a Lanarkshire local paper; reporting a lecture on Stained Glass Windows, it said: 'During the Reformation John Knox, who had a hatred of art in any form, smashed many church windows. St Andrews Cathedral was one which suffered badly. It was completely desecrated; its windows were dumped into deep wells.' There is an element of truth in that, but it is wholly submerged in a mass of utter inaccuracy. It may be true that the popular name for glasscutters now is red devils, and the pliers

272

they use are called grousers, but these terms have in that case changed a good deal from their original significance.

Thinking, however, of the fact that there is wide-spread throughout Scotland an anti-intellectualism and an utter inability to appreciate the arts – and that nevertheless the country which exhibits these deplorable characteristics is still 'my own, my native land' – I wrote the following poem:

> Scottish Jews comin' doon frae the mountains
> Wi' the laws in their stany herts;
> Minor prophets livin' i' the Factory Close
> Or ahint the gasworks – fresh sterts?
>
> Folk frae the Auld Testament are talkin'
> O' Christ, but I'm no' deceived;
> Bearded men, cloakt women, and in gloom
> The gift o' Heaven's received.
>
> Scottish Jews comin' doon frae the mountains,
> Minor prophets frae vennel and wynd,
> In weather as black as the Bible,
> I return again to my kind.

I do not attribute the evil of which I am writing to Knox, or to Calvinism, but regard it as a probably incurable state of affairs due in part to that 'split mindedness' caused by England's reduction of Scotland to colonial status, and in the main to capitalism.

Or, as I wrote in my autobiography, *Lucky Poet*, forty years ago – a conclusion I have not found it necessary to modify since – 'Calvinism is no worse or better than any other religion; its excesses were due entirely to the fact that from the beginning its spread was closely connected with English policy and that it became England's ideological damper for suffocating Scotish action.'

It gives me pleasure to read of its counterpart south of the Border in the latest book on the subject (Daniel Jenkins; *The British: Their Identity and their Religion*) that the Church of England is 'a thinly disguised adaptation and distortion of the Christian faith to serve the purpose of English nationalism'.

MacDiarmid at Eighty-Five

On 11 August 1977, the poet's birthday, BBC Radio Scotland broadcast George Bruce's interview which began with a question about Mac-Diarmid's early literary life.

MacDiarmid: The beginning wasn't really a beginning. What I still regard as a very extraordinary thing is, before I'd written anything at all, a consensus of opinion amongst my teachers and so on at school was that I was going to be a poet. It hadn't occurred to me at that time, at all, but they all agreed about that. You know, there must have been some reason – what it was I can't tell. Because I hadn't written any poetry at that time. I was always interested in poetry, but that came a little later. This realisation that I was going to be a poet pre-dated my own increasing interest in poetry and reading it and so on.

Bruce: Therefore, they must have seen some response – verbal, I imagine – to your circumstances.

MacDiarmid: They must have done that, yes. I was always quite loquacious, you know. If that's a sign of poetic talent then I always had words at command.

Bruce: But then these words that came to you, these words at command, did come out of a very particular environment. I mean, for example, you obviously spoke Scots from the beginning.

MacDiarmid: Oh yes. Everybody did in Langholm at that time. And there was a resentment to speaking

274

English. It was regarded as apeing the gentry, talking fine. But although it was insisted upon in the classroom, in the school, in the playground and in the streets and in the homes, it was all Scots that was spoken. There was no English at all.

BRUCE: And nevertheless, when you began to write poetry, you did begin, I think, in English – am I right about that?

MACDIARMID: Yes. I didn't know anything about Scottish literature. We weren't taught anything about it in the schools, at all. An odd poem of Burns's perhaps – perhaps one of the ballads. That was the sum total that we knew about Scottish poetry.

BRUCE: And yet you were right in the ballad country?

MACDIARMID: Right in the ballad country.

BRUCE: Why was this denied you?

MACDIARMID: It was government policy, Westminster government policy. And it persisted until quite recently. But as it happened, owing to that not knowing about Scottish literature in the school and so on, it wasn't until I was about thirty that I began to study Scottish literature and appreciate it and read it.

BRUCE: But long before that you were writing in Scots.

MACDIARMID: In a little, a little, but I hadn't developed the kind of Scots canon that I developed for myself afterward.

BRUCE: I see, yes. And yet here you were in Langholm – it did provide you with something apart from words altogether. It provided you with a pretty rich experience of childhood, I would say.

MACDIARMID: Oh yes, indeed. It was very radical, for one thing. The Border burghs, as the constituency was then called, was a very radical constituency, and my own family, my father and so on, very radical. Not Socialist, but radical. Extreme Liberal, and of course the Boer War was on – the first of the three wars that I lived

275

through – and my father was a pro-Boer. That threw up the differences in a little community, you see. Pro-Boers weren't popular, so I was used at that early stage to know what it was to be up against common sentiment.

BRUCE: And nevertheless, besides that there was the influence of teachers who were important to you.

MACDIARMID: Oh yes, very important. Francis George Scott. It was through him that I developed my interest in the sciences and botany in particular. He was very keen on botany, and he used to send me out to the moors to find things and come back and show them.

BRUCE: Was it out of that kind of experience you got that excerpt from the *Dìreadh* sequence – 'Scotland Small'?

MACDIARMID: All that came from that early experience. I don't think I've looked at plants since. I wouldn't recognise many of them now, but I knew them intimately then. Langholm lies in a hollow, circled round with hills, and it's the meeting place of three rivers, which I've also celebrated in my poetry. It's very, very rich countryside. There's an old saying, 'Out of the world and into Langholm', you know. It's a world of its own, quite isolated and rich, not only in forests and hills and moorlands but rich in the rivers, fishing of all kinds, and so on. I spent most of my early boyhood in the river actually, physically, building islands in the river and cooking eels that we speared, and cooked and ate with great enjoyment.

BRUCE: There's a richness and vitality in your early Scots poetry but beyond that there's another element altogether. There's this element of mystery; the sense of mystery seems immediately evident, for example, in 'The Eemis Stane'.

MACDIARMID: I had a very religious upbringing, you know. And reacted against it, of course, very quickly.

There's always been that antinomian rebelli-
ous element in me. I reacted against it but
nevertheless there's the persistence of it. And I
was always attracted to these difficult questions of the hereafter and the relation of life to
the universal creation and so on. And the two
things ran together although I reacted against
the direct influence of religion.

BRUCE: I seem to recollect your saying that you sometimes would go to a dictionary but you must
have had an awful lot of words round about
Langholm as well?

MacDiarmid: Oh, there were a lot spoken at that time. But
you must remember, of course, that I was
about verging on thirty before I wrote these
early Scots poems, you see; so the direct Langholm influence had evaporated by that time,
or it was difficult to recall. It came to me later
on, but for the time being it had gone.

BRUCE: On the one hand there was that dimension.
On the other hand, you've also in your poems
created some of the robust characters as, for
example in 'Crowdieknowe'. It is an actual
place, isn't it?

MacDiarmid: Oh yes. My ancestors are buried there, my
grandfather and my grandmother on my
mother's side.

BRUCE: I see at the stage of 'Crowdieknowe' and 'The
Watergaw' two distinctive elements. On the
one hand, the robust comic characterisation
which is a traditional reference, as you know,
in Scottish literature, and on the other hand,
and this is the most surprising thing, the
extension of the Scots lyric into areas which it
had never been before. And having done that,
you then, as it were, apparently throw it all
away and go into your *Drunk Man*.

MacDiarmid: It's a more didactic poem – it's not a pure
poem – the *Drunk Man* I mean – more didactic.
I was arguing a case against the neglect of
Scottish literature, against the over-laudation

277

of Burns, and so on; I was arguing a case all the time.

BRUCE: On the other hand the mystery's also to be found in it. Is there not a ballad element in the *Drunk Man* that comes through?

MACDIARMID: Of course there is. Largely, the engine that motivates the whole poem and keeps it going is the ballad measure, of course. It varies – there's a lot of variation of metre and so on in the *Drunk Man* but underlying all the variations there's that continuing ballad metre. It comes back to the ballad all the time.

BRUCE: I was thinking on another aspect of some of the ballads. There's the mysterious woman who makes her appearance in the *Drunk Man*.

MACDIARMID: In the *Drunk Man* she came from ... I wasn't thinking of elf-land.

BRUCE: No, I know, that is right. But nevertheless there's a carry over I would say.

MACDIARMID: Oh yes. Well, I should think that was a commonplace in my later reading. I mean I was familiar not only with elf-land but with the recurrence of the idea of – not Graves's White Goddess, you know, but the muse.

BRUCE: By the time you'd got through the *Drunk Man*, that's 1926, now where were you? You were by that time in Montrose? And you were, I don't know what your title was, but you were editing.

MACDIARMID: I was editing; I was the reporter of the local paper *The Montrose Review*.

BRUCE: But nevertheless, your poetry at that stage was only getting through to a limited number of people.

MACDIARMID: Oh yes, oh very, very limited number. I wasn't worried about that at all, no, no.

BRUCE: And yet, when after that you began to write in English there was an outcry amongst the people who knew you, was there not?

MacDiarmid: They thought I was reneging on the Scots, you see.

Bruce: Why did you turn to English?

MacDiarmid: I was becoming increasingly preoccupied with political and scientific matters, and there was no vocabulary for them in Scots. There's no vocabulary in English either; you had to use the international scientific jargon, you see, which I did use. As I got more and more interested in various sciences, geology and botany and so on, I picked up the vocabulary which was in use amongst the scientific writers on the subjects, and used that.

Bruce: But as distinct from the scientific writers themselves, you are using these interests in order to define another position altogether, which I would say is beyond the scientific. For example, 'On a Raised Beach'. What are you after there in that long, and if I may say so, magnificent poem?

MacDiarmid: I was trying to define my own position generally in terms of my environment at that time which was the Shetland Islands where, of course, geology is the prominent feature. You've got none of the resources for illustrative material you'd have on the mainland of Scotland. There are no trees, no running water. You're thrown back on the bare rock all the time. So I was trying to re-shape my ideas of poetry, identifying myself in terms of the Shetland landscape. That's what I was doing. I think it's one of my very best poems, either in Scots or English.

Bruce: Mind you, to some extent, that admiration, that awe: that sense of awe you had already given expression to in 'The Eemis Stane'.

MacDiarmid: Quite.

Bruce: But in Scots. I observe, therefore, the same imagery but looked on with a different eye and in a different light, begins to make its

279

appearance in the poems in English. There's a continuity there, is there not?

MacDiarmid: Oh, undoubtedly there is. After all it's one person. You can't divide yourself up, you know. It was the poetry of a whole man that I was seeking, and I couldn't effectively prosecute that search without breaking away from any provincialism that might be implied by writing in Scots. I had to get a wider medium. I wrote in English. You see? That is my own language, too.

Bruce: Yes, of course it is. But there is a search.

MacDiarmid: There is a search, oh yes. It's not finished.

Bruce: No. It is an unceasing search for truth. You had a very hard time in the Shetlands, did you not? It was a pretty hard life there, I gather.

MacDiarmid: Well, it was an isolated life and I had no visible means of support.

Bruce: Yes, I like that phrase.

MacDiarmid: I had no pension at that time, and I had no way of earning money except by writing books. And then you had to wait a long period before you got an advance, you see – a contract and an advance – and then I could pick up my dates. It was very difficult. More difficult for Valda than it was for me because there was no social life really, you see.

Bruce: I mentioned to you as well that though you had written this great poem as it were on stone, on the stones of the world, you write there are 'no ruined stones'.

MacDiarmid: That's right.

Bruce: Though you had written in these terms of reference you also had, kept in touch, as it were, with the human element in your Shetland lyrics, for example, about the blue-jowled fishermen in 'With the Herring Fishers'.

MacDiarmid: Aye, that's right, because I was out constantly with the fishermen, and I went away out beyond Foula, in the main deep as they call it, you see, beyond the continental shelf. Herring

	fishing. I enjoyed it immensely. I had a wonderful time.
BRUCE:	Therefore, you were in at that time still employing Scots as well in the Shetland lyrics.
MacDIARMID:	Oh yes. Oh aye.
BRUCE:	And you were keeping in touch with a full, with a wide range, a wide range of response, and at the same time as you had the scientific interest –
MacDIARMID:	Well, I was always political you see. I was interested in the actual economic conditions of the Shetlands. All this that has blown up in the last year or two about the oil, and so on, you know – I recommended away back forty, forty to fifty years ago that they should follow the example of the Faroe Islands and break away completely from the United Kingdom. I published articles to that effect, you see. I went and visited the Faroe Islands and had an opportunity of finding out just how they'd done it, and I knew it was quite practicable for the Shetlanders too. And they're thinking about it now.
BRUCE:	Yes, indeed. But, ultimately, it's the politics of man in which you are interested, is it not?
MacDIARMID:	Oh yes, of course.
BRUCE:	Because you put my mind, just now, on to your concern for the people who lived in slums. And that referred, if I recollect, to Glasgow again.
MacDIARMID:	Yes, I applied it to Glasgow, yes. Of course, my interest in that kind of thing had been awakened very early. I joined the Independent Labour Party when I was sixteen – 1908 – and I knew all the so-called Red Clydesiders – Maxton, Kirkwood and all the rest of them. I knew them personally, and they came and stayed with me in Montrose, but the I.L.P. democratic socialism ceased to be enough for me. I wanted to go further.
BRUCE:	Yes. As you talk you put into my mind the

281

lines beginning 'I saw a rose come loupin' oot', from *A Drunk Man*.

MACDIARMID: This is the General Strike. I was a magistrate then, and I took an active part in the General Strike. We had the whole area, Angus, Forfarshire, we had it sewn up. I was speaking when the news came through of J. H. Thomas's betrayal of the strike. I was speaking to an audience mainly of railwaymen, and they all broke down weeping. It was one of the most moving experiences I ever had – middle-aged men, most of them, weeping like children, you know. It was such a disappointment, because we knew, we knew we had it.

BRUCE: You see, your politics and poetry seem to arise out of very particular experiences, sometimes, because again as you talk I remember in 'Reflections in a Slum' you have a reference to the woman being tied up, Valéry and Gide. This is another case I think where your human concern is aroused.

MACDIARMID: Oh yes, undoubtedly.

BRUCE: About the woman being tied up, at the end of which you indicate that it is humanity that is your concern.

MACDIARMID: The end of that poem, of course, might be considered by a lot of people to be anti-human, but I say compassion for the woman's plight is not enough. I'm concerned for something that goes far beyond that: the flowering. As I've said before, I'm not interested in human beings, I'm only interested in the higher brain centres. I've said that you see.

BRUCE: I think you're interested in more than that. I will not accept that one. I will not accept that you're not interested in human beings only in the higher ...

MACDIARMID: I was always a loner. It's significant that Langholm is a small town, fifteen hundred people, and very poorly paid, the mill workers

282

and so on, you know. My own cousins – some had fifteen shillings a week – going through the streets in the early morning, came back in the night when the mills were shut. In their clogs. The beat of the wooden clogs upon the pavements. I was always a loner, and I liked it – I got to like it at any rate. That became intensified in my literary interests too. I hated mateyness; its presumption that we're all Jock Tamson's bairns. We're not. I reacted against that right from the beginning and that accounts for this sort of ambiguity in my work, social ambiguity, you see. I don't like most people at all. I think most people are a failure. And I think that's going to lead to the ultimate extinction of mankind. Mankind is not fulfilling the cosmic purpose. They're not alive these people, most people, not alive in any real sense of the term, as Herman Broch called them, the 'sleepwalkers'. That's what they are. They have never been awakened to the realities of life. They've never examined themselves in terms of ultimate purpose, cosmic destiny and so on, you see.

BRUCE: And yet, again, you see, it's surprising me, it seems to me that no doctrine has been allowed to narrow your vision. Take for example 'The Glass of Pure Water'. It seems to me that here we come to a critical issue because here you brought in together so many different elements. You even say one is talking to God. What does that admit?

MACDIARMID: It depends on the definition of God. It'll have to be in inverted commas.

BRUCE: In a fairly recent interview, with Walter Perrie, you said that you agreed that there must be something transcendental in man and that element is given expression in that poem, amongst other poems, is that right?

MACDIARMID: I think so. David Daiches doesn't use the same term but he uses another one that I think is exact – transhuman. I think I've always been aiming at that because of my dissatisfaction, my disbelief in the centrality of cosmic purpose. That reflects back on my interest in geology and so on. I'm trying to get away from this anthropocentric feeling about human beings, all human beings – not all human beings, very few. I'm an élitist, in other words, you see. That's why I'm a communist, of course, because the greatest communist of them all, Lenin, he realised that; that was why he formed the élite, the storm-troopers, the Bolsheviks. He knew that the mass of people were no use for his purposes – he was going to effect a revolution so he had to get stormtroopers.

BRUCE: And yet you show humanity and compassion in your poetry.

MACDIARMID: Oh yes. The two things aren't mutually exclusive, you see. They're usually treated as if they were, but they're not. I don't think there's any humanity at all in any other position except the socialist position.

BRUCE: But I doubt if all that many socialists would use in a poem words 'We must be humble'.

MACDIARMID: That's my biblical training again.

BRUCE: Ah, it's more than your biblical training now, because after all that is nevertheless as appropriate an expression – if I set that against 'The Watergaw', if I set that against equally that beautiful few lines about the Foramenifera, if I set that expression against 'On a Raised Beach', if I set that expression against 'The Glass of Pure Water', it explains, I think, quite a bit about these poems: their gravity.

MACDIARMID: Oh, there is that gravity seen in my work generally, of course. I've always been a very serious person. I've got a sense of humour but it's the servant of a gravity. I had a serious purpose all along; it wasn't going to be fobbed

	off or misdirected by jokes. It didn't mean that I couldn't joke.
BRUCE:	There is one other question. Very briefly, it is – well, I'll put it this way: What matters about all this work? What matters to you?
MACDIARMID:	Poetry matters. I regard poetry as one of the things that matters most in the world. The organic apprehension that can only be achieved through poetry seems to me sadly lacking. There has been a playing down on of the increasing complexity and pace of modern life and so on, playing down of the role of the imagination. The seer, the foreknower, has been displaced in a hierarchy of human beings. It requires to be replaced there.

Valedictory

On 15 September 1977 the BBC Radio 4 programme 'Kaleidoscope' broadcast Tom Vernon's interview with MacDiarmid. Recorded approximately one year before the poet's death (on 9 September 1978) it provides further evidence of MacDiarmid's octogenarian vitality and mental agility.

MacDiarmid: I was born in a small town, devoted to Tweed mills mainly but it's a beautiful little place, three rivers meet in the centre of the town and flow on to the Solway as one. It's surrounded with hills and forests so there's an abundance of all kinds of natural life and I had a very happy childhood indeed. My father was a postman, a rural postman, my mother came of agricultural farm labouring stock. So I had it both ways – both the industrial and the agricultural side of it. They were very strict, they were very religious people, devout and so on and I had to fall in with their wishes with regard to Church attendance and Sunday School. But I rapidly outgrew that. We didn't quarrel over it, I don't remember having any serious quarrel with either my father or my mother, but they knew that I had abandoned all the tenets that they believed in. My father died suddenly when he was only forty-seven. He'd never had an illness in his life, but he went to a funeral and he caught a chill which developed into pneumonia. Now at that time, he belonged to the trade union – The Postmen's Federation as it was called then, and they paid one shilling a week for medical attendance, and the local doctor was an old Tory who had no use for a shilling-a-week patients. So, when he was called to my father, he simply stuffed him with a dose of – injected a dose of morphia, said to my mother, 'He'll be all right when he comes out of that.' Of course he didn't come out of it. His heart gave way and he died at forty-seven.

VERNON: Was this what made you stand for the Working Class or had it begun already?

MacDiarmid: It added bitterness to my whole attitude.

VERNON: Of course Langholm is in a very beautiful part of the country, only just in Scotland though. If it had only been ten miles further south you would have been an Englishman. Would that have made a lot of difference?

MacDiarmid: Well I think it would probably because it accentuated the frontier feeling in me. There was a great deal of animosity towards the English in most Langholm people at that time. They were very radical, I suppose you'd call them Liberal but they were more radical than liberal and they were very anti-English and I inherited that. It's a border spirit, where the differences are accentuated by proximity. As for writing I hadn't so much thought that myself as had it borne in upon me by my teachers. They all concluded quite early that I was going to be a poet. They didn't know anything about poetry themselves. I was somehow different from the other pupils that they were accustomed to dealing with and I certainly had an inclination to write very early – I think my first poem in a local paper was published when I was about ten or between eleven and twelve.

VERNON: Can you remember what it was about?

MacDiarmid: It was about a hedgehog, about the gypsy business of dealing with a hedgehog – rolling it

287

in mud and putting it in the heart of a fire you know, and then you can take off the hardened mud and the flesh is delightful [laughter] ... that was what it was about. And the name for it was the gypsy name, the Romany name for hedgehog – 'parchywechy'.

VERNON: You were writing in dialect at that time?

MACDIARMID: In dialect no. I was writing in English, I was determined to be a journalist and I was a journalist for many years ... in a local paper. I prefer a local paper to the national paper in any case, for all kinds of reasons. And the local paper I went to was in Montrose which is a very attractive small burgh, but it also has a wide agricultural hinterland. I was the acting editor of that paper. There were two papers in the town, the other one was owned by a cousin of the owner of the paper I was on but I had to work for both of them: one was ostensibly a Liberal paper and the other was ostensibly a Conservative paper and I wrote the leaders on both of them without any difficulty at all.

VERNON: Did poetry more and more take over your life?

MACDIARMID: I didn't feel it take over in that sense. I wrote a lot of small Scots lyrics, most of which were set to music. And, I did them when I was going about my daily work. I had to do a lot of cycling – push-bicycle you know – all over the area and an idea of a poem would come into my head. I would push along and I didn't write down anything until I got home and then I wrote it down and perhaps, improved it a little. But that was the way it was done, and I gradually accumulated a sufficient body of that sort of thing too, to publish books. I became immersed in local politics of all kinds, I became a Town Councillor and Magistrate and what not – a member of the Parish Council, a member of the Education Authority and that led on to more and more public speaking. And the Scottish Nationalist movement was just rising at that time, the National Party of Scotland hadn't been formed but there was an older thing – there has always been a Scottish Nationalist movement ever since the union of the Parliaments – but it was the Scottish Home Rule Association which was a much milder thing. I was a member of it and after the War, when the Nationalist movement began to develop, particularly in Universities – in the University of Glasgow, the Nationalist Association was formed – I became identified with it. Now, whatever I might think of Scottish politics generally, on general politics I was always a Socialist and becoming more and more extreme. What triggered me off was the realisation when I was demobbed, of the actual facts of the Scottish position. But it was prior to that actually, I was in barracks, in Sheffield of all places, in 1915, and I was there when the Irish Rising took place in 1916. If it had been possible at all I would have deserted at that time from the British Army and joined the Irish. I took a very active part subsequently, in gun-running for the Irish and I knew a lot of the leaders. It was a little later on before I met many of the literary figures but I met most of them, Yeats and A.E., Sean O'Casey and I have maintained that interest in the Irish movement ever since. But I added to it, in later years, an equal interest in the Welsh movement. I know the leaders of the Welsh Nationalist movement intimately, and my wife is a Cornish woman and Cornwall has its own little National Party now. So I added these things together and I've been advocating for years, a sort of union of the Celtic countries in the British Isles – meaning, that if they get together, four of them against the English one, that we'd be in a position to rule the roost.

VERNON:	How did it happen that you became conscious of your Scots identity?
MACDIARMID:	I think it was largely the First World War. I was abroad in the Services, in the Near East, in Salonika and elsewhere, for about six years. That imbued in me nostalgia for home and also reinforced my sense of the difference of being Scottish, not English. My recollection of the wartime and the hundreds of men that I soldiered with was that when they were Scots, or Irish, or Welsh we got on alright, but we always had a difference from the English, we didn't get on with the English at all and I became more and more anti-English as the time went on.
VERNON:	But you didn't stay in Scotland, you ended up going to London. Why was this?
MACDIARMID:	That was after I became fairly well known, after my first three or four books in Scots had appeared. A friend of mine, Compton MacKenzie, was starting a small weekly magazine called *Vox* – a radio critical magazine, critical of all the programmes – and he asked me to go to London and be the London editor of it, and I did. But it was under-capitalised and it was much too early anyway, people weren't interested and it only lasted a few months. It was a great mistake on my part but I was hard-up at the time and I couldn't resist the temptation.
VERNON:	You have always kept closely in touch with Irish writers, haven't you?
MACDIARMID:	The Irish poet whom I knew best was A.E. – George Russell – who ran a paper called the *Irish Statesman* at that time. And he and Senator Oliver St John Gogarty made a fuss about my *A Drunk Man Looks at the Thistle* in the *Irish Statesman* and they had revived this part of the developing Irish Free State business, they developed what they called the Tailltean Games. These were a revival of Celtic games of all kinds, held in Dublin annually and they

invited me over as a guest. I went over there and had a very happy time and met them all. Every Friday night, Yeats and a few others would meet in A.E.'s house for talk. They were both great talkers, both Yeats and A.E., and they didn't allow any sort of general conversation – they had to indulge in monologues. However they asked me along, and I went along and Yeats particularly wanted to know something. What he wanted me to do was to explain to him about Douglas's social credit, and I rapidly discovered of course he didn't know anything about the existing banking system, so it was useless trying to tell him and I told him so. I was horrified at that meeting by another thing too; nothing was dispensed in the way of liquor except natural lemonade and it's not one of the drinks that I am partial to – natural lemonade. However I did swallow some of it. I was with Yeats and, walking along, he said, 'Well if you'll excuse me,' he said, 'I must urinate' – which he did in the middle of the road, you see. And I thought to myself, well, what an Irish Senator can do there's no reason why a Scottish Magistrate can't do, so I crossed swords with him and we became very friendly after that. He used to go about reciting poems of mine.

VERNON: You are very fond of the wry comment, the twist in the tail, the thought that ascends to Heaven and turns on its back and nose-dives into the mud. 'Millions o' wimmen bring forth in pain/Millions o' bairns that are no' worth ha'en.' It's a combination of soul and sinew that perhaps is not only characteristically individual, but racial.

MacDiarmid: Yes, it's one of the things that differentiate the imagination in Irish or Welsh literature from the imagination as you find it expressed in English literature – very different indeed.

There's always that comic element as well as a very fierce strong element.

VERNON: But of course, the English have always admired Scots poetry. Perhaps they have admired it sometimes for the wrong reasons?

MACDIARMID: I think they've admired it for the wrong reasons. They've never acknowledged their debt to Scottish and Celtic poetry generally. But they had no nature poetry at all until they derived it from Thomson of *The Seasons* and others. They had a false attitude to nature and they regarded the big mountains and the Highlands of Scotland as savage – beyond bearing, beyond tolerance. They may have expressed admiration for Scottish ballads and so on, but compare the Scottish ballads with the English ballads, compare the Scottish ballads – the best of them, with the ballad traditions of any other European country and it's like comparing whisky and milk.

VERNON: Did your early education emphasise your linguistic heritage?

MACDIARMID: At school we were taught nothing whatever about Scottish literature and although we spoke Scots and all the people in the little town that I belonged to spoke Scots when I was a boy, we spoke Scots to each other in the playground, in the streets and in the homes and so on, but in the school if we lapsed into a Scots expression then we were punished. And that subsisted until quite recently. I was interested, and had been for years, in foreign literatures of all kinds, and it had never occurred to me to write in Scots at all, although I spoke Scots as a boy. Then, in the London Burns Club, they started forming what they called vernacular circles, to try to encourage the greater use of Scots in poetry and other literary forms. And I took violent exception to that because I knew that what they wanted was a continuance of the Harry Lauder debased Scots tradition. I wanted something very different from that indeed. So I wrote, oh I suppose hundreds of letters to various papers and so on, protesting again the London Burns Club's ideas and so on, and then one day it occurred to me it was the attitude of these people to Scots that I was objecting to. I didn't want to see it continued.

VERNON: Is the Scots language not a limiting medium for poetry?

MACDIARMID: I think not. It's argued that there's a limitation involved in that people who speak Scots nevertheless think in English. I don't think that's true. If language is something more than just a medium use, if it's something that's organic with us then it must be true that languages that are part of our whole nature afford a medium that can express things that can't be expressed in any other language. I think that is true. I remember a critic saying that even Burns in some of his poems had to eke out his Scots with English. Of course he did – he wasn't sufficiently educated in Scots and too much under the influence of a very bad period of English literature, the Augustan period with poets like Shenstone who don't matter a damn. But I pointed out that on the contrary, in various poems of mine, when I was up against a real problem of expression, instead of falling back on English, I just plunged deeper into Scots.

VERNON: There's no question but that we do have a tired language in English English: perhaps a transfusion from across the Border might not come amiss to the making of poetry with some blood and bones to it.

MACDIARMID: The poetry you are looking for is the poetry of the whole man. Not a fraction of a man who is a good citizen or a good father or something like that but a real man. We're a hard drinking, woman loving race of people – the Scots – and we have no real inhibitions. This idea that the Scots are inarticulate – you know the

	expression mean mou'd – very careful and canny in their speech – is nonsense. That's been foisted on us. Nearly everything that is regarded by the Scots themselves, and by the world at large, as typically Scottish is a later substitution for the real thing.
VERNON:	You're talking about the poetry of the whole man. And you've also talked about your identification with the working class. But I question whether it is possible to be a whole man and drive a capstan lathe day in and day out, or worse – to work on a car assembly line?
MacDiarmid:	Oh, very difficult I agree. That's the reason why it's necessary to be a Communist – it would transcend that condition in which people are slaves to the machines, where they don't get a chance, where they've no access to the arts and to culture generally. That was what Lenin said. He said that without a knowledge of literature and the arts it would be impossible to call oneself a Communist, one was simply a faker. I'm depressed because of the low level of cultural insight or knowledge amongst the broad masses of the people but I don't see a solution to it except through Socialism – ultimately under Communism of course. I've an instinct against anything that's popularly accepted. I don't want to be a popular poet. I said that Burns had achieved a degree of world popularity unparalled by any other poet in the history of literature. I said it was high time that Scotland was having an unpopular poet. And I've become that. I don't believe the majority of people know anything about poetry – or can know anything about it at all. When you've got a poet who achieves a big public that's generally a very bad poet. I think my whole course is exemplified by what is said by Thomas Hardy – 'Literature is the written expression of revolt against all accepted things.' I think that sums up my whole position.

PART THREE

Fiction

Casualties

C. M. Grieve, then serving in the RAMC, sent this from Marseilles on 12 June 1919 as a contribution to his old school magazine at the request of George Ogilvie, the teacher who had a decisive influence on his early development; it appeared in The Broughton Magazine *in Summer 1919.*

For three weeks the working hours of the unit had been sixteen out of every twenty-four, and at length, in the centre of that sloppy and muddy field, appeared what was to be known to the Army as the Nth Casualty Clearing Station.

Tired enough from the strain of continued and unremitting road-making, tent-pitching, and the innumerable heart-breaking tasks incidental to the shifting of stoves and equipment, and the improvisation of those diversely essential things which cannot be secured except by indents which take many weeks to circulate through the chain of offices, the unit disposed itself, as units do, to snatch some sleep before the first rush should begin.

None too soon, it shortly appeared, for as we stumbled to the Fall-In, headlights began to appear on the road from Albert, a long trail of ambulance cars stretching back into the rainy dampness which hid the tremendous business so casually referred to as 'The Big Push'. The turn of the first car into the little road found a quietly active camp, for hasty preparations had been carried out in just such improbable corner-grounds many times before.

Here, as always in the track of armies in the Somme region, the salient element was mud – thick, deep, insistent and clinging mud that the strongest will could not treat as negligible. There it was and it made the smallest errand an exacting fatigue. The cars manoeuvred through it with the casual air that comes of much experience. Even London taxi-drivers might have learned something from the dexterous and undelaying way in which Red Cross cars were juggled over that boggy land. One by one the cases were slid out by stretcher-bearers working deftly and surely with a sort of tired ease. Car after car rolled up – just the price of 'strengthening the line and solidifying positions in the neighbourhood of ——', as it would appear from the day's official report. Men of all units, tired, pale and dirty, were carried into the hut that a party of engineers had finished feverishly that very day. Their khaki barely showed through the encrusting mud save where it had been slit to rags to allow of temporary dressings being put on at Field Ambulances and First Aid Posts and now showing in curious patterns of white and red. Among them were some to whom this station would be something more than a wayside resting-place, men to whom the doctors up the line, working in dugouts where immediate attention to all could not be given, had given a desperate last chance. They died on the way or slipped off without fuss in the Receiving Room, but one or two were pulled through by efforts and methods that would stagger civilian practice.

All night the slow heavy labour of stretcher-bearing went on. And great grey cars pulled up with loads of less seriously wounded who straggled brokenly into the room, muddied and shivering, hatless and coatless often, and with that complete apathy of look and bearing which tells of strain that has gone beyond endurance.

The detached onlooker might have found it moving enough, but here, fortunately, there were no detached onlookers. Lady friends, of the type we all know, were compelled to find stimulants for their sentiment somewhat farther down. But, here, a man who had been shovelling mud from the road during a back-breaking afternoon was now booking particulars of the arrivals. But some stared blankly through the interrogator, deaf and speechless, shaking and quivering, and that matter-of-fact fellow entered them as 'Shell-Shock. – No particulars available', and they were led off in that new world of theirs to a mattress, and ultimately who shall say to what strange and undesirable destiny.

The slightest cases walked or limped casually up to the keen deft-handed doctor and his alert assistants with the air of men to whom this was but one more incalculable phase of a business whose immensity made all impressions unseizable. To them, indeed, it had been overwhelming, and many of them were so youthful that one felt that the first instinct of their mothers, could they have seen them, would have been to reprove them for being out without overcoats on such a night!

The lashed rows of marquees that had been dignified by the name of 'wards' received these exhausted men on straw palliasses and blankets, and even, for serious cases, cot-beds. Casualty Clearing Stations belong not to any particular division but to an army, and therefore hither came representatives of most of the troops of an Army – Canadian, New Zealanders and South Africans, as well as famous British regiments and new raised battalions, and sick from locally quartered West Indians, Artillery, Engineers, and billeted troops. And there were men in mud-stained grey, stoical as our own, who somehow seemed mere ordinary men again and enemies no longer!

Serious cases speedily filled every available cot and an overflow lay around on stretchers. From all sides came the accustomed moaning for water and the close and heavy breathing of those past even moaning. A strapping sergeant of New Zealanders, gasping out his last unconscious moments, was the first to go. There was no more than time for a quick laying-out (with the boot which was hanging so unnaturally to one side, the foot came off too, despite bandages). His transit must have been a desperate gamble from the start – a wrapping in a rough blanket with scrawled particulars attached, and the big fellow who had travelled so far to his fate was taken on a stretcher to the marquee that served as mortuary.

Many joined him that night. With these hopeless ones there was no time even to stop to watch by the ebbing life, so many bedside fights there were where a forlorn hope still remained. Work went on without respite, changeless save for the occasional sudden appearance of officers who would leave a few hasty directions for the special treatment of cases which had just left their hands in the operation theatre. Those worst hours before the dawn passed in hectic attendance – the tiredness of the body had perforce to be treated merely as a clogging dream – and the day-staff came to the relief of worn-out men.

The peaceful dawn-wind smote the workers as they stooped to pass through the low canvas doorways and the first faint flush of red showed behind a tree on a far ridge.

Up to that ridge wandered the indescribable waste of the countryside, trenched and pitted and ploughed until it had become a fantastic and nightmarish wilderness. On this dreary tract nothing remained of the gifts once showered by nature. But the grim legacies of man at war were countless – chaotic and half-buried heaps of his machinery, munitions and equipment, and the remains of his hasty meals. And he himself lay there, shattered in thousands, to give a lurking horror to a treacherous and violent surface of mud and slime and unlovely litter. The very weeds which might have graced the desolation refused such holding-ground.

Pale now beside the compelling splendour of the reddening day showed the yellow stabs of our guns, flashes that had lit the sky in the night watches, and only the long road, never varying, told that the unspeakable harvest on the Somme was still being gathered in.

The Never-Yet-Explored

A story from Annals of the Five Senses *(1923), C. M. Grieve's first book. It is a collection of poems (such as 'A Moment in Eternity') and (generally autobiographical) prose pieces completed before the assumption of the MacDiarmid pseudonym in 1922.*

'Here in the flesh, with the flesh, behind,
Swift in the blood and throbbing on the bone,
Beauty herself, the universal mind,
Eternal April, wandering alone,
The God, the Holy Ghost, the Atoning Lord,
Here in the flesh, the never-yet-explored.'
—Masefield.

'All creation gave another smell beyond
what words can utter.' —George Fox

She was like Galsworthy's lime-tree, coldly fair, formal in her green-beflowered garb – which yet shakes, when the wind enters her heart, with the passion one sees when bees are swarming, a fierce humming swirl of movement, as though she had suddenly gone mad with life and love – tumults soon dying away; leaving her once more perfumed, gracious, delicately alluring.

Are you, did not Galsworthy ask (with that terible accent of his), the esssential tree when you are cool and sweet, vaguely seductive as now, or when you are being whirled in the arms of the wind and seem so furiously alive? When shall I see your very spirit? ... And as he fought in his dream towards his vision of the Lady of the Lime-tree, separated from him by a gulf of nothingness which was soft and cool to the touch of his face and hands, one of her ears lit up by a great buttercup, her eyes velvety and dark and dewy there, her body lovely though nearly hidden by creamy flowers growing stiffly round her as might asphodels, 'on her lips came the sweetest and strangest of all smiles'. Seeing her smile thus he struggled desperately against the cold smooth nothingness, and while he struggled he saw her quiver and writhe as though she, too, wanted to come to him. Her breast heaved, her eyes grew deeper, darker, they filled with glistening moisture and seemed to entreat him. ... Straining with a furious strength he never thought to have had against that colourless impalpable barrier, he crept forward inch by inch, and as he came nearer and nearer to her he saw her eyes liven and begin to glow sweet and warm as the sun through heather honey; shivers ran through her limbs; a lock of her hair drifted towards him.

A lime-blossom loosened by the bees and wind had drifted across his lips, its scent was in his nostrils. There was nothing before him but the fields and the moor and close by the lime-tree. He looked at her. She seemed to him far away, coldly fair, formal in her green-beflowered garb, but for all that he knew in his dream he had seen and touched her soul. ... And in her dream? There was nothing before her but the red and yellow expanse of the carpet, the familiar furniture gleaming or misty in the strong sunlight beating in through the windows, and herself, this Mrs Morgan, far away, coldly fair, formal in her pale silks. ... She looked at herself.

She tried to define her nature. 'Colourable and plastic, fashioned by the words, the looks, the acts and even by the silences and abstentions surrounding one's childhood; tinged in a complete scheme of delicate shades and crude colours by the inherited traditions, beliefs or prejudices – unaccountable, despotic, persuasive, and, often, in its texture, romantic,' – 'a mobilised and moving equilibrium! Much once central is now lapsed, submerged, instinctive, or even reflex, and much once latent and budding is now potent and in the focus of consciousness for our multiplex, compounded, or recompounded personality....'

She left it there and took, as it were, as the terms of reference for the particular inquiry she was now about to conduct, certain quotations from her recent reading which timeously recurred to her. The first of these was Richard Middleton's dexterous observation that 'nearly all the real sorrows of youth are due to this dumbness of the emotions. We teach children to convey facts by means of words, but we do not teach them how to make their feelings intelligible.' The second was Pearsall Smith's statement that 'the older kind of names for human passions and feelings we may call 'objective'. That is to say, they are observed from outside and named by their effects and moral consequences.... Most people must have felt at one time or another the incongruity of ugly names like greed or malice for feelings delightful at the moment, and a non-human observer from another planet might be puzzled to find that the passions and propensities that were called by the least attractive names were the ones that mankind most persistently indulged.' Introspection, she thus realised, was often, quite rightly, condemned as an unhealthy tendency, for it was very common and very disastrous to study feelings in order to increase their pleasantness. As a consequence language had become quite apathetic, generalised until it was without meaning. It was necessary that she should (sitting up a little and drawing her legs in) not sink into a warm bath of self-contemplation but make the coldest effort to regard her own organism as merely one among others. Her physical intellectual being was the sensorium of Nature, but it was also one thing among natural things whose number was legion. It was the mirror in which she viewed the world, but it was also part of the world, the part most necessary for her to know and work upon, and its value to her depended upon her knowledge of its natural distortions and how to test and correct them. Next she 'staked down' as it were, with an odd sensation of sudden successfulness, a quotation the source of which she could not remember, 'Immaturity, degeneracy, disharmony, aberration are conditions of consciousness in which no communion with reality can take place' and her mind seemed to tremble with an imminent efflorescence of spirit, an opening-up of faculty, the breaking forth of new life upon high levels of joy, and she was full of the strange and insatiable craving for reality, 'the diadem of beauty'.

This brought her swiftly to her next point. 'The essence of life lies in the movement by which it is transmitted.' And she felt that she had satisfactorily completed a most delicate and difficult task when she discovered ready for this end in her mind these lines from that strange drama 'In the Name of Time':—

> If there be judgment it shall be required
> Of women what delight their golden hair
> Has yielded – have they put its wealth to use
> Or suffered it to lie by unenjoyed?

And now she saw as from a wooded height the land of fulfilment but not the road thereto.

She knew that she was in a most subtle and successful fashion alienating the affections of her youngest son Frank from his *fiancée* Jessie Butler – adopting methods against which Jessie was too young to defend herself, and against which, constitutionally, Frank had no defence – for reasons which were so indistinguishably woven into the texture of her incomprehensible life as scarcely to admit of being most fugitively recognised by herself in her keenest moments of self-analysis; reasons which expressed themselves definitely, effectively, and yet indefinably, without her volition and often against her will, in the arguments of her eyes and the subtlest persuasions of her contours and colours. That was all – and yet it was proving enough. No! It was subtler even than that – a matter of involuntary tremors and unaccountable viewless vibrations; of co-intuitioning nerves; of incessant arterial heliographing in codes of infinitesimal pulsations indecipherable by any of the separate senses; of obscure and unseizable interactions of personality, wine-like and wind-like; going by unknowledgeable personal channels ... by flames passing from sensation to sensation.

In the recesses of her own consciousness Mrs Morgan admitted that she did not care. She was never, when she was in a genuine introspective mood (whatever she might be when her consciousness was limited and hampered by the presence of her husband or others, or when the functioning of her mind was altered by the pressure of any of the various normal external preoccupations incidental to wifehood and housekeeping) a victim to that uneasy pain of conscience 'which seizes both the head and the parenchyma of the heart and thence the epigrastic and hypograstic regions beneath'.

It was an instance of a specific aboulia. 'Specific aboulias in real life,' she knew, 'invariably prove when analysed to be due to our unconscious repulsion against the act that cannot be performed' (*i.e.* her acquiescence in this proposed match). 'In other words, whenever a person cannot bring herself to do something that every conscious consideration tells her she should do, it is always because for some reason she does not want to do it. This reason she will seldom own to herself and is in the great majority of cases only most dimly if at all aware of.' ... It was even with a tonic and penetrating thrill that she recognised the extensive abnormality of her awareness.... In other moods she went through the customary conscious processes that so involve and conceal the core of an aboulia. Time and again on such occasions (generally when her husband or other members of her family, all unsuspecting and safely external, were present) she worked herself up, pointing out to herself her obvious duty, with the cruellest self-reproaches, lashing herself to agonies of remorse and once more falling away to calm and by no means unpleasurable recognition of the impotence of her conscious self to control even in her own case the hidden effective factors of human intercourse guiding and enticing all life irresistibly and incessantly to unimaginable ends.

She frankly admitted that she could put into words no conceivable objection to their union. She knew of no bar or impediment. On the contrary, she was perfectly satisfied that Jessie was in all likelihood a more suitable mate than any other Frank was likely to choose or have chosen for him; that she would beyond doubt make him a true and faithful wife, that she possessed graces of mind and person which in conjunction with Frank's would almost infallibly conduce to what the world (and themselves) would recognise as a happy and successful mariage – quite as happy and successful as her own had been, which was, as matters went in the world at the time,* no inconsiderable happiness and no small success from any normal point of view.

She recognised it as typical of her character that in realising that she was thus working, involuntarily but no longer unconsciously, against what in all likelihood were her son's best chances of human happiness (not to take Jessie into consideration) she was not so much concerned with the direction in

---

* The beginning of the twentieth century – a terrible period.

which her influences were operating, or with the probable consequences, as with the unphraseable puzzles of the causation of that tendency, with the mysteries of her own motivation. If means only existed or could be devised not so much for expressing in words, but for thinking exactly about, such matters, how much nearer she would get to herself; vast regions of perceptions and correspondences eluded the imaging powers of her surface consciousness. What a small part of the whole real experience could the tiresome cerebral pantomime of voice and vision contrive to represent! She sought after clear instances of audition, distinct 'interior words', whereby she might translate her intense intuitions into forms with which her surface mind might deal. She was actuated by motives conforming to a rhythm too great for her to grasp, so that manifestations of it appeared erratic and unprepared.

She rubbed the tip of her nose between the ball of her thumb and the knuckle of her forefinger. For a moment she was startled as it occurred to her to ask what had prompted her to do so. She had stumbled on a clue. Instantly, however, she realised that it was a clue which she could not follow up, and it was with impatience that she permitted her thoughts to seize upon it, knowing that they would require to come back, in a little while, nonplussed, to this point of departure. . . . Undoubtedly, so far, it seemed that the solution must lie in the direction of rendering intelligible her obscure olfactory intimations rather than those of any other sense. Was the nose the key to many of the closest mysteries of human motivation – the nose, that strange winged instrument of an incalculable sentience, which, as it were, contributed to the mental atmosphere potent and pervasive elements appreciable only – and even then unintelligibly – in the crudest terms of their most obvious effects? How could she read the riddle of this sphinx squatting between her eyes? It was not any abnormal fineness of smell she possessed, but far-reaching intuitions that were somehow obscurely bound up with her olfactory sense, appreciable even by herself, and that only in a most rudimentary and fugitive fashion in their relation to nasal sensations, not to be disengaged by the subtlest efforts of her intelligence from the general complex of any normal psychological and physiological situation and yet most potently determinant of action, bound up most intimately and effectively with the innermost secrets of her personality – in themselves, in fact, almost solely determining her 'disposition'. She felt that if she could only 'clear her nose' she would come instantly to self-knowledge. Her thoughts turned back again, as she had foreseen, slinking like dogs with nasal catarrh:

> My thoughts are fixed in contemplation
> Why this huge earth, this monstrous animal
> That eats her children, should not have ears and eyes.

She recognised from the outset that to endeavour to arrive at any systematised conclusion as to the reasons for her attitude was bound to prove futile, reminding herself that we cannot concede even to the brute data of sense that fixity and security which a comfortable realism demands. Only by noting an infinitesimal and fugitive detail here, the flitting shadow of a sensation there, by patiently recalling the tiniest nuances of difference in the effect upon herself at different times of different perceptions – shining shadows of difference – by making as it were here and there points in the shifting landscape of that part of her recent emotional history relevant to the matter in mind, and so endeavouring to triangulate that district of her soul whence these influences emanated, could she hope to arrive at even the most fragmentary conclusions.

She cunningly discerned, however, that to imagine that this district or these purposes were central to her nature was probably fallacious. And to understand that her husband (that strange man, with his lumbaginous licence of movement, at once ponderous and erratic), her children, her friends, her enemies, each of all her acquaintants, had in relation to her more or less definite, and widely differing, conceptions of what her nature was – none of which, of course, in any way approximated to the indeterminable reality any more than her own conception before she adopted her present agnostic position had done – made her problem multitudinously difficult.

Her realisation definitely that the whole 'amazing reality of her concealed nature', for no reason that could be discerned by her conscious self, was set dead against this marriage had come one afternoon when she had been going out with Jessie's mother for a saunter down the river-side. When she had arrived, Mrs Butler was in the act of dressing. Her face shone rosily. She tried hard to recall in their initial vividness every sensation she had experienced in the presence of that phenomenon. She failed to discover by ransacking her memory that she had received the slightest unhealthy (unhealthy, not disagreeable – unhealthy for some incomprehensible but very urgent reason was the quality of which she was in search, and not unhealthy in any virtual way but merely in antipathy with the secret standards of her own functioning!) impression.

Patiently her visual imagination recreated the big red face, the smile, the little twinkling eyes, half-birdlike, half-piggish, each separate crow's-foot in itself and in respect of the contribution it gave to the expression as a whole, the under-swell of the chin, the disposition of the throat, the way of the hair – over the ears particularly, and in the effect of the fashion in which it was pulled up from the nape.... Mrs Butler had been in petticoat and camisole. The petticoat was negative – a cancelling stripe – that was to say, it did not affect her as if it had been one of her own (it would be to overrate her perceptions, however, to say that its effect upon her was exclusively Mrs Butlerian), but it aroused no speculations of any kind, and the legs beneath it were apparently quite irrelevant. There had been something, however, about the bust – unconnected with the quality of the linen into which it was somewhat negligently stuffed, with the details of the lacework or the ribbons or the way in which they were crossed and tied. Nor could she definitely attribute it to the remotest sense of geometrical impropriety in the fashion of the bunching and gathering.

It was a matter of a line, some indescribable faint flaw in moulding, an almost invisible 'indisposition' of flesh just over the right breast, an elusive indetermination of form. She endeavoured with a conscious impossibilism to reproduce it on paper, to achieve with the stub of a pencil the faintest approximation which would in any way make this feeling of hers more definite. The effort was hopeless. Then, suddenly, with a swift, soft movement she crossed the room displaying as she walked that lengthening of the joints as when a desert mare canters along the sand. Her fingers glided swiftly down the buttons of her gown. In a second she had freed herself from its ensheathing. Garment after garment fell until she stood almost naked – naked but for a single filmy garment, slipping slightly off her shoulders. Then she turned to the mirror. The light deepened the hollows of her delicate temples and the double furrow between her clever irregular eyebrows. Her eyes held the shady look of long-suppressed desire. Her ears threw red stubs down the shadowy orange of her neck. Her glittering ear-rings were reflected like flecks of moonlight in the clear golden skin at the angles of her cheeks. Her face was more characteristic than beautiful, belonging as it were to 'an upper plateau' with a 'savage poignancy in serenity' stamped upon it, intrepid, individual. Nine men would pass it: the tenth sell his immortal soul for it – if he had one. . . . She had never met one of these tenth men. . . . The paleness of some strong feeling tinged her face. A slight trembling ran through her frame. Her inner soul struggle was acting like a strong developing fluid upon a highly sensitised plate. Passion, self-contempt, cruelty, ruthless curiosity, humour, impotence chased one another like shadows across her cheeks. Naked flesh, her own or another's, always affected her thus. Her bare wrist, slender and nervous, had something of the look of a leopard's claw or the leg of a gazelle. . . . She pressed her palms slowly down under her thighs. A purple vibration waved across her face. Then with a sudden gesture she ripped off her remaining garment and stood squarely in all her throbbing nakedness.

She was conscious now that her thought was pursuing a passionate method that was ubiquitous, that was inadmissible, a method ancillary to a conception not as (impotently recognised in an atmosphere of competing flashes of insight!) one could claim to function, but as, for two pins, one fine afternoon, it might become pathologically patent that one did, insomuch as the carnalities inherent even in the best could no longer be subordinated. 'She looked out of herself,' westwards in the flesh as it were, 'into the world of men and there she saw a sight which filled her with unspeakable distress. The world seemed simply to give the lie to this great truth of which her whole being was so full. The effect upon her was in consequence, as a matter of necessity, as confusing as if it denied that she was in existence herself.' If she looked into a mirror and did not see her face she would have the same sort of feeling which actually came upon her as she looked upon closely woven humanity in which such a small moiety of the incommensurable sentience of which she was so throbbingly conscious was utilised – a panorama of insensate maceration. She felt capable of producing a wholesale labefaction of life by simply daring to be herself. Civilisation made life 'a sad science of renunciation', – condemned her to a fractional existence, her permitted courses an inconsequent commentary on the margin of her uncomprehended soul, ending in the intolerable anti-climax of her animal death!

She had never felt before to any similar extent the cruelty of Nature's law, exciting sensations which could not be gratified and desires which could not be justified – never realised so clearly that Nature had no respect for the conventions of society about sexual commerce. 'Blessed,' said Hawthorne, 'are all simple emotions, be they bright or dark; it is only the mixture of them that is infernal.'

She rigged up in the forefront of her mind hasty skeletons, characterless as Pope's women, of civilised conceptions – hollow colourless forms in postures of paralysis corresponding to nothing ever entertained in a human heart – grotesque puppets – and her mind quivering anew with a simultaneous recognition of the wild unphraseability and utter ordinariness of her sensations and desires, destroyed them again 'with a crash of broken commandments'. 'Women' – she remembered Meredith's dictum – 'who dare not be spontaneous! This is their fate only in degree less inhuman than that of the Hellenic and Trojan princesses offered up to the gods.'

Who was this mighty and magnificent and terrible female creature, with lightning in her flesh and thunder in her hair – with hooded imponderable eyes and bosoms like fog-bound mountains; allied with the ultimate precipitous splendours of life; a votarist of incalculable powers and majesties rather felt than conceived; a lonely, passionate and hungering spirit in a marvellous and intolerable form, set apart for tragedy to come? ... She was carried headlong by the rushing rhetoric of her longings.

> *Impériales fantaisies*
> *Amours des somptuosités,*
> *Voluptueuses frénésies,*
> *Rêves d'impossibilités.*

She thought of her pitiful measures of accomplishment, the preponderance of her forced renunciations, her impotent hungers of heart, outwith the swirl of blood, the trampling of pulses, the violin play of lightning muscles – bound in upon her silent bones, sealed into anaemic courses, marooned in barren continences!

The reduction of the intricacy and wonder of womanhood into a 'rag and a bone and a hank of hair' was not more inhuman than would be her present dwindling back from this amazing stature of her spirit into a commonplace size in suburban wives.

By what secret mechanism did she and all other human beings so dwarf and confine themselves, and why? It made her think of the author who wrote that 'he followed a small maid into an even smaller room'. Because civilisation exalted morality at the expense of life its conventions seemed abortive and unconscionable and its effect unnecessarily withering. Such intuitions as these portrayed a clear outline of the appalling commonplaceness which scenes of involution assume when they become a conscious environment – and yet to how fine a degree a woman might develop her sensibilities and her balance in a monotony of needless inhibition!

This Mrs Morgan that she was – would become again as instantaneously and effortlessly (slipping on a *peignoir* and having had 'one of her headaches') if her husband or one of her children should come in just now – was so aptly and economically contrived, to all appearances spontaneous and free in the consciousness that conceived her; moving with a specified grace, displaying a recognised variety of discreet and appropriate gesture. So tense and subtilised was this accepted fiction of herself, that she had her being within it without any sense of imprisonment. Thought of it did not affect her as if this Mrs Morgan was any mere automaton, any stuffed shape staring glassily out of irremediable posture ... nor even as a separate personality assumed at her convenience for certain purposes ... but as a fairy, the face of which was but a screen, vividly visible on which the suitable selection of her emotions was cast like the lights and colours of a film. With a curious sense of pride she recognised the artistry of that life she was able to contrive under such unconscionable limitations, conjuring up the effects she made as sharply painted as recollections of a dream; and saw herself doing so – leading that usual life of hers, being so perfectly, dexterously and daintily what people thought her (people who could not think) – and her husband and the rest of the company like flittering ephemerides of the spirit under the profound and radiant gaze of her real self.

The artistic temperament. Did not most artists at the end of their careers become discontented with the form in which they had worked? They had succeeded through obedience to that form, but it seemed to them that a rare success lay uncaptured outside these limits. They were tempted by what seemed lawless in life itself: by what was certainly various and elastic in life. They were impatient with the slowness of results, with their rigidity, inside these inexorable limits. The technique which they had perfected seemed too perfect: something cried out in chains and they would set that voice, that Ariel, free. ... But could she?

She stood square to the mirror and drew herself up to her full height, hollowing her back a little, like a gymnast on the horizontal bar, and, looking at herself, she realised with a sudden fear how her new knowledge imperilled her in her relations with her husband and her sons, remembering what Angela of Foligno said ... 'because of this change in my body therefore I was not always able to conceal my state from my companion or from the other persons with whom I consorted, because at times my countenance was all resplendent and rosy and my eyes shone like candles'.

Closely she scrutinised her breasts. In the shifting of a contour, in the motion of a shadow on the skin, she sought for the slightest clue to this elusive recollection of – was it a movement? – an effect. All in vain! Beyond a vague tantalising sense (as when something is 'on the very tip of one's tongue' yet stays unspeakable) of knowing that somewhere along the line of this strange and subtle speculation lay the truth, she achieved nothing. Before leaving the mirror she closely examined her nose, breathing 'nostrils of investigation' as if in some incomprehensible fashion, the effect for which she was seeking – that fugitive sensation of shape – would be reproduced in a quivering motion of the wings. But no!

Turning again with a sense of having been arrested suddenly in the wild course of an inexplicable aberration and becoming, as with eyes like those of a dreamer suddenly awakening from a vivid adventure to confront familiar things (a good instance of a common and somewhat indescribable sensation analogous to by-psychic duality – the fortuitous phenomenon by which spirits are often uncertain as to whom they really represent), related again to the actual facts of her existence – vulning herself, as heralds say of the pelican, in her piety – like a Greek chorus the furniture awkwardly obtruding its crude signifi-

312

cances stood round her passionate soul in travail. Oh, the grotesque, stupid, pitiful interpositions of pictures, chairs, ornaments, needlework! Her household gods had acquired all the repulsive and puerile crudity of heathen idols – the whole room was stuck like an incongruous gargoyle on the tower of her mood.... And through the window in the oblique light 'mere circlings of force there, of iron negation, of universal death and merciless indifference!' with, nearer, a light shallow, an outer reach, a swaying edge of the deep metropolis (like a windless tide invading an unknowledgeable shore, remotely and with infinite gentleness, lapping the absymal dark foundations of the soaring house, alone of all things alive with its dark and durable secrecy, in which she so inconceivably lived), making an electric ravel, full of inconsequent glitter, and with little black unsteadinesses of people, like masses of flies on the broad blond pavements between which the streets were hung like long fine nets, quivering with a close-working subtlety of movement, holding a congested haul of cabs and cars and vehicles of all kinds and colours, endlessly miscellaneous but merged and dwarfed and suppressed into the tiniest courses, almost indistinguishable ... all so small, swarming infinitesimally away down there, sown through the thready complicated radiance ... seeming little more than swarms of midges hung in endless fine nets of flashing and failing light in a nether sky; drifting through strands of light and heat ... now, with a sense of panic, steepening about her as if the lines of her vision were miraculous dry paths between precipitous seas and all these but exposed sections of the infinite fisheries of fate ... now quiet, and decided and remote, rather beautiful, and yet seeming to have some strange cold power over her ... and again all so mild, so very old, so faint and floral, with a far-off life of its own that came stealing in upon her, very faint, swelling, sinking, festive, mournful, ... lustrous, mild and illusionless. This thin glitter and fume, this white and fawn presentment below, the shaken kaleidoscope of a metropolitan fragment, did not exist really ... it rested upon solid darkness, one with the mighty irresistible darkness, upon which she was hoisted into this bright room and existence of hers ... like a gleam of coloured oil upon dark water ... like a fair faint dream in an Egyptian night (her ears appraised the marvellous *fioritura* of the view, a graduation of small light sounds) ... but what was it? – nothing! Just nothing!

313

'It is amongst such communities as these that happiness will find her last refuge on earth, since it is among them that a perfect insight into the conditions of existence will be longest postponed.' Very strange and immaterial were these glitterings of a toy civilisation away down there in the fair blind fabulating streets, a pale calm through which the generations flew like shadows, and the windows high as her own over the way were blue as crystals full of sorcery, shining with a fascinating fatality. In a sudden dizziness as she looked they seemed to rock a secret and their panes seemed luminous, transparent, as if the secret were burning visible in them. Was it true of her, as of Coleridge, that the further she ascended from animated nature the greater in her became the intensity of the feeling of life? . . . Could she dismiss her problems merely by going downstairs?

She crossed the room and threw herself down on a sheepskin rug in front of the fire . . . turning her thoughts now into another channel, recalling the way, or rather the ways, she had been affected by seeing Jessie's father walking in front of her up the street. He was a tall man, spare, with a slight stoop, a stiff fashion of the arms and legs. It seemed impossible that in that precise and mean *ensemble* she could find anything so stupendously objectionable as to mobilise her every instinct to avert this marriage, despite the fact that it was so pre-eminently a satisfactory proposition from every social, material, sentimental and ordinary point of view. Yet such was the case. And she could not discover wherein her objection actually resided, or how it had been stimulated by a back view of Mr Butler. It was, of course, pathological or psychological – practically, here at all events, synonymous terms. It was the invisible and indefinable power that controlled her life. Vaguely she felt that the purposes to which these instincts were directed had practically nothing to do with herself as an individual, or with Frank or Jessie – that they were phylogenetic, intimately implicated with the whole reproductive mechanism of humanity, that in something similar if not identical lay what beneath all the *camouflage* of love, interest, ideals, beauty and so forth, occasioned the suicidal attraction of this man or that man to this woman or that woman. . . . Every crease of his trousers, the whole geometrical arrangement of his frame, the clicking black boots, the bony hands, the shape and angle of his head, and the way in which his ears were fastened to the sides of it, the curves

314

of his bowler, came back to her, but nowhere could she isolate the slightest suggestive detail.

She evoked Jessie herself, with her sherry-brown eyes and flat back, visualising her with an indescribable completeness and accuracy, subjecting her to a thorough pre-mortem, going over her from head to heel, every line, every tint, every habit of her body and mind – unavailingly. She only got near it when the concentration of her mind reached such a pitch that this visualised Jessie seemed to become part of herself, sharing the same vital functions. Then she had the most obscure sensation of something that did not harmonise, that escaped from this imaginary unification, of an unplaceable flaw – of a tiniest discord, as it were, immediately swallowed up and lost in the orchestrated sentience of which she was conscious, of a some-thing unamenable to this twining of their entities. Somewhere the wind of passion failed to keep the sails full and the foam at the bow. Jessie was a pitiful bow for the brave bending of sex . . . a glittering toy where she should have been a golden torment.

Thoroughly she worked this demoniac strain of sensuality which she had found in herself . . . criticising every movement, detecting every little inadequacy in her, every tiny congenital inability to respond to the uttermost, to give all and to give enough. Frank would probably be only very remotely if at all conscious of a disappointed muscle here and of there a vainly clamouring pulse, but . . . ! She thought she saw Jessie looking up at him with her mildly bulging eyes shaken and with a batlike bewildered flicker in their depths. Were these to be given to him in lieu of his birthright – 'eyes terrible as an army with banners'?

These speculations were full of that notion of being captured by the incredible which is of the very essence of dreams. How to understand, then, what made the truth of her mood, its meaning, its violent and invisible essence? It was impossible. No processes of thought could convey that sense of blood running blindly through a net of glimmering surmises; of thought that was but as a mesh of cheating gleams on the verge of the incalculable floods of life.

She who had thought of herself bankrupt (and whom civilis-ation insisted upon treating as if she were) discovered in herself a secret hoard of evolutionary momentum. Wave followed wave from the sea of her soul. She was taken by new billows of largesse. After a period of stability and rest her unstable tendency to variation had broken out with tremendous force, with an abrupt access of vitality, rolling up she knew not whence, breaking old barriers, overflowing the limits of old conceptions, changing her rhythm of receptivity, the quality of her attention to life. She was entinctured and fertilised by a new upwelling of her submerged life. She was on the vergy of saltatory developments. The Cloud of Unknowing had passed over. This realisation came like the winds of March. Experiencing it she participated in the deathless magic of eternal springs, full of emotional efflorescence, with an enhanced vitality, a wonderful sense of power and joyful apprehension, as towards worlds before ignored or unknown, flooding her consciousness. Her life was raised to a higher degree of tension than ever before, and therefore to a higher perception of reality.

How like Frank was to what his father had been when she married him. How curiously the same body had been transmitted from father to son and how tragic was the likeness when these two bodies of the same flesh were made to contain so different a spirit. At a little distance it could hardly be told which was the old and which the young, so exact a copy was the son of the father. Close, Frank made her forget the years almost, made the relationship between them impossible, so exactly did he reduplicate not only what his father had looked like but what she had thought he really was when she married him, and renew the sensations and desires within her which she had had then and had long ago had to suppress so cruelly. How much happier she would have been if his father had had her son's nature – how much more she could have had from life – how much more she could have given. If she had married Frank instead of his father surely she would not have remained a mere adumbration of her destined meaning, a magnificent provision of organs intended for functions which had never developed. She thought of Frank – the bright burnish of his crisply curling chestnut hair, the back of his splendidly moulded neck, full and round and strong, bronzed to the collar line, white as milk below, the first two or three articulations of his spine softly rounded, so deeply embedded in muscular tissues as to be scarcely discernible ... of 'his clean blueness of eye and whiteness of tooth and puissancy of neck and wrist ripe brown with stored sunshine'.

Oh, merry love, strong, ravishing, burning, zestful, stalwart, unquenched! ... She saw herself again with parted lips and panting rounded breasts and a dancing devil in each glowing eye and a throbbing darting tongue and quick biting teeth, giving muscle for muscle and vein for vein, while the wild music in her heart rose, now slow, now fast, now deliriously wild, seductive and intoxicating.... She could feel the answering shiver that quivered up to her.

'Is it beyond thee', her spirit seemed to challenge Jessie's, 'to be glad with the gladness of this rhythm, to be tossed and lost and broken in the whirl of this fearful joy? All things rush on, they stop not, they look not behind, no power can hold them back, they rush on, keeping steps with this restless rapid music, seasons come dancing and pass away ... colours, tunes and perfumes pour in endless cascades in the abounding joy that scatters and gives up and dies every moment.'

It was getting dark. The furniture shone in the fitful firelight dull and livid as old armour.

> Her white breasts gleamed;
> Her neck seemed conscious of its loveliness;
> Her lips, tired of tame kisses, parted with
> The expectancy of proud assault; she was
> As one who lives for a last carnival
> Of love in which she may be stabbed and torn
> By large excess of passion....
>   Her heart now leaps with life
> And now lies sleeping like a coiled snake.
> But in to-night's cold moon she burns and glows.
> Her heart is housing many a mad desire....

Nisbet, an Interlude in Post War Glasgow

This, the first composition credited to 'Hugh M'Diarmid', appeared in two parts in the first two issues of C. M. Grieve's monthly magazine The Scottish Chapbook *in August and September 1922. On 30 September 1922, in the* Dunfermline Press, *Grieve presented 'The Watergaw' as the work of an anonymous friend. When the third issue of* The Scottish Chapbook *appeared, in October 1922, 'The Watergaw' was attributed to 'Hugh M'Diarmid'.*

(*Scene – A Street Corner.*)

Duthie—Hullo! Fancy running into you of all people and here of all places! (*Draws back a little, still holding Nisbet's hand, but speaking as if to himself.*) What made me add that now? I run up against thousands of all sorts of people every day in life. Why should I feel it funny to run up against you, and why should I feel it particularly curious to find you in Glasgow? It's a tribute to your personality in some way....

Nisbet—But one it is difficult to know how to take.

Duthie—No more difficult than to imagine what prompted me to make it. I've no reason for such a feeling. But that's how one does form personal opinions, isn't it? No rhyme or reason. Yet these things strike deeper – right to the roots, I believe. What breeds likes and dislikes? Inexplicable. The mystery of Life. That you and I should know each other at all in such a world is incredible, even more incredible than if we didn't. (And yet I don't know. It is such an extraordinary thing to meet people one doesn't know, never will know, is constitutionally incapable of knowing, and it happens a thousand times a day. Appalling!) But what are you doing? Where do you live? How long are you to be in Glasgow?

Nisbet—One at time – one at a time! I live in Glasgow – been here for six months.

Duthie—Stupendous! You don't say so.

Nisbet—Why?

Duthie—Oh, go on! We'll take it for granted. I feel you shouldn't be here, that's all, in fact that you're not here except physically.

Nisbet—Now, you strike me as part and parcel of the place. It's people like you that are Glasgow. But for you and such as you it would be simply any old city in Scotland, or a rubble slide. Except when I analyse what you're saying I feel that I am speaking not to you in particular but to almost any Glaswegian. You look composite. And yet your conversation is all wrong. The tone or rather the tune is perfect, but the sense is utterly out of keeping. You speak Glasgow, but seem to think – Chinese. You've already said things that I am perfectly certain only a small minority of Glasgow folks could ever either think or say.

Duthie—But you've no grounds for that conviction. You've only talked with the smallest fraction of Glasgow folks. No matter how stupid a chap looks – and probably is – you can never tell what he'll get mixed up with in the course of talk. A crowd's a curious thing – impossible to form any opinions but false ones about. Nothing easier than to say, 'What a lot of sheep.' But are they? If you could only hear what they are saying individually Babel isn't in it. The miracle of pentecost is repeated on an ever increasing scale every second. Their topics are a hundred times more numerous than themselves and far more interesting. . . .

Nisbet—Diversity of topic is nothing. The most impecunious minds generally have enough conversational small change to make some sort of rattle. Only corpses are absolutely stoney broke. What I mean is that your turn of talk is unusual. You look so typical to me that I am all the more struck by the peculiar run of your ideas.

Duthie—Hasn't every man's mind a move of its own in this super chess?

Nisbet—No! Within certain limits I am sure that 99 per cent. of Glasgow people think in the same way – no matter how the things they think about, or think they think about, or at any rate talk about, vary. You belong to the odd 1 per cent.

319

You select your subjects and not only your sentiments about them. Everybody says things – you are one of the few who . . .

Duthie—You've nothing to go upon. You're like a snake. You haven't a leg to stand upon.

Nisbet—Haven't I? I feel different. You say I strike you as different. I am different. I can't talk to the majority of Glasgow people at all – except in the way that a ventriloquist talks to his dolls. But I can talk to you. I haven't found any other Glasgow person I could talk as much to as I have talked to you already. So you must be different too.

Duthie—What does it matter? I do belong to Glasgow in any case.

Nisbet—The devil belonged to Heaven.

Duthie—I shall stay in Glasgow. I'll be the last person to rebel against the Lord Provost. Believe me or not, I am the roundest of pegs in the roundest of holes – but what are you doing here anyway?

Nishet—Nothing.

Duthie—How long are you going to stay here?

Nisbet—I don't know.

Duthie—Where do you live?

Nisbet—Partick.

Duthie—Good God. Married?

Nisbet—No.

Duthie—You look pretty fit – now.

Nisbet—I am.

Duthie—Then what the devil's the matter with you. You're a fish out of water. A blind man could see that if he heard your feet. Don't people turn round in the streets to look at you?

Nisbet—I don't know and don't care.

Duthie—Hmm.

Nisbet—How long have *you* lived here?

Duthie—All my life bar the Army.

Nisbet—You look pretty fit.

Duthie—I am.

Nisbet—Then what's the matter? You look like an outside without any inside – as if you'd lost your personality.

Duthie—Probably I have. Did I ever have one? Does it matter?

Nisbet—In my opinion it is one of the few things that do matter – for ordinary individuals.

Duthie—That's it. That's why you look so disturbingly odd. You're still a mere individual.

Nisbet—While you've lost your soul and gained the whole of Glasgow.

Duthie—A bargain. I was never proud of my little peculiarities.

Nisbet—You're a Socialist?

Duthie—Of course! Aren't you?

Nisbet—I suppose not. We couldn't both be, could we – or it wouldn't mean anything, would it?

Duthie—That's why you look so desperate. Glasgow is enough to turn anybody but a Socialist into a gibbering lunatic. But Socialists are at home here; you see it takes places like Glasgow to make them. 'Socialism is not an antithesis to, but the crowning stage of, the one-sided bourgeois civilisation.' (*Aside*—It's no use trying to make a good collectivist of a fellow like this – like sending Christ to the YMCA.)

(*Silence for a little.*)

Duthie—You used to write? (*Nisbet nods.*) Poetry wasn't it? Ever do any now?

Nisbet—No. I keep trying – it's no go. Brainlock.

Duthie—Bad business! I do yards. Verse too. In the Ham and Meat Column. (*Fails to create any impression: and adds a little defiantly*) They pay jolly well too.

Nisbet—(*Ironically.*) Do they?

Duthie—You despise money? (*As if he had solved the secret.*) Excuse me for saying that you're in a critical condition. If I were you I'd toddle right off home and do a love story the *People's Friend* could accept – or die in the attempt. You might as well die that way as any other. You've just a bare chance. If you don't try for it you'll burst. You're bottled up. A set of verses in the Column . . . at 7/6 . . . is better than a score of epics in the head. You haven't even written your war book, I suppose? That's fatal. Like internal bleeding. The only cure for modern war experiences is to write a book about them. An inexpressible emotion must be Hell . . . who's a b—— fool?

Nisbet—I said it to show you that my case isn't quite so hopeless as you make out. I can express myself all right – but what I am concerned to say isn't printable, that's all – and what I feel I'll be compelled to try to express soon won't even be intelligible – to the sort of people you resemble.

Duthie—Hmm! I never try to say anything that could possibly give me dental hernia ... Oh! Here's Young! We'll ask him. He'll know – if he's sober. (*Grabs him.*) ... This is Nisbet, Young. (*Aside*—It's like saying Jesus ... Judas.) Nisbet and I were together in France. He was gassed. (*In a whisper*—Body and soul.) But he's not like me. You're not a Territorial, are you?

Nisbet—No.

Duthie—Would you join up if there was another war?

Nisbet—I'd see the King ... (*The clatter of a passing motor van makes the remainder of the remark inaudible.*)

Duthie—(*Sarcastically.*) Spoken like a comrade. Young, thank me. You get him on the rebound. And he's a virgin – doesn't know the difference between Blatchford and Lenin. Doesn't want to.

Young—Shut up. You're not a human being. You're a mere sorting house for mixed motives. That letter of yours in the *Herald* yesterday on the necessity for caution and method in the disbursement of doles was the work of a mental degenerate.

'Organised charity, measured and iced.
   In the name of a cautious, statistical Christ.'

(*Duthie laughs unconvincingly. Young turns to Nisbet.*) You mean it? (*Nisbet looks puzzled.*) What you said.

Nisbet—Absolutely. I am constitutionally incapable of rendering any more to Caesar. Nothing is his and that's all he'll get from me.

Young—Constitutional inabilities of that kind constitute dungeons in the present state of society.

Nisbet—I know.

Young—Do you like it?

Nisbet—No.

Young—What are they giving you?

Duthie—Solitary confinement – the straight waistcoat.

Young—Why?

Duthie—He's utterly intractable.

Young—Where does he live?

Duthie—Partick, poor blighter.

Young—What does he do?

Duthie—Nothing.

Young—How long has he been doing it?

Duthie—Ever since he was demobbed.

Young—Choice or necessity?

Duthie—Choice, in a way. ... But he's quite unfit for civilised life.

Young—What is he to trade?

Duthie—A poet – but he complains that modern Scottish acoustics are so bad that it isn't worth while trying to make himself heard. He's trying to invent a new insubmersible sort of song. ... But tell him all about your sad case, yourself!

Nisbet—Verhaeren visited Glasgow. He didn't say anything about it.

Duthie—Its modesty's at the root of his disease.

Nisbet—It's all so hopeless.

Young—What?

Nisbet—This. (*With an all-embracing gesture.*)

Duthie—He means that he can't tuck it all away neatly into a sonnet, like I can. It's the old problem – what happens when an irresistible force comes up against an immovable object? He hasn't found the answer yet. All that he knows is that if he's the irresistible force he's getting the worst of it – but he isn't quite sure any longer that he is. ... He'd have been all right if he'd stayed in Nazareth or Auchtermuchty or whatever his native village was. But he would come to Jerusalem – and he'll be crucified on Gilmorehill.

(*They watch a dog-fight which commences near-by and develops into a battle-royal between a drunk Irishman and a pregnant woman. Police come up, and drag the struggling, cursing combatants away.*)

Nisbet—How can a fellow see that sort even once – all that despair of humanity – and then go home and write verses?

Duthie—And yet you would if you could. What's wrong with you is that you can't.

Nisbet—(*With savage inconsequence.*) I agree with MacGill – Glasgow's a RAT pit.

Duthie—(*Indulgently.*) Tuts! Adam and Eve would feel perfectly at home in Rouken Glen.

Nisbet—(*Doggedly.*) Sodom and Gomorrah weren't a patch on this. Sin isn't even original here: it's mechanical.

Duthie—(*With an effect of triumph.*) Harry Lauder's here next week.

Nisbet—(*Blankly.*) Who's he?

Duthie—Eh – oh – um – quite! (*Obviously staggered: one to*

Nisbet, who knows it, and preens his brain tantalisingly: but recovers adroitly and proceeds with increasing rapidity.) Our High Priest – eat-drink-and-be-merry-for-tomorrow-is-another-pig-by-the-ear-old prophet. Laugh and the world laughs with you; weep and you wet your hanky sort of thing, don't you know.

> 'I have covered up with laughter
> More than you have drowned in tears.'
> Let Glasgow flourish . . . but there's no fear.

Nisbet—(*Brutally*.) There doesn't seem to be. What's the emblem – a what-d'you-call-it rampant?

Duthie—Tut, tut! There's quite as many decent married women in Glasgow as . . . the thingummyjigs you say . . . despite the police. (*Laughs solicitously*.)

Nisbet—(*Taking no notice of the invitation, and reverting to mock-sententiousness*.) Glasgow, like every other city, is a cannibal that feeds on its own children.

Duthie—You quarrel with the nature of existence – and you've precious little room to speak. You're eaten up with your own thoughts.

Nisbet—Ever been to Clydebank?

Duthie—I've passed through it several times – on the way to Baloch.

Nisbet—You know the song 'John Brown's body'?

Duthie—(*Enthusiastically*.) Yes, and 'Wash me in the Watter' and 'One Grasshopper Leaps' and . . .

Nisbet—(*Austerely*.) It's Clydebank's soul that lies mouldering in the grave while John Brown's body goes marching on. He never had a soul.

Duthie—(*Pityingly*.) But Clydebank isn't in Glasgow.

Nisbet—(*Not quite over-emphatically enough*.) No! It's in Hell.

Duthie—(*Severely*.) Look here! This has gone far enough. I'm a member of the University Fabian Society and the Scottish Home Rule Association and half-a-dozen other things . . . keep me busy . . . Satan still . . . (*Turning to Young, who has been standing in patient puzzlement*.) but they'd suit him about as well as an eldership in St Columba's would suit Jesus. You can see what he needs just as well as I can. Take him away to your lair. . . . (*Reverting to Nisbet*.) Young's Propaganda Secretary of the Glasgow Branch of the Communist Party of Scotland! You know – bloody revolution, hacking a way through, dictatorship of the proletariat, deeds not words, propaganda of action, all that sort of thing. No pink politics for pale people about him. He's the man for you. There's no satisfaction for your type except in active political propaganda.... Out of the mouths of miners and dock labourers...

Nisbet—I'm not interested in politics.

Duthie—Oh, yes, you are! But you don't know it. You soon will.... It's the only way. I'm a mere conventional worm, quite pleased to become another Neil Munro or Wee Mac-Gregor. But it's different with you. That's why you look so – so inappropriate, here. It's an axiom that our agitators are always foreigners, Jews and so forth – like Shinwell and Christ. We crucify them all if they give us half a chance – even when the only thing foreign about them is that they agitate, or the only thing agitating is that they are foreign. Don't dis-appoint us. Go and become the prophet you are. There's nothing more foreign in Glasgow to-day than a real Scotsman. Young will betray you at the psychological moment. He has had sufficient experience now as a labour leader to know that the only way to give the People the bread that doesn't exist is to give them circuses. That's his job – to make dummy-bombs and get fools who think they are real to hurl them at us; and we treat them as if they had been. It's a great game. – Yes. Dummy-tits and dummy-bombs....

Young—(*Impatiently, to Nisbet.*) What's *your* idea?

Duthie—(*Triumphantly.*) There you are! What did I tell you? (*Admiringly.*) You're the chap to size them up, Young ... 'Strordinary! (*To Nisbet.*) He notices right away that you're an embodied idea. People like me have only opinions and he has no use for us, but to you it's 'What's your idea?' He's looking for a Man – a Messiah. 'I am not he, though few feel the curse as I do.' He stands before you like a sculptor before a mass of marble, and he'll chisel out the figure that's hidden in you with his questions. He's a maker of men, is Young. Don't be frightened when he begins to chip you up. He knows his job – although he made a botch of me. Puzzled you ever since, hasn't it, Young? – My veining's all wrong. Every now and then he thinks he sees just how to give me the finishing touch and makes a dive at it, but his chisel slithers, and I am transformed into something quite different from what he intended. I am continually being born again, but – I always distress my proud parent by turning out an illegitimate child, don't I, Daddy?

Young—(*Fiercely.*) For the love of Mike, shut it!

Nisbet—(*Solidly.*) Our literature is bankrupt?

Duthie—(*Sotto voce.*) Not quite sepulchral enough.

Young—(*Indifferently.*) Indeed.

Nisbet—(*Passionately.*) But yes, I say! There's no arguing about it. All forms of literary and artistic expressions, equally with other phenomena of intellectual and spiritual activity, have reached in our Western civilisation the point beyond which they can go no further. Western Europe, with America, has exhausted her energies, as Greece, Rome, Assyria, Babylon....

Duthie—(*Anxiously.*) Don't forget Peru!

Young—(*In a bewildered but hopeful way.*) Leave him alone. He's finding his voice.

Nisbet—... exhausted their energies before her. She can add nothing more to the sum of vitally new human knowledge, of fresh and adequate channels of self-expression. We must wait....

Duthie—(*Sadly.*) ... for the inevitable end?

Nisbet—(*Austerely.*) Or rather the new beginning which will come from a civilisation other than ours.

Duthie—Rats! There isn't any.

Young—(*With immense relief.*) I don't know a great deal about literature and art; but I believe you're right and that if you care to go into the matter you will find that the renewal is coming, has begun to come, from Russia. I have been told – by Moira, I think – that in Dostoevsky, if that is the correct pronunciation....

Duthie—An open sesame to the great inane!

Young— ... is to be found the first delineation of that new world.

Duthie—That's just the sort of thing Moira *would* throw out in passing. A wonderful lassie! Chokeful of world-intuitions of the most concise and comprehensive kind. It's ages since I saw her. How is she?

Young—Full of Sinn Fein!

Duthie—Go on!

Young—Fact! No balance. Brain's like quicksilver.

Duthie—Thinks a rebellion in Ireland is worth two revolutions in the bush?

Young—Can't see beyond her nose!

Duthie—I shouldn't want to myself if I'd half such a pretty one. I'd spend all my time crinkling it and counting my freckles. Hot stuff, Moira!

Young—Not a bit. Mere red paint!

Duthie—She hasn't set fire to you, eh? You Marxians are made of asbestos.

Young—Bah! The Celtic fire is only pyrotechnics. Moira looks the real thing – but her politics are crackling tinsel. She's a flash in the pan – a myth in motion.

Duthie—The poetry of motion! (*To Nisbet.*) You must meet Moira. She's the Dark Rosaleen in the flesh. Young cast her for one of his Red Virgins, but he's just discovered that he's colour-blind. ... She's some bird: but no Phoenix. Too downy, eh Young? You've discovered that she's not only a force but a female. ... How about Ireland, Nisbet? There's an opening for you there perhaps.

Nisbet—My soul is no shillelagh. Deirdre was Mrs Grundy's maiden name.

Duthie—(*Impatiently.*) Sigma all that, but you haven't seen Moira. ... You're not built on Young's foundations. Utopia may withstand her, but Moira's the trumpet for the Jerichos. I think you'll turn out a mere Jericho after all! ... Perhaps not! Pearse and Plunkett and MacDonagh were only minor poets – only a half-size bigger than me. 'I see his blood upon the rose' sort of thing – 'winds trampling and militant upon the hill'. ...

Young—Come on then! (*With deliberate asininity.*) All men are sinners, but it's better to be a Sinfeiner than a cynic. (*Pretends to laugh at what he pretends to regard as his delightful wit.*)

Duthie—By-by, Nisbet! I look upon you as two of the ten just men of Glasgow ... full of the saving grace of tragedy. Young'll straw the deserts of your impotence with the guano of Bolshevism till they bloom with beauty and bloodshed and bunkum. There's no hope for a man who isn't full of despair. ... Remember me, poor thief of *vers-de-société*. ... But what can you expect of a *nouveau pauvre*? (*Exit Nisbet and Young.*) Poor souls! It's easy enough to say that little else is worth studying than the development of a soul: but the trouble is to tell just whether it's a soul or not that you're looking at, and then to discover what constitutes development, and so whether there's any to study or not. (*Looking round dissatisfiedly.*) How can one be sure of anything in this light?

'The best of what we do and are
Just God, forgive!'

They go one way and I go another, but we're all going the same way – further and further away from home! (*Exit.*)

Some Day

First appeared in The Scottish Nation, *30 October 1923; reprinted in* Scottish Scene *(1934).*

(*Scene—A winter afternoon. An ordinary Scots lower middle-class kitchen. Round the fire are John Macfarlane, a rugged middle-aged man whose natural bluffness is overclouded by a mixture of awe, bewilderment and humility; his elder daughter Polly, thin-lipped, severe-looking, in the thirties; his younger daughter Jeannie, a fine lively girl in her late teens, obviously excited. Both are intent on their father's cautious, hesitant narrative; but while Jeannie is obviously all agog, Polly affects a sort of disdainful impatience, and knits away as if to say, 'Talking's all right – and I suppose the thing's got to be discussed – but one can talk and work. But in this house I've got to do anything that's done. Jean never puts her hand to a mortal thing: and Father's too soft to notice how idle she is. If Mother had been alive. . . . '*)

Macfarlane—Mony's the funeral o' man an' wumman an' bairn I've seen at Sleepyhillock i' the past forty or fifty years. There's a gey population there noo. A' kinds – auld an' young – deein' in a' kind o' ways. Maist o' them i' the ordinary coorse o' natur' – an' yet ye'd wunner ... accidents, suicides, aye, an' even murders. Twa at ony rate. Na, three – i' my time. An' that's no mentionin' auld Mrs Peters, puir body. But the richts or wrangs o' that were nivur fun oot – or made public. Some thocht ae thing, an' some anither. ... But a' through I've seen nocht tae approach the day's ongangans, no' even the biggin' o' auld Granny Nisbet's airch. ...

Jeannie—Oh, what was that faither?

Polly—Ye've heard the story owre and owre, Jean.

Jeannie—What aboot it? I've nivur heard Faither on't.

Macfarlane—Deed, there's no muckle tae tell. She was a bit

329

lame body, an' as perjink as they mak' them. 'Ears afore she dee'd she had the airch made – an' it's there to this day, but gey ill to see unless ye ken juist whaur to look, owin' to the way the plantation's grown fornenst the wa'. . . . I juist min' o' her an' nae mair, gaen' hirplin' aboot, an' a tongue that wad clip cloots. But the biggin' o' the airch made a gey like stir at the time. Ye see she's a lair next the wa'. An' she wad hae an airch biggit i' the wa', aye, an' steepulated i' her wull that she sud be buriet wi' her feet pointin' that airt. . . . She didna' mean tae be behindhand whan the Resurrection comes. 'I'm a wee wommun,' she yaist to say, 'an' a crippled ane at that, – an', seein' whaur ma bit grun' is, the feck o' the folk'd be up an' oot and owre the hill afore I kent whaur I was. I'm a lang wey frae the yett, an' I could never sclim' the wa'' . . . So she'd her airch put intae the wa' to gi'e her a fair chance wi' the lave. It cost her a braw penny. An' the Pairish meenister mad' a sermon o't – takin' for his text 'The Deil tak' the hindmost'. Opeenion was sair divided wi' regaird to the maitter. Fowk didna ken whether to lauch at the auld wumman or gin there michtna be somethin' in't efter a', or gin it wasna juist eindoon supersteetion. She yaist to talk in a silly kind o' way aboot the Last Day: 'It'll be a sair how-dye-doo, I'm thinkin',' an' her remark was lang debatit i' the Pairish. It seemed to thraw a kind o' queer licht on the Resurrection. It was deeficult to ken what to mak' on't. . . .

Jeannie—Aye. It mak's yin think.

Polly—It depends what she meant. But as for the airch the deid'll rise in a different frame o' min', I'm thinking. There'll no' be ony siccan rush.

Jeannie—(*Seriously.*) Ye nivur ken.

Macfarlane—But I've nivur seen onything the equal o' the day's ongangin's.

Polly—(*Impatiently.*) What juist did tak' place?

Jeannie—The warst o't was that naethin' happen't – as it sud. Wasn't that it, faither?

Macfarlane—Well, yin micht gae the length o' sayin' that, Jeannie, yin micht say that. . . . (*Turning to Polly.*) Whan the coffin was lower't into the grave, Hugh an' Alick kneelt doon by the gravemou', an' baith cried out in a muckle voice, 'I' the name o' Jesus, Arise!' Ye could ha'e knocked doon the hale jing bang o's wi' a duster. It was sic' an unlooked-for thing. We didna' ken whaur to look or what to dae. There bein' nae meenister there made it a' the waur. There was naebody ye could look to – naebody to gie's a lead, as 'twere. Sprung on's suddenly that wey, it was deeficult to ken hoo to tak' it – whether to approve o't, or to regaird it as pure blasphemy, or to keep an open mind. I was fair at sixes an' seevins wi' mysel' . . . No' that I didna sympathize wi' the lads, of coorse . . . but, somehow, it wasna canny. It didna seem richt.

Jeannie—Why ever no'?

Macfarlane—(*Confused.*) Weel, it's no easy to say. We a' believe i' redemption thro' the grace o' the Lord Jesus Christ – every yin o's – an' in the resurrection frae the grave. But still an' on. . . .

Polly—(*Roused.*) It was an awfu' like way o' daein'. Silly laddies like Hugh an' Alick sud nivur hae been allo'ed to hae their way i' a maitter o' that kind. I dinna ken hoo they'd the hert . . . their ain mither! I dinna suppose either of them shed a single tear. It's no' natural. Fowk that's makin' the best o' this life dinna worry muckle about the neist. Hugh M'Taggart'd be better employed playin' fitba than prayin' . . . an' as for seekin' to perpetuate his puir auld mither, wha's she that he sud ha'e nae een i' his heid for the lassies he'd be coortin' gin he was a man ava. . . . Can you really imagine RESURRECTION DAY at Sleepyhillock . . . a' the graves crackin' open an' the fowk loupin' oot. No' me . . . There'd be some gey objects amang them. Mony o' them wad be better bidin' whaur they are . . . aye, an' kent it themsel's when they dee'd.

Macfarlane—Weel, they were baith deid calm an' as confident as ye like. A' the rest o's were vera far frae either, I can tell ye.

Jeannie—But they believed in what they were daein'!

Macfarlane—Oh, aye. They were baith i' deid earnest. There was nae doot aboot that.

Jeannie—An, efter a' if miracles could happen i' Palestine lang syne what's to hinder them happenin' i' Scotland noo?

Polly—But it was Jesus wha performed the miracles himsel'.

Jeannie—But the Bible says gin ye've as muckle faith as a grain o' mustard seed ye can move mountains. An' I believe baith Hugh an' Alick had as muckle faith as onybody ever could hae. (*Turning to her father.*) The rest o' ye were confused juist because ye didna believe richt thro' an' thro', beyond a shadow o' doot the way they did. It's a kind o' death in itsel' – this sayin'

'I believe, I believe' until yin really thinks yin does, an' hasna an honest doubt or a real live hope left. If I didna believe onything micht happen ony meenut I'd become a doonricht atheist.

Macfarlane—I dinna ken. But juist suppose for the sake o' argument that their faith had been rewarded there an' then. Suppose a bit cry had come frae Mrs M'Taggart's coffin doon there – what then? An' they'd hauled it up an burst aff the lid, an' she steppit oot again as large as life? . . . Half the population o' Scotland would ha'e been here the morn. An' the rest o' the warl' afore the en' o' the week. The papers would ha'e been fou' o' nocht else. The hale coorse o' history would ha'e been changed . . . I'm no' sure it would ha'e bin for the best.

Jeannie—(*In sharp protest.*) Faither!

Macfarlane—(*Doggedly.*) Weel, I'm no'. I believe i' Heaven an' i' reunion there wi' oor loved yins. But I honestly confess I wadna' like to ha'e seen Mrs M'Taggart brocht back to life . . . an' yer mither lyin' there a' thae years . . . an' my faither an' mither . . . an' a' the ither deid men an' weemun an' bairns I kent. But, mind ye for a meenut or twa, every yin o' us felt that something wad happen. In a way we were prepared for't. We wadna ha'e been surprised at onything. There was something in the way it a' happened, in the way Hugh and Alick behaved, that fair took awa' a' oor poo'ers o' thocht. Their voices rang oot like commands that couldna be ignored.

Polly—It was takin' the Lord's name i' vain. Neither mair or less. There's a hantle difference atween a prayer an' a command. Hugh M'Taggart's no' in a position yet to gi'e his order to Almichty God.

Jeannie—They didna mean't that way, as ye weel ken. They had faith. An' noo they've lost it, it's mair than likely. Ye couldna blame them if they've turned into pure atheists. It's a lang time sin' Jesus raised Lazarus. It's high time it was happenin' again. Even yae case 'ud gang a fell long way. Fowks losing faith, an' nae wunner. The kirks are a' gaen back an' back. It wad ha'e dune a pooer o' guid. I'm deid sorry for Hugh an' Alick. If there's a man I ken guid eneuch to perform miracles it's Hugh M'Taggart. (*Blushes as Polly looks at her.*) It's true.

Polly—Muckle learnin's made him mad. I dinna haud wi' this faith-healin' ava', an' neither does God apparently. It's fair fleein' i' the face o' Providence. Hugh's got his heid swelled at the College. He'd be better advised to be studyin' the things he needs to study. Christian Science 'll no tak' him fer i' the teachin' profession, even as things are ga'en noo-a-days. An' he's leadin' Alick fair aff his feet tae . . . Noo look here, faither, gin I was to say to ye, ye'll no' dee. Ye're gaen to be the a'e exception. Ye'll leeve for ever . . . ye'd think I was oot o' my heid a'thegither . . . An' I wad be tae . . . but gin it was true, an' ye kent it was true, wad ye like it?

Macfarlane—Weel.——

Polly—Feint a bit. Ye'd be the maist miserable man the warl' ever saw. Ye ken yersel' ye'd be far better deid. . . . It's got to be a'body or naebody, an a' the same time, if there's to be ony Resurrection at a'. An' even then it'd be a fell queer mix-up. Eternal life'd be a gey puir thing compared with this. If it wasna for disease an' death life wadna be worth leevin'. . . . Och, I believe in a life beyond the grave . . . but I canna imagine ony that'd be worth ha'en. An' I dinna think onybody else can. I've nivur heard ony Heevun described yet that ony sensible body could tolerate for a . . .

Jeannie—(*Who has been following her own thoughts.*) It's my belief Mrs M'Taggart wad nivur ha'e deed at a' if Hugh had been at hame. The doctors expected her to dee months an' months syne. They canna mak' oot hoo she kept on leevin' ava'. But she wadna let Alick sen' for Hugh i' time. She did improve wonderfu' efter Hugh cam'. The doctors were fair dumfoonert. If Hugh'd come a day or twa sooner he'd ha'e pulled her thro' a'thegither. But she'd let things gang owre far afore she sent for'm. She didna gie'm a chance. . . . It's a puir kin' o' God that canna reward faith like that yince in a while.

Polly—Jean! Faither! D'ye hear her – but ye're as bad yersel'!

Macfarlane—(*Who has been sitting completely bemused.*) . . . Ech! Oh, it's deeficult to ken what to think. Weel, as I say, we waited in complete dumfoonerment. Naethin' wad ha'e surprised me – mair than the fac' that naethin' did happen. It didna seem richt that naethin' should happen. Everybody meltit awa' as soon's they could – scared-like. Ye can tell what like it was, when even auld Tom, the gravedigger, hung back an' daurna pit his wisp o' hay doon an' begin fillin' in. . . . He was still staunin' switherin, loathlike, when I lookit roon frae the yett. An' the twa laddies were still kneelin' by the grave-mou' prayin'. . . . As

Jock Greig said to me i' the road back, 'There's only twa ways to't – either Mrs M'Taggart sud he'e been brocht back to life there and then – or Hugh an' Alick sud ha'e been struck doon. As it is it's almost as if there wasna ony God ava' – if ye ken what I mean.'

Polly—(*Deliberately*.) I'm no' sae shair that ye dae yersel', faither.

Macfarlane—I'm no' sayin't i' ony irreverent way. .... Jock Greig was very bitter about neither o' the meenisters attendin' the funeral juist because they waurna asked to offeeciate. Of course, ye couldna wunner at a stickler for form like auld M'Queen – but Latimer's different. He mak's oot to be sae unconventional – an' oot-an'-oot evangelical. Hoo did they ken onyway that God wadna side wi' Hugh an' Alick? What a drap that'd ha'e been to them. An' they could ha'e dune wi't. The reeligious life o' this toon's a' ga'en to wind and stour. A miracle yince in a while wad quicken the souls o' the folk. Sic patient believin' an' believin' year in an' year oot, wi' naethin' ever happenin's no' natural. Fowk believin' even on like that's nae incentive to God. Still an on God micht weel tak' a thocht. ....

(*Knock at the door, and, opening it, a woman thrusts her head round the corner.*)

Polly—Come awa' in Mrs Thomson.

Mrs Thomson—(*Coming forward a little in great excitement.*) Na! Na! I ha'ena a meenut to spare. Ha'e ye heard the latest?

Polly and Jeannie—(*Together.*) No!

Macfarlane—(*Amazed – half-rising from his chair.*) Ye dinna mean ...?

Mrs Thomson—(*Portentously.*) Alice M'Taggart's had a veesion.

Polly—A what?

Jeannie—Oh, ye dinna say so! What? When?

Mrs Thomson—(*With unction.*) Aye! Her mither appeared to her, no' quarter o' an 'oor syne, an' said her speerit'd return to her body at fower o'clock. The news has run like wildfire. Half the toon's up at Sleepyhilock, an' Hugh an' Alick are fair garin' the dirt flee.

Macfarlane—Puir laddies!

Mrs Thomson—I'm jist on my way up mysel'. Yin nivur kens. An' maister M'Queen's had a shock, a' doon the left side. It's like a judgment.

Polly—I wunner at ye – a wumman come to your time o' life. Ye can spare yersel' the trouble. Nocht'll happen.

Jeannie—Ye mean ye hope nocht wull. Ye dinna ken mair than the lave o's. Faith's no' that common that God can afford to squander't, an' gi'e mean swee souls that ha'ena the strength to haud a decent hope leave to craw owre their betters. (*Jumping up and grabbing her hat.*) Oh, I hope it's true, I hope it's true. (*Suddenly drops onto her knees.*) O God, answer this prayer. We believe ye wull. Fulfill the veesion. Gi'e back this mither to her sons an' dochter. Amen!

Macfarlane—Amen!

(*Exit Mrs Thomson and Jean.*)

Macfarlane—(*Squirming under Polly's look.*) It's bound to happen some day – an' as weel the day as ony ither ...

Polly—(*Unrolling a bundle of knitting wool and passing a cut to her father.*) You'll mebbe gi'e's a haun' wi' this i' the meantime. (*Macfarlane puts the cut round his wrists and Polly begins briskly winding it into a ball.*)

The Dead Harlot

First appeared, under the title 'In the Fulness of Time', in The Scottish Nation, *18 December 1923; reprinted with present title in (ed) John Gawsworth,* New Tales of Horror *(1934).*

'She had the foul disease of animal existence in its most enfevered and terrible form, complicated to an unthinkable degree by that quality which men, baffled by their blood, miscall beauty,' he said quietly, and then, with a note of exultation, almost of gloating, added, 'I do not remember a more radical cure. Peace to her bones!'

As he spoke a dark ray seemed to accentuate 'the strange superfluous glory' of the autumn air. Looking up at him, momentarily silent, I remembered these lines:

> Then did Ormuzd stand
> Silent, the monstrous silence of the sky
> Dwarfed by his own. Fathomless was his eye,
> His face the cloister of his thoughts, his head
> A still lone summit.

I recognized that our acquaintanceship was for me an Alpine adventure.

'She is driven hither and thither no longer – her real nature obscured – by the lusts of the flesh with its shivers and heats,' he continued. 'She has entered into the antique order of the tongueless dead. She is set in silence, a prey no more to the sickening pulsations of life. Her incredible courses have at last exhausted themselves, and she has come to the peace that passeth understanding. You remember what the Amida-Kyr says? "All who enter into that country enter likewise into that state of virtue from which there can be no turning back."

336

Flesh fade and mortal trash
Fall to the residuary worm; worlds wildfire leave but ash,
In a flash . . .
This jack, joke, poor potsherd, patch, matchwood,
    immortal diamond
Is immortal diamond.

'– I am afraid I do not make myself quite clear.' As he looked
at me it was as if a great bird had swooped down from the height
of the heavens and sliced my sight with the points of its pinions.

'If cleanliness is next to godliness,' he proceeded, 'how high
now is her estate? Her bones are free of the toils and torments
and embroilments of the flesh. The cannibal clay has picked
them clean as starlight on a night of frost. A miraculous
reduction to ultimate reality! They have thrown off for ever and
a day with one swift white gesture the restless tyrannical
burdens which battened so unendurably upon them – the
insatiate flesh that lives upon itself and the flesh of others,
shapeless and impotent but for these! – shifting and straining
upon them, from birth to death, this way and that, now surging
to incontinent heights, now sagging in the troughs of delusory
deliverances – and have sprung out, for the first time, into their
free and natural shapes, white, inveterate, turned on the lathe of
Eternity, unsearchable, compact with silence. What artistry
has wrought such sculpture from such chaos, with this finality
of form, this economy of means, this undeluded surety of touch?
Think of the antiseptic vision, the unnerving eye for essentials,
the ruthless mastery – the consummate finish! No mawkish
sentiment here, no pandering! He has probed his subject and
come to unanswerable conclusions, profound, exclusive, universal! No straining here after originality, no needless elabor-
ation of the theme, no moralizing! His work has the
impersonality of all great art. It lies before us, stark, simple,
pitiless, unpalliated. A bone taken away – a missing rib – and
you would have realism; a bracelet loose on the wristbones or a
pendant garish on the sternum, and you would have sentiment;
as it is you have reality. As a study in the elimination of
unessentials it is incomparably successful, an inexorable
victory, accentuated by the one wild flourish of her living hair, a
virgined and vehement art voiding without compunction all
that most men praise as beauty, fulness and fertility! Cold,

controlled, complete, bladed and pointed with cardinal justice, it is the final tribute of time to eternity, the loneliest masterpiece of human art. ... Who that knew her unstable, bright, voluptuous life could have dreamt that it lay in her to sign her forced renunciation with a signature such as this in the page of fate, decisive, neat, unalterable? She had such a volatile, enticing and exciting concupiscence that even I had difficulty, looking upon the living woman, in determining her morphic values. She always brought ot my mind Meredith's:

> Ravishing as red wine in woman's form,
> A splendid maenad, she of the delirious laugh,
> Her body twisted flames with the smoke-cap crowned
> ... who sang, who sang,
> And drew into her her swarm
> Revolved them hair, voice, feet, in her carmagnole!

But now – this! hard, intrinsic, whittled down to the last essentiality and directness, cruel yet so unswervingly sure in its concentration, so distinct in its surety! Who would rather have diffuse heats, blind hot livingness, than this keen hard separateness? Does it not make you aware of another freer element in which each fate is detached and isolated? Here is no confusion. Is not this our natural element? Who does not envy such a faculty of sharp incontrovertible response to all the lapping, suffusing, swamping, endless conspiracies of life? ... Complexity has laboured and brought forth the most signal of all the simplicities. The last gaunt midwife has delivered this travailing creature of the final issue of her ravelled womb – this naked and incorruptible offspring, building in ivory, the heir of Time!

> Wanderers eastward, wanderers west
> Know you why you cannot rest?
> 'Tis that every mother's son
> Travails with a skeleton.

'Whenever I think of a section of flesh, I remember that indispensable phrase "bizarre, compliqué, nombreaux et chinois". Ah, that flesh of hers, blazing and blurring, full of malady and murmuration! Perhaps you do not understand. Did it never strike you as horrible, as intolerable, that these slim, shapely bones, so calm and clear and capital, that these immaculate blades, these cups and balls of polished ivory,

338

should be so grossly overlaid, beslimed, befouled, and bloodied, by the abominations of the body – hemmed in so noisomely by masses of clogging corruptible flesh, rank with blood, raging with carnal lusts, hideous with livid rioting muscles (lightnings in the oppressive thunderous atmosphere of animal being) instinct with incipient death – tugged this way and that under the incessant drumming of the pulses – obscenely put up on? Do we not know it all – "the brute betrayal, the dead load, the cry of worlds, the laughter of the pit? ..."

'All the vain violence is over. No trace remains of the stenchful ichor of her lustful life. No memory of passion confuses or corrupts these incontestable symbols of purity. Only the clean cold light of death streams straitly through her liberated, bare, and unvibrating bones, ranking in silence here, radiate in finality, cradling the invisible, unpulsating heart of eternity, "the general gender", the organs of oblivion, the largest rhythm, the inviolable spirit ... dominant upon her little satiate teeth ... proclaiming in sheer white accents on the glittering edges and in the opalescent hollows of her pelvis (emptied of that little hot incontinent belly we knew) – set, as it were, like the ivory wings of an immortal bird immobilized on the very bit of passion! – that out of corruption cometh forth incorruption.'

His voice fell. 'The awful devices of her breasts are shredded away. Level and stirless lie the bones of her passioning thighs. The fingers caressing are fingers of naked bone. The slant green eyes conjure no longer. The red enchantments of her lips and quick, exciting tongue are flames that have faded and fled. The smile is the smile of fleshlessness and the places of her eyes are darknesses and voids. ... Only her hair streams still like seaweed over the alabaster shell of her head, decorating her cervical vertebrae with the remnants of ravishment, the impotent lustre of this last sexual symbol life's ghastly tribute to the stern omnipotence of death. ...

'And it is well with her now as it was in the days ere she was born.

> So let this fire of sense decay.
> This smoke of thought blow clean away,
> And leave with ancient night alone,
> The steadfast and enduring bone.'

He fell to silence, pulling upon his pipe, and was lost in clouds of smoke; and, lonely upon this withdrawal, meditating eyried as it were in inhuman resignation, I recollected another passage of verse:

Were you to see
The graves gape wide asunder
Cracking with noise of thunder
The marble monuments and thenceforth rise
Strange things with cavernous emptiness for eyes
And wormy horrors in a ropy mesh
Where there should be round limbs and veined flesh
Your brain would reel and spin –
Turn you your eyes within
On us – even such, even such as these are we.

Old Miss Beattie

From The Gallovidian Annual, *1927*.

It's as faur back as I can mind. I maun hae been a gey wee laddie at the time. I aye gaed wi' my mither on her veesits to the seek and the deein', and whiles wi' my faither tae. My brither didna. He juist point-blank refused. I kent I sudna want to gang either – but I did. I didna let my faither and mither ken hoo keen I really was. No' that I was ony feart o' them jalousin' that it wasna naitural for a boy to want to see auld dottlin' craturs o' men and wimmen leevin' their lane in a'e-room hooses in out-o-the-wey corners o' the toon, and stertin' to think oot my real reasons. But I kent that ither folk (includin' my brither) had different opinions and wadna be lang in expressin' them. My faither, and still mair, my mither were different frae the feck o' folk – they were mair religious. That was hoo they'd aye sae mony silly auld folk to veesit. And they thocht their sons sud be different tae. As a maitter o' fact they were puzzled owre my brither; he took life that easy. He was aye oot playin' wi' a pack o' ither loons. It took my faither and mither a' their time to get him to bide in long eneuch to dae his lessons at nichts. I wasna like that. I had to mak' the best o' lads and lassies aboot my ain age in the schule – I managed no' sae bad wi' the lassies. But outside schule 'oors I'd nae use for the lads ava', and nane for the lassies either unless I was fair stuck for something better. Folks that saw e'e to e'e wi' my faither and mither used to say I'd an auld heid on young shouders. I'd learned the knack o' sayin' byordinar' pious things – in the richt company. I could gar them forget I wasna as auld as themsel's. And I could dae't withoot lookin' the least bit self-conscious tae. 'Losh me,' folk used to think efter a bit when they mindit again that I was only a

341

wee laddie at the schule, 'the boy's lost his ain mooth and fund a minister's.' But it was only the kind o' folk that were mair or less like my faither and mither themsel's that I could strike in that way. Ithers took a vera different view.

And they took a vera different view o' my faither and mither tae. A' they did for auld folk and badly folk never brocht them a penny piece, and whiles it brocht them nae end o' ill-wull – but ither folk got it into their heids that there was 'mair in't than meets the e'e'. Noo I ken vera weel that it was naethin – sae faur as my faither and mither kent – but eindoon Christianity. My faither's wages werena abune the average – but mither and him seldom gaed onywhaur empty-haundit. And the funny thing was that the mair they gied the better they got on themsel's. That's what took folk to the fair. It was aye a couple o' oranges or a quarter o' tea, or twa three scones, or, in the warst cases, a bunch o' grapes. And mony's the auld cratur, as it cam' near the end, they sat up wi' nicht aboot, and weel they kent it was a thankless job. Even the bodies themsel's were fell suspicious and ill-to-dae-wi'. Tho' they'd naething in their bit hooses worth a bodle they followed your every move as tho' you were a thief, and every time you gied them their drap o' medicine you micht hae been poisonin' them. Whiles, gin the illness was lang-drawn-oot or o' a delicate and fiky kind, the mair you did for them the mair they hated you. They couldna help needin' you tae handle them – but the mair they needit it, the mair they resented it. And abune a' they hated deein' and you watchin' them. Afore the end cam' they'd send their een through you like reid hot needles. It was a' vera weel for you to want them to tak' it easy and to pass oot quiet – a' vera easy for you – when it was them that was daein' the deein'! You were fell clever – but no' clever eneuch to help them – even if you wanted to, which was questionable. Hoo can onybody ever be deid shair o' onybody else's motives? Few o' thae folk were when they cam' to dee. Suspicion and dislike were uppermaist. It's fine for doctors and ither folk roond a bedside to keep a calm sough, but it's no sae easy for the cratur in the bed.

Noo I'm no' gaun to probe into the real reasons that gar'd my faither and mither tak' up sae mony cases o' that kind. I ken what they themsel's thocht. I ken that that didna juist exhaust the maitter. But they had baith ony amount o' patience, and naethin' was owre muckle bother for them, and, for a' that was thocht and even said to the contrary, they never got a brass farthing or a stick o' furniture for their trouble. Mair than aince when there was onything o' ony consequence left it was claimed by relations that had taen precious guid care no' to come near as lang as there was onything to dae, and they werena slow in suggestin' that faither and mither had poked in their noses whaur they werna needit, and hintin' that there micht be reasons for't. Mither used to get fair in a wax when onything o' that kind happened, and the angrier she got the mair colour attached to the suspicion.

Speaking' for mysel', I dinna think I was ever the least bit concerned owre ony o' the craturs. A' that I wantit was to see what happened and hoo. And to watch my faither and mither 'in action', as it were, and speculate owre the sense o' pooer – or, as the case micht be, pooerlessness – a body feels at somebody else's daith-bed. Yin got a' kinds o' eerie thrills. I used to watch a' that my faither and mither did and listen to a' that they said – but ahin' the twa three oranges, or the bit prayer, or the medicine, or the talkin' aboot things, or the 'wheesht, wheesht noo, an' no' tire yersel' oot – ye're bringin' on the cough again' – ahint a' the Christianity and humanity, as it were, I saw an eindoon animal drama. Whiles I thocht that, though they keepit up the surface play, my faither and mither got a blink o't tae, but nearly aye I kent the body that was deein' saw naething else. A' that was said to them or dune for them then seemed to gang alang a different plane a'thegither and never come into contact wi' them ava'. It made you feel that the Doctor and whiles the Minister, and your faither and mither, had made a queer mistak', and were treatin' a beast juist as if it had been a human bein'. It was like bein' at the theatre – only me and the body that was deein' mindit that we were only watchin' a play; a' the rest were like the silly wumman at the pictures that whiles forgets they're no real and bawls oot a warnin' to ane o' the characters.

But the craturs were generally owre faur gane when they got to this stage, and it didna last lang eneuch for me, besides being' maskit maistly by the effect o' the medicine or me no' bein' there at juist the richt time. Auld Miss Beattie was an exception. She was in that state frae the vera beginnin' – lang afore she was bedridden even. She lookit like a monkey to stert wi' – and had the brichtest and broonest pair o' een imaginable. As a rule, there was naething else in them but juist pure glossy broon. But whiles they seemed to slip and slither aboot and syne to reel in her head wi' excitement, and whiles they narrowed to the thinnest slits and syne you'd see eindoon malice keekin' roon' the corners o' them. She wasna to be trustit. My faither and mither used to whisper to each ither aboot her – when they thocht I wasna listenin'. I dinna ken juist what they said, but she wasna to be trustit, no' even wi' hersel', and I kent better than let mysel' be left alane wi' her. Yince we were in her parlour and my mither had to gang into the kitchen to get something or ither. She was nae suner i' the lobby that I saw Miss Beattie movin' – as if she wasna' movin' ava', and wi' the blandest and maist benevolent licht in her een – to get atween me and the door. I made a dive for't juist in time. Sic a snarl o' rage she gied! I dinna ken what 'ud hae happened if she'd got me, and I dinna like to think. I was mair carefu' efter that; sae were my faither and mither. We never turned oor backs on her again. You couldna move in that hoose but the auld cratur's een were on you – like a snake's, waitin' to strike. There was a queer atmosphere about it – as o' something no' human ava'. You couldna pit it doon to onything in particular, but it was a' roond you. Uncanny wasna the word for it. And nae maitter what she said, or what onybody else said, in that hoose it soondit unreal, as if it was juist a pretence, a disguise for something else that didna bear thinkin' aboot. Whatever was wrang wi' her made a'thing but itsel' seem wrang. A big book o' texts hung on the kitchen wa' and it was aye open at the same page. 'Ho, all ye that thirsteth.' I wadna hae taen onything to eat or drink in that hoose for love or money, but I never lost an opportunity o' gangin' there a' the same – especially efter the time I've juist tell't ye aboot – and it's little my faither or mither ettled the kind o' stimulant I was aye imbibin' there. But auld Miss Beattie kent – and 'ud fain hae gi'en me a stronger dose!

The Common Riding

This story appeared in The Glasgow Herald *on 12 March 1927. The Common Riding is a local celebration deriving from the ancient custom of riding round the boundaries of a burgh's common lands; Langholm's Common Riding, held annually on the last Friday of July, is a spectacular ceremony led by the bearer of a huge thistle. MacDiarmid, who liked to visit Langholm for the Common Riding, refers to the festivities in* A Drunk Man Looks at the Thistle*:*

> *Drums in the Walligate, pipes in the air,*
> *Come and hear the cryin' o' the Fair.*
>
> *A' as it used to be, when I was a loon*
> *On Common-Ridin' Day in the Muckle Toon.*
>
> *The bearer twirls the Bannock-and-Saut-Herrin',*
> *The Croon o' Roses through the lift is farin',*
>
> *The aucht-fit thistle wallops on hie;*
> *In heather besoms a' the hills gang by.*

'Ambition's a queer thing,' he said, 'and grows in the maist unlikely places and tak's the maist unaccountable shapes.

'The queerest case o' ambition I ever kent o' here in the Muckle Toon was that o' puir Yiddy Bally (Bally for Ballantyne). Yiddy was a puir bit eaten-an-spewed-lookin' cratur a' his days; but even afore he left the schule he was Common-Riding-daft. He seemed to leeve for naething else. This year's was nae suner owre than he begood talkin' aboot next year's. Ye could scarcely get him to say a word aboot onything else – but mention the Common Riding! But at first he hadna muckle to say aboot that either – only if onybody mentioned it ye could see that he was a' lugs. And he was aye spierin' whenever he got a

345

chance at auld folks aboot Common Ridings lang syne. It sune becam' a standin' joke – Yiddy Bally and the Common Riding. And at first he didna' like bein' lauched at, and ye could see him pretendin' no' to be interested if it was mentioned, and even gan' oot o' his wey to cheenge the conversation. But that didna last lang, and he sune got used to being' lauched at – and, aiblins, to like it. It gied him a kind o' distinction o' its ain, and he was sherp eneuch to ken that folk are apt to be gratefu' whiles to the cause o' their amusement. For a while, tae, he used aften to get his leg pu'd – some o' the wags 'ud mak' up the maist ludicrous fables o' past Common Ridin's and puir Yiddy swallowed them a' like lamoo. But a' the same his real knowledge o' a' the oots and ins o' its history was growin', and it wasna lang afore he kent the guid coin frae the fause.

'Naething could stop him. He even got at the files o' the local paper and read every line aboot the Common Ridin' that had appeared in't since the year one. And, forbye, he kept a' that ony leavin' body cud tell him. And the mair he learned the mair thrifty o' his lear be turned. He wasna aye talkin' aboot the Common Ridin' noo, tho' a'body kent he was aye thinkin' aboot it. No. It was only as a special favour he'd talk aboot it. And syne it was only to a wheen carefully-selected cronies. In ord'nar company if Common Ridin' was mentioned he'd never let cheep unless he was appealed to to settle a knotty point. He was the final court o' appeal. Whatever he said was richt. Frae the time he was oot of his teens he was never kent to mak' a mistak'. He was like that memory man in the papers – only the Common Ridin' was Yiddy's a'e subject. On a'thing else he was as toom as a cock's egg. But ye couldna riddle him wi' the Common Ridin'. He'd the names o' a' the Cornets aff by hert frae A to Z, and no' only the Cornets, but the dogs that wun the hound trail; the horses that wun the races; the men that wun the wrestlin' and wha' cairried the Croon o' Roses and the Thistle and the Bannock and Saut Herrin', and wha cried the Fair, and hoo mony horsemen followed the Cornet, and wha was his right-hand man and wha was his left-hand man, and whatna year saw the first wumman rider, and what like the weather was – and dod! I'm no shair that he didna ken the name o' ilka bairn that ever toddled wi' a heather besom and got a thripp'ny bit. He was a fair miracle. And forbye, he was an authority on the rites themselves – the size o' the Thistle, the bakin' o' the

346

bannock, the twal' penny nail that hauds the saut herrin' to the bannock, the order o' precedence in the procession, the exact wordin' o' the Cryin' o' the Fair, and a' the ancient details o' the burgh boonds and the rights o' the freemen.

'But he hedna wun on the Committee yet. Ye ken what a Committee is in a place like this. It's aye in the haunds o' a certain few, and if ye dinna belang to their cleek ye've nae mair chance o' gettin' on to't than a rich man has o' gaen' through the e'e o' a needle. But Yiddy's cheenge o' tactics showed the steady development o' his ambition – his maister-passion, as the meenister ca's't. It was a move in the right direction no' to be owre free wi' his information to Tom, Dick, and Harry, but he took guid care no' to disoblige ony o' the Committee if they did'm the honour o' askin' his opinion on ony point. He played his cairds well. The Common Ridin' Committee was like a'thing else in the Muckle Toon – kirks, the Masons, freen'ly societies – it was composed o' individuals you never heard o' in ony ither connection. And apart frae the Committees they specialise in, their opinions on onything else arena worth tippence. It only met in public aince a year for the choosin' o' the Cornet. The committee were chosen tae, but naebody ever thocht of no' juist re-electin' the auld haunds again unless there was a vacancy by act o' God or ane o' them leavin' the toon; and a' the ither arrangements were made by the committee. And, to tell the truth, although the Cornet was chosen by the meetin' to a' appearances, the committee aye had it a' cut and dry aforehaun'. For a' his knowledge it wasna until he was in his twenty-third year that Yiddy was elected a member o' the committee. Twa years afore that some bletherin' fule proposed him when there was nae vacancy. If it had gane to the vote there's nae doot he'd hae been elected a' richt and some ither body knocked oot – but Yiddy up and said he couldna allow his name to gang forrit under sic circumstances. Ye should hae heard the applause. It was an understood thing efter that that Yiddy would fill the first openin'.

'And when he did he said that as far as could be ascertained he was by at least ten years the youngest member that had ever had the privilege o' servin' on that committee, barrin' Cornets. Ye'd ha'e thocht that that would ha'e been eneuch for the maist ambitious man. But Yiddy was cast in a different mould. I aye had the reputation o' bein' a gey lang-sichted customer, and I kent weel eneuch that Yiddy had fish to fry naebody else had seen. But what kin' o' deep sea craturs they could be was anither question. Somebody asked me what I thocht he hed at the back o' his mind, and it was on the tip o' my tongue to say, – "What price Cornet!" By guid luck I was juist in time to check mysel' frae sayin' ocht sae foolish. Yiddy was young eneuch and licht eneuch in a' conscience to be Cornet, but he'd nane o' the ither qualifications. Apairt frae the fact that he didna' ken a'e end o' a pownie frae the ither, the Cornets are aye drawn frae the sprigs o' the gentry or young bluids o' fairmers – no' factory haun's. It tak's a bonny penny to be a Cornet, and Yiddy was the last man on earth to want to lower the dignity o' the Standard-bearer and ha'e the committee at their wits' end for the cash to cairry oot the programme in proper style. Sae I juist said: "Yiddy kens what he's efter – and it'll no' be common property till he says the word," and, juist to keep up my reputation and forgettin' that mony a true word is spoken in jest, I addit, "And ye can guess till ye're tired, but ye'll no' fin' oot."

'It sune becam' perfectly obvious that Yiddy was playin' a deep gaim. Ye'd hae thocht he'd hae dominated the committee aince he got on t' it. But no' him. He did the lion's share o' the donkey wark – and gied the credit to the ithers. Ye never heard his voice in the public meetin's. Even in the committee meetin's he let the ithers dae a' the talkin' – but he'd talked tae each o' them singly first (or as mony as he needit tae talk tae wi' a particular end in view), and maist a'thing they did and said had come frae him in the first instance. Yiddy had them a' on strings withoot them, or onybody else, haein' ony idea o't. And as time gaed on it seemed clearer and clearer that he'd nae axe to cairry the croon o' roses or to mairshal the bairns wi' the heather besoms or gie oot the thrippeny bits or get ane o' their freens on for this or that or the ither thing, and naebody was better at smoothin' oot the runkles and seein' that everybody got what they wantit or as near haund it as possible, than Yiddy. But he aye kept in the backgrun' himsel' – the poo'er ahint the scenes, as the minister says. Aft an' on he got the chance o' maist o' the plooms, but he aye said 'No,' like George Washington – till he had refused sae often and yet dune sae much and obliged every one o' them in sae mony ways that they simply couldna refuse him whatever he did want. Noo ye ken what Yiddy was like –

juist a rickle o' banes wi' the thews o' a maggot. The thistle for the Common Ridin' was grown doon at the Toonfit. A plot o' grun was set apairt for the purpose, and mebbes half a dizzen thistles were grown each year, and for weeks aforehand croods used to gang doon on Sunday efternunes to see hoo they were comin' on. The biggest and shapeliest was chosen, but it was an unwritten law – and a point o' honour wi' the gairdener – that it had to be at least aucht fit high wi' the tap aboot as muckle in diameter. Tied to the tap o' a flag pole it made a bonny sicht, wallopin' a' owre the life, an' a hunner roses dancin' in't, a ferlie o' purple and green.'

Like the suffragette colours, I thocht.

'It was mair than ae man could cairry, of coorse, for mair than a few yairds at a time. There were aye fower or five hefty chiels tell't aff to gie a hand wi't, but the principal carrier for mony a year had been Neen Ferguson. Ye mind Neen? A buirdly figure o' a man he was, sax fit three in his stockin' soles and braid in proportion. It used to be said that he could hae felled a bull wi' a single dunt o' his nieve. Well, it was aye Neen's pride to cairry the thistle single-handed frae the fit o' the Port into the Market Place – a distance o' mebbe a hunder yairds – and auld folks used to say that mair than ae cairrier afore him had tried the same dodge, but he was the first that had ever succeeded. Weel, juist three weeks afore the Common Ridin' puir Neen was cairret aff wi' the 'flu, and there was a rare howdy-do as to whae was to tak' his place.'

I jaloused it richt aff the reel. 'Yiddy,' I said. He lookit me up and doon and then he gaed on:

'Aye, Yiddy it was. The cat was oot o' the bag at last. There was nae gainsayin' him. He was deid set on't, tho' ye'd as sune hae thocht o' a rabbit settin' in to worry a beagle. And mind you, tho' as I've tell't you, he'd pit them a' in sic a position that his word was practically law, they tried their utmaist to get him aff the notion. They lauched at him and pled wi' him and pointed oot hoo important it was frae the general standpoint o' the programme that the Thistle should be weel and truly cairrit. But it was nae use. 'I'll cairry the Thistle,' he said. 'Im' no' muckle to look at but I've never let the Common Ridin' doon yet through onything I've either dune or left undune – an' I'll no' let the Thistle doon either. I'm mebbe no a Hercules athegether – but guid gear gangs in little buik, and ye'll aiblins be surprised to see what I can dae when I set my mind to't.' 'It disna' maitter aboot settin' ye'r mind to't,' somebody said, 'Ye're no asked to balance't on yer heid. If your back was as strang as your will there'd be nae question aboot it.' 'I'll cairry it,' said Yiddy. 'I'll hae my helpers, but frae the fit o' the Port to the centre o' the Market Place I'll cairry it mysel', and nae ither man'll pit a finger on the pole.' Excitement ran high when the news leakit oot; and shair eneuch when the day cam' there was Yiddy wi' the holder strappit roond his middle, at the howkin' o' the thistle, wi' his helpers roond him. It was a whopper tae.

It took them a' their combined strength to lift the pole aince the Thistle was tied on and fit the end o't into Yiddy's holder. It was perfectly clear then that they'd make a big mistake. The rest left gae o't juist for a meenit, and Yiddy fair doobled up under the load. They'd to tak' haud again at aince. Yiddy never said a word but juist gied reid and white by turns like – like a signal. Aff they gaed to join the procession. The helpers raxed themsel's for a' they were worth tae mak' it as licht for Yiddy as they possibly could – but even then as ane o' them said. "We expectit tae hear his spine crack at ony step." Yet it was wonderfu' tae see hoo the wee cratur braced himsel' up. Heaven only kens what he maun hae been sufferin'. . . . Still they got to the fit o' the Port a' richt, and then Yiddy said: "Noo, haunds aff. I'll manage the rest mysel'." No' a haund slackened, but Yiddy lookit at his helpers first on the ae side, then on the ither with sic a glower in his een that they let gae afore they kent what they were daen. They said efter his een were juist like twa slaps into Hell itsel'. And he moved – cairryin' the Thistle by himsel'. The first twa-three steps maun ha'e shown him that nae maitter what unheard o' strength he'd summoned to his assistance he'd never manage to the centre o' the Mairket Place. That maun ha'e been an awfu' moment for him – for this is hoo I figure it oot. It was the pride o' the Common Ridin' versus his ain. Could he maintain them baith? The first wadna suffer materially if he let his helpers tak' haund again – but the second, wad, mortally. There was only a'e way oot it seemed. Sae he sterted to rin'! Guid alane kens hoo. A'body else stude stock still, their een stelled in their heids and their herts in their mooths; ye could ha'e heard a peen fa'. He reached his goal. The Thistle swung for a meenit in the air. Syne he seemed to crumple juist as if he'd gane fair through himsel', wi' the thistle hidin' the hole. In the deid silence it was the eeriest thing ye could imagine. Then, as sune as he was doon, sic a hullabaloo! I was as near him as you are to me noo, and a wheen o's pu'd the thistle affin'm, and had him up in oor airms afore the crood had time to surge in. We were like herrin' in a barrel noo. "Gangway," somebody shouted – and a lane opened up to the door o' the chemist's shop as if by magic. "Haud on," cried Yiddy: "Alick," he said, turnin' to ane o' his helpers, "Tak' the Thistle. I dinna ken what possess't me – but the Common Ridin' maun go on. A'e man can cairry me – I'm nae great wecht – and I haena faur tae gang. Let naebody else move." Sae ae man cairret him to the chemist's shop, while a'body else stude like stookies and Yiddy made him halt on the doorstep. ' "Gang on wi' the Common Ridin'," he cried, in a voice that soondit richt owre the Market Place. And we did. But Yiddy was deid afore his voice had stoppit echoin'! – and whiles I think it hesna stoppit yet.'

Murtholm Hill

From The Scots Magazine, *April 1927*.

'The warld's like a bridescake in a shop window the day,' he said.

'Weel, see and tak' care o' yersel' noo,' said his mither, 'and no' be comin' back killt.'

'Nae fear o' that.'

She was smilin'. The things that boy said! She'd see him waggin' his heid in a pulpit a' richt – if naething cam' owre him.

He was pleased that he'd gar'd her smile, and wonderin' what had pitten that in his heid – 'the warld's like a brides-cake'. No' bad for a boy of twelve. There wasna' anither boy in the toon could hae said onything like it. He was wishin' he could follow it up wi' anither. It had never really been in his heid ava. It had juist louped frae naewhaur to the tip o' his tongue. He micht sit in the hoose a' day and no' think o' anither to gang wi't. Forbye, for his age, he was as tall and weel-built as ony o' the boys in the toon, tho' he'd never been allowed to rin wild like maist o' them. Sittin' in the hoose and thinkin' o' things like that was fine; nane o' the rest o' them could dae that – but he wanted to show that he was as guid as them at ither things tae. If they could dae things that he couldna that took awa' frae the things he could dae and they couldna. 'Aye, he's clever, but he's no' strang.' That took the gilt aff'n the gingerbread a'-thegither. It made brains nae mair than the result o' bein' silly; a thing naebody envied.

Of coorse, he kent it 'ud be a' richt aince he was a bit aulder. It was only for a while he'd to thole it. He'd grow up into a banker or a lawyer, or, at the vera least, a teacher, and they'd be mill-haunds a' their days; and nae wicer, the feck o' them, at forty than they were at fourteen.

Seein' him dackle, his mither swithered tae. She wanted him to enjoy himsel', of coorse; yin's only young yince, but, a' the same. . . . She thocht she'd try again.

'I wish ye werena gan' to the Murtholm tho'. The Lamb Hill 'ud dae ye fine. Ye'd enjoy yersel' as weel there, and it's faur safer.'

'I'm owre big. It's only the infant schule that gang there.'

'Weel, there's lots o' ither places – up Ewes or awa' oot the Copshawholm Road or the Wauchope, and ye'd hae them a' to yersel' and could dae as ye liked.'

'They're a' richt for sli'in', but no for sledgin'. There's naething worth ca'in' a brae till ye gan' miles oot.'

'Havers! The Copshawholm Road. . . .'

'The Copshawholm's no' steep eneuch to stert wi' – and syne it's owre steep. It 'ud be the best o' the lot if it began suner and endit better – and besides, the bobbies'll no' let ye sledge there. It's a blin' corner and bad eneuch for a bike let alane a sledge. There's been plenty o' accidents there already.'

His mither had had nae thocht o' that end o' the road – and it aboot took her braith awa' him thinkin' she had! – but o' the heichs and howes awa' oot by the White Yett. There wadna be ony danger oot there, and it was quite steep eneuch for him, besides gan' up and doon like the switchback at the fair, but it was juist as weel to say nae mair aboot it. He'd shairly never think o' attemptin' the Lang Brae – but the bare idea o't hadna' been sae impossible to'm or hoo could he hae thocht she'd actually suggested it? The idea fair gar't her shiver.

'The Murtholm's fell dangerous tae,' she said. 'The bottom hauf's steep, and if ye dinna tak' the corner ye gang richt into the water.'

'It's frozen owre,' he said, 'and what's mair, it's as shallow as a saucer juist there. It wadna' come owre your taes, even if there was nae ice.'

'Weel, it's narrow between the wa's. Some o' the bigger yins'll mebbe rin ye doon and coup ye. See and let the ithers awa' first. Ye'll be safer if ye come doon last wi' naebody ahint ye.'

He gied a crookit kind o' lauch. Weemun didna' understaund. Hoo could ye wait till the last when there was nae last?

They were gan' up and doon a' the time. He kent weel eneuch what she was hintin' at tho'! Twa winters syne he'd been on the Lamb Hill, when some o' the bigger yins cam' up and chased the youngsters awa' and took his sledge frae him. It was the finest sledge o' the lot by a lang chalk, wi' lang steel rinners – the roond, narrow kind, no' the braid, flat yins. Maist o' the ither bairns had been on bits o' boxes withoot rinners at a'. Pride gangs afore a fa' – and he'd been fell prood. He'd been ane o' the biggest yins there, and wi' the best sledge he'd been nane owre canny aboot claimin' the croon o' the hill and hustlin' some o' the wee'r and less forritsome yins into the side. What a stound he had at the stertin' place! 'Na, na. You gang first,' said the ithers that were there. And as he flew doon he saw the envious looks o' the ithers that were climbin' back. The best sledge on the field! Gosh! it could gang! Like greased lichtnin'! And aince or twice that efternune as he was near the top climbin' up he saw ithers stertin', and, by rinnin' as hard and launchin' off as quick as he could, he was able to mak' up on them hauf way doon and send them whirlin' and whummlin' into the wreaths at the side. Nae end o' fun. And he was juist in the middle o't when a wheen o' the big yins cam' alang the top road frae the heid o' the Kirk Wynd and clam' the palin' and ordered them aff the coorse. He was climin' up at the time – and heard them. But they didna' mean him? It 'ud be some o' the sma'er fry; and they *were* a bit o' a nuisance and 'ud be apt to get hurt if the big yins were usin' the coorse as well. It 'ud be for their ain guid to keep oot o' the road; but he was a' richt – he could look efter himsel'. Abune a' wi' a sledge like that. Sae he paid nae heed, but trudged on to the stertin' place and clappit himsel' doon on his sledge – and was off. The big yins were still a yaird or twa away. The coorse swoopit doon and then there was a hump, and as you gae'd owre it the sledge flew clean in the air and landit again a yaird or twa doon, and then there was a glorious lang swoop wi' a curve-up at the end that brocht the rin' to a fine finish. But juist as he was toppin' the hump a muckle snawba' dung him clean aff the sledge and sent him whizzin' heid first inta the bank at the side. When he pickit himsel' up and got his e'en and his ears shot o' the snaw his toom sledge was birlin' awa' doon near the fit o' the coorse. And, a' at aince, wi' a shout that gar'd his hert stan' still and made him forget the stoundin' pain in the side o' his heid, ane o' the biggest o' the big yins – Bobby Price – gied a rin' and a jump at the stertin' place and brocht his feet thegither and was off – swoopin' and soarin' owre the hump and swoopin' again like a bird wi' his airms ga'en up and doon as if he'd been dancin' the Hieland Fling, and whiles he coo'ered till his doup was level wi' his heels and up again. By sang! That took some daein'. It wasna mony could dae that. Hoo he wish'd he was as big as Bobby Price!

Bobby Price was at the bottom o' the coorse; and was comin' up again trailin' *his* sledge.

He felt like shoutin' to'm 'Wha cut the yorlins' throats wi' the roostit nail?' and rinnin' awa' as hard as he could. He was a bad yin, Price – up to a' kinds o' ill. Him and his gang used to gang alang the waterside, and when they saw a cat they'd 'Cheechie, cheechie, cheechie,' till it cam' wi'in reach and syne grab it and whirl it roon' and roon' by the tail in cairtwheels – and let gae. And syne there was a splash hauf way owre the water. He'd let them see. He'd ...!

But a' at aince he pit his haund up to the side o' his face and brocht it doon again reid wi' bluid. The hert gae'd oot o'm, and he was as seeck as a dog. There maun hae been a stane in the snawba'. That was like them. He never kent hoo he got hame. Naebody gaed wi'm. He kent them a', juist as they kent wha he was – but he hadna a chum amang them. And he gaed hame withoot his sledge. Bobby Price had it. He grat in his mither's airms as if his hert 'ud brak.

'Never mind', she said. 'Your faither'll gang and get it when he comes in – and gi'e them what for, that's mair. That Price needs a sing on the side o' the lug.' He'd picked up eneuch by this time to say: 'Aye. It 'ud be the price o'm.' He smiled even yet inside himsel' when he minded that pun.

But that wasna the warst o't. When his faither gaed to get the sledge there was nae sign o't. Price denied point blank that he'd ever seen it, and the rest backed him up. It was only when his faither was comin' awa' again that he fund a wheen broken sticks lyin' in the corner aside the yett. It was a' that was left o't. The brutes had kickit it to bits when they were dune wi't. But the rinners werena there. He kent naething o' that till the following mornin', and syne he'd anither greetin' match.

'Wheesht, wheesht,' his mither said. 'Your faither'll mak' ye anither yin – and a bigger yin at that.'

'But the snaw'll be a' awa' again afore its ready. Boo-oo.'

'Nae fear. He'll stert to't the nicht, and mebbe finish't tae, and ye can tak' it doon to the smiddy and get the rinners on't the morn's forenune.'

And his faither did. It was a beauty. But he wasna allowed to gang sledgin' again unless his faither was there to watch. And there had been nae real sledgin' weather last winter at a', and he'd never had it oot. That was the sledge he had noo. It was a real grown-up sledge. But, of coorse, he was big eneuch for't noo.

'Oh, I'll be carefu',' he said. 'Ye needna' be feart. I dinna want *this* sledge broken.'

But he wasna sae shair in his ain mind. He was big eneuch and strang eneuch – but he was only yin. The rest hung thegither in cliques. They micht mix as free as ye like: and they were a' freenly eneuch wi'm on the surface; but if ocht gaed wrang – if there was a row or ither – the rest 'ud split up in their different groups as quick as lichtnin', and he'd be left on his ain. And it wasna only that. He couldna' fecht. He'd never had a fecht wi' onybody. Fechtin' wasna' sae muckle a maitter o' strength as juist kennin' hoo. Ye'd to be used to't or ye were nae match for them that were. And it wasna only in regard to fechtin' that he was at a complete loss as compared wi' the ithers. They had an' understaundin' – ways o' sayin' things, and o' lookin' at each other, and twistin' their faces, and a' the rest o't, that meent faur mair than they could ever hae pitten into words – that he couldna' faddom. It cam' frae a' kinds o' experiences and appetities that he didna share wi' them. Ye needit to be leevin' amang't day and daily, to pick it up. He'd never been let rin' aboot the streets or play wi' the ithers oot o' sicht o' his mither's windas. He kent that he was cleverer than them – but only in his heid; he could think a' kinds o' things – but they did a' kinds o' things they couldna' even think aboot, as quick as lichtnin' afore he'd had time to ken what they were daein'. They couldna follow his thochts; but he couldna follow their actions. Though he was as healthy and as strang and as guid-lookin' as ony o' them – and better fed and better clad than maist o' them – somehoo or ither his body didna' seem as quick and as shair o' itsel' as theirs; or, raither, his body and his mind were disconnected somehoo. What they thocht, when they thocht at a', aye depended upon what they were daein'; their minds and bodies worked thegither. And often the bodies were the quicker o' the twa. No' his. His thocht was aye first, and mair often than no' owre fast and fankled his actions – it made him dackle. He lacked self-confidence. It gied him a miserable feelin' – as if he was shut up inside himsel' and couldna' get oot. There was naething the maitter wi' his thocht if only his body 'ud answer to't. But, as the meenister said, 'the spirit was willin', but the flesh was weak'.

And then there were a' kinds o' things that he daurna even attempt for the sake o' his faither and mither. He didna' really want to – except that the ithers did them, and he juist wantit to show that he could tae. There were some o' the things they were aye sayin' – he could say them tae, but he kent that if he did they'd simply roar and laugh, because it 'ud be perfectly plain he'd nae idea o' what they meant. And he'd nae way o' findin' oot. They were things ye couldna ask onybody. Nane o' them had learned them by spierin' – juist by listenin' and lookin' or aiblins some kind o' instinct he hadna' got. You'd to live in a certain kind o' atmosphere to learn things o' that kind – and he didna, and a'body else did. It gied him a queer feelin' that he was naethin' but a pair o' e'en and a brain lookin' on at life – but withoot ony share in't. This was especially the case wi' lassies. A' the ither lads were aye daffin' and cairryin' on wi' the lassies. Of coorse, maist o' them had sisters o' their ain, or were aye wi' chums that had sisters. He hadna. And in dealin' wi' lassies there was a haill complicated way o' gan' on he didna ken the vera first letter o'. Lassies took nae mair notice o' him than if he wasna there. Or, if they did, it was to cry names efter him – 'Lassie-boy', and the like – or pu' his leg and roar an' lauch at the funny way he acted wi' them – no' like ony o' the ither boys ava.

And (he had crossed the wee brig owre the Wauchope noo and gane alang the side o' the burn and was turnin' up the brae between the wa's: and sledge efter sledge was whizzin' past him and landin' its riders on the bank at the corner, lauchin' and shoutin' in the height o' delight) this was the rub. Ye needed a lass ahint ye on a grown-up sledge to get the best fun oot o't. He hated comin' doon by himsel' and a' the ither lads wi' lassies sittin' on ahint them wi' their airms roond their necks. What was the use o' ha'ein' the best sledge on the coorse if a' the rest were gettin' twice as much fun oot o' sledges hauf as guid? And, besides, ye gaed quicker wi' somebody on ahint. Wecht for

357

wecht, naebody could pass him. Stertin' level he'd be at the fit afore they were hauf-way doon the last brae. But if there was twa or mair on their sledges and only him on his, it was a different story. And nae maitter hoo quick he gaed or hoo fine his sledge was rinnin' or hoo weel she took the corners, he'd naebody to share his pleasure and pride – unless a look noo and then frae somebody climbin' up (but then a'body climin' up envied a'body comin' doon), or wi' a much puirer sledge, or less nerve than he had. But it was different wi' a pairtner! He'd an idea that to ha'e a lassie on ahint was only the last proof o' bein' grown-up – a man in the fullest sense o' the term – and wi' a queer thrill o' its ain owin' to he didna' ken juist what; but, apairt even frae thae twa considerations a'thegither, it mair than doobled your enjoyment.

The wa' at a'e side stopped and a hedge began, and, huggin' the ditch, and keepin' a gleg lookout – for every noo and then a sledge wi' its shoutin' riders cam' swishin' by (and there were some whoppers oot, thought his ain could compare wi' ony o' them, even in point o' size, and for beauty o' design and its thick reid cushion he hedna seen its marrow yet), he got to the top o' the first brae and on to a wee level stretch. The second brae curled awa' frae his taes like the letter S, hauf o't atween a couple o' slopin' fields, and the rest roon' the side o' a wud to the yett to the hill. Crickey, what a lot were oot. The haill way up was dottit wi' knots o' folk climbin' back up, and there was a fair crood at the stertin' place. He'd been ower busy thinkin' to dae mair than notice that maist o' the sledges that had passed him were fu' o' young men and wimmen nearly dooble his ain age. There werena mony as young. Up to noo, for a' his doots and difficulties, he'd felt big eneuch and strang eneuch at a' events – but this wasna the Lamb Hill. Frae top to bottom it was nearly a mile and a hauf lang – and tho' it was heavy gangin' on the snaw, an' it took ye the best pairt o' hauf an 'oor to spiel to the stertin' place, ye gaed to the bottom in five meenits. He'd need a' his wits in a press like this. 'See and let the ithers awa' first.' Gosh, that wadna be afore midnicht.

A wee sledge cam' whirlin' roon the first bend o' the S. He saw at a glance that it was a boy in his ain class at the schule. Tam Montgomery, a cocky wee buffer, wi' ane o' the Fletcher lassies on ahint. But he hadna got to the straucht afore twa big tobaggans – bigger even than his ain – wi' four folk on each o' them – shot oot roond the curve ahint him. They were racin' each ither. The lassie Fletcher lookit roon' and the toboggans were fleein' abreest and no' mair than a wheen yairds ahint them, and she whispered something to Tam. He should ha'e steered the nose o' his sledge into his left side a wee and then strauchtened her – and aiblins baith the toboggans 'ud ha'e had room to pass him or ane o' them micht ha'e pu'd up a wee and let the ither aheid. Mebbe he did mean to dae that, but gied owre sudden a jerk, for he coupit richt in the middle o' the coorse on the tap o' the Fletcher lassie. The toboggans were still abreest; but the drivers were leanin' awa' forrit – each wi' ain o' his airms oot, and as they cam' up (it was eneuch to steeve their wrists) they gied Tam and the lassie a shove that sent them skitin' – ane to the ae side and ane to the ither – richt into the ditch. But the steel-shod rims o' the toboggan catched the wee sledge fair and square and dung it to splinters. ... He didna even lauch as he cam' up past Tam, scramblin' to his feet.

'A narraw escape that time,' he said. 'You're no hurt?'

'No. But there's owre mony big folks', said Tam, 'and they shouldna gang twa abreest. I'd keep aff if I was you. It's no safe.'

'Och, I'll be a'richt,' and then, on a sudden impulse, 'Noo that you've nae sledge, you can come on wi' me if ye like. There's plenty o' room.'

'Na!' says Tam, nesty-like, 'unless I was drivin' mysel'.'

That was owre muckle to ask. And besides, he'd wantit him to refuse. That gied him his chance. 'Weel, if you're gaun hame, and Jeannie's no' tired o't, she can come wi' me.'

Jeannie lauched like to burst – in a kind o' way that needit nae words to complete her answer.

'I'll show them,' he thocht as he trudged on.

He heard them sniggerin' ahint him, and Tam sayin' he hopit something or ither – he didna hear what, but he'd an idea. He'd show them – and yet he kent he'd pit his fit in it again, even offerin' Tam a ride as if he was tryin' to 'come it' owre him, and waur, in regaird to the lassie Fletcher. It was ane o' the kind o' things that werena' dune – except by him – and he didna' ken why he'd dune it. She was nae beauty – wi' a face like a suet puddin'. It 'ud be fine to gang sailin' past them – if the same thing didna happen to his sledge. He hadna' bargained for sae mony big folk. Tam was richt eneuch. It wasna' safe – and a' the less safe him bein' himsel'. Pride gangs afore a fa' – but he wisna prood. Only he'd show them. He'd let them see. The sniggering. . . .

He was nearly at the top, gan' roon the last curl o' the S. He'd been that thrang thinkin' that he hadna' noticed the sledges flashin' by. Sic a crood at the stertin' place – a dizzen or mair at least. But naebody had passed him on the way up and a fell lot had gane doon. He'd aiblins get a clear field efter a' – tho' sometimes that wasna' sae safe either. Some o' the big yins climin' up micht try pranks to whummle him or pelt him wi' snawba's. They were less likely to dae that if a wheen different sledges were comin' doon ahint each ither. Och weel, what did it maitter! He couldna' clim' up and syne walk doon! But he wished there had been naebody at the stertin' place. There was sic a banterin' and cairry-on whiles.

Then juist as he was comin' forrit he saw that the nearest to him was the new minister and his wife, and a lassie wi' them aboot his ain age. It was the minister's niece. The minister had been in his hoose the nicht afore last – his faither was rulin' elder o' the kirk. The minister kent him again: and said, afore them a', 'Hullo, Peter.'

Peter touched his hat and grinned.

'That's a fine sledge you've got.'

'Aye.'

'Its the prettiest I've seen yet,' said the minister's wife.

There was juist a wee thing lackin' here tho' – he didna want them to think that his sledge was owre bonny. That was kind o' Jessie-like.

'Aye,' he said, 'and it can gang like lichtnin'!'

He blushed as he said this, for it had been on the vera tip o' his tongue to say 'like the vera deevil'. No' that he was in the habit o' sayin' things like that. He didna ken quite what had gar'd him think o't, juist at this particular time: and he hadna time to fin' oot. The stertin' place was clear. The last sledge had left juist as the minister spoke to him first.

He whirled his sledge roon wi' an expert air and clappit himsel' doon o't, diggin' his caukered heels in sideways a wee till he was richt to stert.

A'body was watchin' him. He lookit up and was juist gan' to touch his cap to the meenister and be aff, when he catched the niece's e'en. There was nae mistakin' her look. Up he jumped and afore he'd time to think, he'd asked her if she'd like to come wi'm. Afore the words were weel oot o' his mooth he was thinkin', 'What a fule I am! What if she winna?' And he kent hoo a' the folk 'ud lauch and say what a cheek he'd had. It 'ud be a' owre the toon; and his faither and mither would be shair to hear o't, and wadna like it. Forbye, it was sae unlike him. And mair than that, a' at aince, he'd a horrible picture in his mind o' them coupin' and her lyin' deid wi' her heid twisted under her oxter and her neck broken like a stick. He'd never hear the end o't. It 'ud juist be like his luck.

But the lassie was beside hersel' wi' joy. 'Oh', she said, 'Will you?' 'How kind,' and she was dancin' roond aboot her auntie seekin' permission. 'Please, please!'

He could see that her aunt wantit to let her gang, but was feart and yet didna ken hoo to refuse withoot disappointin' her and withoot hurtin' his feelin's tae.

At last – efter what seemed an eternity – she turned to the minister. 'What do you think, Dick?' she said. That was a'. Left it to him. And 'Dick' to the minister! He lookit at him. Nae doot it was something in his e'en – for he was shair the minister was juist aboot to shak' his heid, when a' at aince he grinned.

'I think,' says he, 'if Peter'll be so kind – and (to his wife) if you don't mind, my dear – there's room for three – tho' what the guid folks'll think o' their new minister now I dare scarcely think.'

Peter jumped at the chance. This was different frae Tam wantin' tae drive. The minister! And in twa three seconds there they were – the minister, then him, then the lassie wi' her airms roon his neck. His sledge juist held the three o' them neat.

'Now, hold on tight, Barbara,' said the minister's wife. 'Barbara!' What a wonderfu' name! Barbara! Barbara needed nae second tellin'. She tightened her grip till he was near chokin'. It was rare to feel the lassie snugglin' in: she'd a wee fur coat on – and the sleeves o't were as soft as silk aboot his neck. and had the bonniest smell – like – like a chemist's shop.

'Keep your legs well up,' said her auntie.

And she stuck them oot alangside his. Fine trig legs wi' lang-laced boots.

Juist as they were shootin' oot o' the first curl o' the S, they met Tam and the Fletcher lassie gaen up again – tho' what for, when they'd nae sledge? He didna let his een licht on them, but juist turned his heid roon, lauchin' to the minister's niece. Her een sae close to his made his tail-end views o' the snaw and the sky like farles o' soot – and aince they were past he saw Tam and the Fletcher lassie stanin' gapin' efter them wi' their een like saucers. The sledge was gan' at a terrific rate. It soared oot o' the S like a swallow, juist rocked for a minute on the wee bit level at the tap o' the first brae – then swoopit doon atween the wa's, wi' the folk climin' up, skippin' in the side like a puckle rabbits. He kent he was missin' a' kinds o' looks on the folks' faces – he hedna even time to tell himsel' that he was seein' this body and that body – but it 'ud a' come back to him efter; he wisna really missin' onything – his een were takin't a' in, tho' his brain was owre excited. But he'd mind a'thing later on. It 'ud bear thinkin' aboot for days an' days, and aye he'd mind something new. As the sledge gethered speed – an' there were mair and mair shadows o' folk skitin' oot o' the road – there didna seem to be three folk, but only yin. He was famous as the minister in front, and as bonny as a picter (no like yon suet-puddin' o' a Fletcher cratur') in the lassie ahint, but, still and on, he was himsel', Peter, the seen o' a' een, the owner o' the sledge, here in the middle, feelin' that the minister and his niece were naething but pairts o' himsel' that he'd been able – hey, presto! – to flash oot to impress the folk and show the reenge o' his personality. Of course, the ithers micht tak' it oot o'm efter. He mauna look owre cocky. . . . Bother sic ideas! He was leevin' for the meenit like a bird on the wing. . . .

The minister took the corner at the fit dandy – as clean as a whustle, and they shot alang the level as far as to the wee brig itsel' afore 'the cat deed'.

The Waterside

From The Glasgow Herald, *16 April 1927.*

There was faur mair licht and life – o' a kind – in the hooses
alang the Waterside than onywhere else in the toon. The front
windas lookit richt into the water wi' nae trees to daurken them,
and the lift was clearer and braider there than owre ony ither
pairt o' the toon. There were juist twenty hooses frae the Stane
Brig to the Swing Brig and the toon gaed abruptly up ahint
them through a patchwork o' gairdens wi' grey stane wa's to the
muckle backs o' the High Street hooses and on to the terraces on
the face o' the hill. And on the faur side o' the Water there was
naething but the Factory. But the river was braid and a' broken
up and fu' o' movement there, and, tho' some o' the loons could
thraw a stane frae a'e side to the ither, the Factory seemed faur
awa' and could dae naething to impose itsel' on the Waterside
windas or oppress them in the least. Abune the Stane Brig lang
gairdens, dark wi' auld trees, ran doon to the river frae the
bucks o' hooses that lookit the ither way and formed a continu-
ation o' the High Stret, and aneth the Swing Brig there wer the
heichs and howes o' a lump o' waste grun' in front o' the New
Mill that the Toon Cooncouncil were usin' as a cinder dump, and
owre frae them the Murtholm Woods spielin' the braes o'
Warblaw.

Juist abune the Stane Brig there was the meetin' o' the waters
whaur the Ewes clashes into the Esk and alow the Swing Brig
the Wauchope cam' tumblin' in. But in front o' the Waterside
hooses the bed o' the river was fu' o' muckle flat shelfs o' rock
they ca'd the Factory Gullets that cut up the water into a' kinds
o' loups, and scours, and slithers, and gushes, wi' twa-three
deep channels in atween them through which the main flows

363

gaed solid as wa's. Gulls were aye cryin' there and whiles there was a heron standin' on a rock when the water was low, or a kingfisher even. Sae, in the simmer time, or bricht winter days, the hooses alang the Waterside were aye fu' o' a licht and life that made the ongauns o' their inhabitants o' as little conse-quence as the ongauns o' the rats in the cellars were to them, and the dunt and dirl o' the river was in them like the hert in a man, and they had shoals o' licht and the crazy castin' o' the cloods and the endless squabble o' the gulls in them faur mair even than the folk talkin' and the bairns playin'. It wasna sae much a case o' leevin' your ain life in ane o' thae hooses as bein' pairt and paircel o' the life o' the river. Your hoose wasna your ain. It was wind-and-water ticht in a'e way bit no' in anither. A' the ither hooses in the toon were sober and solid in comparison. And the folk that leeved in them had a guid grip o' their lives. But alang the Waterside they were windy, thriftless, flee-aboot craturs. The sense was clean washed oot o' them. A' the sense – and a' the stupidity tae. It's only some kinds o' birds that ha'e een like what theirs becam' – cauld and clear and wi' nae humanity in them ava.

The folk up the hill lookit doon on the toon and some o' them pitiet it and some o' them felt clean abune't, but the taps o' the hills a' roon aboot that they saw frae their windas kind o' steadied and silenced them. They werena like the Waterside folk; there's a queer difference atween ha'en taps o' hills and taps o' waves aye in yin's life. And the folk in the tree-daurkened hooses were different again – they were slow and secret and aften kind o' sad. And the folk on the High Street had naething but themsel's and ither folk in their lives – they were clannish and fu' o' clash and conceit, and aye comin' an' gaen through-ither. But the Waterside folk kept skitin' this way and that. There was neither peace nor profit in their lives. They couldna settle. Their kind o' life was like the dipper's sang. It needit the skelp and slither o' rinnin' water like the bagpipes' drone to fill oot the blanks. Withoot that it was naething but a spraichle o' jerky and meaningless sounds.

There was only a narrow cobbled street between the hooses and the water wa' that stude aboot twa feet high, and was aboot as braid on the tap and syne fell frae aucht to ten fit to the riverside rocks. And dae what ye wad, naething 'ud ever content the bairns but to be scramblin' up on the wa' and

364

rinnin' alang't, and their mithers were aye at their doors wi their hearts in their mooths. They never kent a meenit's peace.

It was only in the winter time that the water exercised its poo'er owre the haill toon. The hills were hidden in mists then and the folk that were aye accustomed to them were at a loss. They were like a puckle water when a jug braks; they'd tint the shape o' their lives. And the folk in the High Street couldna talk loud eneuch to forget the roarin' o' the spate. It seemed to be underminin' the toon. It was level wi' the tap o' the water wa'. Trunks o' trees, hayrucks, and whiles sheep and kye, cam' birlin' doon on the tap o't. The Waterside folk lived in their doors or windas as gin their hooses had nae insides. They could dae naething but look, or raither be lookit at, through and through, for it was the water that did the lookin' and no' them. There was nae question o' thinkin'. It was faur owre quick and noisy for that. It fair deaved them, and every noo and then a muckle wave loupit in through their een and swirled in their toom harnpans and oot again. That's what I mean when I say that the Waterside folk were brainless craturs. Brains were nae use there. To dae onything ava they'd to use something faur quicker than thocht – something as auld as the water itsel'. And thocht's a dryland thing and a gey recent yin at that.

The Waterside folk couldna stop to think. The High Street folk thocht aboot naething bit themsel's, and a' they did was the outcome o' that. The folk on the hillside were like the sailor's parrot – they didna say muckle, but they were deevils to think. The Waterside folk micht ha'e managed to dae a bit thinkin' in the simmer time when the water was low, but low water, they said, gied them a queer feelin' as if the fronts o' their faces had fa'n aff, that fair paralysed them. They were like the man that tell't the wumman he wanted nane o' her damned silence; and sae they juist stottit aboot like a wheen hens wi' the gapes.

I mind a'e Sunday when the water was higher than onybody had ever seen it afore. They were frichtened for the Swing Brig. But it had stoppit rainin' a wee by dennertime, and the fules o' High Street folks, and a wheen o' the Hillside yins tae, wad send their bairns to the Sunday schule. To get there they'd to cross the Swing Brig. It was weel named Swing Brig that day. It was as crazy wi' unexpectit movements as the flair o' the House o' Fun at the Glesca Exhibition. Every noo and again the rusty contraption wheenged richt abune the clammer o' the spate. Ye could hear nae ither soon' but the roar o' the water and whiles the whine o' the iron.

Juist at skailin' time for the Sunday schule the rain cam' on again waur than ever. It fell haill water. Faithers and mithers cam' rinnin' doon wi' umbrellas and waterproof coats juist as the bairns were croodin' on to the Brig. And a' at yince it brak in twa haufs and skailed a'body on't into the river like a wheen tea leafs in a sink.

The news spreid like lichtnin'. Afore the bairns struck the water the banks at baith ends o' the Brig were black wi' folk. Men that could soom, and some that couldna, dived richt in and brocht bairns oot. Ithers had run to a tongue o' rock that ran oot into the river a bit faurer doon, and were in time to grab a wheen o' the weans there as they gaed whummlin' by. Atween the Brig and the end o' the cinder dump a back swirl had scoopit oot a hole for itsel', and by guid luck maist o' the bairns were spun into that. Men jumpit in wadin' up to their oxters to rescue them, and a wheen wimmen tae. Human cheens were made frae the tap o' the dump to the middle o' the pool. A'e wumman, in particular, was fair awa' wi't; her bairn had been on the Brig, and she slid doon the cinder brae on her hunkers richt into the pool. She grabbit a wee lass frae a man a bit faurer oot, but when she saw it wasna her ain bairn the doited cratur, withoot kennin' what she was daein', pitched it into the water again. She was frae ane o' the hooses on the Hill – a' thocht and nae sense! Nane o' the High Street folk ventured into the water tho' a' their bairns were rescued; and nane o' the Waterside folk's bairns were on the Brig when it brak. Catch them! But they did the feck o' the savin' wi' an air as muckle as to say: 'If the fules 'ud keep their brats at their ain gate-en's they'd be less nuisance to ither folk.' If it had been the faithers and mithers instead o' the bit bairns, I question whether the Waterside folk 'ud ha'e bothered to rescue them, and even as it was I'm no shair they felt in their herts they were daein' richt – especially on a Sunday.

A'body's Lassie

First appeared in Scots Observer *14 May 1927; reprinted in (ed) John Gawsworth*, New tales of Horror *(1934)*.

She turns up at a' kinds o' odd times and in a' kinds o' odd places. Whiles she's dressed in rags and whiles she's in the vera height o' fashion like ane o' the coonty gentry. Her age varies. She may be nae mair than a lassie wi' her hair hingin' doon her back, or she may be a braw figger o' a wumman ye'd tak' for onything atween thirty and forty. But as a rule she looks aboot nineteen. Whatever her age she's as bonny as a dream. And there's nae end to her tricks. Mrs McVittie, the baker's wife, was juist sayin' to me yestreen that ye never ken wha's turn it'll be next wi'r. Ye'll hear a chop at the door and there's a split image o' yer wee lassie that deed o' the diptheria. Ye ken that it's owre guid tae be true and yet ye can haurdly misbelieve yer ain een. And it's no' juist yer een. 'Mummy', she'll say, that lifelike. A'e puir wumman I ken that's aye in a natter wi' her big faimily kent there was something wrang and yet she wisna in time to keep back the words. 'What gars ye knock, ye wee limmer?' she said, 'haudin' me rinnin' to the door when I'm thrang.' She cud hae pu'd her tongue up by the roots efter.

And there's mair than ae mither in this toon has been ca'ed tae the door in the same way to fin' a wee white-faced, waesome bit critter stannin' on the steps. 'Weel, what is't?' or 'What ails ye, lassie?' – but never a word oot o' her heid. 'Ha'e ye lost yer tongue? Noo, noo, nae mair greetin'. Rin awa' hame to your mammy. Whaur d'ye bide?' Or whiles ane o' her bairns 'ud come to the door wi' her or she'd cry ben to see if they kent wha' the streenge lassie was. But they'd nae idea. And it wasna till later on – mebbe efter she'd gane till her bed and hed a meenit to think – that the wumman 'ud say to hersel', 'Losh, but it was fell like my puir wee Jeanie,' or Lizzie, as the case micht be, and begin worryin' hersel' till her man said, 'Toots, wumman, what're ye rowin' aboot at? Can ye no lie still? Ye're like a hen on a het girdle. This is no' a soomin' pond.'

I'm namin' nae names, but I was tell't aboot a'e wumman that lives up the brae, and I hope there's no anither like her in the toon. The chop cam' to her door a'e forenune, and when she gae'd to't there was the bit lassie on the step. 'What d'ye mean stannin' wi' yer clarty feet on my new-cleaned step?' says she. The lassie juist hung her heid. 'What d'ye want, onyway?' said the wumman, but the lassie juist swallowed in her throat and couldna get a word oot. 'D'ye think I've got a' the mornin' to plaister wi' the likes o' you?' says the wumman, 'clear aff oot o' this!' And slammed the door in her face. An 'oor efter, she happened to gang to the door again and there was the lassie aye stannin' on the step. Ane o' the bobbies was gaen by at the time, sae the wumman cried him owre and tell't him aboot 'this silly wee brat that disna ken what she wants and'll no' gang awa''.' The bobbie was a great muckle fat reid-faced man that was a favourite wi' a' the bairns, and he pit his haund doon neth her chin and tilted up her facey. He'd juist time to see her afore she disappeared as gin she'd never been. Neither him nor the wumman saw which airt she gaed. 'Missus,' he said, 'It's your ain bairn.'

By jing, there was a row owre that. The wumman gaed richt in and pit on her bunnet and gaed doon to the Polis Office and reportit the maitter; and the Superintendent held an inquiry int't. The bobby stuck to his guns, and by guid luck the wumman neist door had seen the lassie and said she thocht nocht o't at the time, but later on it struck her that the lassie on the doorstep was the verra image o' the wean that deed. And she said she wisna surprised a bit that her ain mither didna recognize her. 'She's like that,' she said. 'She's forgotten she ever had her – tho' it's nae mair than three years come September that she deed.' But ye ken what neebors are; and besides, wha ever heard o' a deid bairn comin' back hame and stannin' on the doorstep? The Superintendent gaed the bobby a gey tellin' aff in front o' the wumman – but, after she was awa', he spoke to him and the next-door wumman in a different way a' thegither. As weel he might, seeing that he wisna only

Superintendent o' the Polis but o' a Sunday schule, and the faither o' a faimily himsel'!

Whiles the critter's ploys had a different endin' frae that tho! There was the case o' the druggist's hoose-keeper that was engaged to Wilson the plumber and had gien notice to quit at the term to be marriet. Guid kens what she saw in Andra Wilson, the muckle sumph. He wasna fit to clean her shoes to'r. Weel, he was stannin' lauchin' and talkin' wi'r at the druggist's door a'e nicht when a wee lassie cam' fleein' in frae naewhaur into her airms cryin' 'Mummy, mummy'. Afore the wumman kent what she was daein' she was doon on her knees cuddlin' the wee cratur for a' she was worth and lauchin' and greetin' at the same time, but in the verra middle o't – whisk! and the lassie was gane as if it had been a' a dream. Wilson ca'd her a' the names he could lay his tongue to, and rived the engagement ring aff her finger and pitched it into the gutter whaur it rowed doon the cundy. The scaffy had a gey job graipin' in the glaur for't the followin' day.

Sic a crood had gethered. It cam' oot that a gey wheen years afore when she was a young servant lassie she'd had a bairn to a son o' the hoose. Her auld mither brocht it up and it was the bonniest wee thing imaginable. But it deed when it was aboot nine. The wumman was still on her knees a' this time wi' a face like the day o' Judgment, but the druggist – his shop was juist owre the way – cam' elbowin' through the crood and liftit her up withoot a word spoken and took her into the hoose and banged the door on a'body's face. She's still wi'm; and I heard a rumour the ither day that they're gaun to be marriet. He's a guid bit aulder than her, but he's no' juist sic an auld man either.

Then a'e nicht juist efter dark there was a wheen bairns playin' ring-a-ring-o'-roses at the heid o' the Factory Entry, when anither lassie cam' rinnin' oot frae the shadow o' the hooses into the ring o' the lamp to join them and twa o' the bairns let gae to mak' room for her. And juist then they saw what it was and the dance stoppit as if they'd been struck.

'Jeannie Morrison', said ane o' the auldest o' the bairns aince she fan' her voicer, 'whaur hae ye sprung fra?'

'Whaur d'ye think?' said the lassie lauchin' and tossin' her curls.

'But ye're deid,' said the other.

'Deid?' says she, 'What's deid?'

The bairn lookit roon' at the rest for help, but they'd nane to gie.

'Deid's juist deid,' said she.

'You mauna believe a' that the big folk say,' said the lassie.

'Then you're no' deid efter a'?' said the ither.

'Ee!' said the ither, 'Sic a fraud! A' the rest o's in the class had to gie money to the teacher for a wreath for ye.'

'Dinna let's waste time,' cried the lassie, stampin' her feet. 'It'll sune be bedtime and it's a while sin' I'd a game.'

Sae they a' forgot what they'd mindit and clasped hands and danced roon' and roon' in the licht o' the lamp shoutin' and singin' till they were fit to drap. Syne twa-three o' their mithers cam' cryin' to them to c'wa hame and get to their beds and off they ran this way and that. But them that mindit that Jeannie Morrison had been supposed to be deed, and tell't their faithers and mithers aboot her, thocht they took it in a gey queer way and Jeannie didna turn up at the schule the next day or ony ither day, and she never cam' to play wi' them again.

That's sae muckle for a'e side o' her pranks. I could keep on tellin' ye ither stories a' nicht. Nearly a'body else in the place kens them as weel as me; but naebody need think; 'If she comes to my door, I'll say "Ho, Ho! Y'ere no' gan' to play ony o' your tricks on me."' Ye canna gaird against her. She does things that naitural-like you're taen in against your ain judgment. She's mair alive than Life itsel'.

It's a queer body that hasna some unsatisfied desire or some skeleton in the cupboard, or doesna wish that something or ither hedna' happened – even if it's only gettin' auld. If you're a decent kind o' soul at a' she sets your hert agin' your heid (and you're nane sorry efter that it won); and if you're no', your conscience mak's a fule o' you, juist when you're least expectin't. Tak' Mrs Dunbar, the banker's wife, for example. She was walkin' doon the High Street in braid daylicht. And by the time she got doon to Cunningham the shoemaker's, there was the bonniest wee lassie, walkin' alangside her, her hand in hers. And Mrs Dunbar and her was lauchin' and talkin' to each ither as happy as ye like! But juist at the fit o' the Kirk Wynd – whisk! – the lassie was gane. Mrs Dunbar lookit a' roon' aboot and gaed doon juist like an umbrella when the shank comes up through't. She'd to be carriet hame, puir body. She's kinda got owre it noo. 'D'ye ever hear onything sae stupit?' she says, when she's tellin' aboot it. 'I've aye wanted a lassie, and, ye ken, I clean forgot that a' my bairns are laddies.'

Ye ken auld Bauldy, the milkman? They say he hesna been able to see his ain feet this forty year an' mair. He was makin' his mornin' ca' at the Manse no' a month agone, when oot she trippit. Auld Bauldy cocks his een when he sees her, as wild as a turkey cock. 'Ye didna turn up last nicht,' says he. 'I did,' says she, 'but I didna see *you* there.' 'What!' says he, 'Ye leein' besom!' And in his anger he turned on the spigot wi' sic a jaw that he splashed himsel' wi' milk frae heid to fit. 'Noo it seems it's your turn to droon,' says she, and disappeared aff the face o' the earth.

He opened his mooth like a fish and couldna shut it again, and he was stannin' like that and no' a drap o' milk left in his ten-gallon can when the meenister's wife hersel' cam' oot. She'd been withoot a servant for a month – and I dinna wonder at that; wha'd bide wi' a critter like yon. It turned oot that twenty or thirty years back, Bauldy had been keepin' company aff and on wi' a servant lassie at the Manse (and as pretty as a picture she was, they say), and ae nicht he trysted her to meet him near haun' the Wauchope Brig whaur the road turns up to the Bex. Bauldy fell in wi' a wheen ithers doon the toon and got as fou' as a puggy an' forgot a' aboot it, but the lassie keepit the tryst. It was a pitch black nicht and somehoo or ither she had faun into the pool at the Brig and couldna win' oot. . . . Bauldy was in an awfu' state the followin' day. But it's queer he should hae mindit juist what she lookit like sae mony years efter, and him marriet and a widower and marriet again and wi' a dizzen o' a family. Tho' they say the seecund wife's a tartar – he hesna had her lang – and nae doot the puir man whiles wishes things had fa'n oot different. It's haurd to tell.

Then there was the case o' the Provost himsel'! A mair dignified auld josser ye wadna meet in a day's mairch, wi' his white fish-tail beard and his lum hat. He was crossin' the Square a'e day, noddin' to this body and that body, and liftin' his tile to the ladies, when, a' at aince, she steppit oot o' Myrtle's fruit shop and gaed a whistle. He whirled to the richt aboot like a young ane and sterted rinnin' to meet her. Of coorse, he flew heels-owre-gowdy and knockit in the croon o' his hat and broke his siller mounted nibby in two into the bargain.

Then there was the time she put her airm in puir Jim

Tamson's. And there was Jim, feelin' twenty years younger and fair forgettin' a' aboot what had happened in the interval, and lauchin' and cairryin' on wi' her, and back in the daft days. But when they turned the corner o' John Street, wha did they rin into but his wife? At the first glance he didna even ken her, but she sune enlightened him. She lookit auld eneuch to be the mither o' the bonnie cratur' swingin' on his airm and it was nae use him sayin' 'We used to be great chums – we were in the same class at the schule.' 'Schule!' said his wife, 'It's easy seen ye're in yer second childhood.'

Och, ye can explain it hoo ye like – but there it is. Mebbe it'll be your turn next.

The Moon Through Glass

First appeared in The Glasgow Herald, *16 July 1927; reprinted in* (ed) *J. Rowland,* Path and Pavement *(1937).*

'Ee!' ... She felt she'd been owre late to haud the exclamation back: but, scansin' owre her shouder at her mither and sister she saw that she hedna gien hersel' awa' efter a'. Wi' a shakin' haund and flutterin' hert she gaed on clearin' awa' the tea things. Should she say onything? It 'ud ser' them richt if she cried oot and gar'd them look up and see the new mune through the winda' tae. But she'd never hear the end o't. No' that either o' them believe't in't the way she did. If they'd seen it themsels they'd never hae thocht twice aboot it, or the ane micht hae drawn the ither's attention to't and made some joke aboot it, prood o' daurin' the auld superstition and kennin' the ither 'ud feel the same way or mebbe pretend to be angry for the sake o' hae'in a row and pittin' the hoose in a steer. Especially if she was aboot, for she hated rows and her no' kennin' which o' them to side wi' for peace's sake aye amused them and suner or later they kent they'd draw her into the row tae and syne they'd baith yoke on her and blame her for the haill todo. If either her mither or sister had seen't they wadna hae swithered a meenit aboot trappin' her into seein't tae and lauchin' thegither at her. But she daurna try ony sic pranks wi' them. They'd mak' the maist o't, tho' she kent weel eneuch – and they kent she kent – they thocht naething o't really and were only makin' a sang because it was her or for the sake o' makin' a sang. If it wasna ae thing it was anither. They'd aye to be wranglin'.

She could hear them and a' the turns and twists they'd gie't.

'You sud think o' ither folk.' On and on and on, as if she had dune it on purpose or, if no', oot o' eindoon want o' thocht which was even waur. 'What were ye glowerin' through the winda at onywey? Dreamin' aboot that muckle sumph o' a man o' yours? Mebbe he'll propose the nicht at last. If he does ye can tak' it the auld sayin's come true for aince.' That 'ud be her mither: she could hear her – and syne her sister 'ud follow suit. 'But cheer up, Meg. It's no' you that need be hingin' the fupple – unless it's wi' disappointment at the kind o' man you've got efter a' your fancy notions (no' that he'll no' be guid eneuch for you whatever he's like) – for it's him that'll hae the feck o' the ill luck, wi' you for his wife.' And on and on and on.

She daurna say onything aboot onything. They were aye doon on her, aye raggin' her. She could dae naethin' to please them. She wished her haund 'ud stop dirlin'. They'd baith sic quick een. Yet she was feart to gang to the back kitchen – she'd mak' sic a rattlin' as 'ud gar them look up, or she'd let the dishes fa'. It 'ud juist be like her luck. What a how-d'ye-do that 'ud mak'! She'd hae to pay for them – and it was Jock's birthday in a fortnight. She'd be tell't her fingers were a' thooms – pity the man that mairriet her! – but nae doot she'd be mair carfu wi' her ain things. Aye gan' dreamin' aboot! That was the main burden o' their complaint – she was aye dreamin'. That was the trouble atween them. They didna' ken what dreamin' was, what onybody could get to dream aboot. And the mair she'd tried to tell them (when she was younger) the less they'd understood and the mair they'd made a fule o' her. Her and her dreamin'! What did she think *she* was? Better than ither folk? Aye moonin' aboot!

And, in the middle o' flytin' at her owre the broken dishes, her mither looks at the winda, and whups roond waur than ever wi' her haunds on her hips. 'Ho! ho! Sae that's the cause. You and that damned mune. The ill-luck's no' frae it, but frae you believin't.' And her sister 'ud chip in: 'And she wasna gaun to say a word aboot it. She wanted us to see it tae! O' a' the mean, dirty, underhaundit ——' On and on and on, the pair o' them! What could she say or dae? Suppose she tried to warn them. Nae maitter hoo quiet she spoke, Jean at onyrate was facin' the winda and 'ud lift her heid and see't – and blame her for no' warnin' her quicker. Even if she did get the warnin' oot withoot either o' them see' in't first, they'd juist lauch at her and look at it to spite her. And syne cairry on aboot her superstitiousness and the curse it was to a hoose, and to a'body connected wi' sic an afflicted cratur. Her best plan was aye to haud her tongue – tho' when she did they ca'd it bein' 'in the dorts' and ranted on aboot her perpetual ill-natur' – she was as blithe in a hoose as a thunder clood – and she kent as a maitter o' fact that no' bein' able to speak to them – to open her heart to them – had made her feel dour and tongue-tacket eneuch in the coorse o' the years. Thank God, she had Jock.

But at the thocht o' Jock the fu' tide o' her ill-luck in seein' the mune through gless – this nicht o' a' nichts – poored owre her. It micht mean ... This was the first time her thocht o' Jock had had a tinge o' doot or fear. This was the first time that she hedna kent for shair that nae maitter hoo miserable things micht be at hame, she'ud find naething but joy wi' him. He was her only ootlet. Only wi' him could she be hersel'. She wasna hersel' wi' her mither or her sister or ony o' the rest o' them. This wasna her life – this wranglin' back-bitin' miserable way o' daen'. But ilka noo and then she won clear o't for a wee – wi' Jock: and she'd been hopin' to win' clear o't a'thegither sune. In fact she'd expectit him to say the word that vera nicht – if she hedna seen the new mune through the winda. Whatna price to pay for a pure accident! And even as this thocht gaed through her heid she kent that there was a waur yin dodgin' through ahint it that she wasna able juist to see richt. It was that mebbe he'd still say the word this vera nicht! The ill-luck 'ud be in her bein' disappointed wi' him – or him wi' her – efter they mairriet; or, frae ae cause or anither their mairriage no' turnin' oot as they expectit. It was the first time *that* had ever entered her heid. Nae wonder it gaed slinkin' through it, she thocht in an effort to tell hersel' that it was oot o' the question – but even as she tried that, it cam' back in again, bigger than ever, and blacker. She sterted to bamboozle hersel' sae that she could imagine it wasna there (altho' a' the time it was gettin' bigger and bigger and blacker and blacker) by tryin' to lauch at hersel' for forgettin' that the ill-luck only lasted for a month sae it couldna affect her mairriage (and, by jings', she'd be mair carefu' in the future in regaird to new munes) and syne, when that didna' work, by tryin' to mind whether or no' the ill-luck couldna' be averted frae something o' consequence to something o' nane by brakin' a plate or some sic thing: and noo she was in sic a state that she was in twa minds either to let the tea things fa' and pit up wi' a' that her mither and sister micht say, or juist tell them what had happened and ask them if brakin' a plate 'ud ward off the ill-luck. But if she did this last they wadna tell her – or they'd tell her wrang; and yet it was an awfu' pity to brak' a' the dishes if ane 'ud dae! She was fair in a swither.

It took her a muckle effort movin' into the back kitchen (it was a God's wonder her mither and sister hadna been at her for takin' sae lang to clear the table as it was) and the dishes jiggle-jiggled in her hands to sic a tune that aince she sterted (near-haund trippin' on the mat) she's to rin to get them safe to the sink. And the warst thocht o' a' struck her then. What if the ill-luck concerned Jock? What if onything had come owre him? What if he jilted her? Or if he'd had an accident and was deid! She catch't sicht o' hersel' in her faither's lookin'-glass at the side o' the sink. Jock hadna missed muckle onyway. What had he ever seen in her? She didna look the least like what she' been feelin' inside hersel' afore she saw the mune. She was faur mair like her sister or her mither than she'd ever imagined. If Jock had been a' that she'd thocht he'd never hae gien the likes o' her a second look. But if love had blinded her to the truth aboot hersel' nae doot it had blinded her to the truth aboot him tae. Her sister had aince said: 'Wait till you're mairriet – he's only a workin' man and you an' him 'll juist be like ony ither workin' class man and wife.' She'd had a horrid vision o' Jock as nae mair than a common ploo-man, and o' mairriage as the same auld drudgery under a different name. Had a' young couples the same high-falutin' ideas – afore they mairriet? If they'd ha' come doon to the level o' the feck o' the folk roon' aboot – o' her faither and mither say – it was a guid job he was deid. He couldna come doon then. She'd keep him the man she'd thocht him as lang as she leeved. He'd aye be the ootlet for her dreams. But in that case whaur was the ill-luck o' seein' the mune through gless . . . Tchah! She couldna' mak' heid or tail o't. But she'd better get on wi' the dishes or she'd be late – for what?

Maria

From The Glasgow Herald, *27 August 1927.*

Maria was gaun to dee. 'But it'll no' likely be till some time through the nicht,' he'd heard his mither say. Still, that wasna long. It was an unco queer thing to think aboot; there she was, talkin' and to a' appearances gey near in her usual – as he'd aye kent her; and even jokin' and lauchin' whiles. Did she ken she was gaun to dee? She didna seem the least bit feart. Ye'd think the prospects o' the weather and the clish-clash o' the toon wadna maitter muckle to a wumman that wadna see the morn. He wondered at his mither. She kent Maria was 'at daith's door', and yet she was as bad as Maria – her tongue gaun sixteen to the dizzen aboot nocht o' ony consequence, and rallyin' and cairryin' on as if deein' was the maist ordinary thing imaginable. He'd expected something a'thegither different – hushed voices and lang faces, and a terrible solemn kind o' feelin' owre a'body and a'thing. He felt disappointed. To a' ootward appearances there was neist to naething oot o' the common in't ava. Maria micht be gaun to dee, but she certainly didna look like it. Yet a' at aince – according' to his mither – something 'ud happen, and Maria 'ud be 'nae mair'; the blinds 'ud be pu'd doon, and syne the men 'ud come and pit Maria's body in a lang black coffin and tak' it awa' and bury it in the grun', and she'd never be seen or heard tell o' again. What a queer thing! What did a body feel like, deein'? He'd ha'e liked to speir at Maria, but something tell't him that he mauna. That was hoo Maria and his mither were gibble-gabblin' the way they were daein' – to keep awa' frae the thing that was uppermaist in baith o' their minds.

Mebbe he'd see Maria deein' and ken a' aboot it. His mither

had to rin hame for a wee; and he'd to bide wi' Maria till she cam' back. 'Ye'll no' be feart?' she'd spiered him, and he'd said he wadna – but he'd felt feart eneuch, till he cam' in and saw Maria lookin' juist as she'd aye lookit.

But, tho' he'd felt real feart, he'd managed to smile a brave wee smile and say 'Na, na! I'll be a'richt,' for he kent weel eneuch that it wasna ilka laddie o' his age that had the chance o' sittin' by a daithbed – alane at that. It wadna be a thing to brag aboot – but to haud his tongue aboot, and that 'ud mak' him a' the mair mysterious and important. He could hear folk sayin': 'There was naebody wi' her when she deed – but Tam Mackie. His mither had had to gang hame, but Tam volunteered to bide till she cam' back. She wasna lang gane afore the cheenge cam'. Puir Maria; she'd a sair struggle at the end. The laddie did a' he could. It maun ha'e been a gey trial for him. He disna like to talk aboot it, but ye canna wonder at that.'

Sae, altho' it was a relief in a'e way to find Maria sae like hersel', it was disappointin' in anither. There was only a'e thing oot o' the ordinar'. Maria was lyin' in the best bedroom – what had been Mary's room – instead o' in the kitchen bed. It was a bonny room – a' licht colours, juist like the water-colour paintings hingin' on the wa's in their gowd frames. He mindit Mary. She'd been an awfu' lady-body; Maria had aye dune a' the wark. It seemed queer to see Maria in Mary's bed. It gied ye the same sensation as when ye crackit open a chestnut. O' a' the unexpectit things in the warl' shairly there's naething mair unexpectit than to crack open sic a pale green shell and see yon bricht broon chestnut inside it – like a muckle doonsin' e'e. Maria lookit juist as oot o' place in Mary's bed. She was that dark o' the skin. Mary had been a' pink and white – like a rose. And if Maria lookit a kennin' paler than usual it was mebbe owin' to the whiteness o' the sheets reflectin' in her face. If there had been naething but the blankets, there micht ha' been nae cheenge at a'.

'Weel, well, I'll no' be lang,' his mither was sayin'. 'Juist lie back and see if ye canna get a wee sleep. I wadna talk ony mair ... Tam'll juist sit owre here by the winda and if there's onything ye want he'll get it for ye ... Sit here, Tam.'

And she gar'd him sit beside the winda. 'Gie her a look ilka noo and then', she whispered, 'I'll no' be lang. I think she'll be a' richt till I come back. Keep quiet an' she'll mebbe fa' owre.'

His mither was gane. As sune as the door closed ahint her, he lookit owre; Maria was lyin' back wi' her een shut. She lookit afa' faur awa' tho' and he could hardly mak' oot her face at a' for a shaft o' sunlicht that cam' slantin' in. Bairns were playin' in the street ootside. It was queer to think his brither was up on the golf course somewhere caddyin'. He wadna come and sit like this. Nae fear. 'Tam was his mither's boy.' What gar'd folk say that in sic a way as to mak' ye feel a wee thing ashamed – as if ye were a kind o' lassie-boy? Shairly it took mair courage to sit like this aside a deein' wumman than to cairry a kit o' clubs roon' the hill. Hoo quiet it was in here – like bein' cut off frae life a'thegither. He was mair feart noo; he felt his hair risin'. He wished Maria 'ud wauken again. It hadna been sae bad when she was talkin' awa' to his mither. If he moved and made a wee noise mebbe she'd wauken. He lookit owre to the bed again, movin' his heid forrit to get clear o' the sunbeam. She hadna stirred. There wasna a soon' o' ony kind. It seemed a lang time since his mither gaed awa'. Mebbe she'd met somebody an' was standin' talkin'. He wished she'd come noo.

Wheesht! Was that her? He thocht he'd heard a door openin'. Could it be Daith comin'? His hert was dirlin' inside him at an awfu' rate. He felt like runnin' owre to the bedside for protection – but he couldna move. The bedroom door was openin' – tho' you could haurdly see it move; it couldna be a human bein' that was open'n't. His mither's heid keeked in; he'd been sittin' wi' stelled e'en, haudin' his braith – he could hardly believe it was really her and no' – no' what? He couldna conjure up ony picter o' the terrible sicht he'd expectit to see.

His mither stepped owre to the bedside. Had she seen hoo frichtened he was?

'Wheesht', he felt like sayin', 'She's sleepin',' but something hindered him. And his mither turned roon'. He kent at aince frae the look that it was a' owre. Maria was deed – and he hadna seen her deein' efter a'. It didna seem possible. He felt awfu' disappointed. He micht as weel no' ha'e been there awa. If he'd only f'und oot afore his mither had come back – and been able to tell her, to show her he kent. Even if he hadna seen anything he could ha'e claimed to ha'e seen a' kinds o' things. She couldna ha'e contradicted him. Could he no' pretend even yet to ha'e kent? What could he say? He wished his brain didna feel sae stupid-like.

'Rin and tell your faither, Tam', she said.

He was off like a shot – rinnin' thro' the streets for a' he was worth. Shairly folk 'ud see frae his face and the way he was runnin' that he was cairryin' important news. That was aye something. But he was wishin' in his hert o' herts that his thochts were gaun as quick as his legs. He couldna mak' up his mind what to say.

The Visitor

From Scots Observer, *1 October 1927.*

I mebbe haena got the hang o't just richt. It's a queer story. But, as faur as I can mak' oot, here it is.

It seems that in the middle o' the nicht there cam' a rappin' at the door. Mrs M'Ilwrath's a licht sleeper – no' like him. She heard the first chap but wisna shair it was their door. It was a bricht munelicht nicht but fell cauld. There's this to be said for her – that if it had been ony ither wumman in the toon and they'd heard a chap at that time o' nicht, and thocht it was at ony ither door than their ain, they'd have been out o' bed and hauf oot o' the winda like a shot. They wadna hae waited to wauken their men – let alane lippened to them to find oot. It 'ud only tak' a wag to gang roond the streets in the wee sma' hoors chappin' at this door and that in the winter time to gar hauf the wives in the place hirple to the Kirk wi' frost-bitten feet the followin' Sunday. But that's gettin' awa' frae the point. Mrs M'Ilwrath prides hersel' on no' bein' inquisitive like ither folk.

The chappin' gaed on. Mrs M'Ilwrath sat up in bed. Her gude man was snorin' for a' he was worth. She heard first a'e winda and syne anither gan' up alang the street. The neebors were thrang. At last she cam' to the conclusion that it maun be her door richt eneuch. Wha could it be? She tried to think, but it wasna easy wi' the clapper gan' smack ilka twa-three seconds. She wondered if she could lie doon and fa' asleep juist as if she'd never heard it. Whaever it was 'ud be weel ser'd if she could. But the knockin' seemed to be gettin' looder and looder – like to smash in the door. The haill hoose was dirlin' – and the neebors were shoutin' to ask what the maitter was. 'Mak' less din', she heard ane cry. 'ye'll wauken the bairns.' It couldna gang on.

She'd hae to wauken Jock. But she leuch to hersel' when she thocht o' what the neebors 'ud say neist day. She'd never let on she'd heard ava'. It 'ud fair rile them. They'd get nae cheenge oot' o' her.

'Jock,' she said, and gied him a dunt in the ribs. But he juist grunted a wee.

'Jock,' she said, and dunted him again. The knockin' never stoppit. Rat-a-tat. Tat-a-tat. Rat-a-tat. It was beginnin' to get on her nerves.

'Jock,' she said, and gied him a third dunt. That waukened him, but he was slow in comin' to himsel', and it took a bit time to tell him what was what.

'Wha can it be?' she spiered.

But he'd nae idea.

'You'd better gang doon the stairs an' see.'

'I'll thraw up the winda first and look oot.'

'You'll dae nae sic thing. Doon stairs and get the kitchen poker, and cry through the door to see what it is and what they want afore ye open't.'

Aff he gaed, and syne she heard him at the door: 'Wha's there?'

But there was nae answer, and the knockin' gaed on withoot a break.

'Wha's there?' he cried again.

There was nae answer; juist rat-a-tat, rat-a-tat. Even on.

Syne she heard him open the door, and – efter a wee – speakin' to somebody.

Then the door shut. She waited to hear his fit on the stairs, but it gaed alang the lobby and into the parlour instead.

The muckle sumph! Wha could it be? He micht hae shouted up the stairs at ony rate to pit her mind at ease. She swithered a while, thinkin' first ae thing and syne anither, and a' the time ca'in' hersel' a fule for thinkin' at a' when she'd nocht to gang by. They were takin' a lang time. It was queer that Jock hadna come up for his breeks even. She tholed the suspense as long as she could. It seemed an eternity. At last she shouted, 'Jock,' twice, but there was nae answer. Sae there was naething for't but to rise. Up she got and put her claes on. She could hear them talkin' frae the heid o' the stair. The clock struck three juist as she got to the fit o't. She gaed alang the lobby and threw open the parlour door.

Jock stude dumfoonered in the middle o' the flair. There was naebody else in the room.

'Wha' was't?' spiered his wife.

'Naebody,' he said.

'But I heard you talkin'.'

'I was talkin' to mysel'.'

'What keepit you doon here ane lang then?'

'I dinna ken.'

'Ye needna tell me naebody could clour the door like yon.'

'Ye can look for yersel' then.'

And that was a' she could get oot o'm. As a maitter o' fact he hasna' muckle mair to gie. 'When I opened the door,' he says, 'who was standin' there but mysel'? Plain as a pikestaff. For a' the warld as if the street was a lookin' glass. D'ye think I dinna ken mysel' when I see mysel'? "Guid sakes', I said, "whaur hae ye been to this 'oor o' the nicht?" "I wish," said he, "I kent whaur I've been for a lang time back." "Dinna talk nonsense," says I. "What I want to ken is, wha' I am if you're me? Ye'd better c'wa ben and let us thrash it oot." I took him into the parlour and we argled back and forrit, but neither o's could mak' heid or tail o't.

' "If you're the real me," I said in the hinder en', "hoo in a' the wide warld am I to accoont to Mrs M'Ilwrath for haen the presumption to act sae lang in your place?"

' "Accoont to wha?" says he.

'And juist then I heard the wife upstairs shoutin' "Jock".

'He jumpit as if he'd been stung.

' "Wha's that?" says he.

' "The wife," says I.

' "Then I'm for oot o' this," says he. "I'll no fash ye again. You needna be feart." "Haud on," says I. "What am I to say to her?"

'He suggested ae thing and anither, but a' they showed was that he'd nae idea o' the kind o' critter I've to deal wi' in the shape o' the wife. Ye'd ha'e thocht he'd nae idea what a wumman was, tho' he was gleggit at the very thocht o' ane.

' "Look here," says I, "I was sleepin' beside her, as canny as a lamb, when you sterted to batter at the door. You're no gan' to skedaddle noo' and leave me to tell her a cook-and-bull story nae wumman on earth 'ud believe. I'd hae nae peace efter that. Juist you stan' your grun' and let her see wi' her ain een. Then she'll no' blame me, whatever else she does."

'I got atween him and the door as I spoke, and juist then I heard the wife comin' doon the stairs and alang the lobby. Wad ye believe it – ye can either believe it or no' – juist as she opened the door the man vanished as if he'd never been there. Disappeared into naething afore my verra een. Guidness kens hoo!

'What could I dae or say? It's bad eneuch as it is, but if I'd telt her that it was my ainsel' that was chappin' at the door and syne o' oor conversation thegither, it 'ud hae been faur waur. Mind ye, I'm nane sorry the man vamoosed the way he did. If he stude his grun' it 'ud hae helpit me in ae way but it 'ud hae complicated maitters beyond a' bearin' in every ither direction. I daurna imagine what the wife 'ud hae thocht if she'd opened that door and seen me – twice. Ance was eneuch. And it's faur better she shouldna believe what I tell her than no' be able to believe her ain een. As for the neebors, maist o' them hae gane oot o' their way to get unco friendly to me sin syne. They'd been wont to imagine I'd nae spirit o' my ain – but when they saw me at the door at three o'clock o' the mornin' they drew their ain conclusions. They didna see wha opened the door, and think it was the wife. I haena thocht fit to undeceive them. Considerin' the circumstances, a' thing's fitted in nane sae badly, but, mind ye, mum's the word.'

Andy

From The Glasgow Herald, *22 October 1927.*

He juist hated fishin' – but he couldna refuse. For a'e thing, his mither 'ud be on his top in a meenit wi' a voice that could clip clouts. She'd nae patience wi' him – 'aye sittin' in a corner mumpin' owre a book!' If it had been his schulebooks it wadna hae been sae bad – but poetry and novels and guid kens what! Stuffin' his heid wi' a lot o' useless nonsense. His faither was faur owre saft wi' him. 'Let the laddie abee,' he aye said; 'there's waur things than readin'!' But he'd to pey for his faither's support in a' kinds o' ways, and his mither and Andy saw that he did.

If there was a message to rin or a hank o' yarn to wind, he was aye there or thereaboots and had to pit doon his book tae dae't. He daurna complain o' bein' interrupted in his readin' tho' it was a hunner times a nicht, for his mither 'ud appeal to his faither, and his faither 'ud side wi' her then. It was only when he wasna wantit for something else that his faither stuck up for him bein' suffered to read in peace. But the mair he did for his mither, the mair she thocht him Jessie-like. And ahint it a' was Andy's influence – aye sneerin' at him, tormentin' him, eggin' his mither on. Andy was his mither's Jacob. She thocht he was that manly – aye oot fishin', or caddyin' at the golf course and makin' money. Nae books for him – barrin' his schule books, and nae mair o' them than he could help – and syne he'd to be helped wi' them. Andy – and his mither – took fu' advantage then o' his superior learnin'. But tho' his mither wanted Andy to get on, at hert she sympathised wi' his contempt for book-lear, and tho' she made him help Andy she didna like him ony the better for bein' able to dae't.

Ilka time he did gang oot fishin' it was a fresh humiliation. The fact o' the maitter was that he couldna fish. He never catched onything but auld tin cans, or the brainches o' a tree or his ain breek-bottom; and he never heard the end o't. He'd an idea that if he could gang oot aince and catch a guid fry o' troot his mither and Andy 'ud never want him to gang again.

His faither, of coorse, was a crack hand either wi' worm or fly. Andy wasna muckle better than himsel', to tell the truth, but he never got into sic predicaments and he aye managed to catch something, even if it was only a smout. It wasna his wyte he didna' catch a' the fish ever made wi' ae cast, and in ony case his mither aye said, 'The wee'r the trout the sweeter.'

His faither was wonderfu' patient wi' im. He never leuch at him – till the ithers began it. And he never lost his temper and said his fingers maun be a' thooms – or no' often! It 'ud ha'e beena' richt if Andy hadna been there. He believed he could ha'e explained his feelings aboot the haill thing in a way his faither 'ud understand – but he haurdly ever saw his faither alane. There was never ony fishin' unless Andy had naething better to dae and got his mither to get his faither to tak' them.

Andy was aye wi' them if they were ootside and his mither if they were in the hoose. The kind o' things he wanted to say were fell ill to say – and he kent that even if he could say them it 'ud hae to be to somebody he trustit and likit, and if he tried it on wi' his faither he'd nae suner get stertit than either Andy or his mither 'ud see he got nae faurer. They kent, deep doon, the difference atween him and them – better mebbe than he did himsel' – and they took precious guid care he didna' get a chance o' expressin' it. And the things they could aye say to side-track him and pit him in the warst possible licht and gar him mak' a fule o' himsel' were that muckle easier to say than the verra first words o' ony defence he could mak'!

A' the same it was a kind o' fear that gar'd them aye chip in afore him and prevent him frae sayin' what he kent he wad hae said – whatever that was – gi'en time and fair play; and that gied him hert. He kent his faither jaloused something o' this – but no' juist eneuch. He lookit at him in a queer switherin' way whiles – and syne sided wi' his mither and Andy; it was that muckle easier. But he felt that if he could juist explain things to his faither aince he'd hae nae mair bother.

He liked bein' ootside a' richt (tho' he liked readin' better).

But he'd hae preferred bein' alane – wi' his ain thochts. It was haurd eneuch thinkin' ootside onywey, even if ye were alane – haurder than in the hoose; mebbe because there was faur mair to gar ye think. What he couldna stand was Andy aye yabble-yabbling aboot things he felt sae sma' and silly in comparison wi' nature or books. The wild skelp and slither and swish o' the spate was eneuch for him – withoot makin't a' juist a side-issue to fishin'.

He could hae stood for oors daen naethin' but watchin't. But that was exactly what Andy and his mither couldna understaund or thole. Fillin' yer heid wi' a lot o' wild ideas that ser'd nae purpose – no' like fishin'! Sensible folk didna gang oot to gape and glower at the flood – they gaed to catch fish, and the degree o' their sense was determined, if no' a'thegither by the number o' fish they catched, at a' events by the evidence they gied that that was what was first and foremaist in their minds.

He kent that he was seein' a thoosan' things that Andy 'ud never see – twirly bits, shades o' colour, queer wee soonds that werena tint in the general roar, crochet-patterns o' faem – and he'd see a thoosan' mair if his mind was free.

He'd fa'n into a broon study. A' at aince he heard a yell and the birlin' o' a reel. Andy had yin on – and 'By jings, it's a whopper,' he bawled to his faither. His faither was comin' back owre the rocks as fast as his legs 'ud cairry him to help to land it. 'Gie't plenty o' play,' he cried. Andy's face was a picture – fair eindoon determination, like a thundercloud – as if there was naethin' in the warld but him and this wallopin' troot and the need to land it.

He felt he was seein' the haill truth aboot Andy noo. He'd aye be like that – deid serious aboot something that didna maitter a docken and blin' to a' that did. Puir Andy, he felt wae for him – wi' a face like that, makin' a life-or-daith maitter o' something you could buy for tippence for breakfast frae the man that cam' roon wi' the lorry. His face like that was like seein' the flair o' the sea – a'e meenit a' jobblin' waves, and the next – naething but dour black glaur. He felt he could gang richt through the bottom o' Andy's mind noo to the promised land like the Jews gaen through the Reid Sea; but it was a fell clarty road. If it 'ud only bide like that it micht dry; but nae doot in a meenit or twa the muckle treacherous flood that generally hit it 'ud sweep owre't again and naebody that hadna seen't for themsel's 'ud ken the horror it covered.

Whether Andy hadna heard his faither's advice or thocht he kent better or was juist owre anxious, he'd rung in till his rod was like a hauf-hoop and his line as ticht as the gut o' a fiddle – and there was its heid! It was a whopper and nae mistak'! Andy wadna hauf craw owre him noo! His faither was juist at him when – snap! – the line broke, and in the blink o' an e'e, afore his faither could lift a haund to stop him, Andy dived into the pool heid first – efter the troot.

It was a deep pool and a dangerous ane. There had been twa-three folk drooned in't. His faither's mind was slow in workin'. For a second he saw him – standin' wi' his een fair stelled in his heid. He saw as faur ben into his faither then as he'd seen into Andy a meenit afore. Andy bobbed up in the centre o' the pool, brakin' the bonny swirl o' the waters like a muckle blot in an exercise-book, and still wi' the same determined look on his face – he hadna had time to alter it. It had been that fixed. He was conscious o' hauf a dizzen different thochts at aince – the pure comicality o' Andy gaen in efter the troot; the fact that he'd be spared a lot o' trouble and humiliation if Andy was drooned; a hauf-waesome, half-ashamed sense o' his faither's flabbergasted condition – and a' at aince he dived in tae.

It was pure accident – juist the way o' the current and the angle he struck the water at – but the next thing he kent he'd Andy by the jacket-neck wi' the ae hand and a haud o' a rock on the faur side o' the pool wi' the ither, and his faither was comin' splashin' through the shallower water a wee bit higher up, and in a meenit or two he'd hauled them baith oot.

Ane or twa ither anglers cam' rinnin' up. 'Weel dune, Tammy,' a voice shouted frae the ither side o' the pool. 'It's the bravest thing I've ever seen.' It was Macrae, the banker, nae less. It 'ud be a' owre the toon in nae time. He was a hero. It was a guid job ither folk had seen it tae, or Andy and his mither 'ud hae whittled it doon to naething. But he kent they wadna like him ony the better – tho' for a while they micht hae to pretend to. That micht be still waur to stand than onything he'd had to pit up wi' yet.

What had gar'd him jump in to the rescue? He couldna soom. He micht easy hae made things waur instead o' better. That 'ud juist hae been like his luck. A' this ran through his heid in less time than it tak's to tell while he was sittin' up tryin' to get the water oot o' his lugs and listenin' to the human hubbub aboot him and the stoond o' the spate that seemed looder than ever noo he'd had a mair intimate acquaintance wi 't. A' at aince he louped to his feet. He'd thrawn his rod doon when he dived and it had got jammed by the reel in the rocks; but – look! He couldna get owre to 't. He was dancin' like a hen on a het girdle. But the banker had seen't at the same time. 'A' richt, Tammy, I'll see to 'it for ye' – and he did. Played it bonny! And, by jings, it was a whopper!

But Andy aye declared that it was naething ava compared wi' the ane he'd lost – 'And, besides, ye didna' land it yersel'!'

The Scab

From The Glasgow Herald, *15 August 1932.*

In the very heart of these beautiful policies there is a malign piece of ground, called The Scab; and, talking with others who come here, I have been interested to discover how obscurely but overwhelmingly important it is. This is no peculiarity of my own temperament; it is shared by many others different enough from myself. Willy-nilly, all steps gravitate thither oftener than to any other part of the grounds. The beauties of the setting become negligible in the light of that abject gem, a jewel of horror whose rays, as it were, annihilate the rest of the word, and can destroy the heavens themselves. Its fascination (for we are conscious of the element of pleasure even when we are most insistent upon describing our feelings as repulsion) remains almost entirely a secret to us: we can hardly begin to explain it. Anything we can say seems inept and absurd. We have, moreover, a constraining consciousness of our ingratitude, a sense of shame; the grounds are so magnificent, so perfectly laid out. We are ashamed to prefer the canker to the rose. It is difficult to admit that all loveliness goes for nothing as against this appalling eyesore; that ugliness, naked and unashamed, is a far more potent magnet than beauty. But it is so. I have been amused to see how some of the visitors have sought at first to hide the fact that it atracted them so irresistibly, but gradually shed their pretence – one or two with unrestrained terror of the lure that had so inexplicably enslaved them, as if it had revealed some evil predisposition of their souls – as no doubt it had. Others of us never attempted any dissimulation; we were hurried, open-eyed, to this patch like flotsam is to the heart of a whirlpool. It is our Sargasso Sea.

The Scab is unnatural. Any grave is soon covered over; fields champed out of all semblance into obscene messes of mud bestuck with blasted parodies of trees are very soon recaptured by the green grass and the wild flowers. Nature lies just round the corner, ready to seize the first opportunity to recover any territory that is taken from her. But Nature does not lie round the corner here. It is as if Nature recognised that this had never belonged to her and never could, or had been somehow compelled to give it up as forever irreclaimable. There is an invisible barrier beyond which no blade of grass, no runner of a weed, no thread of a root, attempts to pass. Chance of wind may deposit a seed there from time to time, but without result. Nothing grows there. I think that nothing has grown there since Time began, or ever will – that it might be ploughed and reploughed as deep as the centre of the earth and filled with fertiliser, to no end, and that, even were it possible to remove that sterile soil, such of it as was transferred eslewhere, in bulk or in separate particles, would there again produce sterility, in patches or in specks according to proportion, while the place from which it had been taken would remain a ghastly pit which nothing else could fill. I may be wrong: I am of a fanciful disposition, but that is how I feel about it, and others who know it as I do share my feelings despite the most radical differences of temperament.

So far as I can ascertain, it has no particular history. There is no reason why it should be thus infamously differentiated from the rest of the world. It had a common origin with spots which are now gardens or glades or green fields. In the beginning of things no one could have foretold that it would become so unlike these, or, witnessing the stages of its alienation, if there were any such, could have suggested any reason for its monstrous and unparalleled development. While Nature holds aloof, however, and, so far as human eye can see, attempts no reconciliation, the Scab is stealthily but incessantly encroaching on Nature. Even in my experience it has extended perceptibly, and Nature, while falling back inch by painful fraction of an inch, never attempts to regain the ground she so loses. This is unlike Nature, unlike her infinite patience, her inexhaustible resource. One would expect some sudden sally, some surprising circumvention. But no. Things take their course. Nature knows when she is beaten! – and the Scab apparently has her beaten. All that she can do is to yield only by degrees as infinitesimal as the eternal concentration of her enormous opposition can contrive.

In putting matters thus I am only too conscious, of course, of the inadequacy of language to deal with such a situation. I have called the Scab unnatural, and spoken of it as impervious to Nature. But that is not quite true. It is to green life. But there are forms of life which infest it (apart from the fact that it is a kind of living death itself). Ants, for example! They have succeeded in forming intricate establishments in that sinister and inhospitable soil. They maintain a perpetual traffic on and, to some undetermined extent, within it. Seeing them following their incomprehensible courses (a vicious circle if ever there was one) – which they support upon nothing found within that desolate circle, but upon material they abstract from Nature, to and from which they journey incessantly, without let or hindrance – an extraordinary similarity presents itself to one's eyes between them and this barren soil. They are simply like mobile particles of it, well-nigh indistinguishable from it. Not so is an ant that one may encounter in Nature. The foil of greenery, of infinite variety, sharpens such an ant to our sight, and endows it with lively qualities of enterprise and dexterity and even a tiny burnished beauty these sordid insects entirely lack as they pass and repass (to no other end than the multiplication of their kind) on this wretched surface mechanised to so unendurable a degree that the sight of them going and coming afflicts the conscious but baffled spectator with a sense of meaningless and endless motion alien and repugnant to the human soul. Other insects and tiny reptiles are found here too. The evidences of their existences uncorrected by the diversity of Nature assume a hideous relief: their *formes*, and other commotions or indentations of the earth, are an unsightly testimony to insensate activity. The whole plot has been mined and honeycombed and corrugated throughout the ages, in countless ecstasies of futile ingenuity: the product of a mindless itch.

And some of those with whom I have discussed the phenomenon believe that the Scab will, slowly perhaps, and perhaps at an incalculably accelerated rate, but surely, spread over the whole earth, and that in the end the blessed light will fall only on an immense panorama of empty 'workings,' established in their time by myriads of ants and other insects and tiny reptiles the last of which are dead.

The Last Great Burns Discovery

From At the Sign of the Thistle *(1934)*.

So Charlie Crichton has gone to his reward!

Well, he will rank for all time as one of the Great Burnsians, in the direct line of Duncan MacNaught and Thomas Amos and John Muir. Their like will not be seen again. The whole field of Burns lore has been 'redded' with a small-tooth-comb – there is no scope left for the development of such Titans now. Crichton was the last of them. Only minor gleanings, the veriest *minutiae*, remain; these cannot feed the indomitable will of such men. What pigmies in comparison are even the best of our Burnsians to-day! There is no help for it. It is 'beyond remeid'. Yet even when Crichton first became prominent in World Burns Circles over thirty years ago the same might have been said – it seemed almost equally unlikely that he could find anything sizeable either or be destined to do more than stroke the t's and dot the i's of his distinguished predecessors. Those who thought that reckoned without their host however. The secret perhaps is just that Crichton knew better than anybody else all that had been done already. Heavens, how he applied himself! He had the whole thing at his finger-ends. He wasted no time on false trails. He knew the whereabouts of every scrap of holograph and every relic of Burns himself and his family and his relatives and everybody mentioned in his poems or letters or in any way connected with him, and the birth-places and various dwelling-places and last resting-places of them all. Yet he did not give up hope; he was sustained, I can only suppose, in addition to infinite tenacity of purpose, by some premonition of his high calling, of the momentous discovery which despite all the probabilities, had eluded the myriads of indefatigable searchers who had gone before him and been reserved for his humble self.

I stress the adjective – his *humble* self; since his natural modesty must have had a great deal to do with it – that, and his profound common sense, as the direction in which his researches finally took him, and the very nature of his discovery, show. If he subsequently – and most naturally – became less humble the question is whether he did not remain to the end infinitely more humble than anyone else would have done in like circumstances. I think he did.

All this, of course, is an old story now. It is nearly twenty years since he gave to the world what I feel amply justified (there are certainly no indications to the contrary) in calling the Last Great Burns Discovery. It came at an opportune moment. The Burns Movement had fallen on lean years; and there was a ridiculous attempt in certain would-be-clever quarters to switch it off its traditional lines and concentrate attention on highbrow stuff and nonsense. Crichton put an end to that.

I know what I am writing about because of a fact which I have never disclosed before, simply because, for his own good reasons at the time, he asked me not to. *I was the first man to whom Crichton disclosed his epoch-making discovery.* I divulge this at last with a full sense of the title to immortality Crichton thus – I think deliberately – conferred upon me; and am, of course, in a position to prove it up to the hilt. The time was not ripe then – nor for another couple of years – to make it public. Crichton judged it unerringly; those of us who remember the effect of his disclosure, the worldwide furore, when he decided that the moment had come, can vouch for that. It was a veritable bombshell; the biggest thing in Scottish literary history since the Kilmarnock Edition itself – and probably the last big thing Scottish literary history will register!

Few men could have kept the secret of having been Crichton's first *confidant* as I have done, and I have frequently in these intervening years laughed up my sleeve at nobodies bragging of some petty detail and posing as Great Burnsians without knowing that, like little Jack Horner, I too had had my finger in that pie and had pulled out such a stupendous plum!

I remember that evening as it were yesterday. We had been sitting in Crichton's parlour discussing some teasing, if very trivial, points in current Burnsian controversy – on the musicology side. He worked up to it very gradually; probably afraid of the effect a too-sudden disclosure might have upon me. Finally: 'Now I've got something to show you', he said, 'something really big. We are going for a walk before the light fails. It isn't very far.'

Off we went, across a field and over a medium-sized hill and through the valley on the far side of it, until we came to the 'larach' of an old cottage, and, beside it, a patch of jungle running down to a little burn. That patch of jungle had been the cottage garden once upon a time. Now, even then I knew my Burns topography as well as most so-called expert Burnsians, and my excitement began to rise. I suspected what Crichton was leading up to; I was right up to a point – Burns *had* lived for a while in the cottage that had stood on those old founds. But Crichton – though I saw him noticing out of the tail of his eye that I had already jumped to that conclusion – had something far greater to show me. He plunged breast-high into the tangled growth of the old garden and I followed him until, close by the burnside, he threw aside a last swathe of rank vegetation, as if it had been a curtain, and said: 'There!'

What I saw was a little ruined old dry closet. There was no door to it; but the roof had been recently repaired, and the seat inside, though rotted away in parts, was wonderfully preserved.

'You don't mean . . . ?' I cried.

He nodded solemnly.

It was an august moment – the most impressive moment of my life – as we stood there in the gathering twilight, and he told me the slow but sure steps, the ten years' unremitting study, that had led to his discovery and his final and absolute proof that (though, alas! there was no scrap of writing on the walls, no carved initials on the woodwork even) Burns himself had used that very place, that very seat; the only convenience he had used that was still extant – Burns himself, and Jean Armour.

'Since then,' he said, with a break in his voice, ' . . . you will understand . . . It has become a sort of temple to me; a Holy of Holies. I am not a rich man, as you know, but I have bought this property . . . to preserve it for all time.'

What a wonderful thought! That strip of semi-decayed wood bridging the years and bringing one into almost direct physical contact with our national Poet – and on no adventitious grounds but on the immutable basis of common human necessity, of constitutional at-one-ment! Darkness was descending upon us but I felt a glow of supreme exaltation and looked with awe into my friend's eyes.

We stood silent together in unspeakable communion for a little while.

Then swift upon the rapture of revelation came the tragic cry which showed the real genius of the man – his power of thinking of *everything*; literally nothing escaped him – and the way in which the achievement and failure are hopelessly twined together even on such great occasions.

'But the pail', he cried, 'the old pail wasn't there. If only . . . '

We left it at that.

Five Bits of Miller

Five Bits of Miller *(1934).*

First of all, there is my recollection of a certain fashion he had of blowing his nose: the effect of the sound mainly, and my appreciation of the physiology of the feat. A membraneous trumpeting. Fragments of a congested face, most of which was obliterated by the receptive handkerchief. Like an abortive conjuring trick in which, transiently, certain empurpled and blown-out facial data meaninglessly escaped (as if too soon) from behind the magic cloth which, whipped off immediately after, discovered to the astonished gaze not the expected rabbit or flower pot but only Miller's face as it had been before the so-called trick (the trick of remaining the same behind the snowy curtain when literally anything might have happened) or, rather, Miller's face practically unchanged, for the curious elements that had prematurely broken out of their customary association were to be seen in the act of reconciling themselves again, of disappearing into the physiognomical pool in which they usually moved so indetectibly. – I had invariably present in my mind on such occasions moreover a picture of the internal mechanism, the intricate tubing, as if Miller's clock-face had dropped off, disclosing the works. I never really liked the way his wheels went round; the spectacle offended some obscure sense of mechanical propriety in me; I felt that there should have been a great deal of simplification – that there was a stupid complexity, out of all proportion to the effects for which it was designed. I was in opposite case, regarding Miller, to the guest who took for a Cubist portrait of his host a plan of the drains that hung in the hall.

Then the condition in which this weird aggregation was kept

revolted me. It was abominably clogged up. What should have been fine transparencies had become soggy and obtuse: bright blood pulsations had degenerated into viscid stagnancies; the tubes were twisted, ballooning or knotted in parts and taut or strangulated in others. Miller could never hoist his eupeptic cheeks with sufficient aplomb to hide this disgraceful chaos from me or dazzle my contemptuous eyes with that lardy effulgence of his brow from which his hair so precipitately retired. 'Yes, yes,' I would say to myself, 'a very fine and oedematous exterior, but if you were all right behind instead of being so horribly bogged – really lit-up from within, instead of disporting this false-facial animation – man!; if your works could only be completely overhauled and made to function freely and effectively, what a difference it would make!'

Then there was his throat. I hated to hear him clearing it. He was top-heavy as I have just shown. That appalling congestion behind his face consumed practically all his energy. The consequence was that any movement of his throat sounded remote and forlorn, a shuttle of phlegm sliding unaccountably in a derelict loom, the eerie cluck of a forgotten slot, trapping the casual sense that heard it in an oubliette of inconsequent sound. It was always like that; like the door of some little windowless room, into which one had stepped from sheer idle curiosity, implacably locking itself behind one. A fatal and inescapable sound, infinitesmally yet infinitely desolating. How many stray impulses of mine have been thus irrevocably trapped! I feel that a great portion of myself has been really buried alive, caught in subterranean passages of Miller's physical processes as by roof-falls, and skeletonising in the darkness there. Miller clearing his throat was really murdering me bit by bit; blowing bits off me with those subtle and unplaceable detonations of his, of which his over-occupied head behind that absurdly bland face must have been completely unaware –

Thirdly he had a way of twirling his little fingers, almost as if they had been corkscrews, in his ear-holes and withdrawing them with lumps of wax on the nail-ends. Uncorking himself by degrees. But his brain was never really opened: it remained blocked, or rather it had coagulated – his hearing never flowed clear into one. Just an opaque trickle devoid of the substance of his attention. – One felt always that one was receiving a very aloof incomplete audition. The wax itself was inhumanly stodgy and dull – not that bright golden vaseline-like stuff one sometimes sees, silky skeins of it netting the light, flossily glistening, a fine live horripilating honey. But orts of barren comb that had never held honey; dessicated fragments of brown putty that made one sorry and ashamed.

Even yet I cannot trust myself to do more than suggest in the most elusive way the effect his cutting his fingernails had upon me. He did it so deliberately and his nails were so brittle and crackling. Dead shell. His finger-tips under them were dry and withered. Shaking hands with him was like touching dust and deepening reluctantly but helplessly into the cold clay of his palm. – But meanwhile I am speaking of his nails. They literally exploded. He affected to use scissors like the rest of us: but, watching him closely, I was never deceived. It was not by the scissors that he cut his nails. He blew them off with his eyes. I know that sounds absurd and impossible. But if you could only have seen the way in which he looked at his finger-tips while he was engaged in this operation, and the extraordinary crepitation and popping-off that ensued –

Lastly, there was the way in which he used to squeeze a black-head out of his chin. He was the sort of person who more or less surreptitiously permits a horde of these cattle to enjoy his cuticle for a certain length of time for the queer sport of killing them, and, at the appointed time, he slew them with amazing precaution and precision. I think this process gave him some strange dual effect of martyrdom and ceremonial purification. I cannot attempt to describe here the rites with which he was wont to sacrifice a black-head of the proper age on the altar of his complexion. For the outsider the ceremony was to a great extent masked by the fact that he only obliquely faced any congregation through the medium of a mirror. In a fragment of it that eluded the blocking back of his head and a thin slice of side-face decorated with a whorl of ear, one saw all that one might, heightened in effect by the liquid light in which such a reflection was steeped. The squeezing-out process was a delicate and protracted one. Black-heads do not squirt out under pressures like paint from a tube, but emerge by almost imperceptible degrees. A very slim yellow-white column (of the consistency of a ripe banana) that ascends perpendicularly and gradually curves over and finally, suddenly, relapses upon its base again.

Yes! I think that perhaps the most vivid recollection of Miller I still retain is that of some knobly fragment of his chin on which under the convergent pressure of two bloodless, almost leprous, finger-tips the stem of a black-head is waveringly ascending; and then of the collapse – lying there, thready, white, on a surface screwed and squeezed to a painful purple, like a worm on a rasp!

You remember the big toe-nail in one of Gogol's stories? Well, I have only these five somewhat analogous bits of Miller left – mucus, phlegm, wax, horn, and the parasitic worm – five unrelated and essentially unrepresentative bits of the jig-saw puzzle that I used to flatter myself I could put together with blasphemous expertise. All the rest are irretrievably lost. But see what you can make of these five.

Wound-Pie

From (ed) John Gawsworth, New Tales of Horror *(1934). An earlier version of the story, published in the* Scots Observer *of 19 March 1927, was entitled 'A Dish o' Whummle' – a phrase used in place of 'wound-pie' in the text, which was otherwise identical apart from the conclusion:*
  ' "And what's a dish o' whummle?" I asked.
  ' "Wund-pie," said he, and stumped off doon the close.'

'Ou, aye. She's aye leevin' – for ocht that onybody kens,' he said.

'Hoo d'ye mean? – for ocht that onybody kens?' I spiered.

'Weel, up to a wheen years syne – mebbe five or sax – she was whiles seen gan aboot. But ane or ither o' them was aye wi' her. Naebody ever got chance of speakin' wi'r by hersel'.'

'That was unco queer, was't no'?'

'Mebbe aye and mebbe no. It's haurdly for me to say. It's only lookin' back yin minds o't. Naebody noticed it at the time – or at first at onyrate. Gin onybody tried to hae words wi' her whichever o' them happened to be alang wi' her spoke for her and gin the auld body spoke hersel' at a' it was juist to repeat what they had already said. She never said a word that wisna pit into her mooth. There was nae gettin' roon' them; and ye'd to watch hoo ye tried. Ye ken what it is in a place like this whaur everybody's connected through ither.'

'Which o' them does she bide wi'?'

'I canna tell ye that either. There's a fell big family o' them and when she cam' here at the first go-aff she'd bide a wheen weeks wi' Jock in Henry Street, and syne a wheen wi' Dood in Back Mary Street and syne wi' Leeb in the Factory Entry, and whiles she'd gang doon to Mirr'ns at the Tail. And sae on. She was aye on the go. It stude to reason. They were a' keen to hae'r and sin' she couldna' be in hauf-a-dizzen different places at aince she'd to dae the neist best thing.'

He pu'd on his pipe for a meenit or twa as gin he was wunderin' whether to say ony mair or no'; and then he gaed on.

'Of coorse ye ken what a place this is for talk. When she cam' first she'd onies amount o' gear, bonnets an' cloaks an' costumes. Twa three kists pang fu'. An' she stoppit wi' Jock to start wi'. Dood and Leeb and the rest were nane owre weel pleased but Jock was the auldest and what could they dae? And Jock's wife is sic a managin' wumman. Besides he'd the biggest family, and the sma'est pey. Jock was a prood man when he ushered her into his seat at the Kirk the first Sunday, and a'body noticed his wife had a new costume on. There was a lot of talk. Ye see, naebody kent juist hoo the auld body had been left. There were different stories, but, by a' accoonts, she wisna' bare. I forget juist hoo lang she stoppit at Jock's – five or sax weeks onyway; and afore she left Jock's faimly was gey weel riggit oot. Their mither was a skilly craitur wi' the scissors and needle, and the bit bairns lookit' better than they'd dune for mony a lang day when she'd finished makin' doon some o' their granny's things to them. But I will say this for Jock and Jock's wife and some o' the rest o' them – it was a guid while efter that afore there was ony cheenge in the auld body's condition – to a' ootward appearances.'

He took anither sook at his pipe.

'To cut a lang story short, it was noticed that by the time she'd made her first twa roons' and wan back to Jock's, she'd a sicht less luggage wi' her. And the claes she was wearin' at the Kirk werena the claes she'd worn the first Sunday and she wasna quite sae lang at Jock's as she'd been the first or even the seecund time afore she went on to Dood's and she wasna sae lang at Dood's either afore she went on to Leeb's ——'

He seemed to hae lost himsel' a'thegither tryin' tae mind a' the oots-and-ins, sae I asked, 'But which o' them was she wi' the last time she was seen?'

'That's juist what naebody can mind,' he said. 'An' it's no' for want o' tryin'. Every noo and again even yet the weemum argie themsel's black in the faces owr't but they never get oot o' the bit. And every noo and then ane o' them plucks up courage and pits a direct question at Leeb or Jock's wife, and I've heard them wormin' at the bairns, but the bairns are every bit as fly as

their mithers. And whiles they've fair provokit me or some o'
the ither men to spier at Jock or Dood, but it's nae guid – drunk
or sober, there's nae gettin' ony faurer forrit wi' them. Jock'll
say she's at Dood's and canna win' oot o' her room, puir body,
and the doctor'll no' hae her fashed wi' visitors; Dood'll say
she's at Leeb's; Leeb'll say she's doon at Mirr'ns at the Tail –
The fact o' the maitter is that she's a'whaur and nae whaur at
aince; and like to bide there.'

'An' that's a' that onybody kens?'

He noddit.

'Onything may hae happened?'

He noddit again.

'But it's no' the thing – it canna be left at that.'

He lookit as if he'd been aboot to nod a third time but had
thocht better o't. And I noticed that he didna' pey me the
compliment o' askin' me if I'd onything to suggest that hedna
already been tried.

'Yet they're aye talkin' aboot her?' I persisted.

'Ou aye! They'll talk richt eneuch – gin onybody spiers.'

'No' unless?'

'Whiles if they think ye're like to spier.'

'It's a queer business.'

'It's a' that,' he said.

'There's naething ye haena' telt me?'

He was slow in answerin'.

'Weel,' he said, 'there's juist this an' ye can mak' o't what ye
like. I canna vouch for the truth o't. But Bob Mackay was
courtin' Leeb's man's sister at the time the auld cratur gaed to
Jock's for the third time, or mebbe, the fourth. And it cam' frae
him. He says that she'd got to sic a state she didna ken whether
she got ocht to eat or no'. And – I'm gien ye his vera words –
Jock said: "If it's a' the same to her there's nae need to waste the
guid mercies." . . . Sae, accordin' to Bob Mackay it cam' to this
that sae lang as she was set doon at the table she'd sit there and
gang through a' the motions, and be juist as weel content as
though she'd been eatin' like the lave – and never hae a bite.'

'Guid sakes!'

'Mind ye, I canna swear for the truth o't – but there's juist
this. The verra last time my wife saw the auld cratur maun hae
been as near as we can reckon juist aboot that time. She met
Jock's wife an' her a'e efternune and Jock's wife and her talkit

back and forrit first about a'e thing and syne aboot anither till my wife said she'd had to rin' a' the way hame to get my tea – I'd been awa' in the country a' day wi' naething but a piece in my pocket and ud be as hungry as a hawk. And wi' that the auld wife opened her mooth and licked her lips and said: "Naething beats a wound-pie." Juist like that.'

And he gied an imitation – like a cuckoo clock.

'My wife says you could hae knocked her doon wi' a feather. She was that taen aback that she fair missed her chance. Jock's wife took an awfu' red face and sterted takin' aboot something else sixteen to the dizzen, as if it had been something unco important she'd near hand forgotten aboot – and she never took the slightest notice o' the auld wife's remark and my wife couldna' get a word in endways tho' she tried sae hard that she's never since been able to mind what Jock's wife *did* talk aboot – and as faur as we can mak' oot the auld wife's never been seen since – And, mind ye, even supposin' for the sake o' argyment that she's aye leevin', there's mebbie a guid and sufficient reason for her never bein' seen oot. Accordin' to the best calculations o' the gear she cam' wi – and' I'm nae coonter mysel' – checkit wi' a' that her dochters and guid-dochters and grandbairns hae been seen wearin' since, it appears that at the time my wife saw her last she canna hae hed a steek left barrin' what she was stannin' up in; an' it's a weel established fact that that particular dress was rinnin' up and doon the braes a month or twa efter that on the backs o' Leeb's brats.'

'And what's wound-pie?' I asked.

'I recollect aince readin' o' cannibalism,' said he, and stumped off doon the close.

The Stranger

From (ed) John Gawsworth, New Tales of Horror *(1934).*

'All I can say is that he wasn't born of man and woman any more than the man in the moon,' said old Ben wiping his whiskers and relighting his pipe.

'But how could you possibly know that, even if it were true,' replied young Jake.

'Just the same', said old Ben tartly, 'as most of us can tell that a horse is a horse and a cabbage a cabbage and a man a man.'

'I don't see that,' said young Jake.

'You wouldn't,' said old Ben. 'You've never even been married.'

'But that's not to say,' Peter interposed. 'that he doesn't know the difference between a man and a woman.'

'Or,' added young Jake, nettled, 'that all the rest of us are so blind that if there's an equal or greater difference between him and a mere human being, we can't see it – and you can.'

'What I can't see,' said George, 'no matter what he is – and to my eyes he looks just as human as any of us, which isn't saying much – is why you refused to have a beer with him when he offered it to you.'

'I am not the man to say no, when anyone offers to stand treat,' replied old Ben, 'and the beer would have been just the same paid for by him or anyone here. All I can say is, that I had better not. It's a queer thing – but it goes to prove that I mean what I say. Otherwise I wouldn't have refused the beer. Surely that's plain enough.'

'Well,' said George, 'he's a fine free-handed creature whatever he is and all the rest of us drank with him and aren't suffering any ill effects – as far as I can see.'

'So far as I can see,' repeated old Ben, 'it all comes back to that. But it's a good proverb that warns us never to judge by appearances.'

'Dammit!' said Philip, 'he belongs to the next village to my own home town, and I know his father and mother.'

'That settles it,' said young Jake.

'Pardon me, but it does nothing of the sort,' said old Ben. 'The world has been quarrelling about a very similar problem for the last two thousand years. I have no doubt all sorts of people knew Jesus Christ's father and mother. A fat lot that mattered!'

'Here! here!' said the landlord. 'None of that now, this argument has gone far enough. I served the man and he paid me in the ordinary way, and as the responsible party in this licensed-house, I say that he was a stranger, but otherwise just an ordinary sober human being, fit to be served in any well-conducted bar. An argument's an argument but when it runs into blasphemy I'll have none of it here.'

'Blasphemy be damned!' said old Ben, 'it's a well-known fact that Jesus Christ wasn't born of man or woman in the ordinary way, and all I am saying is that the same thing applies to the gentleman in question.'

'Well,' said the landlord, 'I don't care a sniff whether that's true or not, but I've warned you. No names, no packdrill. Argue away as you like as long as you don't get too rowdy, but to mention Jesus Christ by name is blasphemy, and if you do it again, out you go.'

'The only thing to do,' said Philip, 'is to ask him point blank if he comes in again.'

'You and he seemed to get on particularly well,' said old Ben, to the landlord.

'I liked him,' said the landlord. 'I could do with a lot more customers like him these days. He seemed to have plenty of money and to be of a very lavish disposition.'

'Yes,' said old Ben, 'I understand all that, but I was thinking of something quite different.'

'You would be,' retorted the landlord. 'What was it?'

'Just that his kind seem to have one thing in common – a curious predilection for the company of publicans and sinners.'

'You're just tryig to be blasphemous again in a less direct way, you nasty old man,' said the landlord, 'but I haven't noticed that the gentleman in question was any different in that respect from anyone else here – and you're all human enough, God knows.'

'Who's being blasphemous now?' asked old Ben.

'Here he comes again at any rate,' said George.

'Well, I'll ask him plump and plain,' said Philip, and as the stranger came forward, rose and said, 'We've just been having a friendly argument about you. Do you mind if I ask you a simple, straightforward question?'

'Not in the least,' said the stranger, 'but let's have a drink first. Landlord, drinks round, please, on me.'

They all filled up except old Ben, who refused.

'Why won't you have a drink with me?' asked the stranger.

'Because I don't think it is right,' said old Ben.

'What?' asked the stranger, 'the beer? There's nothing the matter with it. It's damned good beer. The landlord knows his business all right. Besides, he's drinking the same in any case.'

'No,' said old Ben. 'Not the beer. You.'

'What's the matter with me?' asked the stranger.

'It's like this,' said Philip, 'we've just been having a little argument, as I said. The question I want to ask you is this – were you born in the ordinary way of a man or a woman, or were you not?'

'What an extraordinary question,' said the stranger. 'How in the world did it arise?'

'Old Ben says you weren't,' said Philip, 'that's why he won't drink with you.'

'It doesn't say very much for old Ben's experience in the world, to refuse a perfectly good drink, no matter whether he's right about my birth or no,' said the stranger, 'but I am sure the idea did not originate with old Ben himself. Who started this hare?'

'You're right there,' said old Ben. 'It was my missus told me. She saw you across the jug-counter here the last time you were in.'

'How did she know?'

'Well, it's hardly for me to say seeing she is my missus,' said old Ben. 'I'm the last man in the world to base much on women's nonsense as a rule. But one of the others will perhaps tell you that what my missus says is a good deal more worth paying attention to in such connections than most folk's talk.'

407

'Yes,' said George, 'we're bound to admit that his missus is a very remarkable woman. She sees far into the future. Time and again, to the knowledge of all present, she has prophesied rightly.'

'There's no question about that,' said the landlord.

'Does she drink?' asked the stranger.

'Keep your insulting remarks to yourself,' said old Ben.

'I meant no insult,' said the stranger. 'I wasn't inferring that her predictions were the by-products of fuddling. I only asked in a perfectly friendly way. Does she like a drink? The bearing of my question on the argument will be clear as soon as it is answered – in the affirmative, as I am sure it will be.'

'She's very fond of a bottle of stout,' said the landlord.

'Well,' said the stranger, opening his wallet, and laying a ten shilling note on the counter, 'will you kindly supply her with stout to the value of ten shilling with my compliments and best wishes?' He glanced at his wristwatch. 'Good gracious! Is that the time? I must be off. Good night, all.'

'Good night. Good night.'

'Just a moment,' said Philip. 'The point is, was Ben's missus right or wrong?'

The stranger had passed out, his hand on the handle of the swing door.

'Right,' said the stranger, and was gone.

The Dean of the Thistle

From New Scotland, *9 November 1935.*

The Very Reverend Doctor Thomas MacPhaid, Dean of the Thistle, a courtier, one of the leaders of the Church of Scotland, a brilliant ecclesiastical statesman, and the foremost public orator of his day, stopped suddenly in a wonderful passage of eloquence at the very height of his theme while the crowded congregation – they had even had to have chairs put in all the passage-ways – hung on his words. Many of his hearers had not been competely rapt away, if they had retained the very slightest critical power, it might have occurred to them that this unexpected pause was for the sake of effect. If so, it showed the man's miraculous resource – his supreme self-confidence in the presence of the Divine itself. Any other man would have been carried on inevitably on the tide of his own discourse. Or had he over-reached himself – did the sudden pause indicate that he had come to the verge of the unutterable, 'breathless with adoration'? Would a little downward gesture of those hands which could gesticulate so marvellously confess the limit of their powers and the quiet resumption of his seat say all that needed to be said? In the meantime he kept the congregation poised on the edge of the unspeakable. The silence was intolerable; surely such a tension could not maintain itself a second longer; a terrible cry must arise somewhere – probably no one in the whole church had not a desperate feeling as if his voice or her voice were struggling against the impossible restraint and must instantly burst out in some unthinkable noise. If one had given way they would all have given way and howled together like a pack of dogs. Not to be the first was the prayer in every heart.

Then it was seen that up there in the high pulpit the reverend Doctor was smiling. Ah! Was this to be his way out of it? It was as good as – nay, far better than – a little downward gesture of the hands and a quiet relapse upon his seat. Such a smile was a benediction; it resolved the unutterable into the ineffable, signifying that they had passed into it together, not overcome – but having overcome. What splendid terms it would leave them all on with themselves and with each other! A genial and glorious experience!

The beautiful smile that should have signified all this had suddenly gone too far and gone awry, however. It had spread to his ears and become distorted into an extrordinary grimace. It was difficult to recognise the handsome lineaments of the great preacher in what was now declaring itself as the facial express-ion of a paroxysm of uncontrollable mirth. A second later he was hanging on to the woodwork of the pulpit and howling with helpless laughter. There could be no mistaking the quality of it either. It was genuine laughter; there was no cruelty in it – it rang through the grey old building with a sheer simple humanity that no one could misunderstand. Surprised and shocked as the audience were, every one was sensible of a sudden access of a feeling of well-being – of, somehow or other, the essential rightness of this laughter at such a moment. They had a sensation of delight, an imitative impulse, a feeling of at-one-ment, in spite of themselves. It was a supreme mani-festation of the humour of the Saints. It was redeemed by its utter humility. Gone were all the reverend Doctor's conven-tional attributes – his learning, his high social and ecclesiastical position , his political acumen and experience, his splendid physical presence, his superb address, his unrivalled rhetorical prowess. He was striving for no effect. He had forgotten the existence of the congregation. He was lost to the considerations of this world altogether. He was just a man laughing helplessly in pure delight in the presence of his God.

And yet, it seemed, not so completely lost after all. Some sense of his position had entered into him again. By a tremen-dous effort he regained partial control of himself and began speaking. 'I beg your pardon,' he said. 'It was a private joke that carried me away. But I could not share it with you in advance. I did not foresee it myself. You heard my sermon; I was never more sincere in all my life. I was never more moved by what I was saying. I felt inspired as I had never been before. Just before I paused it seemed to me that the very heavens were about to open – that my voice was about to modulate itself into the very accents of God Himself. But there is so very narrow a margin between the sublime and the ridiculous that one sees at such a moment that they are really interchangeable terms – or, at least, merely aspects of each other. The unutterable absurdity of the whole business struck me with irresistible force. We laugh at the quaint ideas of our forebears – we laugh at old ideas of our own that we have outgrown. I suddenly outgrew all ideas, and broke into a new dimension. If, I said to myself, instead of the priestly convention, if instead of myself in this established guise, the familiar pose, with all my reclamé, and ruffling of phylacteries, and the other tricks of the trade, I was here as I really am, what would the effect on the congregation be? If I were suddenly to become myself, they would think I was mad. They could not accept me as God made me, they require that I shall hide myself behind the regulation pulpit robe and the coloured hood. If I tore these vestments off with out pausing in my sermon, until as I entered upon my peroration I stood here stark naked, what a sensation there would be! I question if I could keep the thread of my discourse in the hub-bub I would set up by trying to do anything of the sort – and certainly I could not, at least my words would not, continue to hold the attention of my audience. And yet that is just what I am. In my mind's eye at least, all these externals dropped away and I saw myself standing declaiming here in the state of nature. My Doctorate of Divinity, my Royal Chaplaincy, and all the rest of it went by the board – and here I was, in the year of our Lord nineteen hundred and thirty-five, set up in these highly artificial surroundings over this great and hopelessly unreal congregation, just like a monkey up a tree. My friends, I am, of course, fully aware now of what the practical consequences of this will be – and fully reconciled to them. But I like to think that as far as you are concerned it will not be easy for you at any future time to sit at the foot of any minister, not even the most self-righteous and owlishly humourless of my brethren, even a creature who cannot see the contemptible farce in His Majesty, King George V., being offered, and actually accepting, from the Iron and Steel Institute the Bessemer Medal for scientific metallurgy, as he did last year, and listen to his sermon without (and here he dropped his voice to a whisper which nevertheless penetrated with perfect clearness into every corner of that great building), saying, to yourselves in your heart of hearts with devastating effect, 'a monkey up a tree – just a monkey up a tree.'

And he stood there laughing merrily, with great goodwill to all, and making rapid movements of his hands as though he were furiously scratching his armpits.

A Sense of Humour

From New Scotland, *23 November 1935.*

As you say, a sense of humour is a queer thing. The trouble is that it varies so much, and, here as elsewhere, what is one man's meat is another man's poison.

A little practical joke that I didn't like probably changed the whole course of my life. But for it I would almost certainly have married my cousin Winnie Harrington. We were extremely fond of each other and, child like, gave all our friends to understand that we would be married as soon as we grew up, and live happily ever afterwards.

But as things turned out I have never seen her nor any of the family since I was ten years old, and am exceedingly unlikely ever to see any of them again. Winnie married into the teens of years ago and is the mother of a large family. Winnie and some of her brothers and sisters were often enough in our home, but I had never been to hers and had never met her father and mother. They lived about sixteen miles away, and her father, my Uncle Will, was a village blacksmith, and the very image of the one in the poem. He stood six feet three in his stocking soles and was broad in proportion and had a beard like a crop of hay. I had long looked forward to going to Lochwood, as you may well imagine, and at last the happy time came. My brother and I were to stay there for a week. I was at once thrilled by and afraid of my gigantic uncle. But the visit came to an end abruptly at breakfast-time the morning after our arrival. It was a glorious sunny morning and we were all at table together. I was sitting next to Winnie and felt as happy as could be, though I was usually very shy and it took me a good while to get on easy terms with people I had not met before. I had a boiled egg, and as I topped it I felt that something was wrong – the top seemed to fly off of its own accord instead of requiring to be cut. There on the top of the egg was a horrible live greeny-black bettle. My stomach heaved inside me, but I saw that all the others were looking at me, and just then my Uncle gave a howl of laughter in which they all joined. This was too much. I caught him fairly between the eyes with the egg which I was glad had not been hard boiled, but was nice and 'runny,' and before anyone could say or do anything I was up and out of the door and on to my bicycle and off towards Waterbeck as fast as I could pedal. They could have caught me easily enough, I suppose, but no doubt they were too disconcerted at first to think of it, and in any case probably thought it better to leave me to myself for a little until I got over it. They can never have imagined that I would take it as seriously as I did and not come back. I went to my Aunt Meg's, just beyond Waterbeck. which was about half way home, and stayed there the night, and then completed my journey the following day. First my Aunt Meg and then my parents did their best to induce me to go back to Lochwood, telling me that Uncle Will had always been 'a great one for a joke', but was really as kind and goodhearted as any man could be, and would be dreadfully upset if I took it so hardly and wouldn't forgive him. And what about Aunt Lizzie, and all my cousins, and, above all, Winnie? But it was no use. I had an idea of all that must have been said as time went on after I dashed away from the breakfast table, and they realised that I wasn't coming back. And I could imagine the attitude my brother adopted – the airs he gave himself as quite the little man of the world of the two of us, and all that he suggested rather than said of my silly sensitiveness and petted and unforgiving disposition. So you see, what with one thing and another it was impossible for me to go back, even if I had wanted to; I had been put in a wrong light altogether. I never thought of my Uncle Will or heard him mentioned for years afterwards without feeling a surge of hatred against him proportionate to the disappointment I had felt in being done in this way out of a holiday I had looked forward to so keenly, and though I came to see that I had been too hasty and that the beetle in the egg had been just an innocent joke on his part – not really intended for me, either, for it was only by accident that I, and not my brother, had got the doctored egg – I could not admit it nor modify my attitude in the least. I swore I would never go to Lochwood again as long as I lived or see my Uncle Will if I could possibly help it. And I never did. He died about fifteen years ago and I would neither go to the funeral nor write a letter of sympathy to my Aunt. I only heard once from Winnie after that affair. A week or two afterwards she sent me a postcard, with a few kind sentences designed to show that she was still as fond of me as ever, and with a lot of multiplication signs for kisses. But I happened to be at the door when the postman came that morning. I put the postcard into my pocket and said nothing about it. I wasn't going to stand any more teasing. Later on I shoved it under the linoleum on the kitchen floor and there it remained until mother found it about a dozen years afterwards, when she was moving to another house and took up the floorcloth.

As I say, a sense of humour can mean so many different things. For example, I suddenly remembered all this about the Lochwood Smithy affair last summer when my brother's oldest boy was staying with me – about the same age as I was at the time in question – and I thought I would try out the same joke on him and see how he reacted. But I varied it a little – not intentionally, but just as it happened. I put the egg in the holder with the end containing the beetle at the bottom instead of on top. And what happened? Nothing. He ate the egg all right and when he came to the last spoonful I got a glint of the beetle and was on the point of saying something, but he was looking at me and not at the contents of his spoon and before I could get a word out he had swallowed it up. He never knew and suffered no ill-effects.

A Scottish Saint

From New Scotland, *25 January 1936.*

> The mind of man, upturned,
> Is in all natures a strange spectacle,
> In some a hideous one.

When Peter MacIntyre came out of prison he was a changed man.

It was not that he desisted from the criminal practices which provided his means of livelihood – he was then close on forty and would have found it difficult, if not impossible, to make his living in any other way, even if he had wanted to, especially at that time when Glasgow, to an even greater degree than the rest of Scotland (and that was to a considerably greater degree than England) was suffering like all other so-called civilised countries from unparalleled trade depression, unemployment, and widespread hardship and destitution. It was not, so far as I have been able to find out, that he committed crimes more frequently or sought to earn more by means of them than he had previously done. He remained content with a certain modest enough income, and, to secure it, does not appear to have committed more crimes in any subsequent year than he did in the year before his imprisonment, or one or two years before that. It was not that he ceased to drink as much. But what did happen is that he not only got drunk less but ceased to get drunk at all. The essence of the matter, however, is that – except for strictly 'business' purposes – he is not known to have ever again gone outside the Cowgate area of the city, and even that portion of it triangularly bounded by Hogg Street, Bruce Street, and Anne Street. In other words, the very worst section of all the slums of Glasgow. He had lived prior to going to prison close by,

416

but nevertheless in ever so slightly less infernal a section of those 'backlands' which were notorious as the worst slums in Europe, if not in the world; but one of his first actions on being released was to plant himself thus in the very heart of that sore which a contemporary writer well-styled 'the cancer of Empire'. The action was symbolical of that change in him which, effected by his imprisonment, was only realised by any outsider in conjunction with the events it produced three or four years later.

Another thing was that he ceased to associate except with the fixed population of that quarter. Previously he had been ready enough to talk to whoever stood next him in a public-house, for example. That ceased, and I believe he never spoke again to anyone who did not live in that particular densely-populated triangle.

It was only very slowly that an outsider here and there began to notice that something very strange was taking place. There had, for example, been gang feuds, outbreaks of razor-slashing, and the like in the area. These became fewer and fewer and ultimately ceased in the most unaccountable fashion, although there was every reason to believe that the general criminality of the denizens had not diminished. It had simply changed its tactics – but how and why?

Along with this went another phenomenon; the complete withering of Salvation Army and similar activities of all kinds. The so-called 'social workers' in the area were absolutely nonplussed; they became conscious of a frustrating force with which they had no means of coping. It became more and more difficult, and finally impossible, to get into contact with the denizens at all. Any attempt to enter into conversation failed; any proffer of tracts or anything else was simply disregarded as if it had not been made; street-corner meetings ceased to be able to detain any one at all except 'a crawl of bairns', or, occasionally, members of the 'floating population' which used to be as large as the fixed population of the area, but became steadily less – not that the numbers in the area decreased, but that 'coming and going' ceased; the population became as fixed as MacIntyre himself. All these manifestations were exceedingly intangible at first; it was only a year or two after his release that they became appreciable in their full effect to a few keen observers who remained baffled, however, as to exactly what was happening, or, rather, as to what it all meant.

417

It was in the autumn of 1935 that a friend drew my attention to the matter, and I remember his saying to me that he did not think the people of the area had become any less criminal or less drunken and otherwise vicious in their habits, but that they had somehow or other ceased to do anything that would prevent their deriving the fullest possible enjoyment from, and freedom in, their manner of living and had evolved a pride in being precisely the sort of people they were with which no attempt to change them in any way had any conceivable means of coping.

'It is,' he said, 'just as if they had come by a full realisation of themselves as a distinct species of humanity. They are as insusceptible of being influenced by other types as dogs or cats are from trying to be fish or birds. Their motto might be Shakespeare's

> Simply the thing I am
> Shall make me live.

'What other people call crime is their natural mode of life, what other people call law and order is an organised crime against them on the part of their natural enemies. They feel completely justified in their attitude – and it is impossible to deny that despite the hellish houses in which they live, their debauchery, and all the rest of it, they are just as intelligent and physically fit (and a damned sight hardier) as any other section of the community. Not only that, but they are far more intelligent and physically fit now than similar communities elsewhere that have not succeeded in insulating themselves in their inexplicable and extraordinarily complete fashion from Christian and philanthropic agencies and other influences inimical to their chosen (or at least, fully and finally accepted) mode of life, or than they were themselves before the change took place. The result of this insulation, with

> No orifice for a point as subtle
> As Ariachne's broken woof to enter

has been to make the work of the detectives and police a thousand times more difficult than it was before, and not by any organised or at least obvious defiance – the whole thing is amazing, tacit and undesirable. I am afraid that all the provocation comes nowadays from the police themselves. Nevertheless, the whole population are far warier than they used to be –

418

they do not fall into the hands of the police anything like so easily, and above all they have almost wholly eliminated "aggravating factors" and consequently get off, when they are caught, with lighter sentences. It is an unheard of thing now for any criminal from the Triangle to do physical injury gratuitously when the robbery which is the real object can be accomplished without it. It is an equally unheard of thing for the sleuths to come by the information they are seeking through drunken blabbing. The whole population are on their guard to an unprecedented degree, they keep themselves to themselves and give nothing away. But they have lost both the old furtiveness and desperate defiance. It seems that they have no longer any sense of inferiority, of being at a disadvantage. They are different – that is all, and perfectly understand the margin upon which they operate and are only anxious to have the "necessary intromissions" with the rest of the world. Of what the police are doing by way of retaliation in these circumstances – or rather our suspicions as to the steps they must be taking, when they get the chance – to extract information and secure a reasonable average of prosecutions, the less said the better perhaps, but that can only be intensifying the criminal discipline. The question is, where has that discipline come from – how is it being maintained?

'Although it is operating to criminal ends – ensuring in a far more confident and efficient fashion modes of lives the authorities and all the agencies of religion and public morality deplore – it is unquestionably a moral force, and, having regard to the nature of the human material in which it has manifested itself, perhaps the strongest moral force in Scotland today – though that isn't saying much; "moral forces" are few and far between, and generally associated with the free-masonry and practical interests of more favourably situated groups at the expense of their "inferiors". My own idea – though I have nothing to go upon – is that this Cowgate business must all be traceable to some single individual, and a very remarkable individual at that.'

He was right. The individual was Peter MacIntyre. I had occasion (for reasons that need not transpire) to make the matter the subject of intensive study for a long time afterwards, and it was only with the utmost difficulty after months of work that I got on the right lines that led back to this spare, reticent, ruthless middle-aged man. I never spoke to him myself; that was impossible – though I was frequently in the little public-house that now constituted his headquarters and near enough and unsuspected enough to hear him talk to his associates (friends, let alone intimates, would not be the right term) and note his influence upon them and the way in which it radiated out from them to every individual in the area. It was enough to closely observe his face and particularly his eyes for a little to know that here was a man dedicated to an implacable purpose, and wholly without personal ambition other than to serve it disinterestedly. He would do nothing to improve his condition; he wished no more than would suffice to maintain his particular mode of life; he drank readily but I never once saw him affected by liquor, nor do I believe that he ever committed a single crime more than he found necessary to give him the money he required to frequent public-houses and drink with the particular steadiness which had become normal to him and defray his other small expenses, for food and room. Beyond that he had no use for money, he was an alcoholic ascetic, a slum saint. He was less an enemy of society than a defender of the particular type of society in the Triangle. He upheld the Triangle 'culture' and was determined that no outside influence would weaken or subvert it. He derived no personal advantage from his unique power, he was content so far as actual criminal practice was concerned to work his own line and make no attempt to outshine his fellows as a master-criminal. It was simply the spirit, and not the activities, of the area he organised – he was not a gang leader; he got no percentage on the loot of the others. I question if he was ever privy to ninety-nine per cent of their efforts – any more than they were to his; he used no force to discipline them, they were not answerable to him in any direct or practical fashion – his rôle was limited to infusing them with a certain spirit.

It was, of course, a situation that could not last. The end came, not through the police after all, but through the social reformers and the sanitary authorities. There was a wave of civic improvement; a fresh epidemic of jerry-building. The Cowgaters were to be transformed into typical suburban rabbits, like bank-clerks, shop-walkers, commercial travellers, and insurance agents. An order went out in August 1936, for the demolition of the entire Triangle: and a wholesale transplanting of its denizens to new housing schemes. It was then for the first time that MacIntyre showed his hand and his complete ascendancy over the population was demonstrated in an astounding way. The authorities were defied. It was seen at once that the completest arrangements had been made to resist the Order, and that only the most drastic measures would serve to enforce it. The most drastic measures were adopted; the police, galled by years of contempt against which all their methods had proved singularly ineffective, were only too glad to have the chance 'of teaching the scum a lesson at last.'

But MacIntyre knew that the end had come. A baton charge or two, men with showers of stones, bottles, boiling water, and what not, resulted in a number of casualties on both sides, but the Triangle as a whole was securely barricaded in its teeming tenements. Daylight the second morning, however, showed the horrifying spectacle of 'a fine blue flower border' – twenty-seven policemen with their throats cut lying side by side along the pavement in Anne Street. No end of a hullaballoo ensued. Detachments of soldiers and armed police were rushed up; but it was found that the denizens were armed too and amply supplied with ammunition. It was to be a fight to the death, and they were determined to sell their lives dearly. They did. The siege of Sidney Street in London was a mere fleabite to the Battle of the Triangle. Finally, as everyone knows, it ended with the firing of the entire quarter – whether accidentally or of set design by the authorities or by the denizens themselves is not known.

I believe that it was MacIntyre's final order and that it was loyally obeyed with the full consciousness that it would mean the death of every man, woman, and child in these densely-populated warrens. It did. Apart from that, the police and military fatalities numbered over 1,100. So ended the last attempt in Great Britain on the part of any community to remain where it was and preserve its own mode of life in defiance of the over-riding forces which insist that even if, in many ways, the distinctive qualities of such communities compare favourably – as they did in this case, and as the final discipline, heroism, and decision to die together show – with the general tone, they must yield to the so-called march of progress and 'become like other people'.

But even yet I sometimes think I see MacIntyre's eyes

contemptuously looking the whole force of civilisation 'through and through', and I have never seen any other Scotsman whose eyes could have made MacIntyre's blink under their scrutiny. Nor, for the matter of that, anyone who wasn't a Scotsman either.

Aince there, aye there

From Outlook, *June 1936.*

The Parish Council of that great, lonely, scattered parish, which included nearly a score of very sparsely-populated islands – rocky, treeless islands with snaggled coasts divided by belts of water so that they presented an endless collection of silver-points in full daylight; and in the twilights of dawn and dusk, by moonlight, or on days of overclouded skies, of wood-cuts – were astounded.

The islanders led a very bare life, and parochial relief was a matter of mites; the old people lived in their little, low, isolated cottages on next to nothing – 'wind pie' the staple of their lives – and in exceptionally hard cases, bedridden or blind or the like, whether an extra sixpence a week or as much as a shilling might be granted was a matter for weighty consideration. Hours of deliberation – little oases of monosyllabic comment in a desert of doubt and difficulty – would be given to such a problem. It was difficult to tell such infrequent speech from the coughing of sheep outside. And most of it was not devoted to the business in hand, but to fragments of gossip, and to matters of fishing and, above all, of crofting interest.

The recent rains have washed off the 'limy' mildew and new green shaws have sprung up from the centres of the 'castocks'. Is this healthy? No. This recovery means the growth of new shaws from the bulbs must take sap and substance from the turnips. ... On cutting the centres, nearly all swedes and yellows have a streaky, mottled appearance inside; later this may induce rotting. There is a 'teuchness' about the tapins and want of sap in all turnips. ... Pigs are in the 'deid thraw' again; retailers are complaining everywhere that pigs bought under the new quota system cannot be sold at a profit, and prices are a little back from those of a fortnight ago. The other side of this is, for years pig breeders and feeders under the chuck-and-chance-it systems were getting far too little for their costs of production. The cure? – further limit the imports of foreign bacon and give home producers a chance. ... Isn't it evident that rough beef-cattle, fat or stores, are out of fashion? ... In the midst of this somehow or other the business of the Board goes forward and decisions are reached. The actual money, of course, was not entrusted to the paupers concerned; they could go a whole year, many of them did, without touching so much as a penny piece; the relief was given in kind – the van from the General Stores allowed the recipients goods to the value which the Parish Council decided upon. Only at the last meeting a month ago the Parish Council had had a particularly difficult case to deal with, and had had – though none of the members could recall afterwards just how they had come to decide in that way – an altogether unusual burst of generosity. It had been a vicious night of wind and sleet, desperately cold, and the members from the different areas having to come considerable distances had no doubt felt they must do something big to justify the ordeal to which they subjected themselves in the public interest. The business in question was an application on behalf of two old sisters living together in a remote spot on the west side for no less than a pair of blankets, and their crave was actually granted, and a pair of nice, thick, winter-weight blankets duly supplied.

It was not pleasant to have the glow of satisfaction – the heroic sense of being ready to defend their action – which suffers members of a Parish Council who make such a gesture replaced almost instantaneously by a realization of the utter unworthiness, the sheer black ingratitude, of the recipients. Yet here they were confronted within thirty days with another application for a pair of blankets from the same parties. The letter of request was handed round like some fearsome curiosity. The members could not believe their eyes. It was incredible.

No mistake had been made. The previous pair – fine, fleecy blankets with a sky-blue line along their borders – had been handed over to the silly old creatures immediately after the last meeting. A joke of any sort was out of the question. It was equally incredible that the renewed application was made in earnest – that they really imagined for a moment that having just been allowanced one pair of blankets they would be given another unless there were wholly exceptional circumstances to warrant such an unprecedented step. Were they too 'dottled' to know they had got them? Had they sold them? Had they accidentally set fire to them? Had they been stolen? Nothing of the sort was specified in the letter. In their slow way the members discussed this grave matter, or rather sat silent about it, for a long time. The more they thought about it the more inexplicable it seemed. Finally it was decided that two of their number who resided nearest the old women should visit them in person, find out all the whys and wherefores, and report to the Council the following month.

In due course, then, Doddy Irvine and Peter Moar came to the dilapidated, ill-lit little cottage on the west side, and found only one of the sisters at home – Molly Shearer, a little, bent old woman with almost the expression of a toad, wrinkled, scaly, yellow skin, and eczema on her left ear.

'Aye,' she said. 'It's the bitter black weather, so it is. A terrible time for old bones without any meat or marrow. There's no keeping a sparkle of heat at all in a poor done body in a winter like this. The cottage is so damp and draughty, one might as well be out on the open hill-side, and, dod, in these long nights the back of a peat-stack would be cosier than a bed like mine.'

She told them how she took two cats in beside her and put every scrap of cloth she had in the house on top of her, and yet lay dirling with cold and loneliness as if she'd been standing bare naked on the seashore and the wind from the north.

'That's just what we've come to see about,' said Peter Moar. 'You've applied for blankets from the Parish Council, but the Parish Council is responsible for laying out public money and has far more to do with it than can possibly be done, especially in such uneasy times and seeing that the whole of the money at our disposal is drawn from people scarcely any better off than yourself. So we've got to be careful – very, very careful indeed. It is a very serious matter. Now, about this application for blankets, you got a pair granted to you by us just a month ago. We can't understand why you are applying for a second pair, so soon at any rate. Where are they anyway? You got them all right, didn't you? But I don't see any sign of them on the bed there.'

'Och aye,' Molly replied, 'we got them all right. And a rare heavy pair they were too.'

'Well, they must have made a heap of difference to you. You couldn't be too cold at nights with a couple of comfortable, thick fleeces like that tucked round you, and with two of you in the same bed to keep each other warm.'

'Two old women don't warm each other any; they simply double the misery and cold. It's not like having a man in the bed. I'm not saying that the blankets did not make a lot of difference though. They did that. We were right glad to get them.'

'Well,' said Peter, 'it hardly looks like it. You might have been content for a while at least to be so much better off than you'd been. But instead of that you pop in a second application right away. Do you think the Council's made of blankets? You're keeping something hidden. It's all very mysterious. But where are they? – that's what I want to know – where are the new blankets you got only last month?'

'Eh,' replied Molly, 'I'm just coming to that. You know old Henry Polson lives just through the wall, in the cottage adjoining this – going on for his ninety-third year and nobody to look after him. It's a great age – and Kirsty and I have to do what we can for the poor old atomy. It isn't much – but there are things a man needs a woman body for. And the poor must help the poor. He's a lot older than us, and far more helpless.'

'Well, well,' said Peter, 'but what's that to do with the present business of Kirsty and you and the two blankets you got from us only a month ago.'

'I'm coming to that – I'm just coming to that,' said Molly. 'Poor old Henry feels the cold terrible. In fact, it seems he gives out cold just as some folk give out heat. It doesn't matter how cold the weather is, he is always ten times colder. And this winter he's been worse than ever – just frozen to death all the time. It's his back that's worst – he scarcely ever says anything else but just how mortal cold his back is – cold water running up and down it all the time. He was awfully bad one night about three weeks ago – cruelled with the pains, and cold, you wouldn't believe a man could be so cold and still alive. So Kirsty – she's eighteen months younger than me, and always a one for her own way. I could never stick out against her even if I wanted to. So Kirsty said we must lend him our new blankets;

and before I could get in a word edgeways she pulled them off the bed and took them in and happed him up. But he said he was no warmer and nothing would satisfy him but she'd to get in behind him ...'

Molly's voice tailed away as if she was musing profoundly on the mysteries of life and death; there was silence for a while; and then she added: 'So you see – that's why we had to put in a second application for blankets.'

'But,' said Peter ...

'Well,' said Molly, 'it's like this. I told you she'd to get in behind him, and you know – well – aince there, aye there!'

Old Eric's Hobby

From The West Fife Annual *(1938)*.

There is no man in the archipelago who knows more about the history of the islands and the psychology of the people and the secret, subtle, almost indetectible dramas that move beneath the seemingly grey, featureless, and uneventful surfaces of their lives than old Eric Laurenceson – no man with better stories to tell, and, alas, no man less able to tell them. People from the Scottish mainland are apt to think the life of the islanders essentially the same as their own, only much duller and poorer. You have to live a long time on the islands and to shed all the outward signs of being a stranger until the islanders almost forget that you are and accept you as one of themselves, before you begin to realise how utterly different all their little ways and promptings are – how completely different they are in their attitude to the most fundamental things, in the intimate texture of their beings. And once you have got to that stage – and it would be a very exceptional incomer who could ever get any further – you will be in a position to appreciate the great gulf that lies between your insight and the intimate understanding of a man like Laurenceson.

The trouble with Laurenceson, however, is that eagerly gossipy and voluble though he is, his speech is all but wholly incoherent. It is not that he has any actual impediment in his speech, but his manner is an endless outpouring of broken phrases, unfinished sentences, a most disconcerting scrappiness, with lapses into the ancient Island language, insinuations and innuendos, a general taking for granted that you are far more familiar with the background than you can possibly be which makes him obscurely allusive and maddeningly ellip-

428

tical, and these fragments of speech are eked out with a range of inflections to the significance of which you have no clue, queer little giggles, sly looks, nudgings, and gestures of all sorts. These mannerisms are partly due to his extremely alcoholic past; he has gone all to bits and pieces. He is upwards of seventy now, and though he very seldom goes on a regular 'skite' and indeed cannot afford any longer to spend the pound to thirty shillings a week he used to continue to do regularly until a couple of years ago or thereby on going out in the flit boat to the bi-weekly mail-boat out in the voe (for the mail-boat cannot come in to the little jetty and the flit boat has to convey passengers and cargo out and in), he still pays his visits twice every week without fail to the steward on the steamer and has his sufficient ration of whisky. For there are no licensed houses on the island, and it is impossible to buy any strong drink retail. The only way is to visit the mail-boat; or to buy the stuff by the case or the barrel, which isn't a good plan because one loses the social stimulus, and, drinking by oneself, one drinks more and it becomes at once too expensive and too harmful, besides being a case of a feast and then a famine.

His wife runs the shop now, or, at least, does ninety-nine per cent of the work. Old Eric only diddles back and forward, making faces and mumbling away to himself; but he always carries his gun. He is the sworn enemy of the Shags – the Green Cormorants. These queer bottle-green and black birds are not eaten; he simply pops them off one after the other – he must shoot an incredible number of them every year – and leaves the shattered corpses to float about, bloodying the diamond-like transparency of the waters of the voe.

There are, of course, any amount of them and all that Eric kills has no perceptible effect in reducing their numbers. They are here, there, and everywhere – especially when the shoals of sillocks (the first year saithe) are close to the shore. It is an amazing sight to see these sillocks; in the voe, close up to the jetty, you can see them in the clear water like an enormous army drawn up on parade – the water is simply solid with them, line after line, column after column, thousands upon thousands of them. To catch them is child's play. Throw out a line and twenty of them will leap at the hook at once. You can fill a basket in less than no time. Fine fat little fish they are too, though too oily for some people's taste. The island folk clean them as soon as they are caught and boil them; then leave them to cool and eat them the following day, when they are simply delicious.

The sillocks hang in the waters of the voe like a vast dense swarm of midges. And any day and every day you will see old Eric standing there on the jetty, with a scrubby unshaven chin, a short clay pipe screwed into his toothless mouth, and an overdone look of grim determination, potting away at his detested Shags. The crack of the shots echoes alarmingly over the still waters and along the rocky shores and away over the drab, treeless peat-moors. There is no movement, however, among the interminable lines of the sillocks. Are they deaf? The shattering one after another of these avian periscopes above them and the ruddy staining of the waters has no effect upon them whatever. Crack, crack, crack! On and on and on. He is never tired of smashing the life out of these ludicrous-looking birds, these misshapen ducks, with the ugly oily gleaming plumage.

It may seem wanton brutality. The birds are of no human use; or at least he never attempts to make any use of them, though, of course, their breasts are eatable, if intolerably salty for most people's liking, while in Greenland their jugular pouches are (or used to be) employed as bladders to float the fishing darts of the natives, and in the Far East they are often tamed and trained to fish for their owners, every bird wearing a ring round its neck to prevent it from swallowing its catch. In Britain they used to be trained for the last-mentioned purpose too, but a rather different system was used, the birds being allowed to swallow the fish but being forced to vomit them immediately afterwards. Three hundred years ago a gentleman held the office of 'Master of the Cormorants to King Charles'.

If they are put to no use, at least in the island voe they are doing no harm; and even if they were, the number he kills would make no appreciable difference where they are so limitlessly plentiful. But old Eric justifies himself. He is a man with a mission. It seems that the Shags are hideously greedy and devour the sillocks in incredible numbers. The poor sillocks! Eric's mouth trembles so agitatedly with virtuous indignation that his pipe almost falls out, and there is more than a hint of tears in his bleary old eyes. With the possible exception of the golden eagle there is no other indigenous species of bird which

430

eats so much that it cannot fly. Yet cormorants are often caught when suffering from surfeits which not only prevent them from flying but also – from all appearances – cause them considerable pain. Nor is that the only manner in which they finally over-reach themselves. Salmon bass have been the undoing of many a cormorant. When a certain cormorant versus bass fight, witnessed some months ago, was ended by the death of both combatants the fish, stuck half-way down the cormorant's throat, was found to weigh four lb. Conger eels, too, have often proved too big a mouthful. A cormorant can certainly eat seven to ten lb. of fish a day. Words fail old Eric to express his hatred of the rapacious shags with their inordinate appetites, and his disreputable old figure struggles queerly to asume a worthy pose as the defender of the innocent defenceless sillocks.

But, of course, nobody likes a good boiling of these delectable little fish better than old Eric himself. He is, in fact, just a human shag, and if you get a close-up of a Green Cormorant and compare it with Eric himself you will see a really startling resemblance. For seen close up the birds have a similar sordidness of aspect, a like tipsy unaccountability of movement, and suggest crude caricatures of their iflended forms – birds gone wrong – just as Eric himself does in relation to normal humanity. And if you catch the eye of one of them cruising about with its head held up like a periscope you cannot fail to recall Eric's expression as he takes sight along the barrel of his gun. Finally the sea is almost as much in his blood as in theirs.

In the crude black and white drawings which constitute the aspects of these islands when the sky is overclouded, it is only by an accident as a rule that his figure is distinguishable from its rocky background; but at other times when everything seems to melt into the endless encompassing clarity – when one can scarcely see life's appearances and happenings for the ubiquity of the light in which they immediately pass away – he emerges with his diseased onion of a head in a strange and startling way, like a special creation, incredible as all beginnings are. The effect is strange rather than terrible, but that is due to the ethereal transparency in which he is steeped, for old Eric is no beginning – in this life at any rate. And these shocking arrivals of his out of nothingness fill one with the most curiously subtle, and remote intuitions about the light, since it is its nature, and not his – some weakness of its nature, some nasty and futile propensity – that is illuminated on such occasions, and he moves in a brilliant vacuum in which he assumes a sort of enchantment, just as a single sound shows up an immense surrounding silence. One cannot think much or say much about the islands without using such a metaphysic of light as one finds here and there, but very briefly and sparingly, in the dry periods of the *Enneads* of Plotinus; but one must use it not briefly and sparingly, but in the most lavish and inordinate fashion. We remember that light properly so-called is only a narrowly defined part of a far greater phenomenon, that of radiation in general. It is a pity that light should be suddenly employed in showing us only old Eric again, just when we are most aware of the idea of countless kinds of invisible light and of the existence of innumerable colours we can neither see nor imagine – given as we are but one octave out of some sixty octaves of ether wavelengths already explorable by the methods of physics, a gamut reaching from great radio waves at one end to the inconceivably minute waves of X-rays, and cosmic rays bombarding our planet from outer space, at the other end. Present yourself, old man; come into the light.

'Creation was once, is always. The miracle of creation, the unique event of the calling into being of things describable, never repeats itself, but there are always places where it is only just an affair of the past.' It is just here that the scandalous figure of old Eric shuffles into sight, with the slaver of a panting dog at noon – this is what we are brought back to, as if his gunshots – crack, crack, crack! – had riddled the whole illusion of the sun, here where the mind goes out, not in serene reception, but in abstract speculation, disdaining earth.

The Case of Alice Carruthers

From (ed) John Lehmann, New Writing *(1939).*

Alice Carruthers was not only quite good-looking but a really nice, obliging, and capable girl – so they said, though it was difficult to see how they could possibly know. For there was no getting near her. She never spoke to anyone – until she was first spoken to, and then she only made the reply that remark called for, but never carried the conversation any further. She had no small talk and if not a positive distaste, at least a complete incapacity, for tittle-tattle. It wasn't that she was in any way sulky or vain or queer. On the contrary she was open-faced and clear-eyed, happy-natured if extraordinarily quiet-natured, kindly in disposition, and always willing to help in any way she could. But she never made the slightest advance of any kind. Naturally all her good qualities did not make up for this singular deficiency; in a little town like Whitshiels how on earth could people get on without 'personalities', back-biting, flippancy, easy vulgarity, and endless excitement and volubility about trifles. One might perhaps liken the effect she produced in that milieu to the use of verse in drama. The verse keeps the dialogue at a certain remove from actuality, while stressing the rhythm of speech – not that she ever gave any impression of calculation, of formality; it did not seem a matter of choice at all. She was, in a word, not 'innerly' and innerliness is the most prized quality down there – all over Scotland in fact – and any one who lacks it is a social outcast. But Alice was happier than most of these unfortunates; she was not 'outcast' very markedly or with any vindictiveness; she paddled her own canoe without ever colliding with any other in that press of craft and without any

433

other ever colliding with hers, intentionally or otherwise. No mean feat!

Alice was not disliked as a child when the pressure to make one 'like everybody else' is most insistent and cruel; but she was generally alone – she was no other girl's bosom friend, and seldom to be seen linking along with any school-mates. And as a young woman she was more and more isolated. This did not sour her in the slightest. She was completely self-contained. People knew exactly where they had her all the time. She was always there – she never went out from herself to meet anybody else half-way or quarter-way or at all, but if they came in to her she was hospitable enough, she gave them what she had to give, but never tried to keep them by playing up to them in any way. Take it or leave it; there she was. The consequence was they felt defrauded – felt that she was reserving her real self and only fobbing them off with an anteroom; it did not occur to them that if she gave them no more it was perhaps because she was unaware that she had any more – that if she was not entirely open to them it was because she had not yet explored herself. And she had never had a lover. She was thirty and assumed to be definitely on the shelf. It was a very curious case. She was exactly like the other girls – she gave herself no airs and graces; she did not criticise or dissociate herself from their mode of life; she did not feel superior to them any more than she felt inferior – only she wholly lacked this indispensable faculty of small pretences and insincerities, of conventional hypocrisies, which meant so much more to all the others than their genuine qualities, so much more that the latter could scarcely have been discerned at all by anyone who did not know them intimately. And as to love affairs, so far as external manifestations went, these partook of exactly the same nature as the rest of this social life in which she had no share – plus a little squalid danger. They depended upon a series of silly gambits and gambols – senseless catchwords and clichés, and actions in keeping with them. Love is a pretty poor affair in a place like Whitshiels, and ends very quickly as a rule – in a poorer; a little shallow stream soon lost in the morass of marriage. Did the young men realise that a love affair could not take this easy common course with Alice – that her self-contained character meant that she was capable of a great passion – and were they frightened of that, having no deeps with which to speak to such deeps, no ability to live up to anything of the kind? They probably knew it without knowing they knew it – like Alice herself. They kept clear of her at any rate, and it seemed to make no difference to her – she was conscious of no failure, no strange cravings, no hopeless longings. She did not realise that in the life about her she was like one of these rocks that stuck up greyly out of the river that ran past her door but displays strange colours if the waters rise till they flow over it. The waters of life had never submerged Alice.

But all at once the time came when they did. Ted Crozier had a bad name. He had got several girls into trouble. You never knew who he'd be going with next – or how many different ones in the surrounding parishes he'd be having on a string at the same time. Ted was not to be trusted. He had to go further afield nowadays. No girl in Whitshiels would be seen with him. It was more than her reputation was worth. Was it just this scarcity of 'raw material' that attracted him to Alice – was it because he was tired of easy conquests and wanted to try his skill with the hardest case in the place? Did he suddenly see Alice as a sort of challenge – a final test so far as he was concerned – in Whitshiels at least? He was near the end of his tether; was this to be his crowning triumph – the achievement of the impossible? It must have been the attraction of opposites. Alice and he were soon going together, hot and strong to all appearances. Opinion in the town was sharply divided as to whether it was Alice's inexperience, her lack of previous affairs, her ignorance of his real character through holding herself so aloof, that was responsible for her fall from long-sustained grace – or – or not. The alternative was never defined; some people had a vague suspicion, but they did not formulate it in precise terms – the springs of Alice's nature were too remote and obscure for them. But they were certainly on the right lines. If she had been in any ignorance of Ted's reputation she could not have preserved it long after they were first seen together – plenty of people were at pains to enlighten her (not blurting it out of course – they weren't on terms with her which would allow of anything of the sort – but with innuendoes, double-edged remarks, of all kinds). Alice did not seem to notice or understand any of these hints, and gave none of their makers any encouragement to pursue the matter any further. Alice was certainly no greenhorn; whatever she might have missed in direct personal experience it was impossible for any girl working in one of the

435

Whitshiels tweed mills to remain in any ignorance of the 'facts of life.' Alice's father, mother, and brother were in a different position; they had no hesitation once they realised that it was true, that it was no mere scandal but actual incredible fact that Alice and Ted were walking out together, in giving her their whole minds and vocabularies on the subject. They did their utmost to dissuade her from seeing any more of the fellow – they called her all the hard names they could lay their tongues to – they predicted her inevitable ruin if she failed to accept their advice – they implored her to think of their good name if she had ceased to have any regard for her own. It would be wrong to say that she gave them the feeling that they might as well have spoken to a stone wall. Certainly all they said ran off her like water off a duck's back, without making any impression; they scarcely got a glimmer of her unfamiliar colours, but she listened quietly and reasonably enough to all they had to say, she did not flare up or anything, she did not weep or sulk – but they simply got no further with her, she took in all they said hospitably enough but it produced no result, she just did not discuss the matter with them in any way. That was the maddening thing about Alice; she looked so nice and natural, she was so obviously one of themselves, there were no oddities about her to lay a finger on – and yet she did not react to anything the way everybody else did. It wasn't that you came up against a blank wall – there was no sense of any impediment, any resistance – you simply seemed to come to the world's edge and fall into the void. The ground disappeared beneath your feet. The thread of your discourse vanished into thin air. You could make nothing of her. Or almost nothing. They did elicit, much to their surprise, one definite statement. It was when they were casting up about the other girls he had ruined. 'He won't do that again,' she said.

As if he could help it! And yet for a long time he seemed a reformed character. There was no breath of his having any other on-goings. So he couldn't be having any – or the news would soon have been out. For people were on the *qui vive*. Ted couldn't get away with anything in Whitshiels or near it nowadays. Either he was hiding his tracks extremely well – or he had really turned over a new leaf. As to Alice there was little difference except that she seemed to have ripened – to have changed, mellowed inside herself, while presenting an unchanged front, or practically unchanged front, to the world. Then all at once the blow fell. It was a particularly bad business too – Ted's worst yet. Had he had to keep the two extremes going, now that he could no longer have two or more affairs much of a muchness going simultaneously? This would be a criminal case too. The poor little creature would probably die – in any case it would take a Caesarian operation to deliver her – for he had got a little incomer, a little servant girl from the country, of barely fifteen, in the family way. There was a lot of violent feeling against him in the town. 'He ought to be horse-whipped – he ought to be lynched' were the general sentiments. A few groups of the men were for taking the law into their own hands. Alice's folk could make nothing of her. The sensational news seemed to go into her one ear and out at the other without affecting her in the least. From first to last they never heard her refer to the matter in any way. But they could hardly believe their eyes when they saw her titivating herself that night as usual to go to her tryst with Ted. They tried to stop her but it was no use. It was a devil of a night too – pouring 'auld wives and pipe stapples'. That alone should have kept her in. She'd be drenched to the skin; do water-rats make love?

A gamekeeper found her the following morning at the foot of a tree, under a branch from which Ted was hanging dead.

She said little about it – except that that was their usual trysting place. She had not realised how wild a night it was. Struggling through the pouring rain against a terrific wind she must have been late for her assignation. It was pitch-black, which had added to her difficulties. All at once stumbling along the slippery clay path she bumped into something which swung away and bounded back into her and swung away again and bounded back once more. She knew at once what it was and fell in a faint below the human pendulum.

Alice's mother knew that her new clothes-rope had mysteriously gone missing, however – but she said nothing about it, and just went and bought another, but not at the same shop.

People were surprised that Alice did not find herself *enceinte*. If she did it was with that as with so many other things – she never showed it. But people knew what Ted had been ... they were sure ... so they just remembered how deep still waters run and remarked knowingly that 'Alice knows the ropes'. Which was true – in one sense if not in the other.

Vouchsafed, A Sign

From (ed) John Singer, New Short Stories 1945–46 *(1946).*

'Na laddie! Ye mauna say that. Sae mony byordinar things happen that the least a body can dae is to preserve an open and respectfu' mind. It disna dae to jeer at the Unseen, for it aye has the lauch o' us in the hinder-en'. You're young yet, but wait until you've lived as lang as I ha'e and you'll no' be inclined to treat things in sic an off-haun way,' said my Granny.

'Oh, I ken,' I replied, 'There's mair things in Heaven and Earth than my philosophy recks o'. Sae I'm tell't. And nae doot it's true eneuch. But it's real evidences o' that I'm eftir. I may come to scoff, but I'm willin' eneuch to bide to pray – if onything impresses me in that way. Sae faur naething has. I think a' this business aboot spiritualism and second sicht and guid dreams and bad dreams and sae on is juist a lot o' havers. But as you say you've lived faur faur langer than I ha'e, and what I'd like to ken is if you can gi'e me ony convincin' first-haund experiences o' your ain o' this kind. Wasn't there something aboot grand-faither's daith?'

'There was that!' said Granny. 'Comin' events aye cast their shadows afore them, if ony yin can read them aricht. Neither your grandfiather, puir man, nor I had ony reason to be lookin' for his sudden daith, but I got as clear a warnin' a wheen nichts afore the fatal accident as ony human being ever had. There was nae mistakin' it. I kent in a meenut, and tell't your grandfaither.'

'But what was this warnin' you got, Granny,' I spiered.

'The Unseen works wi' the vera simplest means,' said Granny, 'Three nichts afore your grandfaither's daith, juist afore he cam' to bed, he lifted up the chamber-pot – and the handle cam' awa' in his hand! I kent then – and shair eneuch he perished in the pit-accident afore the week was oot. Shairly you canna ask for onything plainer or mair convincin' nor that!'

Sticky-Wullie

From the Scottish Journal, *September 1952.*

Galbraith met her in the licht o' the shop window at the fit o' the toon.

'Och aye,' he says, staunin' sae that she couldna win by, 'and ye'll ha'e been for yer wee bit daunder.

'There's waur things' he says, 'than a braith o' fresh air in the country efter bein' cooped up in a stuffy atmosphere a' day.

'But,' says he, 'Sticky-Wullie tells mony a story oot o' schule.' And he pointit to her legs.

She was wearing a short shirt that haurdly cam' alow her knees and a pair o' what they ca' nylon stockin's: and the tail o' her skirt and the backs o' her stockin's were a' covered wi' the wee green ba's.

She blushed to the roots o' her hair.

'It's a guid job,' says she, 'that everybody's no' a Sherlock Holmes.'

'Aye,' says he, 'for them that ha'e onything to hide.'

'What ill can there be,' she says, 'in a wee daunder on a braw nicht like this?'

'Sticky-Wullie disna grow in the middle o' the road,' says he, 'and there's no' mony hedgbacks here-aboots whaur it's heich eneuch to taigle the knees o' a strappin' young wumman like you. But nae doot ye were a wee thing tired and juist took a bit barley in the syke afore ye turned back. Ye ha'ena been lookin' juist owre weel lately to my way o' thinkin', though ye've a rare colour the nicht.'

'I like a guid sherp walk,' says she, 'it fetches the bluid up.'

'To a' appearances it does,' says he, and on the offshot nae doot, he addit. 'And yin steps oot better when yin's by yinsel'. Ye maun ha'e come back in hauf the time it took yer to gang.'

'What gars ye say that?' says she, wi' a fleggit kind o' look.

'Och, if ye're gaen to ca' man a Sherlock Holmes,' says he, 'for usin' his common-sense, he maun live up to his reputation, and if the cap disna fit ye needna pit it on.'

He said it in a meaningfu' way to gar her wunder no' juist hoo he kent onything aboot it ava but juist hoo muckle he did ken; and as for him he was wunderin' mair and mair juist hoo muckle there was to ken, and at a bit o' a loss what to say neist. It cam' to 'm a' o' a sudden.

'It 'ud set ye better,' says he, 'Mary, if ye kent common-sense when you saw it, and aiblins ye'd no' need to be comin' tearin' back to the toon by yersel' at this oor o' the nicht. It'll be a shock to a' yer freens to see ye hame sae early. It's an oor yet afore the feck o' the courtin' couples'll be turnin' back.'

Wad ye believe it, the cratur sterted greetin'!

'Wheesht, wheesht,' says he. 'This'll never dae at a' – the bonniest lass in the toon staunin' bubblin' and greetin' on the street. He's no' worth greetin' owre. There's as guid fish in the sea as ever cam' oot o't and ye can ha'e your pick at ony time. C'wa and ha'e a bit turn wi' me for a cheenge and it'll mebbe steady your nerves.'

And he yokit an airm in hers and she gaed like a lamb. But when they cam' to the cross-roads he noticed she gar'd him tak' the laich road and he thocht to himsel': 'She's fear'd to meet him again – and mebbe it's juist as weel.'

'I dinna ken what ye maun think,' she says efter a wee.

'Ye needna fash yer heid aboot that,' says he, 'That's juist whaur Sherlock Holmes comes in again. A blush is nae guid but ony fule could tell at the first go aff that you're no' ane o' the hardened kind – and, without bein' that, if there'd been muckle amiss ye'd 'a' been mair particular aboot the incriminatin' evidence. Yet it's something new to see you alane – or at ony rate comin' into the toon – at this time o' the nicht; and it's no' ill to jalouse what's at the bottom o't. But there's juist this; atween you and me, considerin' the kind o' lads you've been knockin' aboot wi' o' late, the wunder is something o' this kind hasna happened lang afore this.'

'You seem to ha'e been keepin' a gleg e'e on my affairs,' says she.

'Aye,' says he, 'I ha'e: and no' afore time – and here's that stuck up guid-for-naething Malcolm o' the Bank. It's no' often you sees him by himsel' either at this time o' nicht,' gien her a searchin' look, and syne, when Malcolm cam' alangside, wi' his face a' workin' and his een like to pump oot o' his heid, he said, as easy-osy as ye like, 'Braw night, Malcolm – juist haen your bit daunder?'

'Ye—,' but Malcolm never got the word oot o' his mooth for Mary was owre to 'm and smothered it wi' ane o' her wee hauns; syne, slippin' an airm into Malcolm's, she turns roon to Galbraith.

'Common-sense,' she says, 'is whiles owre common, and the trouble wi' Sticky-Wullie is that it disna aye tell the same tale. Ye mauna judge ither fowk by yersel'. Guid nicht.'

And she whirled Malcolm roond and awa' they sailed and left Galbraith staunin' like a stookie.

Without a Leg to Stand On
A Shetland Sketch

From the Saltire Review, *Spring 1960.*

'Talking about the mass production of B.Sc.s – agricultural or engineering – by the Scottish Universities nowadays,' he said, 'there's no place in the world perhaps less suitable for the young man in a hurry type than the Shetland Islands.

'A little knowledge is a dangerous thing, and the little knowledge these fellows have is particularly dangerous in such islands where the whole business of life is so largely dependent upon kinds of traditional knowledge that have never been reduced to words on paper at all.

'The natives know what they need to know without knowing how. It's not the sort of thing that can be learned. It's all a question of having knacks like that lucky touch or 'green thumb' old gardeners talk about. You see, things must have reached a certain level – which they have not begun to do in the Shetlands – before the application of a little modern science can be useful, and go-ahead B.Sc.s simply can't realise that.

'The nature of their training makes them aggressive, dogmatic, and quite incapable of seeing all round a complicated issue. They think they are being scientific when they are being exactly the opposite – just advocating the application of a few so-called scientific facts to a situation they do not understand in the least and of which they are too constitutionally impatient ever to learn anything worth knowing. That's just it. They fancy they are the last word in up-to-date enlightenment, when the real truth is that they are simply ineducable ...

'Well one of these fellows got the headmastership of the school on one of the little north islands of the Shetland group I

443

know. He was a very typical specimen of the breed. He did not wait to learn the lie of the land – but assumed that as Headmaster of Houll School and a B.Sc.(Agriculture) to boot, he ought to be a Force To Be Reckoned With and a Power For Good in the Community.

'So he barged right in. Joined the Badminton Club which played in the Village Hall and was soon at loggerheads with the Hall Committee because they wouldn't give him his own way. Became Secretary of the Model Yacht Club and on the Organising Committee for the Annual Regatta. And he talked to all the fishermen and crofters and thought he was doing fine.

'They were flattered to have him to talk to. So far as book-learning was concerned they were utterly ignorant, and over-valued it accordingly – in others. But let any of their own children waste too much time reading! That was another matter altogether; and of course any idea of keeping their children at school after fourteen was out of the question.

'There was far too much to be done on the beggarly little scratches of crofts, and at the herring fishing in the summer time and the haddock fishing in the winter, so far as the boys were concerned, and as for the girls, they were in immediate demand at the gutting stations during the fishing season, and, at other times, they had not only to help their mothers with the housework and looking after the babies, but they were needed in the harvest field, and in the milking-shed and in the hen-ree and for turning the peats on the hill and later carrying them in the plaited baskets (or 'kishies' as they call them) slung on their backs, and for stacking them (a great art in itself) beside the houses, ready for the long black winters.

'And also the second main industry in the Shetlands is the knitting industry, and that is wholly in the hands of the women, who spend every waking moment they have when not busy with some other essential task (and often when doing other things, too – for it is marvellous how many tasks they can fulfil while never ceasing to ply their knitting-needles as well) knitting indefatigably, turning out Fair Isle jumpers, sweaters, stockings and gloves. There is not much time for reading in such a community.

'But the young headmaster I'm telling you about was far too green and too cocksure; he did not realise the shrewdness that lay behind the deference with which he was listened to – he did not realise that these people were shrewd enough to be willing to pick his brains and get him to write their letters for them and get free advice from him in regard to all their little problems without ... well, without taking him exactly at his own valuation: and certainly without rushing headlong to act upon the advice he gave them, instead of thinking very cannily about it first and especially when it conflicted in any way with their traditional practices and prejudices.

'And, of course, I have nothing to say about it so long as it stayed at that. It was all right his taking an interest in local affairs and talking to everybody. There isn't much to brighten people's lives up in these islands, and talking to this fellow was a bit of a change – so long as it didn't go beyond talk.

'The young Department of Health doctor on the island hated this new headmaster – Moar, they called him; Peter Moar – like poison. "He thinks it's all plain sailing," he said, "but wait a little. The surface of the water is smooth and sweet enough just now, but life here is just like the Sound between the islands there – it calls for clever navigation, and a great deal of knowledge and experience that is not to be found in any book at all, and, even with that, as the best skippers will tell you, you can never be too careful and patient. The island people will soon see through this fellow. They'll make all the use of him they can in the meantime, but he'll get jammed on hidden and uncharted rocks one of these fine days. Mark my words! He won't last long here.... But he may do a great deal of damage in the meantime."'

What the Doctor had in mind was the fact that Moar was going round insisting that something should be done to improve the local cattle. The cows were small, as all indigenous animals are in the Shetlands, but in the course of generations, as the Doctor pointed out, the islands had evolved a type of cow precisely suited alike to the needs of the people – and to the resources of the islands in regard to feeding for cattle.

'Moar wants the Department of Agriculture to send a Bull of a bigger breed next season. He doesn't realise the danger. The type of cattle they have get on all right with the very limited feeding these crofts can afford to give them – and they give a splendid milk yield, which is just what's wanted.

'To introduce bigger cattle will upset the local economy altogether – and these people can't afford to experiment, apart from the fact that to ignore all the lessons of the past, and the way the local animal has been evolved to suit the local conditions and needs, is utterly unscientific. With these very small crofts the people have no margin to come and go on in matters of this sort – one bad calving season would ruin most of them altogether. The idea just appeals to their cupidity at the expense of their commonsense. But Moar thinks he knows it all – on the strength of a little book learning, and no practical experience whatever. Mark my words, there'll be trouble. I don't know very much about the Shetlands myself. I haven't been here long enough, but I was brought up in a farming countryside in the South of Scotland and I remember a thing or two. I know it doesn't do for a farmer from Berwickshire to come down into Dumfriesshire, for example, and forget that times and seasons are different in the two counties. Or like a fool try wheat where oats or rye are the only hope. Or sow potatoes too soon and have them cut down by the late frost. Or with the sheep, try to grow more wool, and forget the need for hardihood, and lose a season of lambs.

'And there are thousands of such-like things to consider in regard to stock or land before you can safely make any departure from established practice. And these aren't the sort of things you can learn in books – none of them – and that's just where a fellow like Moar (and he's a very typical specimen of the whole breed of these B.Sc.s) is so infernally dangerous.'

'But surely the Department will have more sense than send a different kind of bull before they've taken all the necessary factors in the local situation carefully into account,' I said.

'Not they!' hooted the Doctor. 'They all hang together – these Government boards and these mass-produced B.Sc.s and what not. You'll see.'

I did. The Doctor was absolutely right. But that is another story – the story of the Bull; and it cannot be told in other than Rabelaisian terms. The new Bull fiasco was a howler to high heaven in all conscience, yet it was in another connection that Moar finished himself so far as these islanders were concerned, and I'm telling you this story not only because it is a good story in itself, but because it is a perfect example of the way in which these half-baked young know-alls of B.Sc.s fall down when it comes not to theory but to practice, not to airing their book-learning but to giving a hand with the actual job. It's the sort of thing that is happening all over the country with these Government Boards and young graduate teachers – only it's rather an extreme example perhaps.

Well, as you know, all the crofting ground in the islands is portioned off with deep, open ditches, and every now and again a cow falls into one of them and the people come running from all over the place to get it out. Moar by his way of it had established himself as quite a progressive public figure and the accepted authority in every contingency, when one day this happened on old Fred Williamson's croft at Whitefields and they got ropes and had hauled the cow out when they saw that something was seriously wrong with her. It was then they made the mistake. Instead of sending, as they had been accustomed to do for long enough whenever anything was wrong with any of the cattle or pigs or sheep or ponies, to old Peter Barclay at Isbister, they sent to Houll School for Moar. And ere long Moar came tootling along the road in his little Morris car, and hopped out, and came down over the field and across the rigs very brisk and businesslike. He was soon acquainted with the facts and with the opinion that the cow had broken one of its forelegs. He stood and pondered, looking very seriously at the cow. And then he knelt and examined first one foreleg and then the other.

'Nonsense!' he said when he straightened himself again after a fitting interval. 'It hasn't broken its leg at all. Look,' – and he half knelt again, pointing first to the one leg and then to the other – 'they're both the same length. Get it carried up to the byre and give it time to get over the fright it's had. You'll see, it'll be all right in the morning.' And with a confident laugh he strode off up the rigs again, a purposeful little fellow, with, as everybody round the cow agreed, 'his head screwed on all right and his heart in the proper place too.'

When the morning came, however, the byre door couldn't be opened, and finally had to be taken off its hinges. When this was done, it was found that the cow was lying on the floor of the byre and its back had been hard up against the door, making it impossible to open it. Moar, they reflected, would be busy in the school; it would never do to send for him during school hours. So they now sent for old Peter Barclay, and when he came they told him just what had happened and how they'd sent for Mr Moar and he had said that the cow would be all right by morning and hadn't broken its leg since, as he had pointed out, both legs were the same length.

Old Peter laughed in a crafty, sardonic sort of way. 'Aye,' he said, 'he was right enough. Both legs were the same! But the truth of the matter apparently just didn't occur to Mr Moar. The trouble is both forelegs are broken!'

And so indeed it proved, and when the news went round the island that Fred Williamson's cow had had to be shot after all, quite a few ungrateful people muttered that Mr Moar would have been none the worse of a little shooting too.

'Tuts,' laughed the Doctor, 'there's no need for that. Just give him plenty of rope and he'll hang himself soon enough – if he hasn't done it already.'

An Epoch-Making Event

Printed from the undated manuscript in Edinburgh University Library.

It was while we were living on that little island that my wife came in one day laughing very merrily.

'Great excitement in the village today.' she cried.

It wasn't a village really – only a place where a few houses were built together at the Harbour (all the other houses on the island stood separately on their own little crofts), and where the general store and the post office were located. The bi-weekly steamer comes into the voe there and passengers and goods are taken off or put on by a row boat.

'Phoebe,' continued my wife, 'is thrilled to bits.'

Well, there was nothing very surprising in that. Phoebe is very easily thrilled. If, for example, any new chap comes to the island – a new teacher, or a new doctor, or anything. Until it is ascertained whether he is married or single. If he is single the excitement continues. Phoebe is an old maid, of over fifty. But the appearance of a new bachelor is a sign that she has met her fate at last. She is all over the place discussing him – contriving meetings with him. All the islanders know this little foible and make the most of it. The island lives on little things; it does not take much to interest and divert it. So Phoebe is led on without mercy. The affair is seriously debated in all its bearings. It is reported on all hands that the stranger is undoubtedly in love with her. Has he really said nothing yet? He must be too shy. It is Phoebe's duty to help him out. Let her only look at him carefully and she will see unmistakeable signs of the passion that is consuming him. No wonder. Phoebe is looking younger than ever. So the poor old creature hunts out all her fineries – and togs herself up in the most fetching fashion. One thing is certain; she can blush and giggle like a girl. You never saw such a foolish old creature. And her lover is to be at the Whist Drive on Friday night? Certainly. That is her opportunity. She fusses round him in the most remarkable fashion, prattles away to him with extraordinary animation and fits of merry laughter, feeling that she is making great progress and has him safely in the toils at last – while he wonders what on Earth is wrong with the fantastic old creature, and everybody else in the Hall is fit to die at the ludicrous spectacle. Hope dies hard. Phoebe is not easily put off, and, finally disappointed in one man, comes up again to the conquest of the next with all her colours flying.

Fortunately I was a married man and brought my wife with me when I came to the island. So I was spared Phoebe's attentions of this sort, though I had to stand a great deal of her senseless chatter whenever I went into the shop. So I stopped going; my wife used to go instead. But I had another reason for avoiding Phoebe. I hate all dogs, but Phoebe had one I particularly loathed. This so-called dog was a midget Shetland collie. Our little boy of three called it 'the baby dog' or, in the island dialect, 'the peerie mootie thing'. You never saw such a flea of a dog. You might as well have gone round with a mouse at the end of a lead. But there was never such a dog! It had all the canine virtues. Phoebe thought the world of it. Wherever she went it went. 'Rob Roy' she called it, but she had, it transpired, christened it under a misapprehension, and a month or two later she found it was a lady and had to rename it. Oslo was its new name; and the orgy of adoration of which it was the subject has never been surpassed in all the astonishing history of pet dogs. No wonder Phoebe was an old maid. If she could lavish such a wealth of affection on this horrible little creature, Heaven only knows what she would have done with a man. To see her with Oslo would have kept her a virgin if she had been the only woman in the world.

On this fateful day, my wife had been going round the corner of the shore towards the shop, when she saw Phoebe waving frantically to her from the window of her sitting-room. My wife waved back but did not want to go in. By the time she got into the shop, however, Phoebe had run in there too through the connecting lobby between her own rooms and the public quarters of the establishment, which, with the assistance of a couple of girls, she managed. Oslo was snuggled – I was going to say *between* her breasts, but in Phoebe's case it is not known that there was any such division. Oslo was, let us say, *on* her breast; and my wife saw at once that something entirely out of the ordinary had happened, that Phoebe was excited to an absolutely unprecedented pitch. And no wonder! My wife naturally had no premonition of the magnitude of the cause; the soul-stirring event that had led to the frantic waving from the window and the wild rush into the shop had cast no shadow before it. Phoebe was dying to communicate the great intelligence. My wife cannot remember whether she asked, or even looked, a question or not, or whether Phoebe just incontinently spilled the beans. Whichever way it was, hugging the little beast in her arms, and dancing about like a hen on a hot girdle, Phoebe cried: 'It's Oslo! It's Oslo!'

My wife is not usually 'slow in the uptake', but there did not seem to be any reason for all this commotion. It wasn't as if Oslo was lost or anything. There she was in Phoebe's arms and nothing seemed the matter with her.

'But there's nothing wrong with Oslo, is there?' she asked.

Phoebe was now a sort of dancing Dervish, emitting looks of tremendous profundity, half-laughing and half-crying and cuddling away at the dog; but in the midst of this whirl of gesture and suggestion my wife at least gathered the central fact ... 'Oslo, my little darling! ... He! He! ... You know ... I don't quite know how to say it ... But you know? ... little Oslo's *unwell* ...'

My wife was now purposely obtuse. She was determined to make the dithering old creature say it.

'Unwell?' she said. 'She looks all right. What on earth is the matter with her?'

'It – it's – you know. It's her first time. My dear little Oslo – naughty, naughty! – wants a mate – He! He! – Don't you, precious?'; and Phoebe hid her blushes in the little brute as in a muff.

Glossary

What follows is a reservoir of Scots words regularly used by Mac-Diarmid, whose main linguistic source was J. Jamieson's An Etymological Dictionary of the Scottish Language *(1808). A.* Warrack's A Scots Dialect Dictionary *(1911) is a convenient one-volume reference work. W. Grant and D. Murison's* The Scottish National Dictionary *(ten vols., 1929–76) is an exhaustive work.*

---

a', all
abaw, abash, appal
abies, except
ablach, dwarf
abordage, the act of getting on board
abstraklous, outrageous
abune, above
abuneheid, overhead
aclite, awry
acresce, increase
adhantare, phantom
adreigh, distant
a'e, ane, one
a'efauld, single
afflufe, extemporary
afore, before
aftergait, outcome
aft'rins, the remainder, off-scourings
agley, off the right line, wrong
ahint, behind
aiblins, perhaps
aidle, foul slop
aidle-pool, midden-dub
aiglets, points
aiker, motion or break made in water by fish swimming rapidly
ain, own
aince, once

airels, musical notes of any kind
airgh, lack, or what anything requires to bring it up to the level
airt, direction
alist, alive
alist (to come), to recover from faintness or decay
allemand, orderly
allevolie, volatile
allryn, weird
alluterlie, utterly
alow, below
alunt, blazing
amows, disturbs
amplefeyst, animosity, contrariety
ana', also, as well
ane, one
antrin, occasional, rare
appliable, complaint
archin', flowing smoothly
areird, troublesome
arnuts, earth-nuts
aroint, clear away
arrachin', tumultuous
arrears, goes backward
arselins, backwards
ashypet, scullery maid
aspate, in full flood

452

assopat, drudging
Atchison, old Scots coin
atour, around, out from
attercap, spider
auchimuty, reduced to a mere thread
aucht-fit, eight-foot
aumrie, cupboard
austerne, austere
averins, heather-stems
avizandum (to tak' to), to defer decision
awa', at all
awn, own, owe, owning
awte, grain
aye, always
ayont, beyond

backfa', side sluice of a mill
back-hauf (worn to the), practically
    worn out
backlands, Glasgow slum tenements
backsprent, spine
baggit, enceinte
bairn, child
bairnie, baby
bairntime, a woman's breeding-time
bait, grains
baith, both
balapat, a pot in a farmhouse for the
    family but not for the reapers in
    harvest
balk, ridge in ploughing
barkin' and fleein', on the verge of ruin
barley bree, whisky
barmy-brained, wanton
barritchfu', troublesome
barrowsteel (to tak' my), to co-operate
ba's, balls
bauch, dull, sorry
bauld me glead, stir up my fire
bawaw, an oblique look of contempt
    or scorn
bawbees, half-pennies
bawsunt, with a white stripe
beanswaup, the hull of a bean,
    anything of no value
bear-meal-raik, fruitless errand
bebbles, tiny beads
beddiness, silly importunacy
beek, show, shine brightly

beganè, decorated
begood, began
bellwaverin', uncertain
belly-thraw, colic
belth, sudden swirl, whirlpool
ben, through
ben (gang), go in
benmaist, inmost
bensil o' a bleeze, a big fire
bern-windlin, a ludicrous term for a
    kiss given in the corner of a barn
beshacht, crooked
betherel, gravedigger
bide, stay, await
biel, shelter
bien, complacent
big, build
bightsom, ample
bike, nest
binna, except
birks, birch trees
birsled, scorched
births, currents
blackie, blackbird
blainy, blemished
blanderin', babbling
blash, sudden onset
blate, bashful, cautious
blauds, fragments
blawp, dull, yawning look
blebs, drops
bleezin', blazing
blether, bladder
blethers, havers, nonsense
blin', blind
blinnin' stew, storm through which
    impossible to see
blinterin', gleaming
Blottie O, a school game
bluffert, squall
bluid, blood
bobby, policeman
bobquaw, bog
boddom, bottom
bodily sicht, to see entire
bogle, scarecrow
bood, should
bool, bowl, curve
boon, excellent

453

boot, matter
borne-heid, headlong
boss (of body), front, torso
bouks, hiccups
bourach, cluster
boutgate, roundabout way
bowzie, misshapen
bracks, interstices
brade-up, with address
brae-hags, wooded cliffs
brairds, grows
bratts, scum
braw, handsome
breeks, trousers
breenge, burst
breist, breast
brenn, burn
brent, wrinkled
brent-on, straightforward
brod, table
brough, ring round moon
broukit, neglected
bubblyjocks, turkeys
buddies, folks
buff nor stye, one thing or another
buik, trunk (of body)
buirdly, stalwart, well-made
bumclocks, flying beetles
'bune, above
burn, stream
burnal, strip of barren land
burnet, brown
bursten kirn, difficult harvest
buss, bush
byordinar, extraordinary
byous, wonderful
byre, cow-shed
byspale, precocious, a child of whom wonderful things are predicted

ca' o' whales, drove, school
caber, a pole or tree for hurling
ca-canny, go slow
cairn, pile
cairney, hillock
camsteerie, disorderly, perverse, unmanageable
canny, cannily, gentle, quietly
cantles, summits

caoin, edge
cappilowed, forestalled, outdistanced
carle, man
carline, old woman, witch
cauld, cold
cavaburd, heavy snowstorm
cay, jackdaw
chafts, jaws
channel, gravel
chauve, black and white
cheatrie, deceit, fraud
cheek o' the gushack, fireside
chests, breasts
chief, very friendly
childing, child-birth
chitterin', trembling violently, shivering
chouks, jaws
chow, chew
chowl, twist, distort
chuns, sprouts, germs
claith, cloth
clanjamfrie, collection
clapt, shrunken
claught, grab at
cleg, gad-fly
cleiks, the merest adumbration
cleisher, monster
cleisher o' a whup, a fine big whip, a dandy 'cracker'
climmed, climbed
clints, cliffs
clout, cloth
clyre, tumour, gland
clytach, balderdash
cock-lairds, empty braggarts
cod, pillow
coinyelled, pitted
come-doon, degradation
connached, abused, spoiled
coom, comb
coonter, counter
cooried, crouched
corbaudie comes in, that is the obstacle
cordage, tackling of a ship
corn-cockles, corn-flowers
corneigh, enough (*lit.* coeur ennuyé, internally disquieted)
cornskriech, corncrake

corrieneuchin', murmuring
cottons, cottar houses
coup, overturn, upset
courage-bag, scrotum
couthie, comfortable
coutribat, struggle
crack, converse
craidle on the ca', cradle being rocked
crammasy, crimson
craturs, creatures
craw, crow
cray, pigsty
cree legs wi' (no' to), not safe to meddle with
creel, in a state of mental excitement or confusion or physical agony, influence
creesh, fat
crine, shrink
crockats up, on one's dignity
crockets, tresses
croon, crown
cross-brath'd, braided
cross-tap, mizzen-mast
crottle, crumble away
croud, murmuring
cuckold, hoodwinked, diddled
cude, barrel
cuit-deep, ankle-deep
cull, testicle
cullage, genitals
cundy, drain
cushie, cushat dove
cwa', come away

daberlack, leek-like lengths of seaweed
dackered, searched, gone into, worn away
dae, do
daffin', playing
dally, stick used in binding sheaves to push in ends of rope
dander, temper
danders, cinders
datchie, sly, secret
daunton, intimidate, overawe
daur, dare
dayligaun, nightfall
deasie, raw, cold, uncomfortable

deed, died
deef, deaf, unimpressionable
deemless, countless
deil, devil
deltit, pampered
depert, divide
derbels, eyesores
derf, taciturn, cruel
dern, hide
din, done
ding, bang down, knock
dirlin', throbbin
dishielogie, tussilago
doited, mad
donnert, dazed, stupefied
dooks, ducks
doonfa', downpour
doonhaudin', holding down
doonsin', dazzling
dorbels, eyesores
dorty, petted
dottlin', maundering
doup, backside, end
dour, intractable, sullen
dowed, faded
dowf, hollow, gloomy, inert
dowless, feeble, imponderable
downa, unable
dowse, quench
doze, immobilisation through great speed
dozent, stupid
draiks (i' the), in a slovenly neglected condition
draughtin', delineating
dreich, dreary, tedious
drings, wretches
drites, drips
drob, prick, fall like hail
drochlin, puny
drodlich, a useless mass
drookit, soaked
drumlie, troubled, discoloured
druntin', whining
drush, smush, refuse
drutlin', piddling, incontinent, slow
duds, clothes
dumb-deid, midnight
dung, knocked

dwamin', overpowering
dwine, decline, diminish, dwindle

eel-ark, breeding grond for eels
eel-droonin', ludicrously vain
eelied, vanished
eelyin', vanishing
eemis, ill-poised, insecure
een, eyes
eerned, clotted
egg-taggle, act of wasting time in bad
    company
Egypt herrings, old name for Saury
    Pike
eident, busy, eager
eindoon, downright
eisen, lust
eisenin', lustful, yearing
elbuck, elbow
elf-bones, hole in a piece of wood
emerauds, emeralds
emmits, ants
eneuch, enough
ettle, aspire, attempt, hope, expect,
    reckon
ettlin', eager

fa', fall
faburdoun, faux bourdon
faddom, fathom
fair, completely
fairin', deserts
fanerels, accessories
fank o'tows, coil of ropes
fankles, becomes clumsy, traps
fantice, imagination, whimsicality
farle, oat-cake
farles, filaments of ash
farlins, fish troughs
fash, trouble, worry
fauld, fold
fause, false
fause-faces, masks
feck, great deal, majority
fecklessly, impotently
feeh, exclamation of disgust and
    contempt
feery-o'-the feet, nimble
fegs, faith, truly

fell, clever (*adj.*), very (*adv.*)
ferlie, wonder, marvel, surprise
fey, fated
fidge, move
fidged, worried
figuration, harmony, musical
    structure
fiky, fastidious, troublesome
filed, dirtied
flauchters, flutters
flaught, abased
flaught, flame
flech, flea
flee, fly
fleerin', flaring, gibing
fleg, frighten
flegsome, frightening
flense, cut blubber off a whale
flet, flit
flype, turn inside out
flytin, railing
fochin', turning over
fog-theekit, moss-thatched
fordel, progressive
forenenst, in front of, opposite, over
    against
forenicht, early evening
forfochen, exhausted
forgaed, gave up
forgether, meet
forhooied, abandoned
fork-in-the-wa', means of diverting
    share of labour pains to husband
fotherin', supply
fou', drunk
foudrie, lightning
fousome, disgusting
fower, four
foziest, most stupid
fozy, rotten
fraise in ane anither's witters, run
    through each other
fratt, fretwork
fraucht, cargo
freaths, plumes of foam or froth
fremit, strange
fremt, friendless, isolated
fu', full
fug, moss

fule, fool
fullyery, foliage
fushionless, dispirited

gaadies, bloomers, howlers, gaffes
gad, fishing-rod
gaed, went
gaff, hook for fish
gair, small patch
galliard, rapid dance
gallus, callous, indifferent, reckless
gammons, feet
gams, gums
gane, gone
gang, go
gangrel, wanderer
ganien, rodomontade
gansel, nonsense talk
gantin', yawning
gantrees, planks for putting barrel on
gar, make, compel
garded, covered
gausty, ghastly, ascetic
gaw (to have a), to have a catch upon
gealed, congealed
geg, trick, deception
gell, on the gell, on the go
gemmell, double harmony
get, illegitimate offspring
gey, very
geylies, very much
gie, give
gi'en, given
Gillha', pub of all weathers, hostelry of life
gin, if
girds, hoops
girles, thrills with horror
girn, snare
glaur, mud
gleg, eager
gleids, sparks
glisks, glances, glints, coups d'oeil
glit, slime
gloffs, dark patches appearing denser than other parts of atmosphere
gloghole, deep hole
glower, gaze at, glare
goam, gaze stupidly at

golochs, earwigs
gorded, frosted
gorlin', fledgling
goustrous, frightful, tempestuous
goves, come angrily
gowd, gold
gowd-bestreik, gold-streaked
gowden, golden
gowk-storm, storm of short duration (sub-sense of foolish fuss)
gowls, hollows (opposite of *gloffs*)
gowpenfu', fistful
gowpin', gaping
graith, tackle, equipment
grat, wept
gree (bear aff the), carry off the palm
grieshuckle, embers
grue, revulsion
grugous, ugly
grun', ground
gruntle, pig's nose
guid, good
guisand, thirsty
guisand cude, a barrel whose staves have sprung apart owing to drouth
guisers, maskers
guissay, pig
gundy, violent
gurly, savage
guts, bowels
gy, spectacle

ha'e, have
hag, peat
haik, drag, hoist
haill, whole
hain, keep, preserve
hair kaimed to the lift, on the go
hairst, harvest
haliket, headlong
hanlawhile, a moment
happit, covered
harn-pan, brain box
harns, brains
harth, lean
haud, hold
haud their row, be quiet
hauf, half

457

hauflins, adolescent boys
haw, hollow
hawdin', holding
hazelraw, lichen
heels-owre-gowdy, head-over-heels
heith, high, height
heich-skeich, crazy, irresponsible
heidstrang, head-strong
henree, hen-run
herried, plundered
hert, heart
hesp, hasp
hinds, farm-labourers
hines, rasps
hinny, honey
hod'n, hidden
holine, holly green
hoo, dog'fish
hotchin', restless
houk, hulk
how'd, shorn down
how-dumb-deid, the very dead of night
howe, bottom, hollow
howff, public-house
howkin', digging
hule, mischief
hullerie, with ruffled feathers
hustle-farrant, clad in tatters
hwll, ululation

ilka, every
ingangs, intestines
ingles, hearths
inklins, intuitions

jag, prick
jalouse, guess
jaup, splash
jizzen, straw, child-bed (*lit.* in the straw)
jouk, dodge
jow, surge, swing

kaa, drive
kail-blades, cabbage blades
kaim, comb
kebbuck, cheese
keeks, looks slyly or suddenly

keethin' sicht, sight of the 'keethin's' or disturbances caused by the movements of fish
kelter, undulate
keltie, bumper
ken, know
kilted in a tippit, hung in a noose
kindle, light
kine, cows
kink, bend or twist
kirk or mill (to mak' a), to do the best one can
kist, chest, breast
kite, belly
kittle, tickle, (*adj.*) ticklish, difficult
knedneuch, sour
knool, pin, peg
knoul-taed, swollen-toed
knurl, knob
krang, hulk of a whale after the blubber has been removed
kyths, appears, becomes known, emerges

lade, mill stream
laich, *laigh*, low
lammergeir, great hooded vulture
langsyne, long ago
lapper-milk, sour milk
laroch, hole in the ground, foundation
lauchs, laughs
lave, rest, remainder
laverock, lark
lear, learning
leed, strain
lee-lang, live-long
leid, language
leuch, laughed
liddenin', going backwards and forwards
liefer, rather
lift, sky
lig, lie
ling, gait
linns, rocky stairway
lint, flax
lippen, trust
little-bodies, fairies
loan-soup, see *white*

458

lochan, little loch
lo'e, love
loof, palm of hand
loon, lad
loonikie, little boy
loppert, coagulated
losh me, goodness me
louch, come-hither, downcast
loup, jump
lourd, heavy, overcharged, cloudy
loutit, curtsied
lowe, flame
lown, hushed, quiet
lowse, loosen
lowsin'-time, stopping-time
lozen, window
luchts, loose locks
lugs, ears

maik, partner
maikless, matchless
makar, poet
'mang, among
mant, stammer
mapamound, map of the world, earth's
  surface
mappiemou'd, rabbit-mouthed
marrow (winsome), a creditable limb
maun, must
mebbe, perhaps
mell, mix
minnie, mother
mirlygoes, dazzle
mocage, sardonic humour
mochiness, closeness
moniplied, manifold
moniplies, intestines
mools, earth, soil for a grave
moosewob, spider's web
mou', mouth
muckin', cleaning
muckle, big, much
Muckle Toon, Langholm in
  Dumfriesshire
mudgeons, mocking motions
mum, silent
munk, imitate
munkie, rope with noose at end
munks, swings away

murgeons, mouth movements
mutchkin, liquor measure, half-bottle

nae mowse, perilous
natheless, nevertheless
natter, rant
neb, nose
neist, next
nesh, full of awareness, nervous
'neth, beneath
neuked, crooked
nicht, night
nocht, nothing

ocht, anything
on-ding, downpour
oolin', crouching
oon, shell-less, addled
oorie, weird
ootby, outside
ootcuissen, outcast
ootrie, outré
or, before
orra, odd, nondescript, not up to
  much
Overinzievar, Perthshire place-name
owre, over
owt, anything

paddle-doo, frog
panash, *Fr.* panache
pang-fu', crammed full
pap o' the hass, uvula
partan's tae (literally crab's toe), cutty
  pipe
peepy-show, cinema
peerie, spinning-top
peerie-weerie, diminished to a mere
  thread of sound
penny wheep, small ale
pickle, small quantity
pirn, reel
pitmirk, complete darkness
plaited, pleated
plat o' shairn, cow's dung
ploys, games, amusements
plumm, deep pool
pokiness, congestion
poortith, poverty

port a' beul, mouth-music
powsoudie, sheep's-head broth
prick-sangs, musical compositions
puir, poor
puslock, dung

quean, lass, woman
quenry, reminiscences of dealings
  with women
quither, quiver
quo', said

raff o' rain, a few streaks of rain
ragments, odds and ends
raim-pig, cream basin
ramballiach, tempestuous
ramel, branches
ratt-rime, incantations for killing rats,
  doggerel
raw, row
rawn for the yirdin', frightened to death
rax, stretch
recoll, reminiscences
reek, smoke (*There was nae reek i' the
  laverock's hoose*, it was a dark and
  stormy night)
reek forth, stream out
reid e'en, according to tradition, the
  one night in the year when harts
  and hinds mate, in November
reishlin', rustling
reistit, dried
renshels, beats
ressum, particle
revelled, ravelled
revure, dark, gloomy, contemptuous
riach, dun, ill-coloured
ribie, stripped of leaves like a bird
  that is plucked
rice, branch
rimpin, lean cow
ringle-een, eyes showing a great deal
  of white
ripe, pillage, search
rippit, rumpus
ripples, diarrhoea
rise, bough, branch
risp, grass
rit, scrape

rived, torn
rizzar, currant
rooky, misty
roon, round
root-hewn, gnarled, twisted, awkward
rouch, rough, plentiful
rouchled, ruffled
rouk, smoke, mist
roup, auction, sale
row'd, rolled, wrapped up
rowin', rolling
rowth, abundance
rowtin', roaring
royat, unmanageable
rude, bold, stubborn
rugs, rives
rumgunshoch, rough
rumple-fyke, itch in anus
runkled, wrinkled

sabbin', sobbing
sae, so
sae-ca'd, so-called
sair, serve
sair, sore
sall, shall
samyn, deck of ship
santit, swallowed up in sand
sauch-like, willow-like
sauls, souls
savin'-tree, sabine, said to kill foetus in
  womb
scaddows, shaddows
scaldachan, chattering
scansin', glinting
scaut-heid, scrofulous, disfigured
scho, vacillate
sclaffer, shuffle
sclafferin', slovenly
sclatrie, obscenities, scandal
scoogie, apron
scorlins, tangles of seaweed
scount, small example
scouth, scope
scrats, hermaphrodites
scrauchin', screeching
scunner, disgust
scunnersome, disgusting, repulsive
scut, fud

460

seggs, insignificant plants
seil o' your face, fortune favour you
seilfu', blissful
send, convoy to fetch a bride
sentrices, scaffolding
ser', serve
shairest, surest
shasloch, loose straw, litter
sheckle, wrist
shog, swing, rock
shoon, shoes
shot, freed
shouders, shoulders
sib, blood relations, related
sibness, relationship
sic, such
siccar (to mak'), to make certain
siller, silver
simmer, summer
sinnen, sinew
sirse, exclamation of surprise
skail, come out
skarmoch, scrum-like
skime, gleam
skimmerin', glimmering
skinklan', shining, gleaming
skirl-i'-the-pan, fried oatmeal
skrymmorie, frightful and terrific
slee, sly
sliggy, cunning
slorp, lap up, slobber over
slounge, sharp fall
sma'-bookit, reduced to small
   proportions, minified
sma'er, smaller
smirrs, drizzle
smoored, smothered
sneith, smoothness
snell, bitterly cold
snod, neat, tidy
snood, see *tint*
snoovin', sneaking
socht, sought
sonsy, contented
sook, suck
sook-the-bluids, little red beetles
soom, swim
soon', sound
soupled, accelerated

soupler, suppler
spales, melts, runs down
spalin', burning away
spatrils, musical notes (as printed)
spauld, backbone
speir, ask
spiel, climb
splairgin', spluttering
stang, blast, paroxysm
starnies, starns, stars
sta-tree, pole for tethering cattle to
steek, shut
stegh, glut
stell, fix
stented, appointed
stert, fright
stertle-a-stobie, exhalations
stilpin', striding
stishie, rumpus, hullabaloo
stoichert, bedizened
stound, throb
stour, dust
stow, stole
stramash, noise, rumpus
stramulyert, panic-stricken
straucht, straight
strawns, strings, chains
streek, stretch
streekit, stretched
sud, should
sumphs, blockheads
sune, soon
swack, active, supple
swallin', swelling
swaw, ripple
swee, jerk, sway
sweetie-pokes, bags of sweets
swippert, active, lively
switchables, earwigs
swith, swift
swith wi' virr, vehement
swither, hesitate
syne, afterwards since, then,
   thereafter

tae, too
taed, toad
taigled, entangled
tak's tent, takes care

talla, tallow
tapsalteerie, topsy-turvy
tash, destroy
tassie, glass
tethered splore, adventure within
  prescribed limits
teuch, tough
thae, those
thaim, them
thegither, together
thieveless, impotent
thole, bear, endure
thorter-ills, paralytic seizures
thow, thaw
thowless, handless, useless, impotent
thrang, busy
thrapple, throat
thraw, throw
thrawart, perverse
thrawn, contrary, stubborn
thraws, convulses
threidin', *thridden*, threading
thring, shrug
thringin', hoisting
tine, lose
tint, lost
tint her snood, dishonoured herself
tirls at the pin, rattles at the
  door-handle
toom, empty
toories, pom-poms
tossils, tassels
toukin', distorted
tousie, rumpled, untidy
toves, moods
trauchlin', troubling
trig, trim
turn-gree, winding stair
twaesome, the two of them
twa-neukit, two-horned
tyauve, struggle

ugsome, horrible, repulsive
ullage, deficiency in contents of barrel
unco, strange (*adj.*), very (*adv.*)
undeemis, countless
unkennable, unknowable

vennel, lane, narrow street

vieve, vivid
virr, stamina force, vigour

wab, web
wae, *waesome*, woeful
waesucks, alas
waled, selected
wame, belly
wanchancy, unfortunate
warl', world
watchet, dark green
watergaw, indistinct rainbow
waun'ert, confused
waur, worse
wecht, weight
wee, small
weel, well
weet, wet
weird, fate
weirdless, worthless
wheen, few
wheengin', complaining
wheesht, be quiet, hush
whigmaleerie, trifle
whiles, sometimes
white as a loan-soup, pallid, as thin and
  weak as charity soup
whuds, dashes, thuds by or down
whummle, overturn, upset
whummlin', tumbling
whup, whip
whuram, crotchet, quaver
wi', with
wice, wise
widdifow, perverse
widna, would not
windlestrae, straw
winnock, window
wizened, shrunk
worm-i'-the-cheek, toothache
wud, wood
wud, would
wunds, winds
wuppit, winding, wound round

yabblin', gabbling
yammer, jabbering
yank, throw
yett, gate

Ygdrasil, Celtic Tree of Life

yince-yirn, once-errand, on special purpose

yirdin', see *rawn*

yirdit, buried

yon, further

'yont, beyond

yowdendrift, counter-swirl of snow from the earth, gale driving down, opposite of earth-drift

yowlin', howling

yow-trummle, ewe-tremble (cold spell at end of July after sheep-shearing)